ROSES AT THE CAPE OF GOOD HOPE

COPYRIGHT © 1988 GWEN FAGAN

PUBLISHED BY

BREESTRAAT-PUBLIKASIES

156 BREE STREET

CAPE TOWN 8001

FIRST EDITION 1988

REPRINTED 1989

REPRINTED 1995

NO PORTION OF THIS BOOK MAY BE REPRODUCED

BY ANY PROCESS WITHOUT WRITTEN

PERMISSION FROM THE AUTHOR

EDITED BY BARBARA KNOX-SHAW

DESIGNED BY WILLEM JORDAAN

TYPESET BY NATIONAL COMMERCIAL PRINTERS

REPRODUCTION BY HIRT & CARTER (PTY) LIMITED

PRINTED AND BOUND IN THE REPUBLIC OF SOUTH AFRICA

BY NATIONAL BOOK PRINTERS

DRUKKERY STREET, GOODWOOD, WESTERN CAPE

ISBN 0 620 11032 5

GWEN FAGAN
ROSES AT THE CAPE OF GOOD HOPE

WITH PHOTOGRAPHS BY GABRIËL FAGAN

All roses and hips in the specimen photographs
are actual size unless otherwise stated.

Cover: Old roses in an 18th century *famille rose*
punch bowl. Arranged by the author and photographed
by her husband in the Boschendal manor house built
in 1818 on the foundations of an earlier house.

Contents page: The four Chinese stud roses in a 19th
century Cape custard glass, at Ida's Valley.

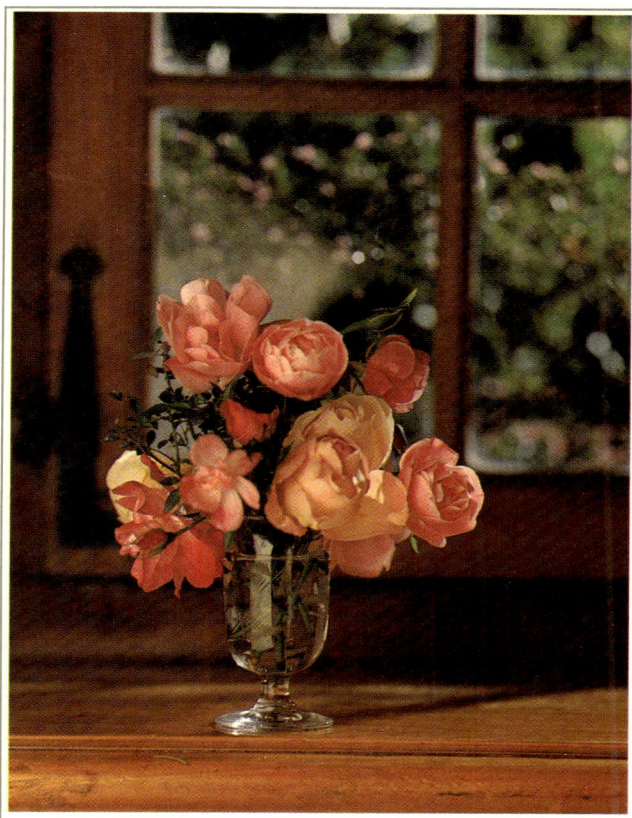

Contents

Preface 7

The Centifolias 9

Red roses at the Cape (the Gallicas) 25

The white roses (the Albas) 47

Damask roses 57

China roses 73

The Bourbons 101

The Noisettes 123

The Tea roses 137

The Hybrid Perpetuals 159

The Hybrid Teas 177

The Species roses 187

Large Climbers 251

Old roses for historic and modern gardens 261

Index 266

Bibliography 271

Preface

*T*his book is about my personal involvement with old roses at the Cape and the places and people associated with them. The period it covers dates from the moment when Commander Jan van Riebeeck picked the first Dutch rose at the Cape on 1 November 1657 until the year 1910 when the Cape of Good Hope Colony was embodied in the Union of South Africa, by which time the new Hybrid Teas were beginning to oust 'old roses' from Cape gardens.

In the Cape where rainfall is often very low, plants haven't always survived as well as they might in more amenable climates. But limited water apart, Cape gardeners have always been as fashion-conscious as rosarians in other parts of the world and have eagerly followed the changing shapes set by the prize-winning show roses. While the older varieties were edged out by new kinds, however, they continued to find a refuge in the simple cottage gardens of small mission villages, in old graveyards, country lanes and tucked-away towns and farms, where I found them when I started my search for old roses.

It was when I was occupied with the restoration of the 18th century parterre garden at Government House in 1968 that I first learnt of the roses that used to thrive at the Cape in those early days, and I began to wonder what they had looked like. It was arranged that a collection of 18th century rose varieties be sent out from Kew for Government House. But unfortunately once the bud-wood had arrived and been successfully grafted at Kirstenbosch, the horticulturist then in charge of Public Works gardens refused point blank to have anything to do with such old-fashioned plants. Consequently the garden, painstakingly restored to a plan which had been drawn by the architect Thibault in about 1791, was decked out with 20th century plant varieties.

After languishing in plastic containers for two years in the Kirstenbosch nursery, the rose plants found a home in the newly restored garden of the old Drostdy at Tulbagh. I had discovered once more a plan in the Cape Archives, this time for a small formal garden at the back of this early 19th century magistrate's court. The Kew roses fitted in perfectly and grew happily until it was decided yet again that modern roses would be more impressive. A friend phoned to tell me that the rose collection was destined for the rubbish-heap.

When the Kew collection eventually found a permanent home in the new garden at Boschendal, a farm complex which we had restored for the Anglo-American Corporation, many of the labels had been lost and I had to do some extensive reading in order to identify the varieties. Few people at the Cape had first-hand knowledge of old roses at that time.

My interest, thus stimulated, took leaf and blossomed into an obsession, though a most enjoyable one. I started collecting slips of old rose varieties wherever I found them to plant with the original Kew collection at Boschendal.

The Cape of Good Hope constituted a halfway-house on the trade route between Europe and the East Indies, and I was accordingly not surprised to find both European and Eastern roses growing here. A number of unidentified roses seem to occur only at the Cape — whether they might be the result of local hybridization, I have not been able to establish. Perhaps, like the last rose of summer, they are, after all, European hybrids which have managed to linger longer here at the Cape, their companions having disappeared long since from Western gardens.

Old roses have brought much beauty, grace and fragrance into my life. They have enriched me with many wonderful new friends, and have taught me that perseverance and patience are a woman's most important attributes — not least when she acts as photographer's assistant, and her husband is the photographer!

I shall be happy if a small part of the pleasure we have had in collecting and photographing these roses over the last eight years communicates itself to the reader. For this must be the first step in any attempt to revive an interest in their cultivation and preservation in Cape gardens.

I would like to give credit to the following friends whose enthusiastic support was a constant source of inspiration and encouragement:

Willem Hefer who started me off on this book, originally intended as a brochure for Boschendal visitors;
Enid du Plessis who encouraged me to carry on;
The many gardeners who generously supplied me with rose slips;
Maisie and Peter Knox-Shaw and Eve Palmer for unabated enthusiasm;
Dr John Rourke of the Compton Herbarium at Kirstenbosch and Mrs Anne Bean of the Bolus Herbarium at the University of Cape Town for advice;
Julie te Groen for valuable help in the SA Library and for checking the footnotes;
The staff of the Cape Archives and Parliamentary library;
Barbara Knox-Shaw for meticulous editing and proof reading;
Willem Jordaan for the book design;
C.D. Brickell, Director of the Royal Horticultural Society Garden at Wisley, for help in identifying rose specimens;
The Librarian of the Lindley Library for kind permission to reproduce illustrations from the Mary Lawrance and Reeves collections;
Peter Beales, David Rustan, Dean Ross, Clair Martin, Trevor Nottle, Toni Sylvester, Barbara Cannon and Pat Wiley, co-speakers at the Second International Rose Conference in Adelaide, 1986, who urged me to publish this book at all costs;
My husband, who by financing this book, has made it available at a reasonable price.

IDA'S VALLEY COLLECTION: SIMON VERELST

·Q·

THE CENTIFOLIAS

·Ò·

The first rose which was picked at the Cape almost three centuries ago was a Centifolia, and although the forms that were so common in sixteenth and seventeenth-century Dutch gardens are now seldom seen, their coarsely-toothed soft leaves on nodding prickly stems, their branched glandular calyces, and above all, their voluptuous, clear pink globular blooms live on in the still-life paintings of the Flemish masters.

Lately some of these have crept back into the gardens of romantic gardeners all over the world. At the Cape, too, respect for its ancient lineage and fascination with its famous fragrance have stimulated a desire to grow again what was once regarded as the Queen of Roses.

No less fascinating, the Moss rose — which arose as a sport of the Centifolia, differing only in the hairiness of the flower-stalks, the much-branched sepals and the numerous fragrant glands covering leaves, sepals, calyces, flowers and leaf-stalks — is being welcomed back into modern gardens. Unlike the Centifolia, many more of the old varieties have remained in cultivation and are still obtainable.

There are many who believe that the original attar or essential oil of roses was first distilled from the petals of the highly fragrant Centifolia roses. Miller in his *Gardener's Dictionary* (1768) describes the process as follows:

The process for making Attar or essential oil of Roses is as follows: Forty pounds of Roses, with their calyxes, are put into a still, with fifty pounds of water. The mass being well mixed, a gentle fire is put under the still; and when fumes begin to rise, the cap and pipe are properly fixed and luted. When the impregnated water begins to come over, the fire is lessened by gentle degrees, and the distillation continued until thirty pounds of water are come over, which is generally in four or five hours. This water is to be poured upon forty pounds of fresh Roses, and from fifteen to twenty pounds of liquor are to be drawn from it, as before. It is then poured into pans of earthen ware or tinned metal, and left exposed to the fresh air for the night. The Attar or essence will be found in the morning, congealed and swimming on the surface of the water.

I could find no record to indicate that attar of roses was ever made at the Cape, but I am sure that many Dutch housewives and British settler womenfolk collected Centifolia petals to dry for pot-pourri. In the following pages the Centifolia hedges which graced the Cape landscape for almost three centuries are described. Of the multitude of gardeners who passed through, I like to think that many were like me in hating to let rose-petals drop and go to waste.

One of the 43 paintings done by Jan Adam Hartman and his son on the plastered walls of the Libertas homestead in about 1789 when the farm belonged to J.B. Hoffman.

Rosa centifolia

PROVENCE ROSE

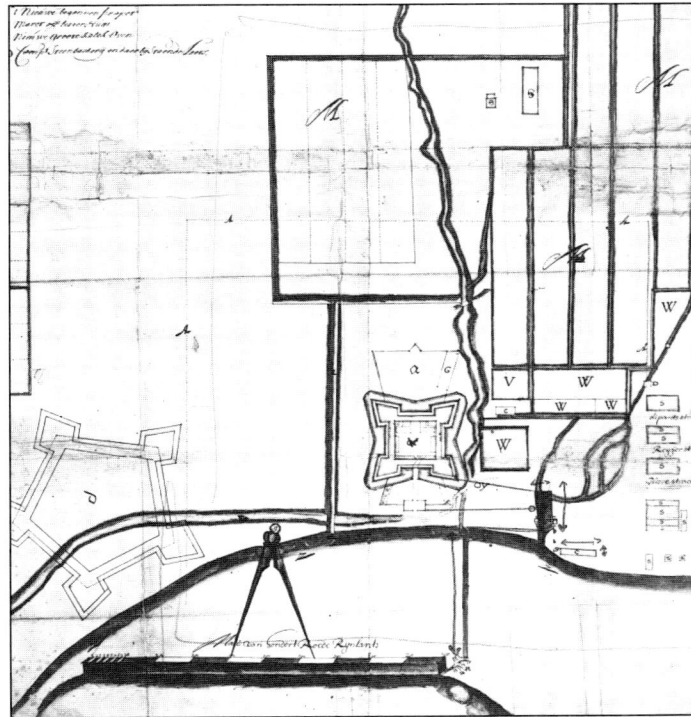

Commander Jan van Riebeeck's
fort and garden in 1665.

Each like a corpse within its grave, until
Thine azure sister of the Spring shall blow
Her clarion o'er the dreaming earth, and fill
(Driving sweet buds like flocks to feed in air)
With living hues and odours plain and hill.

SHELLEY, 'ODE TO THE WEST WIND'

Every year at the appointed time and for centuries unknown, the wild roses of the world respond to the warm spring air and unfold their buds, shaking out fresh green leaves and fragile five-petalled blossoms from the confinement of dormant stems. The rose lover feels the excitement of the coming season and the old curiosity is once again awakened as he wonders: where and in what strange age and land did the first garden rose reveal its glorious many-petalled form?

On Saturday 1 November 1659 Jan van Riebeeck, Commander of the Dutch Colony at the Cape of Good Hope, recorded in his diary:

The south-south-east winds continue to blow strongly and on this day has been picked the first Dutch rose at the Cape from rose trees brought here in the past year.[1]

At the Cape, the spring wind is no gentle zephyr, but a rollicking force of energy blowing endless white clouds over Table Mountain, rushing down to the sea with reckless abandon, tugging and dragging at obstacles in its way and showing respect neither for human dignity nor vegetable fragility. No rose in its pathway would have been left intact. But in his seven years at the Cape, van Riebeeck, a keen agriculturist grown wise through constant experimentation, had learnt to overcome the vicissitudes of the Cape weather. He had been sent to the southernmost point of Africa by the Dutch East India Company for the sole purpose of establishing a garden to provide the sailing vessels on their long journey to the East with fresh produce, for it was hoped that this might reduce the frightening death rate on board ship.

Van Riebeeck had surrounded his garden at the foot of Table Mountain with deep ditches to keep out marauding animals and thieves; along the banks he planted hedges of medlars, cherries and lemons. Oak avenues and clipped bay hedges seven metres high enclosed his vegetable and herb beds, providing further wind protection for all his precious plants.

As he walked through the garden on that spring morning he observed that the fruit trees were in bloom and the corn had been reaped, and I am sure that even the south-easter would not have marred his delight when he picked his first Dutch rose.

Along the foothills of the mountains surrounding Table Valley, the Dutch had come across many new plants, some of which were used medicinally by the local Bushmen and Hottentot tribes. Nonetheless they still felt the need for the familiar herbal remedies from Europe, and van Riebeeck, a surgeon's son, who would himself have had to pass the medical examination required of all officers of the Dutch East India Company, therefore requested in March 1657 'all kinds of Fatherland fruit trees amongst which should be chestnuts, olives, laurel, junipers, medlars, ash and elder seeds in boxes with soil, mast and pine trees, mulberries for worms to try to produce silk, and also rose trees'.[2]

By August the rose trees had still not arrived. 'We are still without Pimper, Rose, Sweet Briar, Raspberry, Lavender and Lovage', he complained to the directors of the Council of Seventeen who controlled the affairs of the Dutch East India Company, and urged, 'We therefore expect trees or bushes'.[3]

There is no record of when these rose trees eventually arrived, nor of the varieties sent, but of all the countries in the world, the Colony of the Cape of Good Hope is perhaps the only one to have an exact record of the day on which its first rose was picked. Far from its natural environment, how strange that *Rosa centifolia*, that most sophisticated of all European garden roses, improved over many centuries of careful selection from a five-petalled wilding to its exquisite 'hundred-petalled' form, should have been the first to bloom on the southernmost tip of Africa where no wild rose had ever seen the light of day.

For by the 'Dutch rose' van Riebeeck was unquestionably referring to the *R. centifolia* or Provence Rose of 17th century Dutch and Flemish flower paintings. In fact, by the time that Jan van Riebeeck landed at the Cape of Good Hope in April 1652, the elder and younger Bosschaert, Jacques de Gheyn II, Jasper van den Hoecke, Jacob Woutersz Vosmaer, Jeronimus Sweerts, Roelant Savery and Jan Davidsz de Heem had all immortalized this rose in their famous masterpieces.[4]

It seems to me that two varieties of *R. centifolia* were favoured by these artists: a large, somewhat untidy goblet-shaped rose, usually of a strong pink colour but sometimes lighter, with outer petals falling back slightly from the central loosely packed cup. This variety appears in paintings of the first quarter of the 17th century.

The second is a slightly smaller rose varying in colour from blush to dark pink, goblet-shaped, with silky petals layered neatly one over the other towards the centre where pouting lips surround a darker pink throat — a voluptuous rose, almost transparent at times.[5] The painters also seemed to be fond of depicting its buds on delicate trailing stems, its oval leaves with deeply serrated edges, and pretty foliated sepals. This variety occurs more often in the late 17th and early 18th century paintings.

There has been a great deal of speculation about the origin of these early Provence roses and one is tempted to say with Parkinson that 'To compare, conferre, and agree together, were a worke of more paines than use: But to proportion them unto the names set downe by Theophrastus, Pliny and the rest of the ancient Authors, were a worke, wherein I might be sure not to escape without falling into errour, as I verily beleeve many others have done, that have undertaken to doe it'.[6]

Yet there is good reason to believe that the Centifolias of the Dutch masters are related to the roses described by Theophrastus in 400 BC and by Pliny almost three hundred years later as 'the hundred petalled rose' which, he tells us, grew in Italy at Campania and in Greece at Philippi, having been transplanted there from Mount Pangaeus. A Roman mosaic depicting a basket of flowers (now in the Vatican museum) might easily have been inspired by Johannes Bosschaert were it not for the gap of 1 000 years separating the two artists! Certainly the meticulously executed Roman 'Centifolia' is as Dutch as any painted in the 17th century.

It is also interesting to note that Roxburgh, who listed the plants growing in the Calcutta Botanic Gardens in 1814, thought that the Centifolia growing there had been introduced from Asia before 1794; he mentions that this rose was well known in Hindustan and Bengal as 'Goolab'. It seems unlikely that *R. centifolia* would have arrived in the East from the Netherlands, even though Roxburgh's list was written

1 *Journal of Jan van Riebeeck*, Van Riebeeck Society, Cape Town, 1952.
2 H. C. V. Leibrandt, *Letters despatched from the Cape*.
3 Ibid., 31 August 1657.
4 I examined prints of over 400 European still-life flower paintings covering the period 1600–1900 and found that 66% of these featured at least one Centifolia rose, and 12% featured Alba roses (mostly 'Semiplena', usually together with a Centifolia). There were a few with Damask roses, but the Gallica roses were conspicuous by their absence.
5 'The petals are so closely wedged together' says Miller 'that the flower appears as if it came out of the hand of the turner'.
6 J. Parkinson, *The Garden of Pleasant Flowers*.

From top to bottom:
Roman mosaic in the Vatican museum.
18th century stucco panel at the Tuynhuys.
Georgian and Victorian cast-iron
fireplaces in the Cape Town Castle
decorated with Centifolia roses.

Gerard's 'Great Holland Rose'.

almost two centuries after its appearance in Holland. It is far more tempting to believe that *R. centifolia* originated in Asia, and that the Persians were responsible for introducing it to the Mediterranean from where it eventually reached Holland.

John Gerard in his *General Historie of Plantes* (1597), which was largely based on the work of the Flemish herbalist Rembertus Dodoens, had his own theory about the origin of the 'Dutch rose':

The great Rose, which is generally called the great Provence rose which the Dutch men cannot endure; for say they, it came first out of Holland, and therefore to be called the Holland Rose: but by all likelihood it came from the Damask rose, as a kinde thereof, made better and fairer by art, which seemeth to agree with truth.

He goes on to describe its flowers, which 'grow on the tops of the branches, in shape and colour like the Damask Rose, but greater and more double insomuch that the yellow chives in the middle are hard to be seen; of a reasonable good smell but not so sweet as the common Damaske Rose'; but his illustration, derived from the German botanist Tabernaemontanus, is too stylized to identify with the large roses of the Dutch painters.

John Parkinson also describes the 'Great double Damaske Province' or 'Holland Rose (that some call Centifolia Batavica incarnata)' in similar terms; he mentions that some people considered the perfume superior to that of the Damask so much so that 'to that end I have known some Gentlewomen have caused all their damaske stockes to bee grafted with province Roses'. Parkinson himself preferred the Damask scent, but tolerantly adds: 'Let every one follow their own fancie'.[6]

Parkinson mentions another rose which was in many respects similar, but of a darker colour and neither quite so full nor so well scented: this he called 'Rosa Provinciales rubra' or 'Batavica centifolia rubra'. A third kind that was white 'whereof I am not oculatis testis' he refrained from describing.

By the beginning of the 18th century the Provence Rose was known to botanists throughout Europe, even though the names they gave did not always agree. The indiscriminate spellings of Provence and Province may cause some confusion, but both probably refer to Provence in the south of France which was first known as Provincia Romana, then Province, and ultimately Provence. I assume that the first Centifolia roses were brought to Holland from here, and therefore became known to the early herbalists as 'Provintie' or 'Provincie roosen' before they were improved by Dutch breeders to become the 'Hollandse provintie roosen' and eventually Provence roses.

In the Cape too the Provence Rose maintained its popularity from

Wall painting at Boschendal. The Centifolia in the 17th century Roemer wine glass is unidentified.

that first day when van Riebeeck picked it in the Company's garden. Johan Schreyer, who visited the Cape in 1668, recorded that 'in other parts there grow only centifolien and Persian roses which grow extremely beautiful and large'. These were probably the same Centifolias which the Company's gardener Oldenland described twenty-seven years later in his herbal, and which Peter Kolbe called 'Rosa maxima multiplex' in the early 1700s.[7]

By the end of the 18th century Centifolias must have been as commonly grown in Cape gardens and as well loved by the Dutch colonists as they were by their compatriots in Europe. The stream of English immigrants that flowed to the Cape after the British annexation in 1806 no doubt brought their own favourites. An early 19th century issue of the annual *Cape Almanac* warned Capetonians, perhaps mistakenly, that 'the Provence and other European roses should be pruned pretty close', or no flowers would be produced.

At about this time the English nurseryman, William Paul, in his book *The Rose Garden*, classified 76 true varieties of the Provence Rose, transferring varieties that resembled the Gallicas to the Hybrid Provence class, and those that resembled the China roses to the Hybrid China class. Apart from these, Paul described six small Centifolias under the heading of Miniature or Pompom roses.[8] Baron von Ludwig in Cape Town seemed to have a special fancy for these smaller varieties; 'De Meaux', 'Pomponia' and 'Maldensis' (*Rosa centifolia parvifolia*) were among the new varieties added to the collection in his Botanic Garden in 1831. The Baron welcomed visitors to his garden and distributed his plants freely, so these small roses would soon have been growing in many Cape gardens.

It appears that the Provence roses attracted visitors to other gardens as well. In the 1855 spring edition of the *Mercantile Advertiser* Capetonians were invited by the proprietor of Topp's Tea Gardens to visit 'Little Paradise' (in Newlands) which was then

splendidly embellished with that Queen of flowers, the PROVENCE ROSE, *and those who really wish to enjoy the sight should pay an early visit, as the above kind of Rose will only last a fortnight. Refreshments of all description can be had in the Gardens at all times, from 6 o'Clock on Monday Mornings, until 6 o'Clock on Saturday evenings.*[9]

Although the growing popularity of the Noisettes, Bourbons, Chinas, Teas and Hybrid Perpetuals led to the eventual decline of interest in the Provence rose towards the end of the 19th century, its fragrance still ensured it a place in many gardens. Lindley in 1820 and Loudon in 1844 both describe a convent in Florence where the friars were continuing to make attar from Provence roses.

Miller alone warns us of its dangerous effects:

The smell is extremely agreeable to most persons; but in too great quantities, these flowers are said to produce sneezing, inflammation of the eyes, faintings, hysterical affections etc. and where persons have been confined in a close room with a great heap of Roses, they have been in danger of immediate extinction of life.[10]

Apart from its fragrance, however, the glamour of the Provence Rose continued to inspire artists, perhaps conjuring up dreams of Persian gardens filled with exotic bejewelled plants, spouting fountains and singing nightingales. This voluptuous rose, so beautifully portrayed by Redouté, has haunted men's minds and still figures in painting, sculpture, wallpaper, furnishing materials, porcelain and all kinds of miscellaneous household articles.

At the Cape the Malayan slaves, the artisans of the day, used to carve ornate stucco swags of Centifolia buds and full-blown roses to decorate the cornices of important buildings and homestead gables. Centifolia motifs also occur in painted friezes around the reception-room walls, window and door openings of 18th century manor houses; at the farm 'Oude Libertas' in Stellenbosch, painted wall panels are embellished with posies of Centifolias.[11]

Even now, some of my older relatives and gardening friends recall the 'Cabbage Roses' of their youth with nostalgia, remembering the wonderful fragrance and the pretty soft pink colour; and so it seems that the Provence held its own well into the early 20th century, retaining its place in the Cape garden and its sentimental hold on Victorian home-makers.

Dr Con de Villiers of Stellenbosch once told me how a wall hanging, beautifully decorated with twining Centifolias and ivy, reminded all visitors to his mother's sitting-room that they were being watched by God's all-seeing eye. As he grew older the text was moved to a passage to make way for an impressive 'Stag at Bay' — an oil-painting done by an aunt who had been sent to Stellenbosch to receive 'finishing classes'. When next he returned home, he was disconcerted to find that the wall hanging, once his mother's pride, had fallen so far out of favour that it had been relegated to the back of the door in the most private closet of the house where 'God Sees You' caused him considerable embarrassment!

Like this 'work of art', the old Provence Rose has had to bow its way out of the Cape garden and we are reminded of its gracious form only by faded Redouté prints on table-mats or more vividly by the paintings of the old Flemish masters, as well as by its later varieties still to be found in a few Cape gardens.

7 P. Kolbe, *Caput Bonae Spei Hodiernum*, Nuremberg, 1719.
8 W. Paul, *The Rose Garden*, London, 1848 (facsimile reprint, New York, 1978).
9 Joyce Murray, *Mid-Victorian Cape Town*, Cape Town, 1968.
10 P. Miller, *The Gardener's Dictionary*, 9th ed. by Thomas Martyn, 1807.
11 Swags on Government House showing groups of Centifolias date to the 1780s; the murals seem to have been painted at the turn of the 18th century.

Rosa centifolia pomponia

'LESSER ROSE DE MEAUX'

Mary Lawrance's 'Rose de Meaux'.

Redouté's *Rosa centifolia pomponia*.

This tiny little rose, which grows only 30 – 40 cm high, is a sport of *Rosa centifolia* and is believed to date back to the early 17th century.

Although it may have been grown by the earliest Dutch settlers at the Cape, it is first mentioned in a list of plants grown in the garden of Baron von Ludwig which was situated on the outskirts of Cape Town in the area today known as Tamboerskloof. Von Ludwig called the rose 'Pomponia' — the name by which Curtis had described it in his *Botanical Magazine* of 1798; it was also painted by Mary Lawrance as 'Rose de Pompon'. Nurserymen of that period called it the 'Pompone Rose', although Aiton had named it 'the smaller Rose de Meaux'. Aiton did not reveal the rose's connection with the small French town near Paris from which the name is presumably derived.

Unfortunately no plants of this very old rose have survived in the Cape, but a plant obtained ten years ago from Kew has suckered so vigorously that it now covers a large area, forming a very pretty ground cover under a bank of Damask roses in the Boschendal garden. It grows only 25 cm high and has very prickly suckering stems like the 'Lesser de Meaux' described by Aiton.

PLANT
This small suckering shrub grows no higher than 40 cm. There are many upright dark-brown sturdy stems with numerous prickles.

FOLIAGE
Five small oval leaflets, about 1,5 cm long, with serrated edges and matt, dark-green upper surfaces, velvety below, glandular along the midrib. The stalks are short, straight and glandular and the stipules adnate and also glandular.

FLOWERS
Small, round, perfectly shaped pink buds open quickly to flat deep-pink rosettes 2-3 cm in diameter. The club-shaped petals, notched on the outer edge and narrow at the shanks, are bright pink, fading to mauve. A few stamens surround the bunch of short green stigmas. The calyx is smooth and globular, the unfoliated sepals glandular on the outside and velvety on the inside. The flowers appear only in spring and have a sweet fragrance which is not very strong.

INFLORESCENCE
One to two flowers on a branchlet off the main stem.

Rose de Pompon by Mary Lawrance.

Rosa centifolia pomponia.

'Pompon de Bourgogne'

The 'Greater de Meaux' rose, also mentioned by Aiton, might be the rose grown today under the name of 'Pompon de Bourgogne'. It looks very much like the rose which Mary Lawrance called 'de Meaux'. The shrub is larger, growing to one metre, and does not sucker like the 'Lesser Rose de Meaux'. It is in all respects a miniature Centifolia with very beautiful globular blush-pink flowers shaded darker towards the centre and with a delicious fragrance.

The photograph shown here was taken from a specimen obtained in the Knox-Shaw garden at Elgin where one imported plant has grown to perfection, producing numerous midget Centifolia blossoms each spring.

This rose is illustrated by Redouté, and Thory mentions that a white and a striped variety also existed in his time. Though he thinks that this is the same rose as the one in Curtis' *Botanical Magazine,* the latter is obviously different. The rose actually called 'Bourgogne pompon' in Redouté has a much larger flower than the one discussed here. It was a variety grown indoors by French nurseries and was therefore often the first to appear on the spring flower market.

'Pompon de Bourgogne'.

15

Moss Roses

Moss rose in the *Botanical Magazine* (T69).

Mary Lawrance's *Rosa muscosa*.

Miller's Moss Rose.

In his list of plants cultivated in the Leyden Botanical Garden in 1720, Boerhaave gave what seems to be the first botanical description of the Moss rose: 'Rosa rubra plena spinosissima, pedunculo muscosa', which Miller in his *Gardener's Dictionary* (1768) interpreted as 'the most prickly double red rose with a mossy footstalk commonly called the Moss Provence Rose'.

Miller states that this rose was unknown in England when he brought a plant from Dr Boerhaave's Leyden garden in 1727. He added, 'The flowers are of the same shape and colour as the common Provence Rose, and have the like agreeable odor'. Miller believed that it was a distinct species, but could not give its origin. Today it is generally agreed that it arose as a bud mutation from *Rosa centifolia*.

It is not recorded how the Moss rose reached Leyden, but it may have been from Carcassonne, the ancient walled city at the foot of the Pyrenees where the rose had been noticed in the 17th century.

Linnaeus, in his *Hortus Cliffortianus* (1737), mentions a Centifolia rose which might be a Moss: 'Rosa hollandica rubella plena, quibusdam centifolia spinoso frutico' (the Dutch double red rose with a hundred leaves (petals) and spiny fruits). An almost identical description of a rose is given by Heinrich Bernard Oldenland, the gardener of the Dutch East India Company, in his herbal of exotic plants growing at the Cape in 1695: 'Centifolia, frutice spinosa, rubra, alba etc'. If this does indeed refer to the Moss rose, it might indicate that the Leyden Moss roses noticed by Miller in 1727 had actually been growing there for a much longer period, for Oldenland's 1695 Moss roses would most probably have arrived from Leyden. Or did the Cape weather perhaps stimulate the initial mutation to mossiness?

Though these are mere speculations, it is definitely recorded that the Common Pink Moss rose was growing in Baron von Ludwig's botanic garden in Cape Town in 1831, and by 1858 'Moss Luxemburg', 'Moss Adelaide', 'Moss Angelique' and 'Moss Lanei' are recorded in Cape Town's Botanic Garden. The white form of the Common Moss known as 'White Bath' was also growing in Cape gardens in 1866. By the end of the century these roses had become so popular at the Cape that most gardens of any pretension had a few varieties.

'The Victorian age would have seemed incomplete without the Moss rose, so firmly did it entwine the hearts of those amiable days' declared a writer in the 1907 *Cape Amateur Gardener*.

My mother-in-law used to tell me how proud her father had been of the Moss roses in his garden at Tulbagh. He was a stately old man, mayor of the town for many years and seldom to be seen without a rose buttonhole, his favourite being the Moss rose with its exquisite fragrance and fernlike calyces.

In Swellendam too, there were admirers of the Moss rose. Miss Rothman, in writing of the old roses there, noted that the pink and white Moss roses were considered to be rarities and were not planted on the same scale as the 'Old Cape Rose' or the Tea roses.

Even in the Karoo town of Victoria West, the Moss rose flourished at the turn of the century, according to Mrs Day who brought a slip from her mother's garden to plant at Villiersdorp where she lives. She remembers how she used to try rubbing the 'plant lice' from the buds

'Nuits de Young'.

Rosa centifolia 'Muscosa'

'COMMON PINK MOSS'

Top: The calyx and pedicel of the Moss rose, magnified.
Below: Stalked glands on the branched sepals, magnified.

PLANT
A shrub with many stems 1–2 metres high. The long stems are often weak and inclined to arch; they are covered with numerous thin prickles of different lengths.

FOLIAGE
The five large, oval, soft, blunted leaflets are inclined to droop, and are covered in stalked glands which are especially prominent along the midrib on the underside of the leaf and along the well-marked serrations.

FLOWERS
The oval buds with longer, foliated, finely-branched glandular sepals open into cupped, quite full flowers about 6 cm in diameter. The petals are soft and of a beautiful clear pink colour. The oval calyx is also covered in stalked glands and tiny prickles. There are many stamens around a column of pistils. The flowers appear in early summer only and are deliciously fragrant.

INFLORESCENCE
A corymb with two to three flowers at the tips of the branches.

Rosa centifolia 'Muscosa'.

17

Moss Roses

'Crimson Moss'.

until her mother explained that the moss was an integral part of the flower!

By the early 20th century Cape plant catalogues listed numerous Moss roses; Smith's of Uitenhage, for instance, offered twelve different varieties in 1906.

Unfortunately I know of very few old plants that have survived in the Cape, but fortunately they are regaining favour among collectors now that local nurseries are re-introducing them.

'CRIMSON MOSS' grows into a large shrub with sprawling branches up to 1,5 metres high. In spring it is covered with very dark crimson, loose, globular blooms, opening almost flat, with the central crimson-purple notched petals curled inwards. The stamens are sparse and short around a bunch of longer hairy pistils. The calyx is very bristly with green mossy outgrowths. The flowers occur in groups of two to three on bristly stalks, appear only in spring and are very fragrant. This English Moss rose (introduced by Lee in the early 19th century) has been growing at the Cape for over a century.

In Basil Bennetts' cottage garden in Wynberg is a Moss plant known as 'CHAPEAU DE NAPOLÉON' or 'CRESTED MOSS'. It dates back to 1827 when Vibert introduced it to the French market, and resembles the Common Pink Moss in all respects except for the excessively foliated edges of the mossy sepals which give the half-opened bud the appearance of a cockaded hat.

The white Moss rose which was introduced in 1880 by Moreau and Robert of Angers in France under the name of 'BLANCHE MOREAU', is also to be seen in Cape gardens. It was one of the three Moss roses advertised by Gowie's Nurseries in their 1905 *Catalogue of Plants*, and Stephen Brett's nurseries were selling it at the same time in Port Elizabeth and Uitenhage.

'Blanche Moreau' is a lax shrub of 1–1,5 metres high; the glandular stems are covered with numerous reddish thorns of unequal length. The creamy-white, full, loosely quartered flowers occur in twos or threes at the tips of the branches and are very fragrant. The flower-stalk, calyx and petals are covered with dark stalked glands which exude the resinous fragrance that makes this rose so particularly attractive. 'Blanche Moreau' is one of the few Moss roses that flower recurrently.

'QUATRE SAISONS BLANC MOUSSEUX' is a less valuable garden rose. Its flowers, which are usually bunched up into untidy clumps, are loosely semi-double, rather tatty-looking and not as fragrant as 'Blanche Moreau' although the mossing is more delicate and of a finer texture and the petals are more fragile. It is a sport of *Rosa damascena semperflorens* and, as the only non-Centifolia moss, of great interest.

'NUITS DE YOUNG' is a very dainty plant, making numerous suckers with thin upright branches to 1,5 metres. This is another of Laffay's Moss roses and was introduced in 1845, but as it is not recorded in old Cape plant lists, it is not known how long 'Nuits de Young' has been growing here. In gardens where it still grows, only a few flowers appear on the tips of the branches in midsummer. But though it is a shy bloomer, the small, neat, dark maroon, full flowers are a pretty sight, and its ease of growth makes this a worthwhile plant to cultivate, especially on banks or in areas where the soil is poor.

'WILLIAM LOBB' has recently been made available by Ludwig's Nurseries in Pretoria, and the specimens I have planted have grown with great vigour. In fact the many branches are so tall that they need support to keep them from dragging their dark pink blooms on the ground. If properly supported, however, there is a great deal of pleasure to be derived from the rich fragrant blooms which are produced in greater numbers than in 'Nuits de Young'.

'Chapeau de Napoléon'

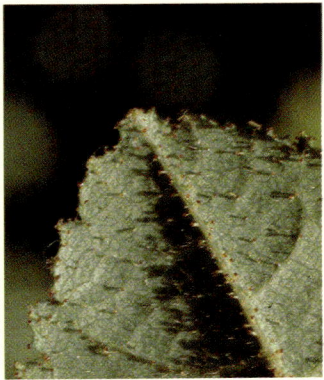

Glands on leaves, magnified.

'Chapeau de Napoléon'.

Ludwig'sburg Garden in Cape Town.
Below: Mary Lawrance's 'Bishop's Rose'.

This magnificent rose of unknown date and origin is sometimes classified as a Gallica, sometimes as a Centifolia and may be descended from both of these.

It is probably the rose recorded at the Cape under the name 'Schoenbrunnensis' in a list of roses imported by Baron von Ludwig for his botanic garden in 1831.[1] Von Ludwig was born in Sulz-am-Neckar, Württemberg in 1784, and trained as an apothecary in Kircheim near Stuttgart. He worked in Amsterdam (where he learned to speak Dutch), and then applied for an assistant's post in the pharmacy of a Dr Liesching in Cape Town where he arrived in 1805.[2]

Dr Liesching not only owned the pharmacy where von Ludwig worked but was one of the four approved physicians in Cape Town and owner of a piece of land, then known as Botany Bay, situated behind the Lion's Rump, where he grew medicinal herbs in his own botanic garden.

Like Dr Liesching, von Ludwig was a keen naturalist and collector of indigenous birds, animals and plants, specimens of which he sent to various institutions in Europe. Eventually he laid out his own botanic garden where he acclimatized numerous exotic plants which he then distributed to the colonists in his enthusiasm to promote agriculture and horticulture. He also became botanical supervisor to the Government Botanical Gardens in Cape Town. Through him many new varieties of roses, like his 'Rosa Schoenbrunnensis', were introduced to the Cape and distributed to gardeners in the vicinity.

The English nurseryman Thomas Rivers (of Rivers and Son, Sawbridgeworth), who describes the numerous colourful Gallicas of the mid-19th century in his *Rose Amateur's Guide* (1837), wrote about this rose: 'Schönbrunn, a brilliant crimson rose, is quite perfect in shape, and most constant and beautiful'.

Redouté's 'Rosier Évêque' which he equated with 'The Bishop', is portrayed as a very large, dark crimson, semi-double to double rose which turns violet to black in the older flower.[3] According to Thory this rose was widely grown in French gardens of the early 19th century and had given rise to several different varieties, either more or less double, but all displaying the brilliant dark colours which make it so notable.

The Cape 'Bishop' resembles Redouté's rose in all respects except that it is more double, forming the most perfect rosette of all roses I know. The dark-mauve petals, suffused with a vivid scarlet especially noticeable towards the shanks of the opening petals, are almost translucent when they catch the light from behind.

A few years ago 'The Bishop' was found growing at the old farm Kromvlei in Elgin by the Knox-Shaws who also found plants at the mission station of Genadendal. I saw my first specimen growing on a grave in the Stellenbosch cemetery where a Mr Devonshire was buried in March 1861 'deeply lamented by Mary Anne and son Walter'. This man had died at Knorhoek, near Sir Lowry's Pass, a farm not far removed from Kromvlei, and one wonders whether both these roses had originally come from the same source, in which case 'The Bishop' has been growing in the Elgin area for more than a century. I found another plant not far from Sir Lowry's Pass, growing in the old Somerset West churchyard which a few years ago was full of old roses, but is now pathetically barren. Cuttings I took from these plants did not grow, so I had to beg for a sucker from the Knox-Shaws who had had more success with their slips.

This sucker formed an elegant large shrub at Boschendal and when in spring it is covered with flowers, I wonder whether I might be looking at a descendant of the 'Rosa Schoenbrunnensis' which flowered in von Ludwig's garden in the 1830s.

1 *S.A. Quarterly Journal*, no. V, Oct. 1831.
2 F. Bradlow, *Baron von Ludwig and the Ludwig'sburg Garden*.
3 J. Redouté, *Les Roses*, Vol. II, p. 29.

'The Bishop'

'The Bishop' with *R. multiflora carnea* at Boschendal.

PLANT
A tall shrub up to 2,5 metres high with upright stems and many slightly hooked, light-grey thorns of different sizes.

FOLIAGE
Five oval pointed leaflets with matt, dull green surfaces; they are inclined to droop from their stem attachment. There are insignificant glands along the serrated edges and on the sturdy leaf-stalk which has small straight prickles on the underside. Stipules are wide and tinged red by many glands along the margins.

FLOWERS
Round blunt buds with sepals slightly longer, open to very full dark-maroon flowers about 8 cm in diameter. The delicate petals are broad, darker towards the centre; they overlap each other to form a neat rosette with some untidily twisted petals in the middle around a column of creamy stigmas. Stamens are insignificant. The calyx is cup-shaped, glandular and small for the size of the flower; sepals have small folioles and are glandular. The flowers appear only in spring and are very fragrant.

INFLORESCENCE
Two to three flowers per head on glandular pedicels. The bracts are short, leaflike and glandular on the edges.

'The Bishop.'

List of Plants in a Wardian Case shipped ♦ "Mauritius" to address W.I.M. Sten ♦w Botanic Garden Natal. September 8th 1865 Freight paid at Cape Town

No s

26	Billbergia zebrina
19	Ilex paraguayensis
55	Ligustrum lucidum
27	Cupressus Rhdeana
25	Melaleuca styphelioides
20	Bouvardia ...
15	Hakea saligna
30	Rose "Paul Ricault" 32 Lane 21 Cupidon
89	Fuchsia "Marie Cornelissen 8 Comte de Sinay
	40 "Camille Bernard 5 "Lady of the Lake"
23	Rose "Marguerite Brunette"

(signed). James McGibbon

One of the first consignments of plants to be
delivered to the newly formed Durban Botanical Society
in 1865 contained thirty 'Paul Ricault' plants.

Whatever Hymie Rabinowitz unpacks his pottery kiln after a firing, friends and admirers from everywhere in the Cape Peninsula flock to Eagle's Nest in Constantia to buy his work.

One Sunday afternoon we found the narrow winding road up the valley to his workshop so packed with cars that we decided to walk the rest of the way. It was then that I saw, in a dell below the road, a dark pink rose flowering in an undergrowth of oak saplings, bramble and periwinkle.

Balancing carefully on the steep slope, I managed to take a cutting and to pick the rose for closer inspection. The globular flower was only half open, but the slightly nodding head and oval, dull, prominently serrated leaves, glandular flower-stalk and delicious fragrance indicated a Centifolia parentage. I was, however, unable to identify the rose positively, though Peter Knox-Shaw, who had earlier collected a slip from Eagle's Nest, thought it was 'Paul Ricault'. A year later, when I saw it at Mottisfont Abbey garden, I recognized the tightly whorled central spiral of deep pink petals in the half-opened flower, and confirmed that it was indeed 'Paul Ricault', a Centifolia hybrid that dates back to 1845 when it was first introduced by Portemer.

More than a hundred years ago this rose was growing in the Cape Town Gardens once owned by the Dutch East India Company.[1] These had long since ceased to produce cabbages and parsley for passing ships and had become a botanic garden. Capetonians who became members by annual subscription had the privilege of walking through on days not open to the public and of viewing many strange and beautiful specimens from the rest of the British Empire. Since the Gardens received only a small subsidy from the Colonial Government, they were financially dependent on the sale of seeds and plants, and it was probably in this way that 'Paul Ricault' rose trees were distributed to many a Cape gardener.[2]

At Clarensville in Sea Point, where the large garden with its sixty pine trees once stretched to the beach, 'Paul Ricault' must have featured prominently when Saul Solomon bought the property in 1865, for in the following year he sent 200 of these rose plants to the Botanic Gardens in Durban.[3] This remarkable man, dwarfed by an early illness, had a gigantic influence on Cape affairs in the mid-19th century, for not only did he acquire ownership of the *Cape Argus*, but in 1854, when the Cape Colony was first granted representative government, he became Member for Cape Town.

The Durban Botanical Society, established in 1865, received in its first year plants not only from Saul Solomon and the Cape Town Botanic Gardens, but also from many other parts of the Empire including Mauritius. From the Royal Botanic Gardens there, today known as the Pampelmousse Gardens, arrived a Wardian box containing 1 000 plants, amongst which were three varieties of roses: 30 'Paul Ricault', 21 'Cupidon' and 32 plants of the Moss rose 'Lane' (which had been introduced by Robert only five years before).[4]

Today one searches in vain for these 19th century gardeners' favourites, and if it had not been for the overcrowded parking on the road to Hymie's pottery, I might never have noticed what appeared to be the last 'Paul Ricault' plant still growing in the Western Cape. From this plant many new ones have been made to distribute among lovers of old roses, for the bright colour, fine form and exquisite fragrance are as welcome today as they were in the 19th century.

1 'Paul Ricault' appears in a list of plants growing in the Cape Town Botanic Gardens published in 1858.

2 In his annual report for 1863, the Colonial Botanist, John C. Brown, complains about the lack of funds for the garden and suggests selling seeds to increase their income. From subsequent reports it appears that this became a lucrative trade for all the botanic gardens at the Cape.

3 Minutes of the Durban Botanic Society in the Killie Campbell Collection.

4 Ibid.

'Paul Ricault'

'Fantin-Latour', another very beautiful light pink Centifolia grown in Victorian Cape gardens.

'Paul Ricault' makes a graceful shrub with its many arching branches.

'Paul Ricault'.

PLANT
A lax shrub with many stems forming a thicket up to 2 metres high. Thorns are hooked and sparse.

FOLIAGE
Five broad, oval, dark green leaflets with small points, prominently serrated margins and dull surfaces. Leaf-stalks sturdy with prickles on the underside. Stipules thin and smooth.

FLOWERS
The fat, round buds have slightly longer sepals and open to very full globular flowers about 8 cm in diameter. The frilled, dark pink petals are tightly packed into a typical spiral whorl before the flower opens completely. The stamens have long thin filaments and are arranged in a column around the short bunch of hairy pistils. The calyx is cup-shaped, sepals longish with small folioles.

INFLORESCENCE
One to three flowers at the tops of the stems on bristly stalks.

23

17th century Dutch East India Company ships off Aden.

·Q·

RED ROSES AT THE CAPE

·O·

'The hedges are of rosemary bushes, in other parts there grow only centifolïen and Persian Roses which grow extremely beautiful and large.'[1]

The Dutch settlement at the Cape of Good Hope was not yet twenty years old when Johan Schreyer, who visited the Cape in 1668, recorded in these words the roses he had found growing in the garden which the Dutch East India Company had established at the foot of Table Mountain. It is not clear what he meant by 'Persian roses', but in 1695 Heinrich Oldenland found not only Centifolias, but also red and white roses growing at the Cape. Schreyer's 'Persian Roses' were perhaps the red roses, since these rather than white roses were more often associated with Persia. The red rose is the one most frequently seen in Persian works of art.

One would assume that the Cape red roses had originally been introduced from Holland together with the Centifolia roses sent out in 1658 at Commander van Riebeeck's request, but Johan Schreyer's reference to 'Persian Roses' could indicate that red roses might have arrived directly from Persia on the Dutch East India Company ships which were sailing regularly between these two countries. Since the Dutch were transporting horses, sheep and slaves from Persia to the Cape, there is no reason why they should not have carried rose plants for the Company's garden as well.

At the time of Schreyer's visit to the Cape, several varieties of red roses were growing in European gardens. Gerard (1596) refers to the Red Rose (known then as *Rosa rubra* or 'Rose de Provins'), which he considered to be identical to the hybrids that Pliny had called Trachinian or Praenestinian roses.[2] Petrus Nylandt also mentions Dutch single and double red roses, known as 'Fluweel' or 'Pat roosen', in his herbal of 1680.[3] J. van der Groen (1696), another Dutchman, called them 'Aert-roosen', 'Fluweel roosen' or 'Provintie roosen'.[4]

There are many references in van Riebeeck's journal and letters to indicate that the Dutch were experienced gardeners and knew how to pack plants for long sea voyages. In 1655, for instance, he gives advice on how to transport apple trees from St. Helena to the Cape, packed 'into tubs with the roots carefully covered with earth and placed in the hold to be protected from the salt spray'.[5] In another letter to Batavia dated August 1658, van Riebeeck wrote: 'We have sent you in the *Parl* one tub containing artichoke plants, one tub containing rosemary trees and one containing seven carnation stools in small cane baskets, packed in soil. Between them are some plants of borage with blue flowers which are added to cabbage and other kinds of lettuce for taste or ornament.'[6]

Whether red roses arrived from the West or the East, they seemed to thrive at the Cape according to early accounts; and Peter Kolbe also noted in 1720 that they were as beautiful there as they were in Holland.[7]

During the last five years of the 17th century, the Company's gardens

1 J. Schreyer, *Neue Oost-Indianische Reisz-Beschreibung, 1669–1677*, Raven-Hart.
2 J. Gerard, *General Historie of Plantes*, 1633.
3 Nylandt, *Kruydtboeck*, 1680.
4 J. van der Groen, *De Nederlandtsen Hovenier*, 1696.

5 This was in a letter dated 6 May 1655, written to Ryckloff van Goens, commander of the return fleet about to leave for Holland. He was asked to instruct the officers in St. Helena to send young apple and orange trees (and young pigs) to the Cape.

6 It was found difficult to send seed of these plants to Batavia as the seed apparently did not remain fresh.
7 P. Kolbe, *Caput Bonae Spei*, Nuremburg, 1719.

DATE	PRODUCT	AMOUNT	DESTINATION	REMARKS
8.1.1696	Oil of roses Conserve of roses Flora rosarum		Mauritius on the *Ten Damme*	Sent together with 85 other 'medicamenten'.
15.12.1696	Flora rosarum Rose-water	40 lbs ¹/₂ aum	Batavia on the *Huis Te Duiden*	Valued at 60 guilders.
1.9.1697	Red rose leaves	30 lbs	Batavia	'We received the opium requisitioned for and also the medicines. We send you the red rose leaves asked for and also the garden seed.' This order was preceded by a letter from Batavia to the Cape complaining that 'The garden seed and herbs you have sent us are so highly charged that it will be cheaper for us to get them from home. Instead of sending us rose petals only roots and stems were included so that we obtained hardly 17 lbs clean from 30 lbs sent!'
11.10.1700	Rose leaves	30 lbs	Requisitioned by Ceylon	Together with 100 lbs absinth, 30 lbs marjoram, 30 lbs salvia, 5 lbs cydomorum, 40 lbs garden seed and three ostriches to present to the King of Kandy, 'who has often asked for some'.
22.12.1701	Conserve of roses	¹/₂ aum	Requisitioned by Batavia	Together with 100 lasts of wheat, 4 lasts rye, 100 bundles Cape onions, 10–12 aums train oil, 110 lbs garden seed, 50 lbs salvia and 20 lbs neyaramia.
30.11.1702	Rose-water		Requisitioned by Batavia	'The onions were spoilt but the oil, seeds and medicines arrived in good order. The rose-water always spoils and therefore no more must be sent.'
30.11.1702	Dried rose petals	50 lbs	Requisitioned by Batavia	'Conserve of roses no longer to be sent as it never arrives in a good state.'
18.5.1703			Batavia	'We send you everything asked for, but no conserve of roses.'
14.12.1705	Flora rosarum	50 lbs	Requisitioned by Ceylon	Together with 6 lasts wheat, ¹/₂ last rye, one bag white beans, a sample Roman beans, 50 lbs rosemary, 50 lbs salvia, seed of cydomorum, rosemary, 122 lbs new garden seed.
16.1.1706	Conserve of dried roses	¹/₂ aum 30 lbs	On the *Ter Aa*	18 muids rye, 1 020 train oil, 9¹/₂ muids onions, 70 lbs salvia and 100 lbs absinth also requisitioned.
23.9.1707	Roses Conserve of roses	50 lbs ¹/₂ aum	Batavia	The Cape was in future to inform Batavia how much garden seed and herbs they could deliver so that Batavia would know what quantity to requisition from Persia, Surat and Bengal.
26.9.1707	Flora rosarum	50 lbs	Batavia's requisition for 1708	Together with 100 lasts wheat, about 100 lasts rye, 120 lbs fresh garden seed, 10 aums train oil, 100 bundles of onions, 100 lbs salvia, and 100 lbs marjoram.
24.3.1708	Conserve of roses	¹/₂ aum	Batavia on the *Jerusalem*	Together with 400 muids wheat, 150 muids rye, 25³/₄ muids Turkish beans, 8¹/₂ muids white peas 'as sample'.
29.11.1709	Rose leaves	100 lbs	Requisitioned by Batavia for supply to India	Together with 150 lasts wheat, 1 last rye, 120 lbs garden seed, 70 lbs fine seed, 50 lbs coarse seed, ¹/₂ aum cydomorum, 100 lbs absinth, 50 lbs rosemary, 50 lbs salvia, 50 lbs marjoram.
3.12.1711	Rose leaves	100 lbs	Requisitioned by Batavia	Together with similar quantities of other medicinal herbs as above, 120 lbs of fresh garden seeds, and 5–6 leaguers train oil.
1.3.1730	Rose-water	1 case (24 bottles) ¹/₂ aum	Batavia	The salted roses were sent instead of the 100 lbs of dried roses requisitioned as these were unobtainable. The key for the case of rose-water was enclosed in a letter.
30.4.1731	Salted roses	1 anker	Colombo	Together with 25 lbs absinth, 10 lbs marjoram, 30 lbs salvia, 40 lbs laurel leaves, 3 lbs cydomorum, 1 lb of rosemary, 10 lbs marmalade, 10 lasts wheat, 2 muids white beans, 1 muid grey peas.
12.9.1746– 26.8.1747	Rose-water	200 bottles	Batavia	Mentioned in a proclamation by Swellengrebel who asked for a yearly inventory of rose-water to be drawn up by the secretary at Stellenbosch and delivered to the Company. This suggests that most of the rose-water was produced in that district.
1778	Salted roses	3 ankers	Ceylon on the *Amsterdam*	Together with one case of laurel, one case of 'dragon' plants, 1 128 lbs butter, 150 lbs dried apples, 146 lbs fine garden seed, 146 lbs coarse garden seed and 50 lbs canary seed.
12.10.1778	Rose-water	100 bottles	Requisitioned by Batavia	The previous year's rose-water had not been properly corked and had as a result lost its scent. The new consignment was to replace the spoilt bottles.
24.4.1779	Salted roses	2 ankers	To Batavia on the *Ganges*	With this went 10 leaguers white wine, 5 aum pickled cabbage, 150 lbs dried apples, and 60 lbs aloes.
17.5.1780	Salted roses	2 ankers (100 bottles)	Ceylon on the ship *Amsterdam* Requisitioned by Batavia	Various herbs, dried apples, seed and 2 840 lbs butter.
10.11.1780	Salted roses	2 ankers	Requisitioned by Ceylon	This was later changed to 4 ankers.
February 1782	Salted roses	To the value of 31:4 guilders	Holland	Together with other 'drogerijen' (herbs).
8.2.1783	Salted roses	3 ankers	Sent to Ceylon per *Carges De Leeuw*	Together with 9 lbs fine garden seed and 50 lbs canary seed.

This list includes some rose products exported from the Cape to the East during the 17th and 18th centuries.

at the Cape were in the capable hands of Heinrich Oldenland, a surveyor, botanist and accomplished herbalist, who had studied medicine for three years at the Leyden academy before coming out to the Cape as master gardener. His assistant, Jan Hartogh, had been appointed for his particular knowledge of plant nomenclature and the cultivation of both exotic and indigenous herbs.

It was during the office of these two herbalists that the Company started exporting rose products from the Cape to the East, and one suspects that they might have been responsible for advising how to cultivate and prepare these products. Oldenland and Hartogh would have known about the medicinal qualities of the red rose — 'its astringency most considerable before the petals expand'. They would have known how to prepare the different medicines — conserve of roses, honey of roses, an infusion and a syrup of roses, for according to Miller in his *Gardener's Dictionary* 'these preparations, especially the first and second have been highly esteemed in pthisical cases, particularly by the Arabian physicians'. Dried rose petals were also useful as a purgative when taken in powder form.

Conserve of roses, salted roses and the dried petals of red roses were regularly despatched from the Cape to the East in varying amounts for the next hundred years of the Dutch East India Company's rule, but exactly what variety of red rose was being used we shall probably never know. In Europe the *Rosa gallica* var. *officinalis*, grown mainly in France at Provins, was most highly regarded for its medicinal quali-

ties, but in the Western Cape this rose does not grow very well and I have not found records or vestiges of old plants. 'Russeliana', on the other hand, is one of the most common of all the old roses at the Cape, growing so vigorously and flowering so profusely that it would undoubtedly be a useful producer of red rose petals. I have a hunch that this rose, which may be very ancient, is possibly the 17th century Cape 'Red Rose'.

The table above is derived from records in the Archives of the Cape of Good Hope in Cape Town, and shows some of the many agricultural products that were loaded onto the Company's ships at the Cape for delivery to Colombo in Ceylon or Batavia, the main ports from where the powerful Dutch East India Company monopolized the vast spice trade in the East. For interest I have mentioned some of the medicinal herbs and other strange items which, together with the rose derivatives, were loaded onto the sailing vessels from the little wooden jetty in the bay.

From these lists it will be seen that *flora rosarum* – dried (red) rose petals – was exported only from 1696 until 1730, when a 100 lb. order from Batavia failed to be met. After this date the dried petals seem to have been replaced by 'salted roses' and rose conserves, probably all made from red rose petals, thought *Rosa centifolia* petals might have been used as well. Rose water (probably made from white and damask roses) continued to be exported regularly from 1696 until the end of the next century. It is interesting to note that no rose attar, or essential

confectio hamech
laud: opat:
rad: jalappae
rhabarbar
Cons ro serum
caro cidoniorum

aq vasculi
ol: ro sarum coct:
anis
juniper
therebinth
succ: cili
Bals: rosanis

Elisc proprii
SpiS: Sal armoniac
Sal solat oles:

1

1 Catalogue of medical supplies sent from
  the Cape to the island of Mauritius in 1696.
2 Persian garden. Products of the red
  rose were also shipped from Persia to
  Batavia in VOC vessels.
3 The Dutch in Mauritius in the 17th century.
4 The wooden jetty near the Cape Town
  Castle, from where the ships were loaded.
5 Johanna Margaretha, born Nötling
  (1757-1807), who was married to a VOC
  official, Capt Francois Renier Duminy, is
  seen holding a red rose in this painting
  by an unknown artist.

2

3

4

5

oil of roses obtained by distilling rose petals, is mentioned in these
records and one assumes that this product was being produced mainly in the East.

Although I have found no recipe for 'salted roses', herbals of the 17th
and early 18th century give the following recipes for the preparations
mentioned:

FLORA ROSARUM
*Pick fresh buds before the sun comes up, preferably those with a dark colour
and strong scent, and dry quickly in a warm place.*
CONSERVE OF ROSES
*Put one pound (0,45 kg) of fresh rose petals into a saucepan with one and a
half pints (0,86 litres) of boiling water. Stir with a wooden spoon and leave
to stand for two to three hours, after which boil gently for a few hours until
the petals are tender. Then add four pounds (1,8 kg) of fine sugar and boil
again for a few hours, stirring now and then with a wooden spoon, after which
the conserve can be bottled.*

A cheaper (and less time-consuming) conserve can be made by beating up the dried rose petals or buds with three times their weight in
sugar, but this is regarded as a much cruder product.

FEHR COLLECTION

Rosa gallica

Rosa gallica.

PLANT
Grows 1,5 to 2 metres high, suckering and spreading easily. There are numerous slightly hooked thorns varying in size.

FOLIAGE
Five oval leaflets with markedly serrated glandular edges and rugose surfaces, velvety on the underside. The leaf-stalks are sturdy, also glandular and have no prickles. Stipules are adnate, narrow, quite long and have sessile glands on the edges.

FLOWERS
Round buds open into expanded single flowers about 7 cm in diameter with light clear-pink cordate petals sometimes blotched with darker pink and having paler shanks. There are many bright yellow stamens surrounding a short column of creamy stigmas. The calyx is globular and covered with many stalked glands; sepals are foliated and glandular on the upper surface and edges. The flowers appear only in spring and have a slight fragrance.

INFLORESCENCE
Three flowers per head on glandular stalks. The short, narrow bracts are green with red glands along the edges.

This wild red rose, which is believed to be the species from which the most ancient of the red garden roses are derived, was first described and named by Linnaeus in 1759. According to most authors it is to be found growing naturally in Europe and Western Asia, but it is generally agreed that it might have spread to Italy, France, Spain, England and Central Europe with the growth of the Roman Empire, having originated in Asia Minor from where it reached Greece perhaps at the time of Alexander's conquest.

Perhaps this was one of the five-petalled roses known to Theophrastus of which he wrote: 'Among roses there are many differences in number of petals and roughness, in beauty of colour and in sweetness of scent. Most have five petals.'[1]

I have never found the single *Rosa gallica* growing in old Cape localities, nor seen references to it in plant lists, but at present it does occur in the gardens of several old rose enthusiasts who have obtained it from Ludwig's Nurseries in Pretoria. Because of its importance as a foundation species from which numerous very showy and valuable cultivars were developed in the 18th and early 19th centuries, it is included here.

1 Theophrastus, *Enquiry into Plants,* translated by Sir Arthur Hort, 1916. Pliny's description is remarkably similar.

Rosa gallica *var. officinalis*

Hip.

PLANT
A suckering plant that soon forms a widespread thicket of many upright stems. The thorns are thin, small, straight and of various lengths.

FOLIAGE
Five large, oval pointed, dark green leaflets with rugose surfaces and deeply serrated glandular edges. The leaf-stalk is sturdy, covered in fine stalked glands and bristles and has very small prickles on the underside. The stipules are wide with free tips and edged with glands.

FLOWERS
The round buds open into semi-double crimson flowers 7–8 cm in diameter. The petals are club-shaped, the outer ones opening flat and the central ones standing up in a twisted haphazard fashion. There are several rows of stamens with white filaments around a bunch of light-green hairy styles. The calyx is small for the flower, cup-shaped and glandular; the sepals oval with small folioles, glandular on the upper and velvety on the undersurfaces. The flowers appear in spring and are slightly fragrant.

INFLORESCENCE
One to three flowers at the top of the glandular stems. Small leaflike bracts are also glandular.

Rosa gallica var. *officinalis.*

29

An enclosed garden in Provins.

The old tower in Provins.

Rosa Mundi in spring.

Rosa gallica var. *officinalis* is one of the most ancient of all garden roses, and is believed to have originated in the Middle East from the single wild red rose at some forgotten time. It is probably the same rose that was used in the religious ceremonies of the Persian Magi and the Median Fire Worshippers of the 12th century B.C. The Persians regarded the rose as the queen of all their flowers, and 'gul', their name for a rose, is used in many flower names e.g. gul-i-narges (narcissus) or gul-i-kukah (dahlia). 'Gulgasht' is a pleasure-ground and 'gulkan' a bed of flowers. 'Gul' could also be used as a general term for flowers.

The rose was an integral part of the Persian poet's language. As Donald Wilbur puts it: 'the beloved's face, her cheeks, her forehead or her entire figure are identified with the rose, her tears with rose water and the world wherein she dwells with a rose garden.'[1] The presence of the double red rose in many Persian illustrations of paradise gardens, as well as in other works of art, is a further indication of its importance and significance in their daily lives.

Pliny described the roses most famous in Roman times as coming from Praeneste and Campania, but equally well loved was the rose from Miletus on the Ionian coast 'because of its brilliant fiery colour, though it never has more than twelve petals'.[2] This was most probably *Rosa gallica* var. *officinalis*, while Rosa Mundi may well be the one that Pliny called the Praeneste rose.

The myth of how roses became red is recounted by Rembertus Dodoneus: Venus loved Adonis better than Mars who then slew his rival. In running to Adonis' aid, Venus fell on a thicket of white roses, wounding her feet on the sharp thorns. The blood that sprang from her wounds fell on the white roses 'which colour they do yet keepe (more or lesse according to the quantite of bloud that fell upon them) in remembrance of the deare and pleasant Venus'.[3]

Not only for its colour was the Milesian rose famous, but for its many uses described so aptly by Henry Duhamel in 1755. 'These roses enter into many medicinal preparations; one finds them in conserves, in simple and composed syrups, in distilled rose water; one uses them in the making of pastries and in many remedies; surgeons use them in fomentations with decoctions of dry roses.'[4] Its lack of fragrance, however, made the red rose less desirable than the Musk or Damask for rose-water.

There is, in fact, no lack of evidence as to the medicinal value which the red rose possessed, for all the herbalists sang its praises. Gerard in 1596 told how it strengthened the liver, kidneys, weak entrails and the trembling heart; how it staunched bleeding and controlled the 'whites and reds' in women; how honey of roses healed wounds and ulcers that needed to be cleansed and dried and how oil of roses 'would not suffer inflammations or hot swellings to rise'.[5] Parkinson in 1640 added to this that a decoction of red roses was good for headaches, pains in the eyes, ears, throat, gums and the fundament. Furthermore, sleep could be induced by binding over the forehead and temples a folded cloth containing dried rose leaves and an ointment of roses made with a little beaten nutmeg and poppy seed.[6] Dutch herbalists like Petrus Nylandt[7] and J. van der Groen[8] published similar remedies, stressing the astringent qualities of the red rose, and Nicolas Lemery regarded the red roses growing in the vicinity of Provins as the most valuable.[9]

The ancient village of Provins, situated in Champagne and said to have been the site of a Roman military camp in 271 A.D., became renowned from the middle of the 13th century onwards for its flourishing rose industry, and the following story of how the red rose was first brought to Provins was obtained from their tourist bureau when I visited the town in 1980:

Thibault IV, King of Navarre and Count of Champagne and Brie, on returning from a crusade in the East in 1240, was saved from drowning in the sea by a young Cypriot named Zupha. In gratitude, Thibault took the young man to live with him at his court, but sensing that Zupha was always sad, and discovering that he was longing for his beloved left in the Orient, Thibault gave him leave to return to his country. After two years the young man returned with his bride Palmyra, bringing with him the red rose as a gift for Thibault. Many fields were then planted with this rose and Zupha was placed in charge of all the rosaries. Soon Provins was renowned throughout Europe for its red roses and people came from far to buy products derived from these flowers at the great fairs of Champagne.

Edmund of Lancaster, second son of Henry III, who became Count of Champagne from 1274 to 1277 by marrying the widow of the previous count, Henri le Gros, adopted the red rose of Provins in his family coat-of-arms and is said to have introduced the red rose to England. When the Yorkists, whose emblem was the white rose, later came into conflict with the house of Lancaster, this thirty-year struggle became known as the 'War of the Roses'.

Products of the red rose are not as plentiful in Provins today as they were when almost every shop in the main street was an apothecary's shop selling dried roses, conserve of roses, rose candies, rose patisseries, perfumes and the renowned rose jelly that over the years had been presented to many famous personages including Joan of Arc, Charles VII, Catherine de Medici, Henry IV and Louis XIV.

When we visited Provins in 1980, we found the narrow streets, grey stone buildings, small courtyards with gay flowers and the curious Tour Cesar towering from the ancient ramparts and dating to before 1137, filled with such romantic charm that we were loathe to leave and extended our visit by pitching camp on a nearby promontory overlooking the old town. We sat around our kettle of tea in the long twilight, savouring the rose conserve we had bought, and contemplated the long history of Provins, once a thriving commercial centre, now a forgotten, quiet French village.

The following morning we were delighted to find a rose nursery that had a large variety of red roses in full flower, some possibly dating back to the end of the 18th century. There too were the *Rosa gallica* var. *officinalis* and its sport Rosa Mundi flowering as lustily as they probably had done more than seven hundred years ago in the fields of the King of Navarre.

We wondered whether these were the same red roses that had flowered in the Cape when rose conserve, dried red roses and salted roses were being carried from the Cape to the East in the vessels of the Dutch East India Company during the 17th and 18th centuries.[10] Some of the Huguenots who fled to the Cape after the revocation of the Edict of Nantes came from Champagne and Brie and one, Isaac Taillefert, was the son of an apothecary. Did he grow the *Rosa gallica* of his homeland at his farms Normandy and Picardy in Paarl? Through his two daughters and two of his sons he had many descendants who lived in the rose-producing areas of Stellenbosch, Drakenstein and Paarl in the early 18th century and one wonders whether they too were involved in the age-old rose industry of their forefathers that made Provins famous for six centuries.

1 Donald N. Wilbur, *Persian Gardens*, 1962.
2 Pliny, *Natural History*, written in 77 A.D.
3 R. Dodoens, *Of the History of Plants*.
4 Henry Louis de Monceau Duhamel, *Trees & Shrubs Cultivated in France*, 1755.
5 J. Gerard, *Of the History of Plants*, 1596.
6 J. Parkinson, *Of the Theatre of Plants*, 1640.
7 P. Nylandt, *Den Nederlandse Hovenier*, 1680.
8 J. Van der Groen, *Den Nederlandtsen Hovenier*, 1696.
9 N. Lemery, *Algemeene Verhandeling der Enkele Droogeryen*, 1743.
10 See the chart on page 26.

Rosa Mundi

The anthers of Rosa Mundi, magnified.

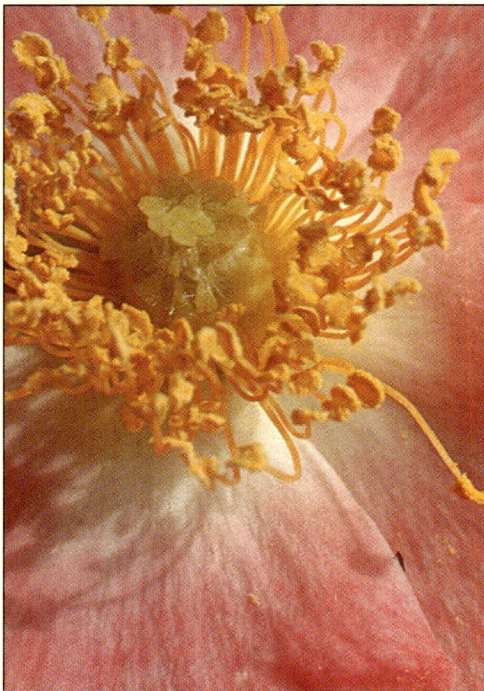

Rosa Mundi, the sport of *Rosa gallica* var. *officinalis*, resembles the parent in all respects but for the mottling of the light-pink petals with darker pink. One often sees these two roses flowering together on the same shrub.

'Tuscany'

In October 1831 Baron C. F. H. von Ludwig, one of the most prominent Cape Town citizens, imported various plants from Württem-
burg and Hamburg for his Botanic Garden situated on land which he
had acquired the previous year in Kloof Road.[1] Amongst the twenty
varieties of roses which arrived with this group of plants, the name
'Tuscany' appears.

This was a well-known garden plant in Europe when the Cape was
first settled, and especially popular for the darkness of its colour. 'The
floures grow at the top of the stalks, doubled with some yellow thrums
in the midst, of a deepe and blacke red colour, resembling red crimson velvet whereupon some have called it the velvet rose', Gerard had
written in 1597.

John Lindley in 1820 thought that the 'Tuscany Rose' was the most
splendid of all the Gallica varieties and one can imagine how impressed
the gardening public of Cape Town, who had free access to the Baron's garden, must have been when these large maroon-black velvety
roses, with their contrasting bright yellow stamens, first came into
bloom. Plants could be bought from Ludwig'sburg Garden and thus
the 'Velvet' rose would probably have found its way into many a Cape
rose garden.

To my knowledge, no old plants have survived at the Cape but at
Boschendal I have raised a hedge from a single plant obtained from
Kew a few years ago when an old-fashioned garden was being planned
for Government House. The government horticulturist refused to plant
any 'old roses' in the garden and so the 'Tuscany' plants found a home
at Boschendal together with a number of other rejected rose plants.

It is one of the first of the Gallicas to bloom in early spring and the
exotic colouring never fails to astonish and delight visitors to the garden.
As it suckers easily, new rooted plants are usually available, but it is
much more difficult to grow them from cuttings.

Gerard's *Rosa holosericea*.

'Tuscany'.

PLANT
*The many thin suckering stems grow to about 1 metre. The
younger stems have many small, thin, hooked or straight
thorns and bristles.*

FOLIAGE
*Five oval pointed leaflets, dark green, sometimes tinged cop-
per, with serrated glandular edges and rough dull surfaces.
The leaf-stalk with prickles on the underside is sturdy and
glandular; the stipules adnate, long and wide with glandular edges.*

FLOWERS
*The rounded crimson-black bud, with flattened top and short
sepals, opens to a semi-double (three rows of petals) flower
about 7 cm in diameter. The petals are heart-shaped, dark
maroon, with paler shanks surrounding numerous bright
yellow stamens.*

INFLORESCENCE
*One to three flowers in a group at the top of the stems on
glandular stalks. Bracts are short, leaflike and also glandular.*

1 A list of these plants appeared in the October 1831 issue
of the *South African Quarterly Journal* under the title of 'List
of Exotic Trees, Shrubs, Plants, Bulbs, Garden Flowers,
Forests and other Seeds, imported lately from Germany
(Wurttemburg and Hamburg) by the Danish ships *Hor-
den* and the *Iona* for C. F. H. von Ludwig . . . Correspond-
ing Member of the Wine and Arts Institution at Stuttgart.'

'Belle de Crécy'

Whenever I enter a clothes shop, I am drawn magnetically to the garments which range in colour from shocking pink to cerise, purple, dull puce or mauve-grey. 'All the old rose colours', my husband explains to amused friends and relations who think that elderly citizens should dress in more demure shades. But I suspect that this passion for the excitingly exotic oriental colours might be more deep-seated in the matrix of my genes and derived through many generations from Angela, the slave girl from Bengal who married my forefather, Arnoldus Willem Basson, a Dutch soldier in Cape Town, on the 16th of December, 1669.

'Belle de Crécy' possesses all these 'old rose colours', from the brilliant cerise of the opening bud to the pinky-mauve petals of the open flower with its bright-green central pistil. Sometimes the cerise is shaded mauve and as the flower fades, the mauve turns to ash-grey before the petals drop. I like to watch this fascinating change of colour by placing buds and open flowers together in a vase on my bedroom sill. Then I wonder for what unknown purpose and by what ingenious power this magic sequence repeats itself year after year.

According to Nancy Steen, 'Belle de Crécy' may have originated in the garden of Madame de Pompadour at Crécy, a little French town in the Somme district, but it is not clear whether this was during the lifetime of this most famous mistress of Louis XV. If so, the rose dates back to the early 18th century.

At the Cape it does not appear on any rose list or nursery catalogue, yet I found it growing in the old graveyard of the mission town Pniel where it flowered valiantly in the spring of 1978 despite the hard gravelly soil.

I guessed that the plant, probably discarded from some well-to-do garden, had been brought to the graveyard by a poor labourer to cheer up the earth mound marking the resting place of a departed relative. Today the cemetery has been cleared and the earth mounds boast gaudy plastic flowers under transparent plastic domes as lifeless as the slate headstones which once bore witness to the identity of the graves.

Gazing at the disconsolate scene, I thought how much more effectively the mourning mauve flowers of 'Belle de Crécy' had paid their rich tribute to the occupant of a simple grave.

'Belle de Crécy'.

PLANT
Slender stems, suckering to form a thicket 1 metre high.
FOLIAGE
Five dull-green oval leaflets with blunt points, leathery upper surfaces, velvety on the undersides. Petioles are sturdy and have many short stalked glands. Stipules are adnate and have glandular edges.
FLOWERS
The short fat crimson buds with blunted tops, open into very full round pompons about 7 cm in diameter. The outer petals recurve and the inner ones curl in tightly to form a ring around the small green pistil. From almost a shocking pink the colour turns maroon-mauve and eventually goes a grey-mauve. There are few stamens. The calyx is round and very glandular; sepals reflex only as far as the corolla. The flowers appear early in November, last only a few weeks and are intensely fragrant.
INFLORESCENCE
One to three flowers per truss at the top of the stems on glandular stalks.

'Violacea'

'Violacea' seedling.

Where the Helderfontein rivulet originates in a bubbling spring amid a tangle of bracken and arum lilies, an early settler of the high-lying country beyond Sir Lowry's Pass, today known as Elgin, was granted a farm in 1836. He called his farm 'Helderfontein' (Clear Fountain) and built a small cottage near to his water source, using mud bricks for the solid walls and locally cut timber and thatch for his roof. Today the cottage has been modernized, but the many ancient oak trees which were planted to create a cool forest around it, its magnificent oak avenue along the approach, together with the superb view from the front stoep, bear witness to the careful way in which this pioneer planned his 'werf' and the sensitive awareness he must have possessed for the magnificence of his surroundings.

It was at Helderfontein that Sir James Tennant Molteno started farming fruit after he had retired as first Speaker of the Union Government in 1915. His three sons and daughter never married and the Helderfontein portion of the farm today belongs to Mrs Maisie Knox-Shaw.

Maisie, who has a beautiful old rose garden, discovered a number of old roses growing in the Helderfontein garden: 'Russeliana' formed a hedge along the banks of the stream; 'Blush Damask' grew in clumps under the tall oaks of the avenue leading to the house, and in front of the stoep was a very large thicket of a Gallica which she was unable to name until a specimen sent to Graham Thomas was identified as 'Violacea'.

How long the roses had been growing in this, the oldest garden in the Grabouw and Elgin area, or who originally planted them, nobody will ever know. From some far-away country these plants would have sailed across the seas to Cape Town and from there transported by ox-wagon over the Cape Flats and the Hottentot's Holland range to be planted eventually in the garden of the Helderfontein cottage.

Redouté illustrates this Gallica, calling it the 'near single Maheka' or 'Rosa gallica Maheka, Flora subsimplici'.[1] He describes it as one of the most magnificent of all Gallicas, needing no special care, though he noticed that only full exposure to the sun would bring out all the brilliance of its colour. It was very well known in his time and according to Thory, was brought from the Dutch nurseries to France in the 1790s where it was distributed by du Pont. The French sometimes called it 'Fair Sultana'. Thory observes that completely single flowers sometimes appear on 'Violacea' shrubs.

In Boerhaave's list of plants growing in the Leyden Botanic Garden in 1720, Number 24 'Rosa Provincialis: flore pleno, atropurpurea, holoserico', or Number 38 'Rosa Provincialis: flore holoserico, atrorubente', might be synonymous with this rose. The master gardener of the Cape Town Gardens, Heinrich Oldenland, who had been exchanging plants with the Leyden garden at about this time, mentions that red roses were growing at the Cape but unfortunately does not name or describe them.[2] However it is very likely that this dark rose which grew in Dutch and later in French gardens, was also growing in Cape Town in the late 17th century.

Mrs Knox-Shaw transplanted some of the Helderberg 'Violacea' suckers into her garden where they now form a magnificent clump in a semi-shaded area. A seedling from this clump has produced very pretty, bright cerise-mauve flowers with fewer petals than its parent, resembling in almost all respects the species *Rosa gallica* except for some doubling of its petals.

1 J. Redouté, *Les Roses*, Vol. III, p. 78.
2 Oldenland's plant list appears as an appendix to Johannes Burman's *Thesaurus Zeylanicus*, 1737.

'Violacea'

Hips.

'Violacea'.

PLANT
Many tall branching stems up to 3 metres high with numer-
ous bristles and thin, hooked white thorns.

FOLIAGE
Five oval to round dark-green leaflets with blunted or pointed
ends. The surfaces are matt on top, velvety below; the edges
are crenated with a few glands. The stem is sturdy, glan-
dular and has prickles on the underside. Stipules are ad-
nate, narrow and have glandular edges.

FLOWERS
Pretty, round buds with slightly longer sepals open to semi-
double flowers 6-7 cm in diameter. The heart-shaped pe-
tals are crimson with dark mauve shades; the shanks are
white. There are many bright-yellow stamens around a
column of pistils in the centre. The calyx is round and glan-
dular; the sepals oval, foliated and glandular. The flowers
appear in early summer and are very fragrant.

INFLORESCENCE
One to three flowers on short, very glandular stalks. Some-
times there is a panicle of many flowers grouped in threes.

Rose hedges at Genadendal.

In a Langkloof cemetery.

'Russeliana' growing in a border together with *Rosa multiflora carnea* and foxgloves.

Over an old wall at Ida's Valley.

'Russeliana' varies a great deal in colour and in the number of its petals: here the flowers are a light crimson and semi-double.

Ehret's *Rosa holosericea multiplex*.

Up and down the Boland, wherever a large sheet of blue periwinkle indicates the ruins of an old house, one is sure to find remnants of the Old Spanish Rose also known as 'Russeliana', 'Scarlet Grevillea', 'Souvenir de la Bataille de Marengo' or 'Russel's Cottage Rose'. I would like to add 'Rosa chameleonensis', for I have never seen a rose with so many variations in colour, ranging through all the dark pinks and mauves to bleached purple.

I have seen the sullen dull mauve flowers on straggling remnants of an ancient hedge in a coppice of oaks alongside Libertas,[1] the old homestead of Adam Tas who in the early 1700s was imprisoned in the castle for rebelling against the corruption of Governor Willem Adriaan van der Stel; the greyer, light mauve profusion of flowers on the hedge still bordering the shady woodland garden of the Retiefs at Welvanpas on plants probably a hundred and fifty years old;[2] the neatly cut hedge in Margaret Lawder's sunny garden in a harlot dress of shocking pink and bright purple; a rambler tumbling over a wall on the Groot Ida's Valley Homestead yard, where the whitewash seemed to accentuate the white streaks on cerise petals.

In the mission town of Genadendal, old hedges separate the long narrow vegetable plots of the small thatched cottages. The lazy, relaxed shrubs, covered in festive pink and purple flowers, sprawl over the water furrows, taking space from one owner and giving it to the neighbour in the informal fashion of all good boundary hedges.

The local inhabitants believe that this rose was brought out from Germany by the three Moravian missionaries who settled in this 'Vale of Grace' to evangelize the Hottentots in 1793.[3] It is known as the 'Rosie Sonder Naam' because no one had been able to name it. In 1737 the Moravian, George Schmidt, had attempted to establish a mission station at Genadendal without success, and these later brethren laid out their garden around the pear tree which Schmidt had planted fifty years before, planting along their pathways the 'Rosie Sonder Naam'.

George Schmidt's pear tree has died down several times and sent out new shoots from the old roots so that there is still a tree where he planted it almost two hundred and fifty years ago. Robust 'Russeliana' roses today border the paths of the missionaries' vegetable garden, and if these are the same hedges which were planted by them in 1793, the plants are now almost two centuries old.

When one walks through these hedges in the spring, as we did one sunny Sunday morning, surrounded by the brightly coloured crimson flowers and the fragrance of roses and pear blossom, the sound of sweet singing through the open church door fills one with piety and contentment, as quiet as the graves in the missionary graveyard within the garden.

There is a lot of speculation about the origin of 'Russeliana' and each rosarian has his own theory: Robert Buist in his 1844 *Rose Manual* classifies it as a Multiflora and says that although considerably hybridized, it had not lost its character as one of the best pillar roses. He adds: 'I have pillars of it twenty feet high, forming during the month of June a very attractive object, having a profusion of flowers of the richest shades of crimson.'

Roy Shepherd in 1954 also classifies it with the Multifloras and dates its introduction to 1840, but does not give his sources.[4]

Graham Thomas thinks that the name 'Scarlet Grevillea' might indicate that it was brought from Japan together with *Rosa multiflora platyphylla* by Sir Charles Greville between 1815 and 1817.[5] Perhaps it was on the homeward journey that some plants were unshipped at the Cape.

A very beautiful painting done by George Dionysius Ehret of a rose which he named *Rosa holosericea multiplex* has intrigued me more and more with its similarity to 'Russeliana'.[6] Here are the same rough oval-shaped leaves, the thorny stems, the round buds, glandular and with leafy sepals, the double flower with heart-shaped petals and white streaks. If this is not one and the same rose, they must be very closely related!

Parkinson in 1620 describes a red rose under the same name, classifying it with the 'velvet roses',[7] so it is likely that the most common old rose in the Cape may have been here long before the Moravians, and it may be that the hedges were originally planted not only for boundaries, but also to supply the red rose petals which were exported to the East in the form of 'conserve of roses', 'flora rosarum' or 'salted roses' while the Cape was a colony of the Dutch East India Company.

But whether the first plants were brought here by the Dutch, the German missionaries or the English after 1800, 'Russeliana' has clung tenaciously to its foothold here in the Cape, and while we no longer need the products of its petals, it remains a hedge of unequalled quality. Resistant to drought, wind and poor soil and quick to strike from cuttings, it could be of as much use to farmers today as it was to their forefathers two hundred years ago.

1 A farm on the southern boundary of Stellenbosch.
2 In the Bovlei valley near Wellington.
3 Hendrik Morsveld, a Dutch tailor from Gouda; Daniel Schwinn, a cobbler from Erbach in Odenwald; and Christian Kuhnel, a cutler from the Neisser cutlery at Hernhut.
4 *History of the Rose.*
5 *Climbing Roses Old and New,* 1965.
6 Ehret's dates are 1708–1770. He worked in Germany, France and England.
7 J. Parkinson, *Of the Theatre of Plants.*

'Russeliana'

At the Boland Farm Museum.

Hips.

PLANT

*This rose can be trained to grow as a shrub, hedge or climb-
er when it will reach up to six metres. It is very vigorous,
inclined to sucker and has many strong stems covered with
small hooked thorns and thinner straight prickles especially
on the young wood.*

FOLIAGE

*Five oval pointed leaflets with well-marked serrated edges,
dull green surfaces somewhat rugose and Gallica-like. The
petiole is densely glandular and sticky and has prickles on
the underside. Stipules are broad, fringed and very
glandular.*

FLOWERS

*The fat round buds have foliated sepals just a little longer
than the petals. They usually open into full pompon flowers 6 cm in diameter, but sometimes into flowers less full
to reveal the few short stamens around the central equally
short bunch of stigmas. The calyx is smooth with a few
scattered glands, but the well-foliated short sepals are very
glandular on the upper surface, velvety below. The flower-
stalk is also glandular. The flower colour varies from bright
cerise to dull mauve and the petals often have odd streaks
of white. They are very fragrant, appear in early spring
and last only two to three weeks.*

INFLORESCENCE

*A panicle with groups of one to six florets per glandular
stalk.*

'Russeliana'.

'Petite Renoncule Violette'

In the Grahamstown cemetery.
Below: Redouté's 'Petite Renoncule'.

When I discovered this very charming small Gallica suckering over and around some of the oldest graves in the Grahamstown Anglican cemetery, it struck me how much the dark-maroon flowers resembled a ranunculus or small dahlia.

Here in 1850 James Estment, aged twelve, was buried, and next to him were the graves of William and Anne Estment who died five years later. If the roses were planted on these graves soon after, these Gallica plants had survived 130 years.

Searching through Volume III of Redouté's *Les Roses* I found on page 35 a painting of 'La Petite Renoncule Violette', described by Thory as one of a series of Gallicas classified as 'Agathas'. This rose matched my new discovery in all respects. Thory had found it in 1823 growing amongst a collection of roses belonging to M. le Dru; he advises amateur gardeners that it could be procured from the nursery of M. Vibert.

Fifteen years later Catherine Francis Gore described numerous Gallica roses that were currently popular in French and Dutch gardens.[1] Amongst her 'light purple' group she mentions 'Petite Renoncule' which she says was also known as 'Felicie' or 'Sultane Favorite'.

As recently as 1954, Roy Shepherd, like Thory, classified 'Petite Renoncule' with the Agathas, mentioning that it was one of the best-known garden varieties.[2] It is strange that I have not come across the little Renoncule rose in present European collections, and that it should not be mentioned by McFarland or other modern rosarians. Why should it have disappeared in such a short time when it suckers so profusely and sets seed so easily?

In Sydney, while staying with my friend Gillian Batchen, whose garden is full of old roses, I was shown a new plant with two small dark-maroon flowers which reminded me very much of my Renoncule rose, but the flowers were not good specimens and therefore difficult to assess. This little rose was called 'Orphiline de Juillet', and was the only one of its kind that I saw.

I am pleased to say that the slips I took at Grahamstown of 'Petite Renoncule' have grown into plants a metre high which flowered profusely after one year. From these I have supplied slips to many friends. In the Cape, at least, the little Ranunculus rose will once again become a favourite, for everyone who has seen it is enchanted with its ease of growth, its delicate form and the charming spherical maroon blooms.

1 C. F. Gore, *The Rose Fancier's Manual*, 1838.
2 Roy Shepherd, *History of the Rose*, 1954, p. 103.

'Petite Renoncule Violette'

PLANT
A suckering shrub with many thin upright stems and fine straight thorns.

FOLIAGE
Five very dainty pointed leaflets with dull surfaces, glandular on the underside and with bidentate serrations on the glandular edges. The young leaves have a distinctive coppery red tinge. Leaf-stalks are delicate and also glandular and have many tiny hooks on the underside. Stipules are adnate, narrow and glandular on the margins.

FLOWERS
The small round bud with flattened top opens into a very full, dark-maroon flower about 5 cm in diameter with central incurving crumpled petals and outer notched petals opening flat to form a rosette. The calyx is cup-shaped and smooth, the sepals foliated and glandular. The flowers are fragrant and appear only in the early spring.

INFLORESCENCE
One to two flowers in a truss at the top of the branches on glandular, delicate, upright flower-stalks. Bracts are small, green, and glandular.

'Petite Renoncule Violette'.

'Duchesse d'Angoulême'

'Duchesse d'Angoulême'.

T his magnificent rose, believed to be a cross between *Rosa gallica* and *Rosa centifolia*, predates 1827 according to McFarland,[1] but Graham Thomas dates it to 1836.[2] William Paul called it the 'Wax Rose' in 1848 and thought it very beautiful, though 'not adapted for exhibition'.[3] He describes the 'Duke' and 'Duchess of Angoulême' as two separate roses, but McFarland supposes them to be the same.

The specimen illustrated here comes from the Knox-Shaw's garden and appears to be similar to William Paul's 'Duchesse d'Angoulême'.

The very pretty fat round bud with short foliated sepals is all Gallica, but as the flower expands it takes on the voluptuous bell shape of a 17th century Centifolia, with a darkened recessed centre and a sweet fragrance as gentle as the flower itself.

1 *Roses 8*, 1985.
2 *The Old Shrub Roses*, 1971.
3 W. Paul, *The Rose Garden*, 1978 reprint.

PLANT
A branched shrub with drooping stems growing 1-1,5 metres high. There are some slightly hooked light-brown thorns.

FOLIAGE
Five large heart-shaped leaflets with dark-green matt surfaces, lighter on the underside. Edges are deeply serrated, sometimes bidentate. The stalk is sturdy with many sessile glands and very small prickles on the underside. Stipules are adnate, wide with loose tips and have many glands on the edges.

FLOWERS
The round bud, with slightly longer foliated sepals, opens into a perfectly neat cup-shaped flower: the many blush petals with wavy edges overlap each other in tidy rows around the central smaller recessed darker ones which curl inwards around the stigmas. There are a few short stamens around the creamy-green bunch of stigmas on hairy styles. The calyx is round and glandular; the oval sepals are foliated, glandular and velvety on the underside. The flowers appear in early summer and are sweetly fragrant.

INFLORESCENCE
Three or more flowers on glandular pedicels. Bracts are 1,5 cm long, leaflike and glandular.

'Charles de Mills'

'Charles de Mills'.

Maisie Knox-Shaw with her 'Charles de Mills'.

This spectacular Gallica grows with great ease and vigour in Cape gardens, quickly forming dense thickets of almost thornless growth. The large flat flowers, of intensely rich dark cerise-maroon, create a mass of brilliant colour in the early summer. It is a very useful shrub for filling up semi-shaded corners of the garden, as long as the gardener is content with the knowledge that the glorious show of flowers will make these areas conspicuous only for a few weeks, leaving them in subdued green for the rest of the year.

No one seems able to date this rose and there is no record to indicate how long it has been growing at the Cape. In Maisie Knox-Shaw's garden in Elgin a number of large thickets all originate from a single plant which she imported several years ago before anyone in the Cape was interested in old roses and when it was easy to obtain whatever exciting plants overseas nurseries had to offer. From Maisie's garden numerous plants have found their way to other old rose gardens, multiplying a thousand times the joy of the original imported plant.

PLANT
A freely suckering plant 1–2 metres high with numerous lax stems which have few thorns.

FOLIAGE
Five oval-pointed leaflets with dark-green matt surfaces and finely toothed margins. The stalk has many sessile glands and hooked thorns on the underside.

FLOWERS
The fat, blunted, cerise buds with short sepals open to large, expanded, very full flowers of about 9 cm in diameter. The numerous dark-maroon to violet petals are small, overlapping each other neatly around a small recessed central cup in which a few stamens and hairy pale-green pistils are crowded together. The calyx is cup-shaped, glandular at the proximal end; the sepals foliated and glandular on the outside. They reflex only to hold the corolla. The flowers appear only in the early summer and have a slight fragrance.

INFLORESCENCE
Sprays of one to three flowers at the top of the stems.

'Libertas Rose' ('Chénédolé'?)

Although I have been unable to identify this rose, it appears to be a Gallica hybrid, judging by its fat round cerise buds and brittle dark-green leaves. The very fragrant quartered flower lacks, however, the purple-maroon sheen of the pure Gallica and this may indicate some China parentage.

I saw it for the first time one November morning as a large shrub in full bloom on the side of a farm road behind the main house at Libertas. This farm dates back to the 17th century and is famous because its one-time owner, Adam Tas, was locked up in the Dark Hole of the Castle in Cape Town by the corrupt governor Willem Adriaan van der Stel in 1705. The story had a happy ending for Tas, who was released when the governor was relieved of his duties and recalled to Holland.

Of all the old roses I found growing at Libertas this one was the most spectacular. It grew easily from the slips I took and I am calling the rose 'Libertas' until someone identifies it more accurately.

William Paul, on page 75 of the second part of *The Rose Garden*, describes a Chinese–Gallica hybrid of vigorous growth with light vermilion, very large double flowers and spiny stems. He calls it a superb pillar rose and a good seed-bearer — all of which fit the Libertas rose perfectly. Could this be Paul's 'Chénédolé' which actually did grow in the Cape Town Botanic Garden in the mid-19th century?

Dr Morley, who has many beautiful old roses in his garden, Lime Kiln, near Adelaide in Australia, has found a rose which appears to be identical to my 'Chénédolé', growing along old roadsides and cemeteries in South-West Australia. He too has not been able to identify it.[1]

1 The Sangerhausen Rosarium has recently confirmed my identification.

'Chénédolé'.

PLANT
A tall suckering shrub growing 1,5–2 metres high with many drooping branches. There are many hooked thorns of varying sizes.

FOLIAGE
Five oval, large, dull-green leathery leaflets with dull surfaces and serrated edges; the stalk and adnate stipules are glandular on their edges.

FLOWERS
Round buds open to large, dark pink, roughly quartered flowers of 10 cm in diameter. The stamens and bunch of pistils are of the same length. The calyx is cup-shaped and glandular as are the branched reflexing sepals. The flowers appear in spring and do not repeat. They are very fragrant.

INFLORESCENCE
Flowers are borne singly at the tips of the main branches on glandular stems.

'Anaïs Ségalas'

'Anaïs Ségalas'.

In the French Hoek cemetery, where many Huguenots lie buried, I found this dainty, light-mauve Gallica growing on the graves of Klaas and Rachel Hoffman, buried on 19 October 1912. I had never seen a similar plant either illustrated or growing in European gardens, and had therefore not been able to name it. When, however, I visited the heritage rose gardens in Australia and New Zealand after the Second International Rose Conference in Adelaide in November 1986, I was overjoyed to see this rose growing in almost every garden. It proved to be 'Anaïs Ségalas', which Nancy Steen had found growing abundantly 'in old gardens, early milling and mining settlements, and cemeteries as well as in the vicinity of the first mission stations' of New Zealand. It is strange that this little French rose had not been more popular at the Cape.

The plant grows very much in the habit of 'Madame Plantier', looking very pretty in the early spring when the many dainty flowers cover the gracefully arching branches. The half-opened flowers resemble 'Cardinal de Richelieu' in shape, but when fully expanded the small light-mauve rosettes are distinctly different.

Although it flowers only for a short period in spring and early summer, the shrub itself is well worth having in the garden for its pretty foliage and the charm of its arching branches. It grows so easily from suckers and needs so little care that I am now using it for large-scale landscape work. Planted with 'Mme Plantier' and *R. multiflora carnea* to cover long road banks, or in the herbaceous border with mock-orange or *Viburnum opulus*, and with pink pamelia, white foxgloves, mauve nicotiana or dark-purple heliotrope as companion plants, what prettier sight can one hope for?

PLANT
Arching shrub about 2 metres high by 3 metres wide. The thin thorns are reddish in colour, short and hooked.

FOLIAGE
Five round to oval, large, coarse leaflets with rugose leathery surfaces and marked serrations. The stalk is strong and glandular, with hooked thornlets on the underside. Stipules are adnate, narrow, glandular and have fringed edges.

FLOWERS
The round, blunt, dark-mauve buds open to very full violet-mauve rosette-like flowers about 7 cm in diameter. The inner petals curl in to form a ring around the short bunch of greeny-cream pistils, while the outer petals lie flat over each other in neat rows. The calyx is cup-shaped and glandular; the short sepals are glandular above, velvety on the underside, and have a few short folioles. The flowers appear only at the beginning of spring and are very fragrant.

INFLORESCENCE
Bunches of one to three flowers all along the arching branches.

'Cardinal de Richelieu'

Cardinal de Richelieu.

'Cardinal de Richelieu's dark purple goes well with dark blue *Anchusa capensis.*

This most beautiful Gallica was introduced by G. Laffay in 1840 and named 'Cardinal de Richelieu' in honour of Armand Jean du Plessis, Duc de Richelieu, who in 1624 became the chief minister and most powerful man in France under Louis XIII. The extravagant and callous manner in which this politician prepared the way for an absolute monarchy in France, and his relentless subjugation of Huguenots and nobles, have clouded his otherwise brilliant career, associating his name with terror and bigotry.

Yet in his time the Cardinal was a national hero and a patron of science and literature. In Paris the Sorbonne, the Royal Printing House, the French Academy and the Botanic Gardens were established by him. Perhaps this is why, in tribute to these accomplishments, Laffay chose to call his most famous Gallica with its particularly rich mauve colouring, reminiscent of dark-purple ecclesiastical vestments, 'Cardinal de Richelieu'.

This rose is a great favourite in gardens of old rose enthusiasts at the Cape and one of the few old roses sold by local nurseries. It does not, however, occur in old plant lists or nursery catalogues, so there is no knowing when it was first introduced to the Cape.

'Cardinal de Richelieu'

PLANT
Sprawling lax branches build up into a shrub 1,5 to 2 metres high. There are few thorns.

FOLIAGE
Five small, heart-shaped, dark-green leaflets with matt surfaces and finely toothed edges. The stalk is sturdy, glandular and has small hooked prickles on the underside. Stipules are adnate, of medium width and have smooth glandular margins.

FLOWERS
As the fat round cerise-mauve bud gradually opens, the outer petals bend back while remaining convex, leaving the central petals folded over each other like a sea-anemone. When fully open, the loose ball of petals assumes a dark purple-grey colour, paler at the shanks. Stamens are insignificant and the bunch of pistils has shiny cream stigmas on hairy styles. The calyx is smooth and round; the sepals short, oval-pointed, with small folioles, glandular on the edges and top, furry on the underside. The flowers appear only in early summer and are very fragrant.

INFLORESCENCE
One to three flowers on short, curved glandular stalks on side branches. The bracts, also glandular, are short and leaflike.

'Cardinal de Richelieu'.

45

A farmhouse in the Worcester district with a rose hedge enclosing the front garden. From the *Illustrated London News*, 1865.

THE WHITE ROSES

The Rose is the honour and beautie of floures
The Rose is the care and love of the Spring,
The Rose is the pleasure of th' heavenly powres:
The Boy of faire Venus, Cytheras darling,
Doth wrap in his head round with garlands of Rose,
When to the dances of the Graces he goes.[1]

Pliny in the fourth chapter of Book XXI of his *Natural History* describes the twelve roses which were well known to the Romans, and amongst these it seems that the only white one was the rose from Alabandia: 'the Alabandian, less highly prized with whitish petals' — less highly prized perhaps because it lacked colour and a strong perfume. Yet when describing the medicinal qualities of roses, Pliny points out that 'by reason of its subtle pungency' the white rose was nevertheless useful for the preparation of plasters and eye-salves.

In his herbal of 1578 Rembertus Dodoneus tells us:

'The first kind of garden Rose, is the white Rose, whose stalkes or branches are long, and of a wooddy nature or substance ten, twelve, or twentie foote high, and sometimes longer, if they be stayed or succoured. In many places set full of sharpe hooked prickles, or thornes; the leaves be long, and made of five or seven leaves, standing one against another, all upon a stemme, whereof each leafe by its selfe is rough, and snipt about the edges like a saw.'[2]

He, too, noted its medicinal use: 'It is likewise good to be layed to the inflammation of the eyes.'

Twenty years later the English herbalist John Gerard (who drew on his own experience of gardening as well as on Dodoens' work for his herbal), completed the description of the white rose by adding

'. . . from the bosom wherof shoot forth long footstalks, whereon do grow very faire double floures, of a white colour, and very sweet smell, having in the middle a few yellow threds or chives; which being past there succeedeth a long fruit, greene at the first, but red when it is ripe, and stuffed with a downie choaking matter, wherein is contained seed as hard as stones.'[3]

Though Gerard does not distinguish different types of 'faire double floures', John Parkinson in 1629 names two: 'The white Rose is of two kindes, the one more thicke and double than the other.' Parkinson draws attention to the characteristics which distinguish the Albas from all other kinds, namely the grey stems and 'white green' leaves.[4]

The white roses of the early English herbalists were probably the same as those described by Pliny a thousand years before, and it is believed that it was the Romans that brought the white roses to England or 'The Isle of Albion' as it was then known. *R. alba semi-plena* is also held to

be the same white rose which later, during the Wars of the Roses, became known as the Rose of York, although some consider that this might have been *R. arvensis*.[5]

Both *R. alba semi-plena* and *R. alba maxima* were well known to the Dutch when they established a victualling station at the Cape in 1652; Jan van Riebeeck, the first Cape Commander, who was well-versed in the medicinal uses of plants and the value of rose-water made from white roses, would undoubtedly have included them in his garden at the foot of Table Mountain.

That he actually used rose-water for eye ailments is documented in an instruction issued on 27 January 1657 to the quartermaster, Gerrit Harmansz, listing items to take on the locally built sloop *Robbejacht* to the seal hunters stationed on islands off the west coast and in Saldanha Bay.[6] Seal skins, oil, and the meat as well (which formed part of the slaves' staple diet) were a valuable source of income in those first days of the Colony.

The quartermaster's list makes interesting reading and includes the following: 1 000 lbs rice in two barrels, 100 lbs bread, 1 barrel meat, 1 anker brandy, one anker arrack, one anker vinegar, one ton butter, 1 ton cheese, 2 rolls sailcloth, bunting and flags, 6 large spars for tents, 200 bludgeons, 2 leaguers full of pegs, empty half aums for oil, 36 knives with sharp points, 2 thick canes, 24 sail needles for sewing up the legholes, 15 strands of twine, 6 pieces of old cable for yarn, 30 pairs of linen men's stockings, $\frac{1}{4}$ piece of Guinea linen for the surgeon and rose-water for sore eyes.

The seal hunters were to be promised an extra month's pay and a merry Christmas if the seal fishing was completed successfully!

Although 'White roses' were recorded at the Cape in 1696 by Oldenland, the official gardener, and again by Peter Kolbe who in 1720 wrote 'the Cape red and white roses rise to as much Beauty and yield as fine odour as the like do in Europe',[7] it is not known whether rose-water was ever prepared from them on a large scale. However, I am sure that most housewives were aware of its medicinal use, and would have known how to make enough for their home dispensaries so that hedges of white roses might have been quite a common sight in those early days of the Cape.

Other Alba roses such as 'Maiden's Blush' and 'Mme Plantier' (which are described in the following pages) have been growing at the Cape for over a century, although their exact dates of introduction are not known. 'Mme Plantier' used to be a popular cemetery plant and old trees are commonly seen growing in mission villages. It is the only one of the old white roses which is still quite often found, for the ancient roses mentioned by Pliny have long since disappeared from the gardens and memories of all Capetonians.

1 Verse written by the ancient Greek poet, Anacreon, and quoted by Gerard.
2 R. Dodoens, *A New Herbal of Plants,* translated into English by Henry Lyte, 1619.
3 J. Gerard, *General Historie of Plants,* 1633 edition.
4 J. Parkinson, *The Garden Of Pleasant Flowers,* 1629 edition.
5 G. S. Thomas, *Old Shrub Roses.*
6 H. C. V. Leibrandt, *Letters Dispatched From the Cape, 1652–1662: A Precis of the Archives.*
7 P. Kolbe, *Caput Bonae Spei Hodiernum,* 1719.

Rosa alba semi-plena

Gerard's *Rosa alba*.

The head gardener of the Company's garden, Heinrich Oldenland, was the first to record in 1696 that white roses were growing at the Cape,[1] and in 1720 Peter Kolbe wrote, 'The Cape red and white roses rise to as much Beauty and yield as fine an odour as the like do in Europe'.[2]

Kolbe drew a map of the garden which had by now become 'one of the loveliest gardens in the world' as F. T. Choisy described it in his travels of 1685. There were four large compartments containing in the one, the rarest fruit-trees and plants of Asia; in another those from Europe; in the next the choicest fruit trees of Africa and in the fourth, plants which had been introduced from America. Some travellers thought that the Cape garden exceeded in beauty the Company's garden in Batavia, and Valentyn enthusiastically said 'Nothing which the ancients have written can be compared with this priceless Cape garden'.[3]

The pathways were lined with avenues of oak, citrus or medlar trees and the flower and vegetable plots were surrounded by high hedges of clipped bay, or shorter hedges of myrtle, hyssop, roses or rosemary. The clippings of these hedges were used in an infusion to wash the sick, or strewn on the floors of the hospital which was usually crowded with scurvy-ridden sailors recovering from the effects of their long voyages. The garden was watered from canals of clear water fed from the streams of Table Mountain.

The gardeners at the Cape, inspired by the great Dutch botanists like Jan Commelin, founder of the Hortus Medicus in Amsterdam, or Professor Hermann of the Leiden Botanic Garden, sent many of the indigenous Cape plants to these institutions and received European plants in return amongst which were, no doubt, the white roses mentioned by Oldenland.

H. Boerhaave at that time had listed the types of white roses growing in the Leiden Botanic Garden, so one can reasonably presume that Oldenland's 'white roses' were those which Boerhaave had called *Rosa alba maxima* and *Rosa alba semi-plena*.[4] These are the roses which appear in 17th and early 18th century Flemish flower paintings, and are probably very similar to those growing under the same names in Cape gardens today.

From the Company's garden the Alba roses would soon have found their way into the gardens of the free burghers, not only in the vicinity of Cape Town but further afield into the country towns and farms. It is interesting to note that Sir John Herschel still found white and red rose hedges surrounding the vineyards at Klapmuts farm when he travelled through the country in 1834.[5] For Cape farmers had found, like the Romans in the 13th century, that the Alba roses made excellent hedges.

There is a further reference to white rose hedges in a description of an inaugural ceremony which was held on 1 November 1859 in Stellenbosch. The ceremony having been completed in the Dutch Reformed Church, the congregation moved in solemn procession down the street to the theological seminary which had been newly established in the old Drostdy or magistrate's court. The recorder of the occasion noticed that a hedge of white roses was in flower along the boundaries of the Drostdy.[6] But these 'white roses' might have been the Macartney Rose or *Rosa laevigata* which were also used for hedges then.

Unfortunately the ancient Alba roses are no longer seen in Cape gardens except where they are preserved by lovers or collectors of old varieties.

Yet the tall, upright, light-grey stems and grey-green foliage make elegant and distinctive shrubs which have the added advantage of growing in the semi-shade where modern roses do not thrive. In early summer, when the shrubs are covered with the semi-double, milk-white flowers of *Rosa alba semi-plena* or the fuller blooms of *Rosa alba maxima*, they impart a lightness to the garden and a coolness which on hot days is wonderfully refreshing. In the autumn the flask-shaped cherry-red hips have quite a different charm. I like to grow these tall white roses near to mock-orange, and to group mauve and white irises at their feet.

The shrubs of the two varieties are in all respects the same except for the fullness of the flowers, and Graham Thomas has in fact obtained the one by sowing the other.[7] It is now known that *R. alba maxima* can revert to *R. alba semi-plena* and *R. alba semi-plena* can sport *R. alba maxima*. Furthermore it is now believed that *Rosa gallica*, *Rosa arvensis* and the white *Rosa canina* were the initial parents of the Alba roses. But where and how these accidental crossings occurred, probably no one will ever know.

1 Oldenland collected and cultivated the indigenous plants which Governor Simon van der Stel and his son Willem sent regularly to Holland. He also prepared a herbal of dried plants which were mounted in about fourteen volumes with a descriptive catalogue in Latin. This catalogue was published as an addendum to *Voyages to the East Indies* by Johan Splinter Stavorinus, translated from the Dutch by Samuel Hull Wilcock (1798). Oldenland's list included the exotic plants growing at the Cape in his time.
2 P. Kolbe, *Caput Bonae Spei Hodiernum*, Nuremburg, 1719.
3 Francois Valentyn, *Beschrijvinge van Oud en Nieuw Oost-Indien*, 1724.
4 H. Boerhaave, *Index alter plantarum*, Leiden, 1720. He was Professor of Botany and Medicine at Leiden University 1709–1729.
5 D. S. Evans et al, *Herschel at the Cape 1834–1838*, Cape Town, 1969. 'About Klapmuts farm the Hedges of the Vineyards are white and red roses.'
6 *Ons Kerk Album*, 1916.
7 Graham Thomas, *The Old Shrub Roses*, 1971.

Rosa alba semi-plena

Mary Lawrance's 'Double White Rose'.

PLANT
A tall shrub up to 4 metres high with many straight grey stems, lax when young. The prickles are light green and more common on the young branches.

FOLIAGE
Five broad oval leaves, blue-green in colour, with well-serrated margins and matt surfaces, slightly greyer on the undersides. The stalks are flattened and velvety with prickles on the underside; stipules are adnate and wide with loose ends.

FLOWERS
The pretty buds with long foliated sepals open into semi-double, milk-white flowers of about 7,5 cm in diameter, with many bright stamens around a bunch of short pistils. The petals have wavy or notched edges, are wide in the outer rows, narrower in the centre. The calyx is oval with many thin white bristles and stalked glands; sepals are delicate, foliated and glandular. Flowers appear only in the early summer and have a fresh strong fragrance.

INFLORESCENCE
One to two flowers on glandular stalks at the top of the shrub on short side branches. The bracts are wide and leaflike, but not glandular.

Rosa alba semi-plena.

Hips.

49

'Céleste', one of the most beautiful of the Albas.

'La Virginale' in a Provins nursery.

THE
SIXT PART
OF THE HISTORIE
of PLANTS,

Contayning the defcription of Trees, Shrubbes, *Bufhes, and other Plants of wooddy fubftance, with their Fruits, Rofins, Gummes, and Liquors*: alfo, of their Kindes, Names, Natures, Vertues, and Operations.

By *Rembertus Dodonæus*.

CHAP. I.

Of the Rofe.

The kinds.

There be diuers kinds of Rofes, wherof fome are of the garden, fwéet fmelling, and are fet, planted, and fauoured, the others are wild, growing of their owne kind (without fetting) about hedges, and the borders of fields.

The defcription.

The firft kind of garden Rofes, is the white Rofe, whofe ftalkes or branches are long, and of a wooddy nature or fubftance ten, twelue, or twentie foote high, and fometimes longer, if they be ftayed vp or fuccoured. In many places fet full of fharpe hooked prickles, or thornes; the leaues be long, and made of fiue or feuen leaues, ftanding one againft another, all vpon a ftemme, wherof each leafe by it felfe is rough, and fnipt about the edges like to a faw: the buds do grow amongft the leaues vpon fhort ftemmes, clofed in with fiue fmall leaues, whereof

Rosa alba maxima

Rosa alba maxima differs from
R. alba semi-plena only in the
greater number of its petals.

'Köningin von Dänemark'

The Alba, 'Mme Legras de Saint-Germain', with flowers as voluptuous as those of 'Queen of Denmark'.

'Köningin von Dänemark'.

Mary Lawrance's 'Great Maiden's Blush'.

No one looking at the full, clear pink flowers of this voluptuous rose would imagine that it could be classified with the White roses, yet the blue-green leaves with their deeply serrated edges betray its origin. It is generally agreed that the parents were probably *R. alba* and a Damask.

I have no record of when 'Queen of Denmark', which was known in Europe since 1826, was first grown at the Cape, but it occurs in a number of gardens today and is procurable from several nurseries.

Although it flowers for a short time in spring and summer only, it is well worth a place in any garden, for the shrub grows vigorously and makes a fine picture when all the fragrant pink roses are out. Companion plants which I like to use with this rose are lavender cotton, the dark-blue Cape forget-me-not and lime or mauve nicotianas.

PLANT
A sturdy shrub 1–1,5 metres high with many stems which have numerous slightly hooked thorns of different sizes.

FOLIAGE
Seven oval dark-green matt leaflets with well-serrated edges on stiff velvety stalks; there are a number of prickles on the underside. The stipules are about 4 cm long and have pointed loose tips. The lower surfaces of the leaves and the stipules are velvety.

FLOWERS
Fat pointed buds open into very full, loosely quartered blooms of about 6 cm in diameter, which have broad, clear pink petals. The calyx is cup-shaped and has numerous small thin prickles and stalked glands; the sepals are much branched, velvety on both sides and glandular. The flowers appear in late spring and do not repeat. They are very fragrant.

INFLORESCENCE
A panicle of five or six flowers on shortish glandular stems.

'Maiden's Blush'

'Maiden's Blush'.

'Maiden's Blush' is the name by which this beautiful member of the Alba group of roses has been known since the middle of the 18th century. The grey-green stems and dark blue-green foliage are typical of all the Albas, but the growth is bushier, the branches more inclined to droop and the flowers are not white, but a very delicate clear shade of pink. It is believed to be a hybrid of *R. alba* and *R. centifolia*. From the latter it probably inherited its exquisitely sweet fresh fragrance and the soft pink colour that inspired the French to call it 'Cuisse de Nymphe'.

Philip Miller in his *Gardener's Dictionary* (1768) mentions the Great, Small and Cluster Maiden's Blush and William Aiton names the same three varieties in his catalogue of plants growing in the Royal Gardens at Kew (1789). As none of these writers described the roses in detail, however, it is difficult to establish which variety it is that we grow today. According to Thory, the *'Rosa alba regalis'* which Redouté painted was similar to the variety commonly called 'Great Maiden's Blush' by the English in the early 1800s.[1]

This is probably the same rose that has been growing in Cape gardens for over a century, and though I have not found any old specimens, recently imported plants are at present thriving in several rose gardens.[2] In 1905 it was still regarded by Smith's nursery in Uitenhage as a superior rose and I suspect that 'Maiden's Blush' was once as common in Cape gardens as it was in English cottage gardens of the early 19th century.

Babette Taute, who represents the fifth generation of her family to live on Mill River Farm in the Langkloof, believes that her great-great-grandfather's second wife might have planted 'Maiden's Blush' together with other rose trees in her garden. She was Albertinia Sophia Meeding, daughter of the Swedish port captain at Plettenberg Bay. Captain Meeding spoke several languages, was an excellent botanist and entertained many of the early travellers. Perhaps he received rose plants from ships that anchored in the bay and passed on cuttings to his daughter in the Langkloof. But although her garden still contains many old rose varieties, this pale pink Alba has disappeared from the Langkloof, leaving only a memory of its sweetness.

1 Redouté, *Les Roses,* Vol. I, p. 98.
2 It appears in a list of plants growing in von Ludwig's Botanic Garden in Cape Town in 1831.

PLANT
A vigorous tall shrub 3–4 metres high with many branching stems. The thorns are fine, slightly curved or straight.

FOLIAGE
Five blue-green oval leaflets with matt surfaces, slightly greyer underneath. Edges have marked even serrations. The leaf-stalk is strong, glandular and has fine, curved, pale-grey hooks on the underside. Stipules are adnate, long and narrow with small free tips.

FLOWERS AND FRUIT
Round pointed buds with longer branching sepals open flat to loosely quartered blooms with muddled central petals, sometimes arranged more neatly to form a button-eye. The clear light-pink fragile petals are crinkled, curly and reminiscent of a modern carnation. The stamens are short like the velvety pistils, bunched together centrally. The calyx is pear-shaped and covered with thin bristles and stalked glands; the sepals are long and foliated. Flowers appear only in November and are exquisitely fragrant. The cherry-red fruit is pear-shaped, smooth and shiny.

INFLORESCENCE
One to three flowers on a spray at the tops of the stems.

'Madame Plantier'

The 'wild' roses of Genadendal.

'Mme Plantier' against the
Groot Drakenstein mountains
at Boschendal.

The road which runs from Stellenbosch over Helshoogte past the Banhoek fruit farms to Groot Drakenstein passes through the small mission village of Pniel. In the spring I always enjoy this delightful drive when white plum and pink peach blossom, lime-green young oak leaves, white may hedges and tiny cottage gardens spilling over with *Rosa fortuniana, R. laevigata,* white and yellow Banksia, purple stocks and multicoloured sweet peas all pass by in a pleasant sequence of colour.

In the old cemetery on the hillside before the road winds down into the village, I spent many happy hours trying to identify the many old-fashioned roses growing on the graves. It was on one of these that I first saw a sprawling thicket of 'Mme Plantier', covered with numerous pure white dainty flowers on the arching branches.

I dug up a few rooted plants and, smiling rather guiltily, tried to explain to the curious children crowding around me that this was a very old rose variety that used to grow in the Cape Town Botanic Garden more than a hundred years ago. The information obviously did not have much impact or inspire respect for the aged plant, for on my next visit the following spring, the blossoming graveyard had been cleaned and was sadly bare of all green growth. I was grateful that I had saved a small part of 'Mme Plantier' which had in the meanwhile quickly formed a large plant in the Boschendal garden.

Missionaries seemed to fancy this white rose, for I subsequently found many thickets sprawling over the earth banks along the streets of Genadendal, where they had obviously not been tended for some time by the inhabitants of the small thatched cottages, who called them 'wild roses'.

'Madame Plantier', a cross between *R. alba* and *R. moschata*, appeared in Cape gardens soon after its introduction by Plantier in 1835 and retained its popularity for the rest of the century. Smith's nursery in Uitenhage still included it in their 1905 list of 'Sundry Roses' together with the 'Green Rose' and the 'Scarlet Apple-Bearing Rose'.

It does well in full sunlight as well as semi-shade, and if allowed to increase without being pruned, the plant builds up into a tall, very graceful shrub. At Boschendal I have planted it between 'The Bishop' and 'Russeliana'. When these three bloom together in spring, the intermingling masses of white and crimson flowers against the bright sky and darker blue mountains make a particularly fine sight. However, the tree which has left the most indelible impression on me is the lost one that used to cover the earthen grave at Pniel.

54

'Madame Plantier'

PLANT
Large shrub with many thin arching stems. The few small thorns are hooked.

FOLIAGE
Five small dainty oval leaflets from 2–2,5 cm in length; these have finely serrated edges and dull dark-green surfaces. The thin velvety stalk has a few stalked glands and fine prickles on the underside.

FLOWERS
Fat round buds, white tinged with crimson, have longer foliated sepals. They open into very full, flat, rosette-like white flowers of about 5 cm in diameter. Small wide petals with wavy edges give the flowers a frilly appearance. Stamens are rudimentary and the short bunch of creamy green stigmas forms a neat eye in the flower centre. The calyx is cup-shaped and smooth; sepals, longish with folioles and leafy ends, reflex back against the stem. They have velvety undersurfaces and glands on the margins. The flowers appear only in early spring and have a sweet fragrance.

INFLORESCENCE
Bunches of one to three flowers on slightly glandular stalks.

'Madame Plantier'.

DAMASK ROSES

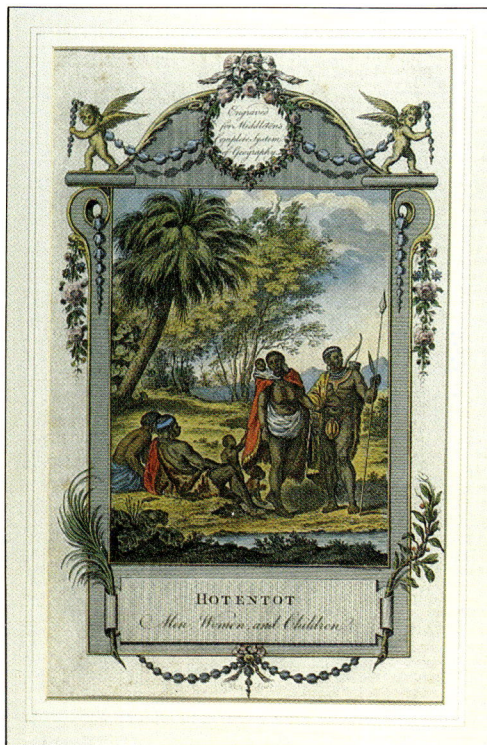

HOTTENTOT
Men, Women, and Children

The Damasks, like the Gallicas and Albas, are garden roses of great antiquity. They are recognized by their large oval obtuse leaves which are soft, rugose and of a light yellowish-green; by their light pink flowers with silky-textured petals, borne in small clusters at the end of long, lax, thorny branches; but most of all, Damasks have always been known for their delicious perfume — a perfume which conjures up romantic images of some eastern garden of paradise — for its sweetness is unlike that of any other rose.

An ancient group, the Autumn Damasks, were among the earliest known garden roses to flower again in the autumn. With proper pruning, these remontant Damasks could be made to flower throughout the season, so that they became known as 'Monthly roses'.

The rose-water made from Damask roses was highly valued for its scent rather than its medicinal properties, unlike the rose-water made from White roses, which was specifically prescribed for eye ailments.

It was customary for Dutch officials to sprinkle rose-water on favoured persons whom they wished to honour. In their relentless determination to uphold the prestige and power of the Dutch East India Company in their colonies, they dispensed punishment of the cruellest kind on disloyal Eastern potentates, but showered favours on those who promised obedience and assistance.

Petrus Conrad describes a ceremony that took place in the Raadzaal of the fort at Batavia in 1679 when the Director General, Cornelis Speelman, entertained rulers of Boegis who had promised to help in the war against East Java.[1] At the height of the festivities Speelman arose and from a silver flagon sprinkled rose-water over Aroe Palaka, his henchmen and their wives — much to their delight, since this was regarded as an act of great honour. Palaka was so overwhelmed that he drew his 'kris', dipped it into water and catching the drops on his tongue, swore lifelong loyalty to the Company!

Also at the Cape, governors who had been instructed to treat the Hottentots with great courtesy and circumspection, honoured them in a similar way by presenting rose-water to their leaders.[2] The Hottentots were certainly very aware of the aromatic content of local shrubs which they applied with fat to rub into their skins. But these perfumes were very strong and even overpowering, so one wonders whether the more subtle scent of rose-water would have pleased them.

It is not recorded when rose-water was first made at the Cape, but in 1681 Governor-General Ryklof van Goens instructed the Commander, Simon van der Stel, to produce it in larger quantities.[3] Van Goens had disembarked at the Cape on his return voyage to Holland at the end of a very successful career in the East where, as admiral and military overseer in Ceylon, Malabar and the coast of Coromandel, he had gained great victories for the Netherland Republic over her English and French rivals, eventually earning for himself the highest position in the Company in the East.

Van Goens' document makes interesting reading:

As has been shown by the Commander and as we have ourselves seen, it would appear that the roses here grow so luxuriously and abundantly that with small cost after two years it would be possible to produce as much rose-water as would be necessary for the whole India even if it were 1 000 cases yearly just like that which comes from Persia, if for that purpose large flasks were sent from the fatherland, which can easily be done, so will Your Highness fill an empty cellar and send 2 to 3 to India first to take a sample to experience what it will be valued at, not doubting that the Company will value a cellar of 15 double jars or 26–27 cases at 8 Riksdollars, which will be of much greater advantage than a whole case of rose water from Persia where as much can be bought. The Commandant will in this way be able to show a discount on expenses and the pleasant smell of the Cape rose water is to be preferred to that of Persia.[4]

This document was drawn up at the Cape Town Castle on 20 March 1681 and subsequent records indicate that after this, rose-water was despatched to the East annually together with other rose products. This continued throughout the Dutch occupation of the Cape and it is amusing to read the complaints when bottles were not properly sealed and the rose-water consequently became spoilt![5] In 1747 Governor van Swellengrebel was anxious to increase the quantity for export and urged all producers especially in the Stellenbosch district to inform officials well in advance how much they would be able to deliver.[6]

It is said that most of the Damask roses were brought to the Cape by the Huguenots when they fled from their mother country to escape religious persecution after the revocation of the Edict of Nantes. They arrived at the Cape in groups from 1688 onwards and settled in the Stellenbosch, Drakenstein and Waveren valleys on farms granted to them by the Dutch East India Company in the early 1690s. Archival records show that the rose-water produced for export to Batavia during the next hundred years came almost exclusively from these farms. The rose most probably planted for this purpose was the recurrent *Rosa damascena semperflorens* which became known as the 'Huguenot rose' and is now quite rare at the Cape, although Centifolia roses were probably used as well.

As new garden varieties of Damask roses were introduced in Europe, they were brought to the Cape and in the mid-19th century 'Noémi' (1845), 'Mme Hardy' (1832) and 'La Villes de Bruxelles' (1849) are recorded from the Cape Town Botanic Garden. 'Blush Damask', though not recorded, was very widely planted and can be seen on many old graves. Surviving old plants of 'Celsiana' indicate that it too, was a favourite.

'Noémi', described by William Paul as 'flowers of a dark rose colour, spotted in a slight degree, large and full' has unfortunately disappeared, but the other Damasks are still with us.

The Cape weather obviously suits this family of roses and perhaps some enterprising person might start producing rose-water once again, for if it was said in 1681 that 'the pleasant smell of the Cape rose-water is to be preferred to that of Persia', might that not still be the case today?

1 Petrus Conrad, *Batavia De Hoofdstad van Neederlands O. Indien,* Amsterdam, 1782.
2 Cape Archives, C495, June 1662. This document refers to a case of rose-water requested by the Governor, Zacharias Wagenaer, to present to the Hottentot queens as a gift.
3 Cape Archives, C700, pp. 357–8, 'Memorie voor den E. Heer Simon van der Stel en den Raad der Fortresse'. This document was also intended to be sent to the Governor-General and Council of India for their commentary.
4 According to Charles Lockyer's *An account of the trade in India* (1711) most of the rose-water came from Persia: 'A Chest of Rose-water is 24 Bottles, but there is a great deal of difference in the Size of them, which the Buyer must have regard to. The best is of a fine Amber colour, and will keep several Years without decay. I have been told, it is made by an Infusion.'
5 See list of rose products exported from the Cape on p. 26.
6 *Kaapse Argiefstukke; Kaapse Plakkaatboek: Deel II 1707–1753* (Cape Town, 1948, p. 226) refers to the original document to be found under C683, f. 265 in the Cape Archives.

Rosa damascena semperflorens

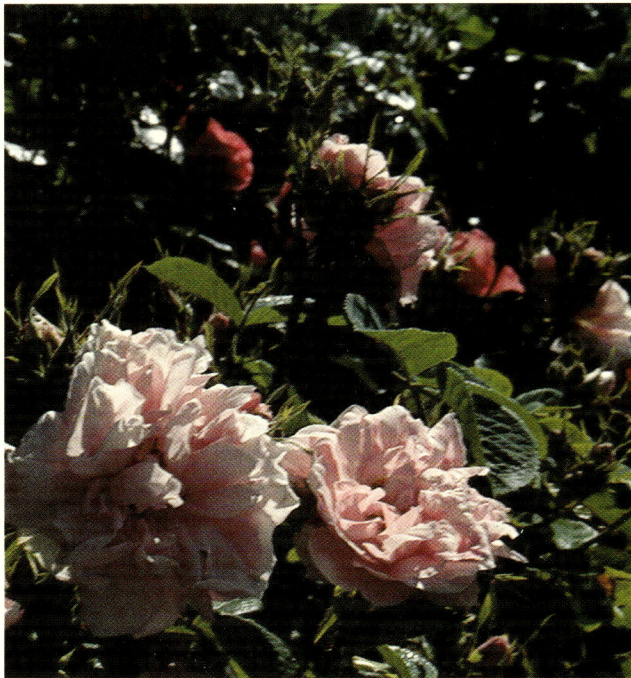

Rosa damascena semperflorens is usually of a clear pink colour. A white variety, like the specimen on the opposite page, is less common.

'I'd sing of rich gardens, their planning and cultivation.
The rose beds of Paestum that bloom twice in a year.'

It is possible that the roses of Paestum, extolled by Virgil in verse written over two thousand years ago,[1] were the roses that are to-day known as *Rosa damascena semperflorens.*

When the Romans founded the colony of Paestum on the Gulf of Salerno in 273 B.C., the remains of the two-hundred-year-old Greek city Poseidonia were still visible; and it is said that the Damask roses, planted by the Greeks in a mile-long bed in front of their temple of Ceres, were still growing there. It is thought that these roses originated in the Middle East and were brought to the Greek colony during the time of Alexander the Great.[2]

The Romans prized the roses from Paestum because they sometimes produced flowers twice a year. Catullus planted them in his garden on Lake Garda and we can still see them depicted in the frescoes of Pompeian homes. Pliny did not associate his twice-flowering roses with Paestum, but his 'coroniola' (little chaplet), which was popularly used for wreaths, may have been a variety of Damask, as may those which grew in the Roman North African colony of Cyrene.[3] Both Pliny and Theophrastus, three hundred years before, had praised the roses of Cyrene for being the sweetest scented and producing therefore the best perfume. Furthermore Pliny noted that in Carthage there were also roses which flowered for a second time in autumn.

These ancient twice-flowering Damask roses were probably cultivated in monastic gardens during the turbulent years of the Middle Ages, chiefly for their perfume but also for the medicinal value of the rose-water made from their petals. During the Renaissance, the works of classical writers once again inspired interest in the natural environment, and we find pale pink Damask roses being wafted on the breath of the Zephyrs that blow Botticelli's Venus to the shore.[4]

Towards the end of the 16th century Damask roses were flourishing in English, Dutch and French gardens. Gerard in his herbal tells us that they were known in Italy as *Rosa incarnata*, in 'high' Dutch as 'Leib-farbige Roosen' and in 'low' Dutch as 'Provencie Roose'.[5] 'The common Damaske rose', he says, 'in stature, prickly branches and in other aspects is like the white rose, the especiall difference consisteth in the colour and smell of the floures for these are of a pale red colour and of a more pleasant smell.'

John Parkinson in 1640 also described this rose and remarked that it was used more for perfumes than for medicine, commenting, 'there is by many times much more of them spent and used then of red roses, so much hath pleasure outstripped necessary use'.[6]

The Frenchman, Le Blond, in his popular handbook on practical gardening which was translated into English, explains how various Damask roses, also named 'Monthly roses', could be made to flower seven or eight months of the year:

The monthly rose demands some particular care without which it will bear but once a year, as the others. This care consists, for instance, in cutting it down to the ground in spring; they are also to be pruned at the end of March by taking the new shoots to the Eyes next the stem, lastly they are to be pruned after each moving of the sap, cutting the Branches below the knots where the Flowers were, after the flowers are gone. 'Tis by this abundance of cutting that this Rose Tree is kept always in flower.[7]

The French also recognized the medicinal qualities of the Damask and we are reminded by Nicolas Lemery in 1743 that it cleansed the bowels, liquified the mucus round the brain, purified the blood and drove away all gallish excretions![8]

Whether for its remontancy, its medicinal use, its sweet perfume or the ease with which plants could be multiplied, the 'Autumn Damask' was cultivated above all others by the French in the early 18th century.[9] During the 19th century, or perhaps even earlier, both the French and the Portuguese took the Damask to their colonies where they planted it to form hedges.

Lowe in his description of the Madeira Flora in 1857, when that island belonged to the Portuguese, writes of 'the old English cottage garden semi-double very fragrant deep blush pink Damask rose with running root and green stems, called Rosa Portugueza occurring everywhere in gardens, often seen in hedges and waste ground on the outskirts of enclosures about houses, growing wholly without culture'.[10]

In the Indian Ocean too a number of travellers to the French islands of Bourbon and Mauritius observed Damask rose hedges growing there in the 18th and 19th centuries. Most rosarians believe that it was on the Ile de Bourbon that this European rose accidently crossed with the 'Pink China', which was also grown as a hedge rose, to form the first Bourbon from which so many of today's roses are descended.

It was also the French who in the late 17th century brought the Damask rose to the Cape, where it became known as the 'Huguenot rose'. Many of the Huguenots who had fled from France after the revocation of the Edict of Nantes were sent to the Cape by the Dutch East India Company particularly to stimulate an interest in viticulture. They were granted farms in the Stellenbosch, Drakenstein, and Tulbagh districts where they proved to be a great asset, for they were hard-working, excellent and skilled farmers. It was probably in these areas where Damask roses were first planted as hedges to mark boundaries, for remnants of these hedges were still evident early this century, 'a relic of the days when nothing but colour and perfume was of any consequence'.[11]

One day, on a trip to Saldanha Bay, I made a detour to the Darling cemetery, having been told that roses grew on the oldest graves there. I soon found the earliest grave where Hildagonda (born Versfeld) and her husband Frederick Duckitt had been buried in 1873. And there, festooning the black headstone was a pale pink Damask rose blooming in small sprays along lanky, very prickly stems.

1 From Book IV of the *Georgics,* which were written in 50 B.C.
2 It is also speculated that these roses originally grew in the vicinity of Damascus, from where they were brought to Europe by the Crusaders.
3 Pliny, *Natural History,* written in 77 A.D.
4 E. A. Bunyard in *Old Garden Roses* thinks that the Damask had died out and was reintroduced into Italy during the Renaissance.
5 J. Gerard, *Of the History of Plants,* 1633 edition.
6 J. Parkinson, *Theatrum Botanicum,* 1640.
7 A. Le Blond, *The Practice of Gardening,* translated into English by John James, second edition, 1728.
8 *Algemene Verhandeling der Enkele Droogeryen,* 1743. This Dutch translation is by C. V. Putten and de Witt.
9 According to Henri Louis du Monceau in his *Treatise on the Trees and Shrubs Cultivated in France,* 1755.

Rosa damascena semperflorens

'AUTUMN DAMASK'

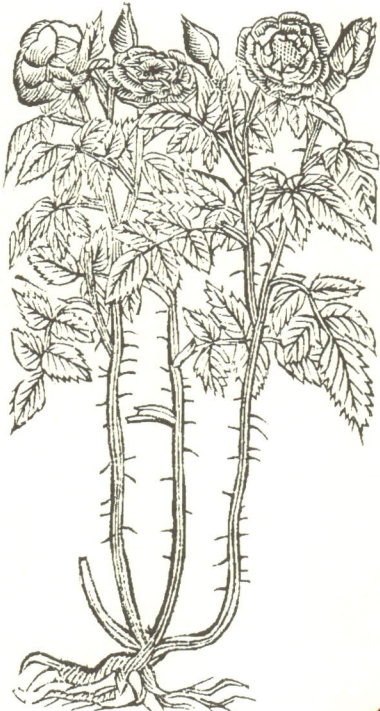

The Damask Rose from
The Theatre of Plants.

Rosa damascena semperflorens.

PLANT

*An upright shrub from 2–3 metres high with many branch-
ing stems inclined to arch and droop. Many curved and
straight thorns of varying lengths.*

FOLIAGE

*Five to seven light green, oval leaflets with obtuse or blunted
ends, crenated edges, and matt, heavily veined surfaces,
duller on the underside. The leaf-stalk is strong and sturdy, glandular with prickles on the underside. Stipules are
narrow, adnate with small free tips and glandular on the
undersurfaces.*

FLOWERS

*Very pretty buds with long branched sepals open to dou-
ble, light-pink flowers about 6 cm in diameter. Petals are
wide, silky and slightly crumpled, smaller in the centre
around well-formed yellow anthers on long filaments. The
pistil consists of a number of short hairy styles and stigmas. The calyx is cup-shaped and glandular. The sepals
are long, foliated, glandular and velvety on the inside. Most
of the flowers appear in late spring, fewer again in autumn.*

INFLORESCENCE

*A corymb of three to four flowers on delicate glandular stalks
which have many fine thorns.*

10 Bowditch in *Excursions in Madeira,* 1823, also mentions
Damask roses growing on the island. The British, on
the other hand, had no Damask roses in their Botanical Gardens either at Calcutta or at St. Helena by 1815
even though they were then common in British cottage
gardens.

11 D. Fairbridge, *Gardens of South Africa,* 1924.

Rosa damascena semperflorens

The late 18th century parterre garden in front of Government House. Perhaps the rose hedges seen here by Lady Anne Barnard shortly after the garden's creation were Damasks.

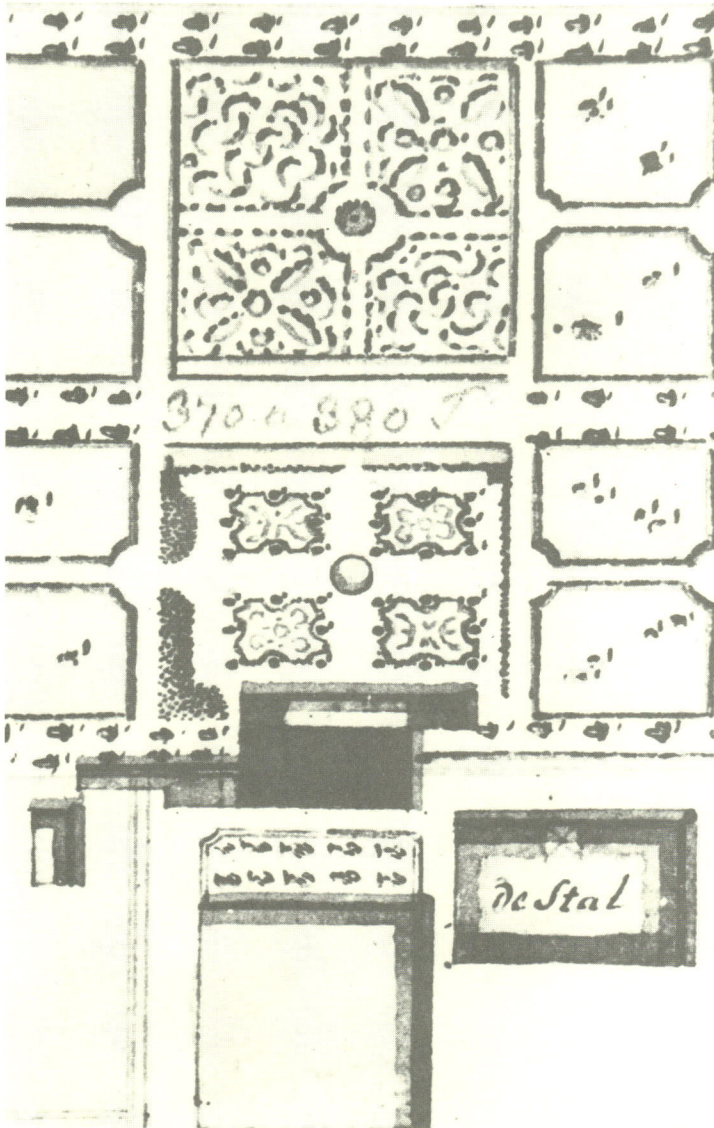

de Stal

Bekendmaking

This document reads:

PROCLAMATION
As the Honourable Lords of the Indian Government in Batavia wish to be informed how much Rose-water can be obtained here annually to be sent there in future, the Quarter-Master or the Secretary at Stellenbosch are requested to indicate how much of this water can be delivered to the Company, and as about 200 bottles are ready for delivery to Batavia, it is hereby proclaimed that those who are at present in possession of Rose-water can supply (the Company) for this purpose.

According to the present Frederick Duckitt of the farm Waylands, their daughter, also named Hildagonda, had planted this rose on her parents' grave. The plant, which had suckered to form quite a large bush, its branches entwined around the cast-iron railings enclosing the grave, was therefore over a hundred years old!

This Hildagonda Duckitt is famous for her cookery book of Cape recipes, *Hilda's 'Where Is It'?*, but what is perhaps less well known is the pioneering role she played in introducing South African wild flowers to Europe. She was the first person to export chincherinchee flowers to Britain and also the first to collect seed of nemesias from the Darling veld, which she sent to Sutton's nursery in London.

In her diary she gives a vivid picture of her life on her parents' farm Groote Post, and describes her mother's garden 'with endless rose-hedges of the sweet old pink Capse or French rose, as it was called (the kind brought to South Africa by the French Huguenots).'[12]

Apart from the Duckitt Damask, I have found no other traces of *Rosa damascena semperflorens*, once so common at the Cape.

When I look at these demure, unassuming, pale-pink roses 'from Damascus' and consider their ancient history and the infinite variety of their innumerable, brightly coloured, voluptuous descendants, I cannot help reflecting on how man's simple pleasures have been changed by his own inventiveness, and I wonder what roses will look like in another hundred years.

12 Quoted in *Quadrilles and Konfyt* by M. Kuttel, Cape Town, 1954.

Gerard's 'Rosa Provincialis sive Damascena'.

Perpetual White Moss

'QUATRE SAISONS BLANC MOUSSEAUX'

The Duckitt grave rose:
Rosa damascena semperflorens
(white variety).

'Quatre Saisons Blanc Mousseux', the mossy
sport of *Rosa damascena semperflorens*.

Rosa damascena versicolor

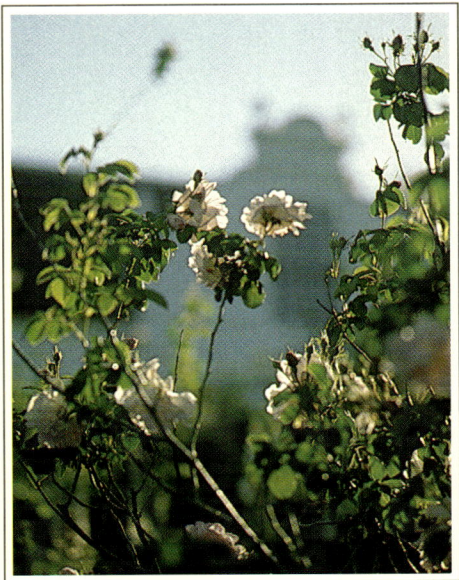

Rosa damascena versicolor at Boschendal.

This rose, which dates back to the middle of the 16th century, appears to be a sport of *Rosa damascena semperflorens*, differing only in the colour variation of the petals which are either pale blush or white, often streaked or splashed with darker pink.

In 1629 Parkinson named it 'York and Lancaster', probably to signify the unity of these two opponents after the Wars of the Roses, in which the Yorkists had fought under the emblem of the white rose and the Lancastrians under the red. He describes the rose as follows:

The one half of it sometimes of a pale whitish colour, and the other half of a paler damask colour than the ordinary; this happeneth so many times and sometimes also the flower has divers stripes and marks on it, as one leaf white or striped with white, the other half blush or striped with blush, sometimes also all striped or spotted over, and at other times no stripes or marks at all, as nature listeth to play with varieties in this as other flowers.[1]

The Dutch certainly knew the rose by 1720 when it was growing in the Leyden botanical gardens, for it was then described by Boerhaave as 'Rosa versicolor flora pleno ex albo et carneo'.[2] There is, however, no record of whether the rose was brought to the Cape in those early days to plant in the Company's or settlers' gardens, where it would obviously have been very useful for manufacturing the rose-water which was being exported annually from the Cape to Batavia.

In 1904 Gowie's Nurseries in Cape Town still had some appreciation for the 'York and Lancaster rose' which they included in their catalogue, describing it as a 'Striped Provence rose'.

Today it still grows happily in several Cape gardens where the two-toned sweetly scented flowers are the first of the shrub roses to appear in September. Though the flowers are never very copious and their season is of short duration, its ancient lineage and sweet fragrance would always earn for the 'York and Lancaster Rose' a special place in any garden of mine. Furthermore I like to pick the flask-shaped, cherry-red shiny hips that appear in the autumn, to arrange indoors with other rose hips, berries and multicoloured leaves.

Hips.

1 J. Parkinson, *Theatricum Botanicum*, 1640.
2 Boerhaave, *Index Alter Plantarum*, 1720.

Rosa damascena versicolor

'YORK AND LANCASTER'

PLANT
Long thin branches form a drooping shrub 2–2,5 metres high with a few straightish grey thorns.

FOLIAGE
Five light-green oval leaflets with blunted tops and matt surfaces. The stalks are bristly and have small hooks at the leaf nodes. Stipules are short, widish and have bristly edges.

FLOWERS
Very pretty buds with elongated leafy sepals open to loose semi-double flowers of about 7 cm in diameter, which are white to a pale blush colour. The wide petals have wavy edges, are of a fine delicate texture, and are either altogether white or pink, or white splashed with pink. The long oval calyx is taken in at the neck and is glandular. The sepals are long, foliated, velvety on the undersurface and glandular, especially along the edges. The flower-stalks are bristly and glandular and have small, glandular, leaf-like green bracts at their bases. The flowers are very fragrant and appear early in spring during the last week of September.

INFLORESCENCE
A panicle of three to four flowers at the ends of the young branches.

Rosa damascena versicolor.

63

'Celsiana' at Boschendal.

'Celsiana' in a Genadendal garden.

When I started to become interested in old roses, Mrs Pam Barlow, who lives on the beautiful old Cape Dutch farm 'Rustenburg' in Ida's Valley near Stellenbosch, allowed me to use her magnificent library in which was an original set of Redouté's *Les Roses*.

I still remember the thrill I felt when I paged through those three volumes for the first time and marvelled at the fragile flowers, drawn with such botanical precision, yet possessed of a spiritual aura and a pervasive light which caught every bloom as if from a mirrored reflection. It was a cold rainy day and as I lay on the warm carpet turning those beautiful pages, time passed into a dream world of never-ending roses. I kept returning to 'Rosier de Cels', for amongst all these strange new roses, I recognized this one as a rose I had seen flowering in front of a small thatched cottage in the Moravian mission town of Genadendal. How graceful the shrub had appeared with its arching branches and many pale-pink loose flowers, and how well Redouté had captured the silky transparency of the fragile petals!

According to Thory the rose was named after the writer Jacques Martin Cels, who first made it known to French gardeners. A flower very

like 'Celsiana' appears in the much earlier 18th century paintings of Jan van Huysum and Rachel Ruysch, however, so the rose was obviously known to the Dutch long before it appeared in France.[1]

The Dutch may have brought 'Celsiana' to the Cape during the time of their occupation, but the earliest mention of Damask roses I could trace occurs in a list of plants growing in Baron von Ludwig's botanic garden in Cape Town in 1831. Perhaps the Genadendal plant was obtained from this gardener, whose plants were distributed throughout the Cape, or perhaps it was introduced to the villagers, together with other roses, during the late 18th century by the Moravian missionaries.[2]

Cape Town was at that time such a beautiful city that it became known as the 'Little Paris' and 'Celsiana' might well have been growing in one of the parterre gardens which were then so fashionable in the Colony.

'Celsiana' lends height and grace to any bed of shrub roses. I have grouped my plants at Boschendal, planted in the semi-shade, with white Albas and other pale pink Damasks, far from the garish Gallicas which would overshadow these fragile colours. These plants, which in five years have never been pruned, have grown into well-shaped shrubs and I expect them to become more beautiful every year.

In Vol. III of *Les Roses*, I found a 'Celsiana' flower with abortive green leaves protruding from its centre. An interesting letter in William Paul's rose book ascribes this grotesque joke of nature to an excess of fresh manure. Having read this with amusement, I was quite surprised when my own plant of 'Celsiana' at Boschendal one day produced a proliferative rose like that of Redouté's, a month after a heavy layer of fresh manure had been applied to the garden!

1 McFarland gives the date 'prior to 1750', but as the name 'Celsiana' was given only after the death of Cels in 1806, the painters must have had another name for it.
2 See 'Russeliana' on p. 37.

'Celsiana'

PLANT
Graceful arching shrub with many stems up to 3 metres.
Thorns are straight and of different lengths.

FOLIAGE
Five large, oval, light-green leaflets with serrated margins
and matt surfaces. The leaf-stalk is sturdy, glandular and
has a few tiny prickles on the underside. The stipules are
wide and long with denticulated edges.

FLOWERS
Pointed round buds with slightly longer foliated sepals open
to large, floppy, semi-double flowers of 8–9 cm in diameter.
The broad wavy petals have a transparent silky texture and
are clear light-pink fading to white. Many stamens with
fine filaments and heavy anthers fill the centre around a
shorter club-shaped hairy pistil. The calyx is oval, constrict-
ed at the top and slightly glandular. Sepals are short with
small folioles, glandular on the outside, velvety on the in-
side, reflexing half-way. The flower-stalk has prickles and
numerous glands. Flowers appear in November and have
a strong Damask fragrance.

INFLORESCENCE
Two to three flowers on a corymb on the tops of the branches.

'Celsiana'.

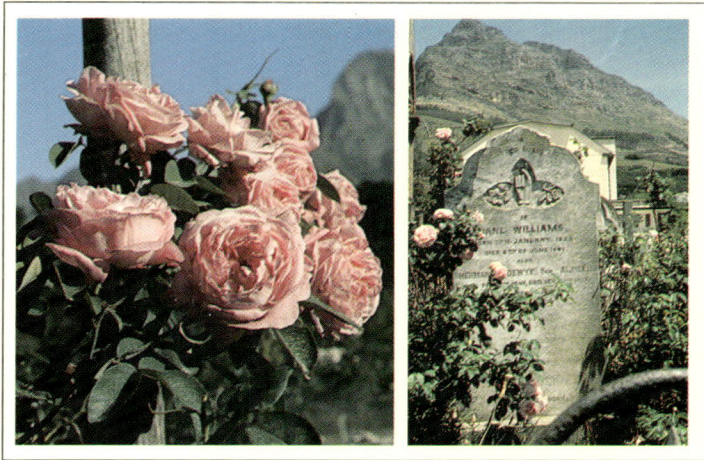

'Blush Damask' makes
a good pillar rose.

'Blush Damask' in
the Mowbray cemetery
with Table Mountain in
the background.

In Australia, too, this was a favourite
Victorian cemetery rose. Here it is seen
growing in the Rookwood cemetery in
Sydney, together with coreopsis.

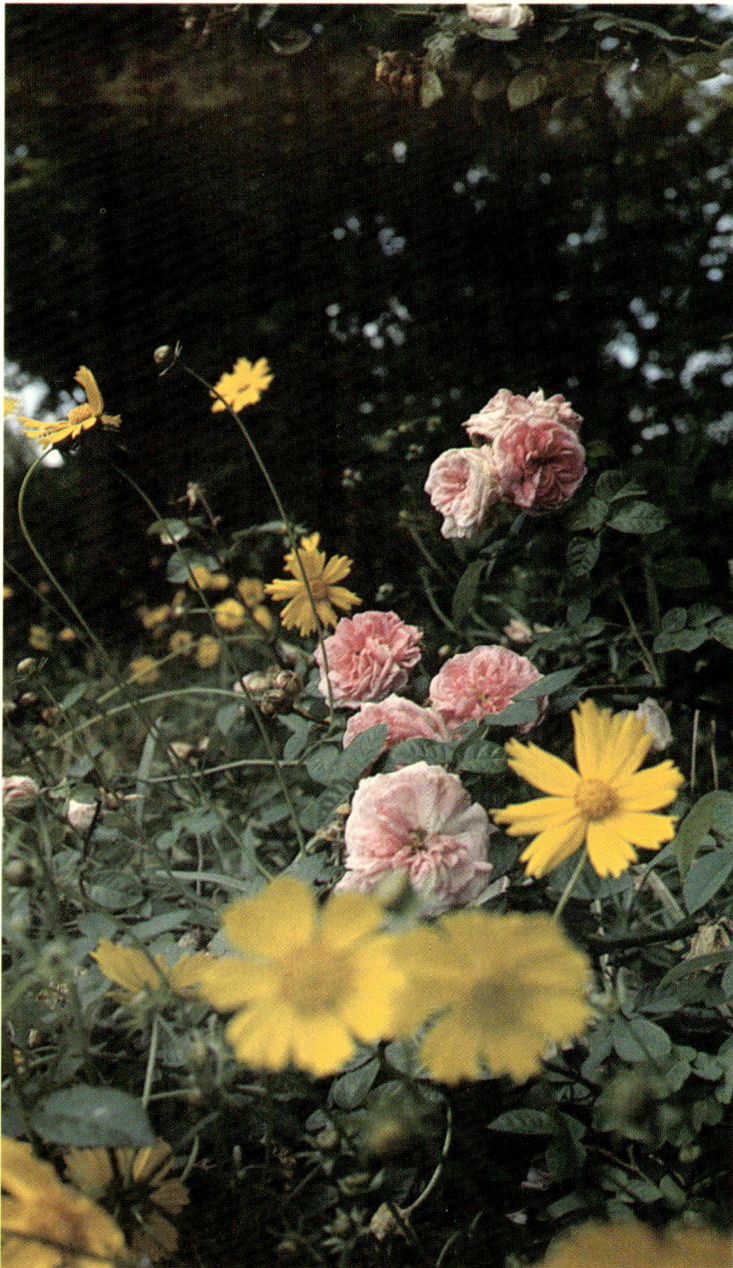

This is the most common of all the old roses to be found growing at the Cape, being especially plentiful in 19th century cemeteries. Towards the end of October, and particularly if the winter rains have been good, the many drooping branches, heavily laden with blossom in shades varying from cerise to pale lilac, fill graveyards throughout the Cape with the most lovely fragrance and colour.

The plants sucker freely and seldom keep to their appointed lots so that Jonas or Karools, in the annual 'skoffel' of the pathways, often cut plants back ruthlessly; but in the next year the lusty young shoots will be there again, for this rose is not deterred by the poorest soils or the most arid weather conditions.

The young rugose oval leaves of a soft olive-green are Damask-like, but as they age they assume the darker, more leathery appearance of Gallica foliage. The fruit, too, is round and of a light orange-red, like Gallica hips.

For several years I did not know whether to classify this rose as Gallica or Damask and indeed found it difficult to identify at all. I noticed a photograph in Edward Bunyard's *Old Garden Roses* which resembled it, classified Damask, but called 'Blush Gallica'.[1] Nancy Steen calls the same rose 'Blush Damask' but admits that it is also known as 'Blush Gallica'.[2] I guessed that this might be my unknown rose, but could find no record of Blush Damask's parentage or date of introduction. Miss Jekyll had known and loved it and found it a common rose in English Victorian gardens.[3]

It was in 1980, while making a tour of European old rose gardens, that I saw a labelled 'Blush Damask' flowering in the Chelsea Physic Garden and realized that it was the same as the Cape 'Graveyard Rose'. Two weeks later this was confirmed by Mr M. Thim, the young new owner of Petersen's nursery near Copenhagen. Old Mr Petersen was then eighty-six years old and though seriously ill, was able to identify each of the roses brought to his sick-bed by the new owner, who had his hands full cleaning a rather neglected garden and labelling all the shrubs in this oldest rose nursery in Denmark.

Mr Thim showed me a 'Blush Hip' growing next to a 'Blush Damask'. At first the two looked similar, but he was able to point out small differences, so that I came away feeling quite satisfied that the correct name had been found for my unidentified rose.

Now, whenever I look at 'Blush Damask', I am reminded of that wonderful sunny day that my friend Gertrud Elling, also an old rose lover, and I had spent at the Petersen nursery where we had been delighted with a most remarkable collection of old roses. Mr Thim had expected us and had baked a fresh brown bread for our lunch which we enjoyed together with local cottage cheese and a bottle of white wine.

On the way back to Gertrud's home we drove through bright yellow mustard fields and, warm with wine and stirred by the beautiful Danish countryside, we sang with great gusto and zeal some old Danish songs that Gertrud had taught me, all the way home to Copenhagen.

Roses, wine and song — what happiness from simple pleasures springs!

1 E. A. Bunyard, *Old Garden Roses*.
2 Nancy Steen, *The Charm of Old Roses*.
3 G. Jekyll, and E. Mawley, *Roses for English Gardens*.

'Blush Damask'

PLANT
A suckering shrub 1,5–2 metres high with many long lax branches on which there are a few hooked thorns.

FOLIAGE
Five round-oval leaflets with serrated edges and dull rugose surfaces, light green in the young leaves, dark green in the older ones. The stem is sturdy with a few stalked glands and very small prickles on the underside. Stipules are thin with free points, glandular on the edges.

FLOWERS
The short, fat, round cerise buds open to very full, flat flowers 7–8 cm in diameter. Many small dark-pink petals, folded on themselves towards the centre, are usually arranged in quarters. When older, the outer petals reflex and the flower turns a faded mauve. A branched, green, hairy pistil and a few yellow stamens show in the centre. The calyx is cup-shaped and glandular; the short sepals with a few small folioles are velvety on the undersides and glandular on the upper surfaces and along the edges. The flowers appear towards the end of October, last about four weeks and are very fragrant.

INFLORESCENCE
Corymbs of three to four flowers appear on small branchlets all along the drooping stems or at the tops of branches. Flower-stalks are glandular and have small to large foliaceous bracts at their proximal ends.

'Blush Damask'.

'Rothman Rose'

'CHAMPNEYS' PINK CLUSTER'

'Rothman Rose'.

This unknown summer flowering rose (which I have named "Rothman Rose"), has now been identified as possibly "Champneys' Pink Cluster" (see page 123). It commonly occurs in old Cape gardens and is often planted in hedges. The flowers have light pink, silky petals and a lovely fragrance. It grows vigorously to two metres and has thorny branches. I have never seen its hips.

'Leda'

'Double Delight'.

'Leda'.

More than a hundred and fifty years before Armstrong Nurseries astonished the rose world with their two-toned 'Double Delight', a garden favourite called 'Painted Damask', also known as 'Leda', was producing flowers with almost exactly the same colour combination and the same type of fragrance, but what a world of difference lies between these two beauties!

The modern Hybrid Tea, large and voluptuous with broad outer petals reflexing in perfect symmetry from the scroll of high-pointed central petals, and the modest Damask with many small petals flatly arranged in quarters around the central green eye, each represents a rose style acclaimed as unsurpassed by their contemporaries. Modern rosarians who cultivate their flowers for exhibition will reject the old Damask with contempt, but the gardener who finds his pleasure in a variety of form and colour will make a place for the old shrub with its luscious dark-green Damask foliage as well as for the modern Hybrid Tea. He will welcome each flower as it opens with the same excitement that he feels for all the wonders which his garden yields.

'Leda' has found its way into a few old rose gardens of the Western Cape, but how long this early 19th century English rose has been here, no one can say. 'Double Delight', on the other hand, is to be found in every rose garden of note, for it is extremely popular not only as a show rose, but also for garden display.

PLANT
A branching shrub 1,5–2 metres high, with many thin white thorns of different sizes.

FOLIAGE
Five large round to oval leaflets with neatly crenated edges and dull surfaces with a few glands on the undersides along the midrib. The sturdy stalk is prickly and glandular; the leaflets sessile. The light-green stipules are wide and adnate with free tips.

FLOWERS
The round crimson-washed bud is small and flat-topped with longer sepals. The flowers are 7–8 cm in diameter, very full, and open flat with a button-eye in the centre. The petals are white with crimson edges. Stamens are thin and delicate with tiny crimson anthers; the pistil is a tight thin column the same length as the stamens. The small cup-shaped calyx is taken in at the top and is glandular; sepals are much branched, glandular and reflexing. The flowers appear only in spring and are very fragrant.

INFLORESCENCE
A corymb of three to four flowers on glandular pedicels. Bracts are short, light-green and leaflike.

'La Ville de Bruxelles'

'La Ville de Bruxelles'.

'La Ville de Bruxelles' was growing in the Cape Town Gardens when Thomas Bowler drew this picture in the mid-19th century.

This beautiful Damask rose, introduced by Vibert in 1849, was listed as one of the plants growing in the Botanic Gardens of Cape Town nine years later.

It is a strong vigorous shrub with many upright stems which form an attractive dense green thicket if left to grow uncurbed. Though it blooms for only six weeks, the numerous large pink flowers which cover the bush are a wonderful sight and well worth waiting for.

Like many of the old roses, this one prefers to grow in semi-shade in the Cape where, with dark-blue Cape forget-me-nots and sheaths of white arums, the pink flowers appear even brighter and the fragrance hangs heavier, protected from the destructive heat of the sun.

PLANT
A dense shrub with many upright stems to 1,5 metres, covered in small bristles.

FOLIAGE
Five medium-sized, dark-green, oval, blunt-pointed leaflets with crenated edges and rough, matt surfaces. The stalk is sturdy, flattish, and glandular, but has no prickles. Stipules are adnate with glandular edges.

FLOWERS
The small fat buds with slightly longer branched sepals open to large, full, clear-pink flowers about 9 cm in diameter. The outer petals are broad and arranged in quarters with the central smaller ones curling in to form a ring around the central bunch of short hairy pistils and rudimentary stamens. The calyx is small, shallow, cup-shaped and glandular; the sepals much branched, velvety on the inner surfaces and glandular on the outside, reflexing back against the stem. The flowers have a marked Damask fragrance and appear only in the early summer.

INFLORESCENCE
Usually three flowers on a truss, the middle one flowering first. The flower-stalks are glandular and have short bracts at the bases.

'Madame Hardy'

'Madame Hardy'.

The very beautiful pure white Damask rose has been growing at the Cape for well over a century, for it is recorded in a list of plants from the Botanic Garden in Cape Town in 1858.

Introduced in 1832 by J. A. Hardy, superintendent of the Luxembourg Gardens in Paris, it was soon hailed as a triumph and declared to be even more beautiful than the white rose, 'Globe Hip', which up to that time had been regarded as unsurpassed.[1]

In our hot climate the vigorous, erect shrub likes a partially shaded spot, and in the half-light and against a cool green background the flower in all its stages appears particularly lovely: first there are the fat round buds with long green branched sepals, then the flushed cup-shaped half-open blooms, and lastly the fully expanded, flat, shiny white, quartered flowers with satin-like petals round a twist of green styles in the centre. A lovely fragrance reminds one that the parents were probably of Damask and Centifolia lineage.

'Mme Zoetmans', which is two years older, could easily be confused with 'Mme Hardy' which it resembles very closely, but the flowers are more blush, the petals smaller and without the satiny sheen of 'Mme Hardy'. It does not appear ever to have grown at the Cape, but I saw it flowering in the Plantskole in Copenhagen, where I took a photograph to compare with 'Mme Hardy'.

1 In 1848 William Paul in his *Rose Garden* predicted that this rose would make M. Hardy famous and Buist in his *Rose Manual* (1844) was equally enthusiastic.

PLANT
Strong compact shrub just over a metre high, with small, slightly hooked thorns.

FOLIAGE
Five to seven large, oval-round, mid-green leaflets with rugose surfaces and deeply serrated edges. The stems are rough, sturdy, and glandular with no prickles on the underside. Stipules are wide with free tips and have many glands along the edges.

FLOWERS
Fat round buds with long foliated sepals open into full, flat, quartered white flowers about 8 cm in diameter. The stamens are rudimentary and the leaflike styles are twisted together into a column which shows as a green eye in the centre of the flower. The calyx is cup-shaped and glandular; sepals are foliaceous, very glandular and velvety on the undersides. The flowers appear in November only and have a strong Damask fragrance.

INFLORESCENCE
Usually a cluster of three flowers with foliated bracts at the bases of the glandular flower-stalks.

71

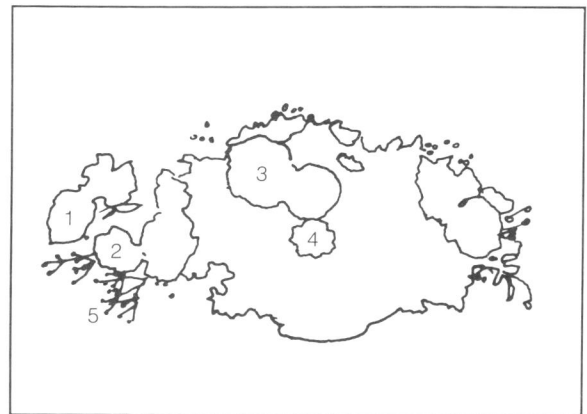

1 'HUME'S BLUSH'.
2 'PARSONS' PINK CHINA'.
3 'YELLOW TEA-SCENTED CHINA'.
4 'SLATER'S CRIMSON CHINA'.
5 HIPS OF 'ROSA MULTIFLORA'.

Late 18th century Chinese bowl with the four China 'stud roses' which reached Europe at the turn of the 18th century.

CHINA ROSES

The first Chinese garden roses to arrive in the West at the turn of the 18th century caused quite a stir in the horticultural world, for they brought a new fragrance, new colours and the most important quality of all — repeat flowering.

The four 'stud roses', as they came to be known, were *Rosa chinensis semperflorens* ('Slater's Crimson China'), 'Parsons' Pink China' ('Old Monthly') *Rosa odorata* ('Hume's Blush China', the first tea-scented rose) and its yellow variant, 'Parks' Yellow China'.

When breeders set to work on these roses, crossing them with existing Western varieties, the results were revolutionary. Entirely new classes were created: the Bourbons ('Parsons' Pink China' x *Rosa damascena semperflorens*); the Noisettes ('Parsons' Pink China' x *Rosa moschata*); the Tea roses (*Rosa odorata* or 'Parks' Yellow China' x various existing roses). And it was by inter-crossing all these groups that the highly prized Hybrid Perpetuals were raised towards the latter half of the 19th century.

Those roses that remain close in character to the original four stud roses are retained in a class known as the Chinas — a rather vague group perhaps, consisting of varieties sometimes placed under other classes according to the classifier's personal preference.

I think the qualities one appreciates in the Chinas are the smooth stems with scattered hooked thorns; the dark green oval pointed leaves, maroon when young; the pretty, loose flowers with silky petals either soft pink or crimson; the oval orange hips; and above all, the very sweet spicy fragrance and the constant flowering.

For over two centuries the China roses have formed part of the Cape scenery. No doubt off-loaded by the early Dutch traders during their halfway rest in Table Bay on their return voyages from the East, they still retain their popularity in old and modern gardens.

For the flat dweller, for the small suburban garden and for the large estate, there is a China rose of suitable size and habit; and if the flowers are cut back regularly, the plant will continue to produce an abundance of colour throughout the year.

From left to right:
Rosa chinensis semperflorens in a cemetery in Mauritius.

R. chinensis semperflorens in the Nancy Steen Memorial Garden in Auckland, New Zealand.

In Mauritius outside the home of Nassar Jugreet in New Grove.

In a Mauritius garden.

Remnants of a hedge growing along a water-furrow next to a Creole house in Mauritius.

Below:
R. chinensis semperflorens in a Creole garden in St. Denis, Réunion.

Famille rose bowl with the red and pink *Rosa chinensis semperflorens* sent to me by Mary Orieux from Mauritius.

On the 10th June 1983 my husband and I landed at Mauritius and, having greeted the taxi-driver who was waiting for us at the airport, we drove off to Grand Baie where we had booked in for a week's visit. Scarcely 10 kilometres from the airport, while driving through an area of many small Creole houses, I thought I saw what looked like a red China rose in one of the little street gardens, and told the driver to stop. On the narrow, traffic-laden road this seemed rather hazardous, but sensing my excitement, the friendly taximan pulled off quickly into someone's yard, and I ran back to behold my first *Rosa chinensis semperflorens*.

While my husband took photographs, I made notes and sketches of the plant growing at the entrance steps of a small cottage. The Creoles are a smiling, friendly people, desperately keen to be photographed, so that it was quite a time before we were able to drive off again, but by then I had with me a large bunch of the dainty red flowers which I had seen illustrated a month before in Jacquin's *Plantarum Shoenbrunnensis* (1798). This painting of Jacquin's had obviously been done from nature, for it very closely resembled the rose which I had just seen and was quite unlike the funny little rose published thirty years previously under the same name in his *Observatorum Botanicum*,

which looked more like the specimen collected by Osbeck in China in 1751.[1]

After this first encounter with the *Rosa chinensis semperflorens*, I saw it many times again in Mauritius and also a week later in Réunion where it grows wild in the Plain de Palmiste.

The two-metre high plants have many rather lanky stems with long delicate oval pointed leaves and very dainty semi-double flowers in small clusters at the top of the bush. Sometimes the flowers are single, but more often they have two or three rows of very delicate maroon petals, though occasionally a flower will be pink. They are very much like the 'Old Monthly' in character, but the flowers are in all respects frailer. In fact I know of no other rose as dainty and as airy as this little China rose, and I can well imagine what excitement it must have caused on its introduction in 1792 when Gilbert Slater, who had financial connections with the British East India Company, procured for his Essex garden live plants of the rose which was later to be associated with his name.

'He readily imparted his most valuable acquisitions to those who were most likely to increase them; this plant soon became conspicuous in the collections of the principal nurserymen near town and in the course of a few years will no doubt decorate the window of every amateur', wrote Mr Wilbour Curtis in the December 1794 issue of his *Botanical Magazine*, when he illustrated and described this rose for the first time as *Rosa semperflorens* or 'Everblooming Rose'.

Because this rose carries in its chromosomes a recessive gene for repetitive flowering, its importance as a 'stud' parent can hardly be over-estimated; and so, not only for its own attractions but also for the revolution it caused in the rose-breeding world of the early 1800s, we must pay our respects to this Chinese garden rose.

Incredibly enough it had gone out of cultivation by the end of the

1 Preserved in the Linnaeus Herbarium (T. 55).

Rosa chinensis semperflorens

'SLATER'S CRIMSON CHINA'

PLANT
This is a graceful shrub with thin lanky branches and a few slightly hooked thorns on the light-green stems. Grown as a hedge it makes a dense thicket up to 2 metres high, with the flowers appearing at the tops of the branches.

FOLIAGE
Leaflets long and tapering, usually three or five on a smooth stalk without prickles. The edges are shallowly toothed. The upper surface is shiny and smooth, slightly duller beneath. New leaves are tinged red as are the stipules which have a few glands on the proximal ends and shallowly toothed edges.

FLOWERS
The small pointed buds have long sepals which soon reflex back against the stalk as the flower unfolds. The silky petals vary in number; sometimes there are only six but mostly there are eleven large broad outer petals with six smaller ones in the centre. The flowers are maroon with paler pink shanks and an occasional white streak, but sometimes the whole flower is light pink. The stamens have long pale filaments and yellow anthers which curl in over a short clump of reddish styles with red-tinted stigmas. The calyx is oblong, taken in at the top and smooth, but the unfoliated long sepals are velvety on both sides and have a few glands on the midrib of the upper surface. The flowers are very fragrant and bloom the whole year.

INFLORESCENCE
Several panicles of three to five flowers are carried at the tops of the young branches on long, delicate, glandular flower-stalks. There are leafy bracts at the beginning of the inflorescence and again one-third of the way up the flower-stalks.

Rosa chinensis semperflorens.

Rosa indica by John Reeves.
(From a collection of Chinese paintings in the Lindley Library)

75

Rosa chinensis semperflorens

Rosa chinensis semperflorens illustrated by Jacquin in his *Plantarum Shoenbrunnensis*.

An 18th century painting on rice paper of the Canton River. (From Nils Parkfelt's collection)

19th century and was thought to be extinct until Richard Thompson discovered it once again in Bermuda in 1953,[2] since which time it has been cultivated at Bayfordbury in Britain. However, anyone wishing to see it grown to its full potential should visit Mauritius and Réunion and keep a sharp look-out in the byways and around the poorer country cottages to catch a glimpse of the small crimson rose 'where amateurs still cherish it'.

I suspect that *Rosa chinensis semperflorens* has been growing on these two Indian Ocean Islands since the middle of the 18th century or perhaps earlier. It was introduced by J. Harrington to the Calcutta Botanic Garden in 1803, and in 1813 Roxburgh recorded it in St. Helena.[3]

There is no clear reference to this rose at the Cape, although 'Perpetual' growing in Baron von Ludwig's garden in 1831 is a possibility. I have never seen it growing here myself, but have been told about a small red rose that used to grow at Alphen in Constantia[4] and in the mission town of Wupperthal.

As there is a good chance that some of these roses might have been off-loaded from Dutch or English ships on their way between the West and East, perhaps via St. Helena or the Indian islands, I may still be lucky enough to find a *Rosa chinensis semperflorens* flowering in some remote corner of the Cape.

A few years ago I obtained a permit to import cuttings of this rose from Mauritius. During my visit there I had made good friends with Mary Orieux who owns the only rose nursery on the island. She did not know the rose but promised to be helpful with the treatment of plant slips to obtain the phyto-sanitary certificate required by import control. While waiting excitedly for the slips to arrive, I received a telegram from Mary to say that droughts on Mauritius had been so bad that there was no suitable plant material to send. The certificate expired and rather than go through the whole wearisome business of obtaining another one, I asked a friend, Helen Neethling, who was going on holiday to Mauritius to visit Mary to find out how the roses were. To my delight ten days later, I received a call from the airport to say that a box of red roses was waiting for me there.

Helen had once been our very efficient secretary and I should have known that she would in some way arrive with the roses which she knew I wanted so badly. My husband was able to take good studio photos of the fresh blooms and I planted the stems under glass jampots on my kitchen window sill. I transplanted several plants into the Boschendal garden, keeping the best specimen for my own patio, where I was soon rewarded with the first red flower. I hope Cape gardens will soon be filled with *Rosa chinensis semperflorens* so that there need be no further fears of its extinction.

2 *The Rose Annual*, 1960, p. 31. Gordon Rowley, *Ancestral China Roses*.

3 W. Roxburgh, *Hortus Bengalensis*, 1814. Roxburgh's list of plants growing in St. Helena in 1813 was published by Capt. John Barnes in 1817 after his twelve-year stay on the island. See also S. Pritchard, *List of Plants Growing in St Helena*, 1836.

4 According to Mrs J. Rycroft. Dorothea Fairbridge also mentions a small single red rose growing at Alphen which she calls *Rosa indica*, 'the somewhat insignificant parent of the glorious Teas and Hybrid Teas of today'.

Rosa chinensis semperflorens

From the *Botanical Magazine*, 1794.   *Rosa chinensis semperflorens.*   Jacquin's earlier illustration in
his *Observatorum Botanicum.*

77

'Parsons' Pink China'

Mary Lawrance's *Rosa indica.*

Factories at Canton. A 17th century painting on rice paper. (From the Parkfelt collection)

The history of Swellendam is inextricably linked with the Barry family in South Africa and it was therefore inevitable that in my search for old roses I should visit the 'Aulde House' in the main street that had been occupied by successive generations of Barrys ever since its construction in the 1820s by the family ancestor, Joseph.[1] It was from this house that Joseph built his famous mercantile empire which eventually encompassed almost all the towns in the south-western districts of the Cape colony.

Joseph's home was admired by several travellers and visitors to Swellendam, but unfortunately no detailed description or plant list survives to give an insight into the exotic wealth of plant material that once flourished in this patriarch's large garden. Later owners, not being keen gardeners, simplified the lay-out, clearing pergolas and shrubs that needed too much labour, but fortunately retained clumps and hedge remnants of old China roses that flower prettily throughout the year. Amongst these were the 'Monthly Rose' and its miniature relative, *Rosa chinensis minima.*

I had hoped to find the 'Monthly Rose' at Swellendam, for I knew that it had been recorded on a farm in the district by the Reverend W. Ellis in 1855, growing together with 'larkspur, purple stock, valera and a curious cactus'.[2] Moreover 'Tant Miem' Rothman had noticed very old plants in Swellendam and at Bedford in the 1930s, growing in quince hedges and deserted plots, and was charmed by the sweet pink flowers of this tenacious rose which she thought had probably been introduced by the earliest British settlers. (Did she have Joseph Barry in mind?) She describes how children used to cut the soft young shoots to serve on poplar leaves at dolls' parties![3]

As I looked at the Barry roses, I remembered my mother-in-law's description of the pink rose hedges along the boundaries of Tulbagh gardens that had enchanted her on her way home from school every day in the early 1900s; I also remembered Stephen Brett's plant catalogue for 1905 in which he advertised the 'Pink-Monthly — the old monthly rose' for planting in Uitenhage and Port Elizabeth gardens; I recalled Dorothea Fairbridge's praise of the 'Pink Monthly' hedges that bloomed in Cape gardens throughout the year,[4] and the description of the mid-Victorian veranda at Camps Bay House 'fragrant with honeysuckle and monthly roses'.[5]

How long, I wondered, had this little rose been a part of the Cape landscape? In the *Cape Almanac* for 1820 gardeners were advised to trim their China roses in January if they wanted their plants to produce many flowers. Could this have been a reference to the 'Monthly Rose'?

The oldest living 'Monthly' plants I know of are growing at Altyd Gedacht, one of the first Tygerberg farms, acquired by another British settler, John Parker, in 1835. His descendants, who still make wine and grow wheat like their forbears, are carefully preserving the plants of 'Old Monthly' planted by John a hundred and fifty years ago.[6] These roses used to be part of a hedge that followed the original entrance road to the old manor house, passing through a clump of bay trees now almost 10 metres high. At Ida's Valley a similar hedge of 'Monthly Roses' also lined the approach to the manor house, but no one knows how old these plants were.

Though the oldest existing Cape plants can be traced back to the British settlers, it is interesting to consider other sources of origin, for the

1 Recently the property has been acquired by Major P. Erskine, whose son, Rupert, is restoring the house and garden.
2 W. Ellis, *Three visits to Madagascar 1853-1854-1856.*
3 M. E. Rothman, *Uit en Tuis.*
4 D. Fairbridge, *Gardens of South Africa,* 1925.
5 *Life at the Cape 100 years ago by a Lady,* 1973.
6 Jean Parker and her two sons John and Oliver.

'Parsons' Pink China'

'OLD BLUSH', 'OLD PINK MONTHLY'

Hips.

PLANT
Light-green angular branches form a rather loose plant of 1–1,5 metres with many reddish hooked thorns.

FOLIAGE
Five smallish oval pointed light-green shiny leaves with shallowly serrated margins. The stalk is sturdy, tinged red, glandular and has small hooks on the underside. Stipules are narrow, adnate with free tips and glandular on the edges.

FLOWERS
Pointed dark-pink buds with slightly longer sepals open into loose semi-double clear pink flowers of about 6 cm in diameter. The outer petals bend back and roll outwards at the edges. The inner smaller ones stand up in disarray amongst a mass of dainty stamens with white filaments and small yellow anthers. In the older flowers they curl in over a bunch of short, loose, maroon pistils. The calyx is oval and smooth; the foliated sepals with velvet undersurfaces reflex soon after the bud opens. They have a few glands. The flowers appear on the tops of the branches throughout the year and have a sweet fragrance.

INFLORESCENCE
A panicle of two to four flowers.

'Old Monthly'.

Rosa indica by John Reeves.
(From a collection of Chinese paintings
in the Lindley Library)

A hedge of 'Parsons Pink' growing at Humayun's tomb, Delhi.

Cape lay midway on the sea route between the West and East and the ships that anchored in Table Bay harbour also had ports of call on the islands of the Indian and Atlantic Oceans, from where plants might have been transported. It is therefore possible that the 'Monthly Rose' might have reached the Cape from sources much nearer at hand.

It appears that the 'Monthly Rose' was introduced to the Atlantic islands of St. Helena and Madeira by the English shortly after 1807. In Madeira it was still being called 'Rosa Ingleza' by the middle of the 19th century.[7]

In the Indian Ocean islands however, China roses are recorded from a much earlier date. Pierre Bernadine, a French officer who was a close friend of Jean Jacques Rousseau, spent some time on Mauritius and Réunion and his correspondence, later published and translated into English, is very interesting on conditions there.[8] In a letter dated July 1769 he describes the exotic island plants amongst which 'the rose tree thrives so well here that hedges are made of it, but the flowers are not so tusted *(sic)* nor is the smell so fine as ours: there is of different sorts, among which a small one from China is in bloom all the year round'. The colour is not mentioned, so the rose referred to could have been either *Rosa chinensis semperflorens* ('Slater's Crimson China') or the 'Monthly Rose', both suitable for hedging. In 1801 Baron Grant, after

twenty years in Mauritius, finds the same exotic plants still growing on the island and mentions 'Indian roses' without describing them.[9]

Twenty years later, when the botanist Bréon arrived on the island of Bourbon to supervise the botanical gardens, he noted that two types of roses were used as hedges: the China 'Pink Monthly' and *Rosa damascena semperflorens*, probably imported from France.[10] At that time Réunion, or 'Ile de Bourbon' as it was known, had no natural harbour and Mauritius (Isle de France) was the port of call for French ships on their long voyages across the Indian Ocean. These two French islands would therefore have had exotic plants in common. Possibly China roses had been introduced to the islands during the governor-ship of either Lozier Bouvet (1753–6) or Rene Magon who succeeded him, for both these men were keen agriculturists and encouraged the inhabitants to plant all kinds of crops on their allotments.

It would appear therefore, that long before the influx of British settlers to the Cape in the 1820s, 'Pink Monthly' roses were growing in abundance on islands that lay on the shipping route to the East.

In June 1983 my husband and I found the 'Pink Monthly' still growing in Mauritius, Réunion, the Seychelles, and in Sri Lanka around the cooler mountainous gardens near Kandy, and to our surprise we saw the same rose flowering in Delhi where a hedge had been planted near Humayan's Tomb. The pink flowers were half-shrivelled and freckled with darker crimson sunspots, probably looking very much as I did myself on that intensely hot day! Unfortunately we did not have the time (or money) to follow the trail of this perpetual-flowering little pink rose to the port of Canton in China where the plant collectors discovered it two hundred years ago and from where they first loaded plants onto their homeward-bound ships.

The Swedish clergyman and naturalist, Pehr Osbeck, is regarded as the person who first brought dried specimens of these China roses to Europe. His specimens, now in the Linnaean Herbarium in London, cannot however be clearly identified, but may include the 'Pink Monthly'.

According to Aiton (1789), a China rose was being cultivated by Philip Miller in 1759 (probably at the Chelsea Physic Garden) and it is likely that these plants were brought from Holland when Miller visited Leyden in 1727.[11]

---

7 R. T. Lowe, *Flora of Madeira*, 1857. 'The comparatively scentless common Pink China or Everblowing Rose (*R. indica* L. a, DC) called by the Portuguese ''*Rosa Ingleza*'' . . . occur everywhere in gardens, are also often seen in hedges and waste ground on the outskirts of enclosures about houses, growing wholly without culture.' It also appears on Roxburgh's plant list of 1807, incorporated in the 'Observations' written by Capt. John Barnes after twelve years residence in St. Helena (London 1817).

8 Pierre Jacques Henri Bernadine, *Voyage to the Island of Mauritius, the Isle of Bourbon and Cape of Good Hope 1768*, translated by John Parish, 1775.
9 Baron Grant, *History of Mauritius*, 1801.
10 T. Rivers, *The Rose Amateur's Guide*, 1846 (reprinted 1979).
11 *Hortus Kewensis*, 1789.

'Parsons' Pink China'

Clockwise.
In the Pampelmousses Garden, Mauritius.
At Fiesole near Florence.
With Pride of India and pink oleander at Boschendal.
Outside the Temple of the Tooth in Candy, Sri Lanka.
Below:
Linarias make lovely companion plants.

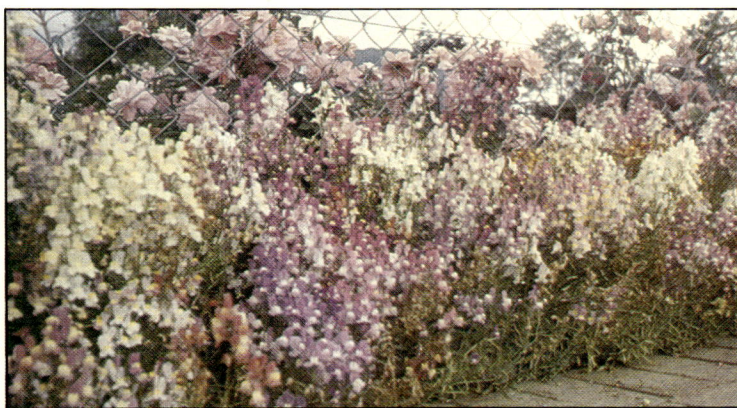

The early Dutch herbalists do not list Chinese roses, however, and the first mention of live plants in the Netherlands appears to be from Baroness d'Oberkirch, Countess de Montbrison, who visited the Haarlem garden in 1782 and was shown 'a shrub that produces magnificent flowers, of which the leaves are soft as velvet, but odourless, that was called the Chinese rose and had been imported within the last year with great care'. She noted that she had seen roses of this species 'delineated on screens and in the corners of fans'.[12]

It seems hard to believe that the captains of the VOC fleets, who were collecting plants for the Leyden Botanic Garden from the earliest years of the 17th century, should have taken so long to bring this important rose to the West, especially when it was already growing in Réunion and Mauritius by the mid-18th century. It is possible, therefore, that the rose mentioned by Baroness d'Oberkirch was not the first Dutch 'Pink Monthly' after all, and that Aiton is correct in saying that this rose was already growing in Leyden in 1727.

Evidence of when the 'Pink Monthly' was introduced to England, on the other hand, is much more positive, for Aiton (1811) informs us that the rose was sent in 1793 from China to Sir Joseph Banks, Director of Kew,[13] and in the Banks Herbarium there are specimens of the 'Pink Monthly' that were collected by Sir George Staunton near Canton in 1792 when he accompanied Lord Macartney's embassy to China. Live plants of the 'Monthly' were first seen to flower in Mr Parson's garden at Rickmansworth in 1793.

From England the rose quickly spread to France. By 1798 it was flowering in Dr Barbier's nursery in Paris and Redouté and Thory were raising seed for Josephine's rose garden at Malmaison. Redouté painted two types of China rose: the semi-double 'Pink Monthly' which was common in French gardens, and a rarer one that had more petals and was of a brighter colour.[14] John Lindley also noted two varieties — the 'sweet scented chinese rose of the gardens with ovate fruit and dwarfer habit' and the more common variety with inferior scent.[15]

The 'Monthly Rose' that grows at the Cape is quite a full rose, has a strong pink colour, a sweet fragrance and is probably the same as Redouté's 'Common China' or *Rosa indica vulgaris*.

We might never know when, from where and by whom the first 'Old Monthly' China roses were planted in the Dutch colony at the Cape of Good Hope, halfway-stop between East and West and meeting-point of the great Atlantic and Indian Oceans. Though the rose is still common at the Cape, very few people realize the enormous effect it had on rose breeding after its introduction to the West in the early 19th century. For with this rose the Chinese had achieved the most important quality of spontaneous remontancy that had been lacking in Western roses up to that time, the Musk rose being the only one to bear a second crop of flowers in the spring.[16]

Malmaison-inspired French breeders had soon created new classes of roses by crossing the existing old once-flowering Western roses with the Chinese 'Monthly' which was quick to set seed and easily raised from cuttings. Thus the 'Monthly Rose' crossed with *Rosa damascena semperflorens* gave rise to the Bourbons; crossed with *Rosa moschata* it gave rise to the Noisettes, and crossed with *Rosa gallica* it gave rise to the Portlands. Further cross-breeding of these new classes of remontant roses led eventually to the Hybrid Perpetual roses of the later 19th century and so to the many varieties that fill contemporary rose gardens.

The China rose that I had found growing in Joseph Barry's garden in Swellendam thus has a most illustrious history indeed and for that alone deserves to be carefully preserved and revered by all Cape gardeners.

12 Baroness d'Oberkirch, *Memoirs*, 1872.
13 W. T. Aiton, *Hortus Kewensis*, second edition, 1811. His father W. Aiton in the first edition (1789) mentions that Philip Miller was growing a China rose from Holland.
14 P. Redouté, *Les Roses*, Vol. I (1817), p. 51: *'Rosa indica vulgaris'*; Vol. II (1819), p. 35: *'Rosa indica centifeuilles'*.
15 J. Lindley, *Rosarum Monographia*, 1820.
16 *Rosa damascena semperflorens* was less constant with its autumn flowers which had to be procured by special pruning.

Rosa chinensis viridiflora

The oldest Green Rose tree that I know of in the Cape was the one that used to grow in the little garden between the old Rhenish parsonage and school in Stellenbosch.

With my class friend, Lydia Baumbach, I often used to slip through the garden gate behind the school at 'play-time' to visit her mother in their home next to the parsonage. On our way we used to pass this large rose tree and gaze with wonder at the strange green flowers.

Lydia was the granddaughter of the missionary, Revd Weber, who after his retirement lived with two unmarried daughters and a son in one of the cottages adjoining the old parsonage. In yet a third cottage lived her 'Tante Agnes' Handelwang, the confectioner's wife, with her family. What a joy it was to visit all these sweet, gentle people and to be offered the wonderful cakes from 'Onkel Paul's' bakery! How I loved to play with Lydia in the large parsonage garden filled with many varieties of fruit trees, flowers and vegetables.

The old parsonage, now restored together with the adjoining cottages, no longer belongs to the Rhenish missionaries and the Green Rose tree along with the beautiful, untidy old garden, has been swept away to make way for a large bare lawn within a white werf-wall.

Mrs Handelwang took a slip of the parsonage Green Rose with her when she moved to a new home in Stellenbosch and from her rose tree I in turn took a slip which soon grew into a large bush at Boschendal. As the Handelwang plant was chopped down by subsequent tenants, I am happy that a descendant of the Revd Weber's Green Rose is still thriving in a safe haven.

Many people consider the Green Rose unattractive, and some have described it as 'monstrous'. I suspect that this is due to the prejudiced idea that flowers should provide a contrast to their leaves. Yet some of the flowers that I find most exciting are in shades of green: the yellow-green ground orchids growing wild in Camps Bay, which we call 'Mother's bonnets'; the strangely scented green lachenalias; the dainty blue-green ixias with black eyes; brown-green gladioli, fragrant only in the evening; green eucomis and green arum lilies. I also love green

hellebores, but my favourite green flower remains *Rosa chinensis viridiflora*!

Sometimes I pick a few sprays of the green rose to arrange in an old lustre mug on my desk, and watch the oval apple-green buds slowly opening. First the sepals curl back showing slightly velvety undersurfaces; then the outer row of broader oval petals folds back, followed by row upon row of narrower silky-textured spoon-shaped petals. Eventually a pyramid of inner blue-green petals shake themselves untidely loose into a flat open flower; at this stage the outer petals have turned a darker rusty-green colour, reminding me that all well-bred China roses darken with age.

According to Roy Shepherd this 'abnormality' has been in cultivation since 1743, but became well known only when the English nursery Bembridge and Hann distributed it from 1856 onwards.[1] In 1817 Breiter had called it *'Rosa monstrosa'*.

At the Cape the Green Rose is mentioned in the 1906 catalogues of Smith Bros, Uitenhage, and of Stephen Brett of Uitenhage and Port Elizabeth. Those recorded in gardens of the Langkloof during this time may have come from one of these nurseries.[2]

There are, however, indications that the Green Rose was very widely grown at the Cape before 1900 and especially fancied, it seems, by parsons — for it grew in the parsonage gardens of both the Revd Hofmeyr of Somerset East, and the Revd W. A. Joubert of North Paarl.

Mrs Corry van Eeden of Stellenbosch remembers seeing *Rosa chinensis viridiflora* growing wild in the veld amongst the proteas and heaths on the farm Blaauwklippen where she went to school in the early 1900s.

I was hesitant to believe Mrs van Eeden's story until M. T. Cadet, botanist at the University of Réunion, told me when I visited the island in 1983 that the green rose grows wild in the Plain de Palmiste. He could not tell me when or from where it had originally been introduced, and I wondered whether this rose, so similar in habit to the 'Old Monthly', had also arrived from the Old Fa-Tee nurseries in Canton.

1 *History Of The Rose*, 1954.
2 Information from Miss B. Taute, Mill River.

Rosa chinensis viridiflora

Rosa chinensis viridiflora.

PLANT
This is a branched shrub growing to 1 metre high, but older bushes can reach up to 2 metres.

FOLIAGE
Five oval pointed leaflets, 4–5 cm in length with finely serrated edges and smooth surfaces of a bright dark-green colour. The leaf-stalk is dainty and has hooked prickles on the underside. The stipules are very narrow.

FLOWERS
The small oval buds with long sepals open slowly as the outer dull-green petals reflex back from the central lighter bluish-green pointed mass of petals. When the whole flower is opened flat, many small wavy petals fill the centre. Stamens are rudimentary and pistils form a tangled bunch in the centre. The calyx is cup-shaped and smooth and the sepals long and narrow, with small foliated edges which have a few stalked glands. The flower-stalk is slightly glandular. Flowers appear throughout the year at the top of the young shoots and are slightly Tea-scented.

INFLORESCENCE
One to four flowers on short to longish flower-stems with elongated bracts one-third of the way up from their attachments.

Above: The farmhouse at Uitvlucht,
Tulbagh in the early 1900's. The rose
in the enclosed garden is 'Indica Major'.
Right: Groot Constantia was once the
property of J. B. Cloete.

Nobody takes much notice of this little rose which is very commonly seen in the Western Cape countryside, especially along road boundaries in the Wellington, Drakenstein, Paarl and Stellenbosch areas. Perhaps it is too closely associated with the unwanted shoots that sprout and have to be removed from the rootstock of cultivated modern garden roses, for until quite recently 'Indica Major' was commonly used not only as hedging material but also as an understock by nurserymen here.

It is a very thankful plant, thriving in almost any kind of soil, in sun or shade, and with little attention growing to luxurious heights against veranda poles or into the tops of old fruit trees. I have not seen it in areas prone to frost.

'Indica Major' is one of my favourite roses and I love to pick the dainty sprays of pale pink flowers when the buds appear in July, for no matter how cold or wintry the weather, the fragile silky flowers, earliest heralds of spring, will open one by one indoors to remind everyone that warm sunny days are at hand. I wake up in the night hearing the rain, and the faint sweet scent of the roses and their airy shadows against the wall fill me with contentment and happiness.

'Indica Major' is an old garden rose from China, where it is known as 'Fun Jwan Lo'. European rosarians generally believe that it is descended from the tea-scented *Rosa odorata* that reached Europe in the early 19th century from Canton. It has the same delicate pink, porcelain petals and the same distinctive tea scent. There is, however, a variety of this rose in which the somewhat paler flowers are blotched with crimson, and a single form of this variety may be the original species from which 'Indica Major' is derived. A fine specimen of the single variety grows at the Swellendam Drostdy museum, but as none of us can remember collecting it, it is not impossible that it was planted as a slip of 'Indica Major' which has now reverted back to its single form.

A painting of a half-open 'Indica Major' in Volume III of Redouté's *Les Roses* (which he calls 'Grand Indienne') indicates that it was growing in France in the early 1800s. In America, where it used to be a popular rootstock, the rose was known as 'Odorata'.[1]

In the Cape 'Indica Major' used to be known as the 'Jacob Cloete rose', but it is not recorded whether the name refers to the Jacob Cloete who arrived at the Cape in 1652 with the first settlers and who, five years later, became one of the first Cape farmers when he was granted land along the Liesbeek River. He and his wife Fytje Raderootjes had two daughters and two sons, progenitors of numerous Cloetes, today still spread throughout the country. Amongst these there have been many Jacobs, but I have been unable to establish which one is associated with the Chinese garden rose which was to become such a useful plant, 'giving much and asking for little in return'.[2]

1 According to McFarland *Roses 8* this rose was introduced to America as 'Odorata 22449', and used as stock, but he gives no date. See also the *Rose Annual 1949* where 'Indica Major' is recommended as stock for countries with a Mediterranean climate and long summer droughts.

Gisele de la Roche doubts whether Redouté's 'Grand Indienne' is the same as the stock 'Odorata'. I think they resemble each other very closely; but it is difficult to compare a painting with living material.

2 D. Fairbridge, *Gardens of South Africa*, 1925.

'Indica Major'

The species from which 'Indica Major' was probably derived.

PLANT
This loosely arching vigorous shrub or climber grows 3–5 metres high and has many sharp, hooked thorns.

FOLIAGE
Five oval pointed leaflets, about 30 cm long, with dark-green shiny smooth surfaces, slightly paler underneath. The stalk is glandular, especially towards the stem, and has prickles on the underside. The stipules are very thin with longish loose ends, glandular on the slightly fringed edges.

FLOWERS
The oval buds have short sepals and open into full, loose flowers. The pale pink silky petals with white shanks bend back and roll outwards on the edges. Many hidden stamens surround a number of short white stigmas. The calyx is cup-shaped and smooth; the oval, short sepals are rough on top and velvety on the edges and undersurface. The flowers come out in very early spring and are sweetly fragrant; the glandular flower-stalk has short bracts at its base, also with glandular edges.

INFLORESCENCE
Usually only one flower appears on a short leafy side branchlet along the main stems.

Hips of 'Indica Major'.

'Indica Major'.

85

'Old Monthly' and its sport, *Rosa chinensis minima*.
Below: My granddaughter Erika is charmed by the small pink roses.

Light pink miniature roses at Mauritius.

Anyone who knows the 'Old Monthly' will immediately recognize the miniature variety *Rosa chinensis minima* which is in all respects identical except for its Lilliputian size.

The tiny plants I found growing at the 'Auld House' in Swellendam were very old, but had grown no higher than 30 cm. I was given one shrublet which I carefully divided into many plants, each with its own roots. I need not have worried however, for even the unrooted twigs I planted soon grew into stout little shrubs which have not ceased flowering in five years.

When John Lindley described this rose in 1820, he thought that it probably originated in China, but had been introduced to England from Mauritius a few years before by a Mr Sweet who named it after Mary Lawrance.[1] Hurst, however, relates that in 1805 the 'Old Monthly' rose gave rise to this miniature variety at Colville's nursery in England, and from there plants were taken by Louis Noisette to France where the rose was called 'Bengale Pompon'.[2] Roy Shepherd, on the other hand, states that the early history of the miniature China rose in Europe is uncertain. According to him there is a possibility that Augustin Pyramus de Candolle might have introduced it to his garden in Champagne from Mauritius before it was known in England.[3] William Paul in his *Rose Garden* (1848) calls the little China rose 'Lawranceana' or the 'Fairy Rose' and confirms that it came from China in 1810, but does not say who introduced it, nor does he mention Mauritius.

William Paul describes fifteen different varieties of 'Fairy Rose', and tells us that thousands of these were sold annually in England as pot plants or for rosarium edgings, 'and beautiful they are when covered with their tiny blossoms'. Five years later their popularity spread to France where they too became well-loved favourites.

An illustration of 'Miss Lawrance's Rose' first appeared in the 1815 *Botanical Magazine* under the name *Rosa semperflorens minima*.[4] This drawing, done by Sims, shows a small single pink rose with pointed petals. A few years later Redouté depicted the same rose under the name 'Indica pumila' or 'Rosier du Bengale'.[5] In his first volume he had already illustrated the double variety which I found growing in Swellendam.[6]

In 1884 Mr Andreas Voss shed light on this rather confused scene by noticing that the small China rose was actually a scaled-down version of the 'Old Monthly' and he gave it the botanical name of *Rosa chinensis minima*, which is now still accepted as its correct name.

In 1920 Dr Roulet of the Swiss army found a variety of this small rose growing in the village of Mauborget. The villagers there had cultivated it as a pot plant and were convinced that it had been growing in their town for over a hundred years. In 1922 it was collected and distributed by M. Correvon, who named it *Rosa rouletii*. This little red rose caused a renewal of interest in the cultivation of miniature roses.[7]

A rose very much like 'Rouletii' (as it is now called) but said to have been pink and more double, known as 'Pompon de Paris', was sold in great quantities as a pot plant on the Paris market from 1839 onwards.

Today the many seedlings of *Rosa chinensis minima*, once the darlings of English, French and American gardeners, are seldom seen. 'Nemesis', described by Paul as having 'flowers crimson, changing blackish',

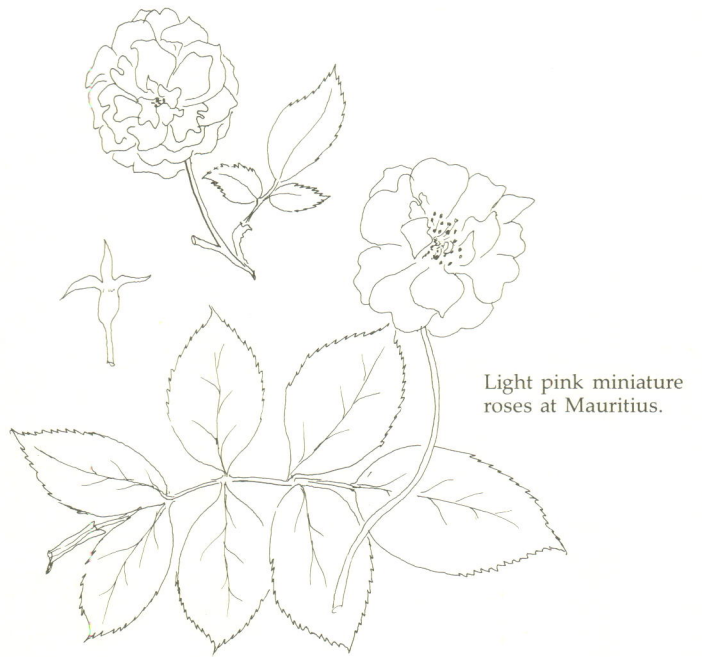

used to grow in the Botanic Garden in Cape Town in 1858, but has since disappeared without trace.[8]

On a visit to Mauritius and Réunion in 1983, however, I was delighted to find how popular old varieties of miniature roses still were. The obvious favourite, to be found in many Creole gardens on both islands, was a shrub one metre high carrying small clusters of tiny pompon flowers of a dull pink colour at the tops of the branches. Though it was not 'the time for roses' many of these rose plants were covered with flowers, making lovely displays either as individual shrubs next to old steps or along garden paths, or massed in large beds. In the garden next to the Natural History Museum in St. Denis such a bed looked particularly charming set in a green lawn.

Mme Madeleine Faubourl, who worked in the Museum, had collected some 'Pompon de Réunion' roses, growing the tiny plants in pots in her kitchen yard. Among them was a very delicate plant with light-green oval pointed serrated leaflets and tiny elongated goblet-shaped calyces enclosing the minute pointed white buds that had not yet quite opened; perhaps Paul's 'Alba', with its 'white, delicate flowers'? There was also a plant with more rounded leaflets and crimson pompon flowers darkening with age, perhaps 'Nemesis'?

One small Creole garden was filled with many rows of identical crimson pompon roses, some slightly paler, some not so double; perhaps 'Gloire des Lawrenceanas', who knows? The local inhabitants call all their small roses 'Pompons'.

The only rose nursery in Mauritius is run by Mme Orieux, generally acknowledged as the rose expert of the island. Her deceased husband had been even more knowledgeable and had experimented with various kinds of rose stock, at one time supplying stock to rose nurseries in India. Mary Orieux told me that before World War II roses used to be imported from France by sea, but of these only about one-fifth would survive. The islanders therefore cherished the hardier old roses and new gardens were mostly supplied from slips out of friends' older gardens. Mme Orieux has a battle growing the more modern varieties, for though they now arrive by air, they are often destroyed by the poisonous sprays used on the surrounding sugar plantations; and then of course, she has to contend with the disastrous effects of cyclones.

Mary showed me 'Annie Muller', a cluster rose which I had never seen elsewhere.[9] It must have been imported from Europe in the early part of this century, for it grows in many gardens both in Mauritius and in Réunion, making a gay show with its masses of curly pink flowers. This rose grows to approximately 1 metre, making quite a strong round bush ideally suited for use as a bedding plant.

'Annie Muller' belongs to the group of cluster roses directly descended from the small *Rosa chinensis* crossed with *Rosa multiflora*. At Lyon, Guillot (Fils) in 1873 produced the first of these hybrids, calling it 'Paquerette'[10] and in 1880 he produced 'Mignonette'.[11] Both these roses were dwarfs, growing only to 20 cm, but because they became the ancestors of most of our modern cluster roses large and small, their significance in the development of the modern rose should not be underestimated.

In the Cape, miniature China roses were growing in the garden of Baron von Ludwig in 1831 and were probably distributed to other keen gardeners from there. They remained popular edging plants until well into the 20th century,[12] for not only do they thrive in our dry soils, but the warm sunshine stimulates a never-ending crop of tiny pink blossoms, especially beautiful when planted together with a ground cover of dark blue lobelia or white alyssum.

1 J. Lindley, *Rosarum Monographia*, 1820.
2 In G. Thomas, *The Old Shrub Roses*, p. 78.
3 R. Shepherd, *History of the Rose*, 1978 reprint, p. 62.
4 T 1762.
5 *Les Roses*, Vol. II, p. 25.
6 *Les Roses*, Vol. I, p. 115.
7 R. Shepherd, *History of the Rose*, p. 64.
8 Plant list of the Botanical Gardens, 1858.
9 'Annchen Müller' was introduced by J. C. Schmidt in 1907, and is a cross between 'Crimson Rambler' and 'George Pernet'.
10 *Rosa chinensis* x *Rosa multiflora*.
11 *Rosa chinensis* x *Rosa multiflora*, second generation according to McFarland, *Modern Roses 8*.
12 D. Fairbridge, *Gardens of South Africa*, 1924.

Rosa chinensis minima

(ROSA LAWRANCEANA)

'Rouletii'

'Rouletii'.

Rosa chinensis minima.

Hip of *Rosa chinensis minima.*

PLANT
*This is probably the tiniest of all roses. It grows from 15
to 30 cm high and is a well-branched compact shrub with
many slightly hooked thorns.*

FOLIAGE
*Five oval leaflets 10 mm long on dainty red-tinged stalks;
there are small prickles on the undersurface. The stipules
are narrow and short.*

FLOWERS
*The tiny pointed pink buds, with slightly longer sepals,
open into semi-double flat blooms 25 to 30 mm in diameter.
The rounded petals are pale to bright pink, turning mauve
as they age. Stamens are very short and the styles even
shorter. The smooth calyx is cup-shaped, and the foliated
sepals are longer in the older flower. The plant is seldom
without a few blooms and these have a sweet fresh fragrance.*

INFLORESCENCE
A panicle of three to four florets.

*'Rouletii' is similar to Rosa chinensis minima, but the plants
are lankier, the flowers are crimson, and the leaflets are a
darker green with more marked serrations.*

Mill River is one of the oldest farms in the Langkloof near Oudtshoorn and probably one of the most beautiful in this valley which is renowned for its delicious apples and pears. On her 1913 visit to South Africa, Pauline Smith stayed some time at Mill River, gathering material on the inhabitants and places which she was later to incorporate in *The Beadle*.[1]

The house has been carefully restored and meticulously furnished with precious family belongings collected over many years by the present owner, Babette Taute, whose great-great-grandfather bought the property in 1815. When I first visited the garden, which lies on two terraces in a walled enclosure in front of the house, it was overgrown with self-seeded hollyhocks, yellow daisies, mauve scabious and irises; the ground was covered with four varieties of violets, and amongst all this wealth of growth were many large rose trees in full bloom. Pauline Smith had counted two hundred in 1913, but when I saw the garden, more than half had disappeared. Of those left, 'Beauty of Glazenwood', 'Russeliana', 'Maman Cochet', 'Gloire des Rosomanes', 'Frau Karl Druschki', 'Mme Isaac Pereire', 'Ophelia' and 'Etoile de Hollande' were old friends, but a number were quite unknown to me.

A drooping shrub covered in large bright-pink roses I subsequently identified as 'La Reine' and a very dark Hybrid Perpetual as 'Black Prince'. But most exciting of all was a tall tree carrying many clear-pink cupped blooms amongst shiny light-green leaves. It was while I was trying to identify the lovely fragrance of these flowers, which reminded me of the scent from a newly opened tin of Earl Grey tea, that it occurred to me that I might be looking at *Rosa x odorata* or 'Hume's Blush Tea-scented China'.

Now as this once famous rose is thought to be regrettably now lost to cultivation,[2] I packed a number of flowers into my coolbag and on arriving back in Cape Town, air-freighted some to Chris Brickell at Wisley for identification. Mr Graham Thomas was able to examine the fresh flowers and sent back the answer, 'could well be Hume's Blush'. I compared my fresh specimens with Redouté's painting and Thory's description and found that my plants agreed in all respects.[3] Thory complained that this rose was prone to odium in wet weather, but plants grown from the Mill River slips were exceptionally vigorous and disease-resistant. But then our weather is rarely wet for long.

A drawing by Andrews done in 1810, which shows a more expanded flower with broad notched petals,[4] has further strengthened my conviction that the Mill River China rose is the same as the original one discovered by an English East India Company agent in Canton's Fa-Tee nurseries and subsequently sent to Sir Abraham Hume in England in 1809. The rose was then considered so important that British ships carried plants across the channel for Josephine Bonaparte's rose garden at Malmaison even while her husband was engaged in war against Britain.[5]

The new everblooming rose set seed easily, but according to William Paul, did not produce anything 'worthy of note' in England except 'Devoniensis'. Paul considered the 'Yellow Tea-scented Rose', a pale straw-coloured variety of 'Hume's Blush', to be a more prolific seed-bearer.

This yellow tea-scented rose was also found growing in the Fa-Tee gardens, and was sent to England in 1824 by John Damper Parks together with the yellow Banksia. It was probably from these same gardens that Parsons had received his first pink China rose some forty years previously. For after China had closed her doors to Europe in 1755, allowing limited trading rights only at Macao and Canton, it was

to these nursery gardens that European plant-collectors turned in their search for new plants.

Robert Fortune described the nursery gardens (about twelve in all, situated three to five kilometres above the city of Canton) where these early stud roses had been found:

'I lost no time', he wrote, 'in visiting the celebrated Fa-tee gardens near Canton, the "flowery land" as the name implies, from where a great number of those fine plants were first procured which now decorate our gardens in England.' The plants were cultivated in pots and arranged in rows alongside the narrow paved pathways. In spring these gardens were a mass of bloom and had a 'singularly gorgeous and imposing appearance' that justified the poetical name of 'Fa-tee'.[6]

There is, unfortunately, no record of when the earliest China roses reached the Cape, and I can only guess that they must have been introduced by the Dutch during the eighteenth century, for by the early nineteenth century Cape gardens were full of China roses. Today still, the China roses and their hybrids are the most common of surviving old roses.

I was one day urgently phoned by a friend with the news that a number of very old rose trees growing in a cottage garden behind the Westerford school in Rondebosch were to be cleared in the week to come to make way for new school grounds. I dropped my work and drove out post-haste to find the garden full of holes where other gardeners had already removed some precious plants.

There were indeed some old rose trees amongst which *R. roxburghii*, 'Céline Forestier' and 'Devoniensis' were spouting a few blooms. Then I saw against the boundary fence what I thought to be 'Hume's Blush' with a few blown flowers. I took many slips, two of which quickly grew into healthy rose trees, but to my surprise, when flowers were produced they appeared paler and of a more creamy apricot colour.

It took me several months to realize that this was definitely not 'Hume's Blush', but probably its so-called yellow variety, *Rosa x odorata ochroleuca*. The only illustration of this rose I have seen is Redouté's *Rosa indica sulphurea*,[7] a very pale yellow, dumpy little rose, closely resembling my Westerford specimen. Like 'Hume's Blush', this yellow rose, also known as 'Parks' Yellow Tea-scented China', has disappeared from European gardens.

If these should indeed prove to be the two lost China Tea roses, there will be no difficulty in raising plants for hybridizers who might like to use them again, for cuttings grow with great ease. Those Cape gardeners who value fragrance might also like to reintroduce these old favourites into historic farmyards as single specimens or in 'endless rose hedges' such as those described by Hildagonda Duckitt in her mother's garden at Groote Post which included 'Odorata as fragrant as attar of roses'.[8]

For no matter what time of the year or how awful the weather, these roses, like the 'Old Monthly' and the crimson China rose, will always provide a splash of colour in the garden or a few gay blooms for a vase. It can be imagined what excitement these Chinese roses caused amongst Western nurserymen in the early 19th century, for while Chinese gardeners had been growing remontant hybrids developed centuries before, European gardeners had had to content themselves with roses that flowered only in summer.

These four China roses became the stud parents from which most of our modern roses are derived, so that their rediscovery and continued cultivation is important not only for their historical significance, but also for providing a valuable gene bank for future rose-breeders.

1 Printed in London in 1926.
2 Baronesse de la Roche in the fourth volume of the Redouté reprints, Antwerp, 1978.
3 J. Redouté, *Les Roses*, Vol. I, 1817, p. 61, 'Indica Fragrans'.
4 Reproduced in the Reverend J. Pemberton's book on roses from H. C. Andrews' *Monograph*, London, 1805-28.
5 Paul comments: 'The late Mr. Kennedy was provided with a passport to go and come as he pleased during the war.' He was at that time superintending the formation of the Malmaison garden. (*The Rose Garden*, 1848, p. 13.)
6 R. Fortune, *A Residence Among the Chinese*, 1853–1856.
7 J. Redouté, *Les Roses*, Vol. IV, p. 119, reprinted Antwerp, 1978. Redouté's flower is slightly darker than mine but may not be accurate, as all descriptions of this rose refer to the light colour. Shepherd in his *History of the Rose* describes it as a pale yellow semi-double variety of *R. odorata* and says that it was also called 'Flavescens' or the 'Amber Rose'.
8 M. Kuttel, *Quadrilles and Konfyt*, Cape Town, 1954.

Far right: Calyx of *Rosa x odorata*.
Right: *Rosa indica odorata* from H. C. Andrews' *Monograph*.

Rosa x odorata

'HUME'S BLUSH TEA-SCENTED CHINA'

Rosa x odorata.

Rosa x odorata ochroleuca.

PLANT
A branching shrub 1–1,5 metres high with medium-sized, hooked, reddish thorns.

FOLIAGE
Three to five smooth, light-green, narrow-oval leaflets, margins with medium serrations tinged red especially when young. The stems have the same reddish tinge, are slightly glandular, and have small prickles on the underside.

FLOWERS
Large oval buds open into globular double blooms. The petals are broad and have notched edges; the inner smaller ones are slightly crinkled. They are of a pale pink colour, darkening a little towards the edges and flushed cream at the shanks. The stamens have long pale filaments and surround a bunch of short pistils. The calyx is cup-shaped, slightly rough on the surface with a few glands on the stem attachment; the pedicel is also slightly glandular. The sepals are smooth to slightly rough on top, velvety underneath with a few glands on the edges, but no folioles. Flowers appear throughout the year and have a strong fragrance.

INFLORESCENCE
One to three flowers on short side branches on the top of the tree. The short bracts are light brown to reddish and have very finely toothed edges.

Rosa x odorata ochroleuca ('Parks' Yellow Tea-scented China') is in all respects similar to 'Hume's Blush China' but the flowers are of a pale cream to apricot colour and the plant itself is not quite so robust.

89

'Gloire des Rosomanes' makes a lovely show high up in an old viburnum.

On a 19th century grave at the Belvidere Church, near Knysna.

The scarlet flowers against winter snow on the Drakenstein mountains.

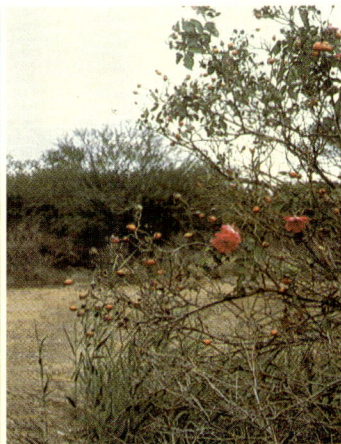

Hips on an old tree at Klipfontein near Graaff-Reinet.

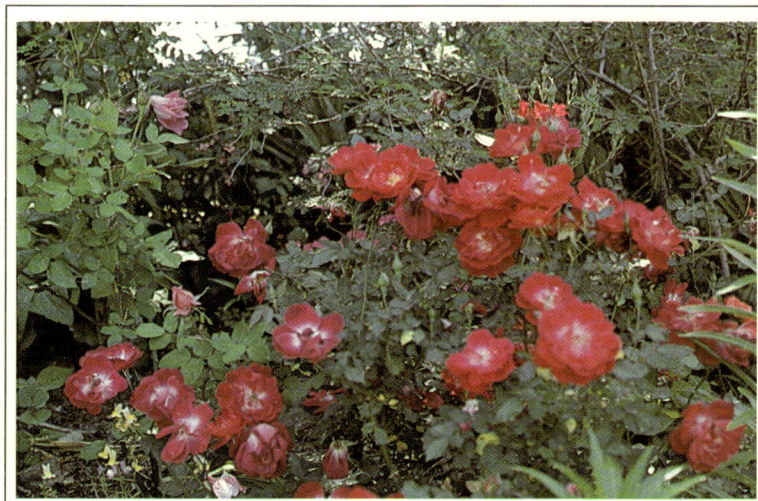

'Fabvier'.

I was first introduced to 'Gloire des Rosomanes' by Dorothea Fairbridge in her book on old South African gardens. She writes: 'A glorious hedge rose, less frequently planted than in former years, is Jupiter's Lightning — the Gloire des Rosomanes of European florists.'

I searched for the 'fine hedge' she had admired in the Company's garden in Cape Town in 1925, but the only roses I found there were rather sad-looking modern Hybrid Teas pruned to the ground, standing self-consciously bare in their well-tilled beds.

A great deal has been written about 'Gloire des Rosomanes', raised from unrecorded parents in 1825 by Vibert. I was consequently disappointed with my first vision of a rather weak plant bearing a few tousled roses in the historical collection at the Roseraie de l'Hay-les-Roses near Paris. However, the loose semi-double crimson flowers streaked with white and with white shanks, made their impression on me and I was thus able to identify the roses blooming in front of a small thatched cottage in the missionary settlement of Zuurbraak near Swellendam when we were collecting old roses in the ensuing spring. In the half-shade of a large oak tree, a rose thicket three metres high was spilling crimson over the pure white blossom of a may hedge, at the same time filling the small garden with a delicious fragrance.

A similar display of crimson and white greeted me one evening when I arrived at the old garden of Babette Taute's Mill River cottage in the Langkloof. This time the white flowers were those of a *Viburnum opulus* seven metres high whose thousands of 'snowballs' were intermingled with crimson sprays of a neighbouring 'Jupiter's Lightning'. In the fading evening light we tried to capture the fantastic spectacle, but no photograph can ever convey the full glow of such living wonders.

I have, since that evening, often had reason to appreciate the apt name of this rose which has been streaking crimson across Cape gardens, even during the most dismally dormant part of the year, for almost a hundred and fifty years.[1]

Mrs Helen Ross, daughter of the Revd George William Stegman of Oudtshoorn, told me that her widowed mother had planted a hedge of 'Jupiter's Light' along the boundary of her semi-detached stone cottage when she moved there in 1905. Revd Stegman had been doing mission work in Rhodesia when he died at the early age of forty-six, leaving his family a pension of three pounds a month. Helen remembered how she was only allowed to use one match to light all the candles and lamps in the house each evening, so poor were they. 'Jupiter's Light' provided flowers for the house in summer and copious red hips for autumn decoration. Furthermore the bright crimson petals, sprinkled on the carpets before sweeping, kept the dust down and filled the house with its delicious fragrance. A useful rose indeed!

In the early 1830s 'Gloire des Rosomanes' was much used for cross-breeding because of its fertility, and so became the parent of many crimson Hybrid Perpetuals. In the U.S.A., where it became known as 'Ragged Robin', it was used as an understock and according to Redvers Blatt, as late as 1933 all roses in California were still being budded onto it except 'HPs and Polyanthas which grow best from slips'.[2]

The cuttings I took from the old Stegman hedge at Oudtshoorn are now growing vigorously in a number of Cape gardens where proud owners are acclaiming the virtues of 'Jupiter's Lightning' with the same enthusiasm that Miss Fairbridge did sixty years ago.

'Fabvier' resembles 'Gloire des Rosomanes' in many respects. It has the same loose flower; its crimson petals are also streaked with white; and the leaves are similar with deeply serrated edges. It is, however, a much smaller rose.

I found it growing in Mrs Johnman's garden in Stellenbosch and thought her name of 'Sunshine Rose' for it very apt. No matter what season or how miserable the weather may be, if she walks into her garden, there is sure to be at least one small smiling crimson flower to greet her and light up the day.

1 The rose appears under the name of 'Eclaire de Jupiter' in a list of plants growing in the Botanic Garden in Cape Town in 1858.

2 Redvers J. Blatt, 'In a Californian Rose Garden', in *Garden and Country Life*, November 1933, Vol. XXIII.

'Gloire des Rosomanes'

'JUPITER'S LIGHTNING'

PLANT
Many branched stems, forming a large loose shrub 2–3 metres high, with large slightly hooked thorns.

FOLIAGE
Five dark-green oval leaflets, pointed at both ends, with deeply serrated edges and shiny surfaces, velvety below; stipules are adnate with loose tips and edges finely serrated.

FLOWERS
Dainty pointed buds with slightly longer sepals open to loose semi-double crimson flowers 8–9 cm in diameter. The outer petals are oblong with white shanks, the central ones shorter, curly and twisted. Stamens are of different lengths, the filaments reddish at their attachments. Multiple pistils form a central hairy bunch, almost as long as the stamens. The calyx is goblet-shaped and glandular; the tapering longish sepals are unbranched, glandular on the outside and velvety on the underside. Flowers appear throughout the year and are very fragrant.

INFLORESCENCE
Flowers occur singly or in a corymb of two to four on glandular stalks which have leafy smooth green bracts at their attachments.

FRUIT
Many bright-orange shiny globular hips.

'Gloire des Rosomanes'.

91

'Cramoisi Supérieur'

'Louis Philippe'
at Bishopscourt.

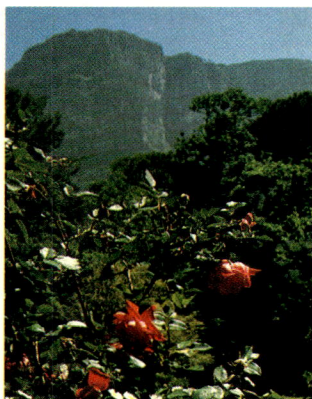

When I opened the letter containing a single mounted slide on which was written simply 'The oldest rose in Durban', I did not doubt that the information was correct, for I knew that it could only come from Barrie Biermann, who has a strange way of knowing many things. The small red rose was obviously 'Cramoisi Supérieur', the China rose introduced by Coquereau in 1832, which soon became a very popular bedding rose in Europe. I knew that it was growing in the Cape Town Botanic Garden by the 1850s and wondered how it had found its way to Durban.

The true story of the oldest Durban rose was subsequently revealed to me by Miss Daphne Child in response to an appeal I made for information on old roses during a Women's World radio programme.

She told me how slips of a little red rose had been brought from Higham in Norfolk, when Mr and Mrs Henry Pratt Harrison emigrated to Natal in 1863. About sixteen kilometres north of Durban they settled on a farm which they called Rosehill. The farmhouse, believed to be the second oldest in the Durban area, is today in the hands of the Misses U. and S. Gillespie, granddaughters of the original owners, and a bush which developed from one of the original slips planted in 1863 is still flourishing in their garden. In 1963, exactly a century after the Harrison's arrival, a cutting of this rose was taken back to England and presented to a Harrison granddaughter in a televised ceremony. The slip was kept under quarantine at Kew and then planted at Higham where it grew successfully.

Three years after the Harrisons had planted their rose at Rosehill, the newly established Durban Botanic Garden received 'Cramoisi' together with a number of other roses from Mr Saul Solomon in Cape Town. I am sure that the Harrisons would soon have seen their rose in many other Durban gardens, for this China rose does not seem to mind the subtropical Natal climate. I found it growing very happily in the Killie-Campbell Museum garden quite recently. 'Cramoisi' is obviously a very adaptable rose — Parsons regarded it as 'one of the most hardy and desirable of old China roses', and a popular forcing rose much in demand for bouquets.[1]

In the old Grahamstown cemetery, a low hedge of 'Cramoisi' covered in red flowers attracted my attention when I was making an inventory of the roses growing there, and I noticed how closely they resembled the blooms on the 'Louis Philippe' hedge I had seen a short while before in the Bishopscourt garden in Cape Town. The 'Cramoisi' blooms were the more brilliant of the two, however; the red extends right into the heart of the rose, unlike 'Louis Philippe' which shows a pink centre as the flowers open fully.

1 *Parsons on the Rose*, New York, 1979 reprint.

'Cramoisi Supérieur'.

PLANT
Branching shrublet 50–100 cm high with smooth shining stems and many reddish hooked thorns.

FOLIAGE
Five oval dark-green shiny leaflets about 5–6 cm long with well-serrated edges. Stipules are adnate and narrow.

FLOWERS
Tiny, round, pointed buds open to quite full crimson flowers of about 6 cm in diameter. The oval petals with white shanks fold inward over each other to form a very pretty anemone shape before the flower is fully open. The many stamens surround a bunch of delicate styles. The calyx is cup-shaped and smooth, but the flower-stalk is glandular like the long tapering sepals. These are velvety on the undersides. 'Cramoisi' is sweetly fragrant and flowers throughout the year.

INFLORESCENCE
Three to six flowers in a cyme at the tops of the branches.

'Louis Philippe'

'Louis Philippe'.

Hips.

Bishopscourt, today the property of the Anglican Church and home of the Archbishop of Cape Town, was originally part of the land granted in 1657 to Jan van Riebeeck, first Commander of the Cape of Good Hope. This farm, situated a few hours by horseback from the small Dutch settlement in Table Valley, was subject to continual harrassment by local tribesmen, and predators menaced the Commander's herds.

Today this area is the Beverly Hills of Cape Town, home of ambassadors and rich businessmen, for the old farm has been gradually subdivided, leaving eventually only the core of old buildings, now much changed, in a small area of garden and forest.

In my search for old roses I visited this garden which was sketched by Lady Anne Barnard before 1800, by D'Oyly in the early 19th century, and which Dorothea Fairbridge describes in her book on old Cape gardens.

I was looking in particular for the 'Cramoisi Supérieur' hedges which she mentions, but though I found a number of old roses, there was no trace of 'Cramoisi' and I could only conclude that Miss Fairbridge had mistaken the hedge of 'Louis Philippe' for that famous red China rose which it so closely resembles.

The hedge, about one metre high, was growing below a stone terrace wall, and was covered in crimson flowers which intermingled with the tiny white daisies of erigeron hanging from the stone crevices. On examining the pretty flowers I found that the inner petals, folded neatly over each other to form anemone-shaped centres, were of a lighter colour than the outer petals which curled back slightly. Having seen 'Cramoisi' before, which is crimson throughout, I sent a slide to Lily Shohan of the American Rose Heritage Society who identified the Bishopscourt rose as 'Louis Philippe', a rose which dates back to 1834.

Like most China roses, this one grows easily from cuttings especially if taken in the autumn, and will start flowering when scarcely 30 cm high. The plants are inclined to grow untidily and should be kept in shape by regular trimming when they will be very useful for edging beds or as specimen plants in pots with other small perennials. For a flat dweller this is an ideal window plant if grown in full sun, for it will provide a bright show of very sweet-scented flowers throughout the year.

PLANT
This small branched shrub grows 60–90 cm high. There are many large hooked thorns with wide attachments.

FOLIAGE
Five oval pointed, shiny, dark-green leaflets with serrated edges; the smooth stalks have prickles on the underside; the stipules are narrow with fine small glands on the edges.

FLOWERS
Fat dark-maroon buds have short sepals which reflex immediately the buds start to expand. The flowers, 4–5 cm in diameter, are full and cupped, with many petals forming an anemone-shaped centre. The longish, slightly bristly, glandular stalks are inclined to nod. The broader outer recurving petals are maroon-crimson, but the inner ones are of a paler pink. The few stamens are insignificant around a short clump of orange stigmas. The calyx is cup-shaped and smooth; the unfoliated sepals are smooth on the outside except for a few microscopic glands, and velvety on the inner surface. Flowers appear throughout the year and have a sweet fragrance.

INFLORESCENCE
There are usually two to four flowers per head.

'Fellemberg'

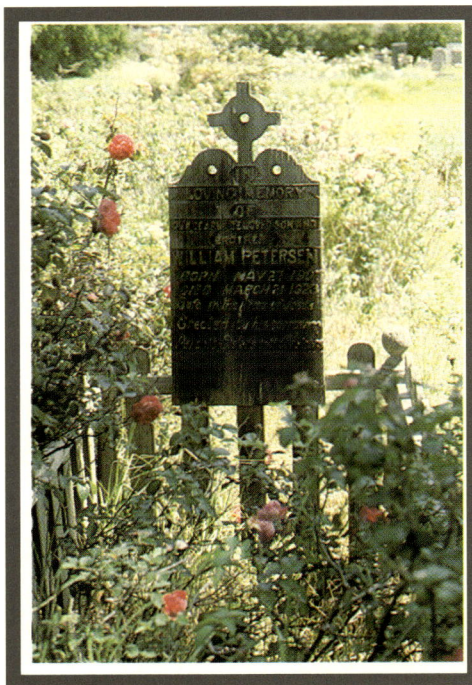

'Fellemberg' in the
Mowbray cemetery.

The origin of 'Fellemberg' is as obscure as its date of first cultivation. Although it was raised and distributed by Fellemberg in 1857,
it was already well known in France before then under the name of
'La Belle Marseillaise' and what appears to be the same rose was seen
growing at the Trianon nursery by De Pronville in 1818 under the name
of 'Bengale à bouquets'.[1]

At the Cape this rose has been in cultivation for over a century, always in demand for hedges, single shrubs, or for massing together in
those peculiarly shaped beds surrounded by low-cut myrtle or rosemary
hedges which were the pride of Victorian gardeners. The ease with
which cuttings strike and grow to mature plants in any soil or climate,
its resistance to disease, and above all its generous crop of flowers
throughout the year endeared 'Fellemberg' to gardeners everywhere.
In the *Cape Garden* of 1909 the editor was enthusiastic in his praise for
this China rose, advising also that 'those who have a low wall to cover
would find this well adapted for the purpose'.

Its virtues were clearly brought to my notice by Professor Felix Lategan who provided the following information on the 'French rose' of
his grandmother, Tant Mieta Lategan:

*'Ever since my earliest youth I remember the large shrub of maroon-red roses
in my Ouma's beautiful flower garden in front of the high stoep of my family's home on a farm near Burgersdorp. When my grandfather retired he took
slips of the rose to plant at his next home in Parys, the small town situated
on the banks of the Vaal River. These slips flourished and produced masses
of flowers.*

*In 1945 I was appointed a lecturer to the Free State University, and a
member of the Vorster family, who had taken transfer of my grandfather's
farm, brought me slips of my grandmother's 'French rose'. To my joy, these
plants flourished on the granite soil of my smallholding near Bloemfontein,
producing their crimson flowers throughout the year.*

*When I became professor of Afrikaans at the University of the Western
Cape twenty-five years later, slips of the rose again accompanied us to our
new home at Stellenbosch where, needless to say, they were as great a success as they had been in all our previous gardens.*

*Once again slips from these plants were taken along when I retired to Klein-
mond, and in the sandy soil of this beach resort, my rose trees did not fail
to maintain their fine performance. I subsequently planted it on my son's
grave where it gets no attention or care, but the miracle rose still flourished.
Nowhere could I find a name for this rose and I saw it in no other garden,
till one day when I visited the battlefield of Amajuba and there, to my great
surprise, I found my grandmother's French rose growing around the house
where the peace treaty ending the first Anglo-Boer war had been signed in
1881.'*

This house, probably built by R. C. O'Neil in 1870, acted as a hospital
where many of the wounded British soldiers were nursed after the fate-
ful battle against the Boer forces. It is not known who planted the red
roses in its grounds. Perhaps the relatives or friends of those ninety-
two men who succumbed with their leader, General G. P. Colley,
wished to commemorate the blood that had been spilt on Spitskop on
27 February 1881.

Professor Lategan brought me some plants of his Ouma Mieta's rose
to identify and plant at Boschendal. But though I had already collected some rooted plants from an old grave in the Mowbray cemetery,
I was glad to add to my collection a descendant of this venerable Lategan rose.

---

1 Ellen Willmott thinks that the parents are *Rosa chinensis*
   (Monthly rose?) and *R. multiflora*.

'Fellemberg'

'LA BELLE MARSEILLAISE'

From top to bottom:
This 'Fellemberg' hedge in Elgin has dark-crimson flowers.

In Nancy Steen's garden in Auckland, 'Fellemberg' has a dark-pink colour.

In 1981 I photographed this clear pink 'Fellemberg' at Mottisfont.

PLANT
This is an angular spreading shrub about 1,5 metres high with small red hooked thorns.

FOLIAGE
Five round to oval pointed, smooth shiny leaflets on sturdy reddish leaf-stalks which are slightly glandular with small hooked prickles on the undersides. The stipules are light-green tinged red, and have smooth edges.

FLOWERS
Round pointed buds open to cup-shaped flowers 4–5 cm in diameter, with six or seven rows of pink or crimson petals. When fully expanded the outside petals bend and fold back while the inner ones fill the centre. The stamens are short with thin white filaments and small anthers; the pistils are a little longer and have hairy styles and red stigmas. The calyx is smooth with a few glands towards the stalk, and the glandular sepals, velvety on both sides, reflex quickly right back against the stem. The flowers are fragrant and appear throughout the year.

INFLORESCENCE
Trusses of three to four flowers in a corymb at the ends of new shoots, often with drooping stalks. Bracts are long and have glandular edges.

'Fellemberg'.

95

'Simonstown Rose'

'Simonstown Rose'.

Below:
'The Warrior' in Anne Endt's
garden in Christchurch,
New Zealand.
Right:
The fully blown 'Tulip Rose'.

Two China roses which I have been unable to identify are shown on these two pages.

The first I have called the 'Simonstown Rose' as this is the only locality where I have found several old trees.

Simons Bay was the name given in 1687 by Simon van der Stel, Commander of the Dutch colony at the Cape, to a cove in False Bay which provided safe anchorage in winter when north-westerly gales made Table Bay dangerous.

Many ships at anchor in Table Bay were however to be wrecked by north-westerly gales before the Dutch East India Company decided in 1741 to use Simons Bay as a winter anchorage. From then onwards a town grew up, frequently visited by sailors and merchants of many different nationalities from the ships that anchored in the bay. In 1814, eight years after they annexed the Cape from the Dutch, the British established their naval base at Simonstown and in 1832 built a church for the growing population.

It was in the garden of this stone church that I found, one autumn morning, an old China rose tree in full bloom. Its many large crimson flowers (10–12 cm across) and its bunches of huge orange hips testi-fied that no one picked from or pruned this plant. I cut away the dead wood and took some slips which grew very well and after two years produced the same spectacular blooms.

Later I found a second tree in the garden of a cottage higher up on the hill where a sunnier position had produced even better flowers on a tree about 2,5 metres high. For this is, without doubt, the largest China I have seen, and perhaps the most fragrant.

How shall I ever discover the story behind this 'Simonstown Rose'? How many homesick seamen or ship's captains have not prayed in the little stone church where the rose flourishes? Did one of them bring slips of the rose from China and plant them next to the church before continuing his voyage? Or was it perhaps brought from Bengal, in which case could it be Redouté's 'Bengale centfeuilles' which has been rediscovered in the garden of the Count and Countess d'Ursel at Chateaux de Hex?

In Anne Endt's Christchurch garden in New Zealand I saw a rose called 'The Warrior' which reminded me of the Simonstown rose, but seemed to be not quite so full, although it may not have been a good bloom.

'Ma Tulipe'

'Comtesse du Cayla'. Half size.

'Ma Tulipe'.

'The Tulip Rose', I named a dark red China in Babette Taute's garden at Mill River farm in the Langkloof, for from the time the bud expands until the rose is fully blown, it retains the perfect goblet shape of a tulip.

I have never seen this peculiar rose shape elsewhere, either in gardens or illustrated, nor could any of my older friends recall such a rose. I was therefore thrilled when I found in Gowie's 1904 *Seeds and Plants List* a rose classified as a Tea, called 'Ma Tulipe'. It was described as 'deep crimson with tulip-shaped buds', and though I try never to identify roses from catalogue descriptions only, this one was too good to be ignored.

McFarland does not list 'Ma Tulipe', so it was probably not a well-known rose when Gowie's called it 'new' in 1904, nor could it ever have become very popular. Perhaps people felt that a rose is a rose is a rose and should not resemble a tulip!

I find the neat globular shape, rich colour and sweet fragrance very attractive and am grateful that my slips have grown into healthy plants which are now producing blooms at Boschendal.

'Comtesse du Cayla' is another China rose of the 20th century, and was introduced by P. Guillot in 1902. The flower has a distinctive orange-bronze colour which sets it apart from the other Chinas. It blooms most of the year and the pretty pointed buds, when picked, will open indoors into loose dainty flowers which look best if a few are arranged alone in a vase.

I have found a number of old plants in Pniel cottage gardens and as far as the Langkloof and Grahamstown. They all appear to be disease-free and vigorous shrubs and are very easily propagated by slips.

'Cécile Brunner'

'Perle d'Or' growing alongside the path in the Murray's Victorian garden at Bloemhof near Graaff-Reinet.

I started gardening when I was seven. Having planted a row of freesia bulbs in my little plot during 'garden time' at school, I became tremendously excited when a week later a row of leafy green heads poked their way out of the brown earth. It became imperative for me to have a garden of my own at home and, having convinced the shopkeeper from whom my mother rented our room to clear his junk yard under our window, I proceeded to create my first garden.

Though digging was done with a stick and watering with a milk-jug up and down two flights of stairs, I managed to produce in that season some pale pink sweet peas and a crop of small turnips. This success produced a gardening addiction which is still part of my life today.

My mother was a singing teacher and our income extremely limited, so plants for my first garden were obtained from friends' left-over seedlings, or plants rejected from their gardens. Although they were far above my means, I longed to have a garden filled with roses like those hanging in splendour from the bowers of the Beast's garden where Beauty's father plucked a rose. I spent many hours gazing at the picture of the hairy beast, the noble father, the beautiful roses and read the story over and over again.

My mother used to sing a song of a lone rose tree in a garden: the owner visited the plant every morning and every evening to gaze upon the one rosebud that had formed, but a storm destroyed it before the rose was fully open. This song saddened me profoundly and I often wondered whether I would ever have the joy of picking roses in a garden of my own, so that a rose garden became for me the symbol of happiness and supreme contentment.

When eventually I did move into a cottage on a small-holding, my preoccupation with a loving husband and baby boy had long since dispelled adolescent rose-dreams and my mind was filled with the more practical considerations of creating a fruit and vegetable garden.

Then one morning early, when the house was filled with sleep, I walked out into my new garden and noticed for the first time that a very large rose tree was growing high up along a veranda pillar of my stoep. The rough black trunk was old and gnarled, the dainty green leaves fresh and shiny, and from the top of the plant a large spray of the tiniest, most perfectly formed pink roses seemed to float on the morning air, spreading a most sweet fragrance. Suddenly I was filled with the old freesia excitement, with the romance of the Beast's garden, with the sadness of the storm-bereft rose tree, and there and then I decided to plant a rose garden.

I picked very many beautiful blooms from this first rose garden in the next twelve years for friends and for my own home, but the most special of all my

trees was the 'Sweetheart Rose' over my front veranda. Throughout the year this generous plant provided tiny pink buds and blooms for all important family occasions: posies for new-born baby girls, sprays for birthdays, Christmas and wedding cakes, cheery vases for sick-trays and tiny arrangements for innumerable dolls' parties.

The older generation of gardeners in the Cape know 'Cécile Brunner' well and from them I learnt that it has been growing in local gardens since the late 19th century. It is the one old rose which owners always identify with certainty and which is always greeted with enthusiastic praise and affection. It must have reached the Cape soon after its introduction in 1881, when M. Pernet-Ducher developed this tiny rose in his Lyon nursery by crossing an unknown Polyantha with the Tea rose 'Mme de Tartas'.

It was many years after we had moved from our first home that I was to see the so-called 'yellow Cécile Brunner' or 'Perle d'Or' growing on either side of the central path in the Victorian terrace garden of the Murray's farm Bloemhof near Graaff-Reinet. The pretty yellow buds with bright orange tips are plumper than those of the pink 'Cécile Brunner', though the shiny neat green calyces with short oval sepals and the full flowers of both are very much alike. 'Perle d'Or' also has a stronger tea fragrance. McFarland tells us that this rose was introduced three years after 'Cécile Brunner' by Dubreuil and that its parents are a Polyantha and the yellow Tea rose, 'Mme Falcot'.

'Bloomfield Abundance' is another rose which resembles 'Cécile Brunner' in many respects. According to McFarland it was introduced in 1920 by Thomas and is a cross between the pale yellow 'Sylvia' and the Hybrid Tea 'Dorothy Page-Roberts'. The flowers are a little deeper in colour and larger than those of the 'Sweetheart Rose', and the plants grow 3–5 metres high.

I came across a hedge of these growing at that very beautiful and famous old Cape Dutch farm, Libertas, outside Stellenbosch; and Mrs Blake, the present owner's wife, assured me that this hedge, which was taller than both of us, had been in the garden when she arrived on the farm as a young bride and would never be removed because her family all had a special love for the perfectly formed small flowers. We agreed that no garden was complete without at least one variety of the 'Sweetheart Rose'!

During the Second International Heritage Rose Conference in Adelaide in October 1986, I was delighted to find a white variety of 'Cécile Brunner' growing in several gardens. This sport from 'Cécile Brunner' was introduced to Europe in 1909 — surely it would have arrived at the Cape soon after? I have seen no plants here, but hope that it will soon be introduced to receive the same acclaim and admiration given to the rest of its happy family.

'Cécile Brunner' has perfect little blooms of a pale pink.

'Cécile Brunner'

'SWEETHEART ROSE'

PLANT
Two varieties of 'Cécile Brunner' occur in Cape gardens. One is a shrub about 1 metre high and of the same diameter; the other is a plant growing much more vigorously up to 5 metres high. Both plants are much branched and form round, dense bushes, and both have small, straightish brown thorns.

FOLIAGE
There are five oval to acuminate, dark green, shiny leaflets 4–7 cm long with well-marked serrated edges. The leaf-stalks are thin, long and have no prickles on the under-side. The stipules are long, widish and have slightly fringed edges with no glands.

FLOWERS
The light pink, perfectly formed, small pointed buds open into miniature clear pink, full flowers 3–4 cm in diameter. The outer petals are rolled back and the inner ones form a perfect point in the half-open flower, filling the centre in a frilly fashion when the bloom is fully blown. The stamens are primitive and the stigmas form a short central column. The calyx is cup-shaped and slightly glandular. The two varieties of plants usually differ in the length of the sepals, those of the smaller shrub being short and un-foliated, those of the more vigorous shrub longer and foliated. These characteristics are not constant, however, and I have noticed short and long foliated sepals occurring on either of the two varieties. Flowers appear throughout the year and are sweetly fragrant.

INFLORESCENCE
This varies greatly in size and number of flowers, ranging from a few blooms on a short branchlet to a 0,5 metre-long spray carrying twenty to thirty flowers. The individual flower-stalks are glandular and sometimes up to 25 cm long; they have long foliated bracts at their bases.

'Cécile Brunner'.

'Bloomfield Abundance'.

'Perle d'Or'.

White 'Cécile Brunner'.

Asiya, who lives next to our office, with the 'Muslim Rose'.

THE BOURBONS

It is generally believed that this group of roses is descended from a chance crossing discovered in 1817 on the Ile de Bourbon, between *Rosa damascena semperflorens* and the old China, 'Parsons Pink China'. This hybrid, named 'Rose Edward', gave rise in France to a new class of roses, the Bourbons.

In Europe the Bourbons quickly became popular because, unlike the old summer-flowering roses, they produced flowers throughout the year. By 1848 William Paul could describe 188 Bourbon roses and list a further 57 as 'Hybrid Bourbons'.

These roses must have been introduced to the Cape soon after their European appearance and the following varieties are named in a list of plants growing in the Cape Town Botanic Garden in 1858: 'Cardinal Fisch', 'Duc de Chartres', 'Eclair de Jupiter', 'Gloire de Dijon', 'Gloire des Rosomanes', 'Lady Montagu', 'Reine des Vierges' and the great favourite, 'Souvenir de la Malmaison'. 'Rose Edward' itself also appears on this list.

Only four of these early Bourbons ('Eclair de Jupiter', 'Gloire des Rosomanes', 'Gloire de Dijon' and 'Souvenir de la Malmaison') are still to be found in Cape gardens although the others, for all I know, may yet be discovered amongst the small group of roses for which I have up till now found no names.

Later on 'Blairii No. 2' (1845), 'Zéphirine Drouhin' (1868), 'Mme Isaac Pereire' (1881), 'Honorine de Brabant' (?) and 'Variegata di Bologna' (1909) were also imported to the Cape, but of these the only one which has achieved a measure of popularity is 'Zéphirine Drouhin'.

Some Bourbons grow more happily and produce better-coloured flowers if planted in semi-shade, but the more vigorous kinds which form excellent climbers for arches and pergolas ('Gloire de Dijon', 'Zéphirine Drouhin', 'Mme Isaac Pereire' and the climbing form of 'Souvenir de la Malmaison') love the sun. These varieties can also be used as pillar roses, but will then need more careful shaping.

Bourbons such as 'Souvenir de la Malmaison', 'Gloire des Rosomanes' and 'Boule de Neige' can be used very successfully in herbaceous borders with companion plants, or for informal hedges. They require the rich soil which all Bourbons love and need little pruning except for the cutting back of dead flowers.

For their ease of growth and recurring voluptuous flowers — rich in colour and perfume — the old Bourbons deserve to have a place in all Cape gardens.

Clockwise:
Serge Michaud identified
this 'Rose Edward' in his
Seychelles garden.
In Mauritius.
'Rose Edward' grows in
various Wellington cemeteries.
Here it is seen on mid-
19th century Retief graves
in the Bovlei.
We found 'Rose Edward'
growing in the Patraia garden
near Florence.

Recently I visited Mauritius and Réunion, the two islands in the Indian ocean which are inextricably involved in the history of the modern rose, to see for myself which roses were still being cultivated there and whether local archives, botanists or historians might be able to throw some light on the origin of the 'Bourbon Rose', ancestor of so many modern roses. I was not disappointed in the many interesting roses which I found there, but as to the history of the first Bourbon rose, the most authentic source still seems to be that of Thomas Rivers, the English nurseryman who, twelve years after the introduction of the rose to England, told the story of its origin according to M. Bréon.[1]

This French botanist, who in 1817 arrived in the French colony of Bourbon (now Réunion) as the curator of the botanical garden, discovered a new rose being cultivated in the garden of a M. Perichon, which he believed had arisen as a natural hybrid of the two hedge-roses growing on the island, namely the 'Common Pink China' and a variety of *Rosa damascena semperflorens*. M. Bréon named the new rose 'Rose de l'Ile de Bourbon' and five years later sent plants and seeds to M. Jacques, the gardener of the Duke of Orleans, who then cultivated the roses at Chateau de Neuilly near Paris. From here they were distributed to leading French nurserymen, reaching England in 1822.

A few years later Redouté obtained a flower from the Neuilly garden which he painted under the name of *Rosa canina Borboniana*,[2] adding in the description of the rose that according to the Duke of Orleans the rose grew wild in uncultivated places on the Isle de Bourbon, a story which I am inclined to believe.

A French officer, Pierre Bernadine, who visited Isle de Bourbon and Mauritius in 1768, mentions European and Chinese roses, the latter 'thriving so well that hedges are made of it'.[3] I suspect that 'Rose Edward' was probably quite common on Indian Ocean islands by the time that M. Bréon arrived at Isle de Bourbon, and that he was not therefore the discoverer of the first one. The Revd Ellis, who visited Réunion in 1855, found 'Rose Edward' growing in the kitchen garden of the Governor: 'the common china rose or Rose Edward forming complete hedges along some of the walks'.[4]

Mr A. S. Thomas of Australia took some trouble to ascertain that the 'Rose Edward' of the Indian Ocean islands was one and the same as the 'Temple rose' of India,[5] which creates a further mystery around the origin of 'Rose Edward': did it arrive in the East from the Islands or vice versa?

During my visit to Mauritius, Réunion and the Seychelles, I saw many roses in private gardens which I suspected might be 'Rose Edward', but since the only photograph I had seen was the rather indistinct picture of Mr Thomas' 'Temple rose' and Redouté's painting, I could not identify these roses positively.

At the Seychelles our taxi driver was extremely puzzled that I should be so interested in every insignificant little rose along the way and apparently unappreciative of their spectacular scenery. My husband explained my strange behaviour and when next we stopped at the top of a hill to admire the tea plantations, the driver went scouting around for roses, while I bought some packets of tea to take home. With great pride he took me to a small garden behind the factory where a beautiful pink rose with delicious fragrance was in full flower and when I asked its name, he ferreted out the owner who told me the delightful news, 'Ah! That is Rose Edouard. My mother and grandmother grew it, and I have known it since I have been a small boy!' Generously he gave me some slips which I smuggled along guiltily through one airport after another, until the heat in India eventually turned them mouldy and I had to discard them.

In Delhi Mr B. P. Pal, the acknowledged Indian rose expert, told me that 'Rose Edward' used to be commonly used as understock, but that its susceptibility to fungus had made it unsuitable for that purpose in recent times. He mentioned that there were two varieties of this rose, the one being a taller shrub than the other. (This was later confirmed by gardeners in the Seychelles with whom I corresponded.)

Now that I had photographs, drawings and a description of this famous rose, I could renew my search for it when once I was back home, for I knew that it had been growing in the Botanic Gardens of Cape Town in 1858 and that from there it had probably been distributed far and wide. Soon I was rewarded by finding plants on farms and graveyards in the Wellington district, and along the road and in gardens of the small Karoo village of Prince Albert.

Slips which I have taken from these are growing well without signs of mildew and I hope soon to have many of these sweetly fragrant pink roses, which flower throughout the year, established in Cape gardens once again.

1 T. Rivers, *The Rose Amateur's Guide*, 1846. 'M. Bréon a French botanist and now a seedsman in Paris, gives the following account, for the truth of which he vouches.'
2 J. Redouté, *Les Roses*, Vol. III, p. 105. According to Thory, this rose was also known as 'Rosier de l'Isle de Bourbon'. This corresponds to the name given by Bréon.
3 J. H. Bernadin de Saint Pierre, *Voyage to the Island of Mauritius, Isle of Bourbon and the Cape of Good Hope*, translated by John Parish, 1775.
4 W. Ellis, *Three Visits to Madagascar During the Years 1853–1854 and 1856.*
5 A. S. Thomas, *Knowing, Growing and Showing Roses*, 1975.

'Rose Edward'

'Rose Edward'.

PLANT

There are two distinct forms of 'Rose Edward'. The one grows into a tall, lax shrub about 2 metres high; the other into a shorter, more compact plant with several upright stems. Both have many hooked thorns of different sizes.

FOLIAGE

Five oval pointed leaflets with widely spaced serrations, often bidentate; the surface is smooth, dark green, duller on the underside. The leaf-stalk is glandular towards the proximal end, rough on the underside but has no hooks. Stipules are adnate and wide, glandular, with free tips.

FLOWERS

Short, fat, dark-pink buds with a few foliated, slightly longer sepals, open into bright, clear pink, semi-double flowers 6–7 cm in diameter. The petals (about thirty) are broad and have irregular, often indented edges; the shanks are lighter. A number of longish stamens with white filaments surround a bunch of pistils with branched stigmas. The calyx is oval and smooth with glands at the proximal end. Sepals are branched, glandular on top, velvety on the underside, and reflex only to hold the corolla. The flowers are very fragrant and appear throughout the year.

INFLORESCENCE

From one to six flowers (sometimes more) on short, sturdy, glandular stalks. Bracts are small, leaflike and glandular.

103

From left to right:
In a Knysna garden.
Guarded by an angel.
The ninety-year-old
Mr MacClaren.

When Philip Erskine of Ida's Valley lent me *A Book About Roses* written by one of his fore-bears,[1] I enjoyed reading it so much that I could not bear to part with it until I had a copy of my own. Amateur enthusiast on the subject of old roses as I was then, I absorbed the firsthand information of the expert as if the century that separated us did not exist. Dean Hole himself said 'I ought to have something to say worth hearing to those who love the Rose', and he had a right to boast, for not only had he grown roses for twenty years and won more than thirty cups 'open to all England', but he had initiated the first rose show and attended most of the subsequent meetings either as a judge or exhibitor until 1868 when he wrote his classic.

In characteristic style he praises his favourite rose: 'If I were miserably sentenced for the rest of my life to possess a single rose-tree, I should desire to be supplied, on leaving the dock, with a strong plant of Gloire de Dijon.'

After this I had a yearning to see this spectacular Bourbon, but though rose lists from the middle of the 19th century confirm that 'Gloire de Dijon' grew in Cape Town's Botanic Garden within five years of its European introduction, I could find no remaining plants.

It was in June 1981 that I saw my first half-open bloom at Bone Hill and a week later the true splendour of the rose was revealed to me at Powis Castle where I arrived one evening in the fading light. Some highly sensitive gardener had trained 'Gloire de Dijon' up against the rustic pink walls of this age-old building and the many blooms in tones of yellow, orange, fawn, buff and salmon made such a lasting impression on me that the Powis Castle garden remains in my memory as one of the most exquisite I have seen.

I subsequently found this climber in a Cape Town cemetery and in the little seaside town of Knysna. The hunt for old roses has often brought me into contact with strangers who have since become dear friends, like the Shands of Rondebosch who brought the Knysna rose to my notice. Or Leslie Whileman, horticulturist of the Worcester farm museum, who turned up one day laden with roses he had collected in the Koo. A few blooms, picked from a fallen climber in front of the old farmhouse at Petrusfontein, turned out to be 'Gloire de Dijon'. The T-shaped house had had its thatch replaced with corrugated iron and was being used as a store, but the rose tree valiantly continued to produce its flowers, indicating better days when the presence of a fond gardener and rose-lover understood its needs.

The resilient Petrusfontein rose reminded me of the Revd Joseph Pemberton's theory that the best Teas were developed in France because seed ripened there in the open, whereas in England seed hardly ever ripened. He also regarded 'Gloire de Dijon', the only rose of its class that could withstand the cold English winters, as one of the very best.

That this rose with its wealth of colour, sweet fragrance and healthy growth should be so rare in our warm Cape gardens is indeed difficult to understand. Mr MacClaren who started working for Leighton's nurseries in King Williams Town in 1906, when he was sixteen years old, told me that they used to send many 'Glory of Dijon' roses all over the country, and that it was still included in their 1940 catalogue.[2]

I interviewed him when he had just turned ninety-one, and like a true nurseryman he said, with slight impatience, 'Nobody grows old roses any more, the new ones are too exciting'. The roses blooming in his garden indicated a preference for vivid orange and yellow: 'Fanny Blankers-Koen' (1949), 'Geneva' (1944), 'Brazil' (1947), 'Mevrouw G. A. van Rossum' (1929), 'Sutter's Gold' (1950), 'Eclipse' (1935) and 'Super Star' (1960). How could the subtle fawn and warm pink of 'Gloire de Dijon' compete against such brilliance?

1 Dean Hole, London, 1869.
2 The roses for the newly constructed gardens at the Union buildings in Pretoria in 1910 were supplied by this nursery.

'Gloire de Dijon'

'Gloire de Dijon'.

PLANT
Vigorous climber to 5 or more metres, with many large hooked thorns.

FOLIAGE
Five oval, dark olive-green leaflets with smooth shiny surfaces; the sturdy petioles are tinged red and covered with scattered glands. Stipules are adnate with tiny stalked glands on the edges.

FLOWERS
Large oval buds, with quickly reflexing sepals, open to heavy cups which expand to form very full quartered and quilled flat blooms. Colours vary from buff-yellow to ochre to warm pink; the shanks are usually a deeper ochre. Stamens are rudimentary and the pistils form a short leafy green mass in the centre. The cup-shaped calyx is smooth and tinged red; the sepals have small folioles, are velvety on the underside and have a few tiny scattered glands on the edges. Flowers appear throughout the year and have a sweet Tea fragrance.

INFLORESCENCE
One to four flowers in a corymb, with long bracts at their attachments and a third of the way up the stalks.

'Honorine de Brabant'

'Honorine de Brabant'.

'Honorine de Brabant' is a striped Bourbon rose of unknown parentage and age. It is found in several Cape gardens but its first date of introduction here is unknown to me. The shrub is one to two metres high, and likes to grow in semi-shade where more flowers of a deeper colour are produced. The curiously striped pink and white globular blooms are very striking especially when arranged with 'Variegata di Bologna', striped mauve and white.

Companion plants which I like best with the soft colours of this rose are heliotrope, white and mauve nicotiana and white foxgloves. At Boschendal I have planted St. Joseph lilies next to 'Honorine de Brabant' where they come up year after year to light up the garden and spread their delicious fragrance to mingle with that of the roses.

At the Cape I have not seen the profuse flowers which impressed me so much in English heritage rose gardens, for Bourbons on the whole seem to be less happy here. Yet I would not be without them and will carry on experimenting to find what soil suits them, and by shifting plants around, find where they like best to grow.

'Bourbon Queen'

'SOUVENIR DE LA PRINCESSE DE LAMBALLE'

This is one of the more vigorous Bourbon roses. It grows very well in the Cape and is occasionally seen in country gardens.[1] When it was introduced by Manget in 1834 there were not many Bourbons with which to compare it, and though it might then have merited the name of 'Queen of the Bourbons', it was soon outclassed by the many new varieties introduced by industrious French breeders who became increasingly enchanted with the perpetual-flowering properties of this new family of roses.

I took my first cuttings from a plant in the garden of Mrs A. E. Heckroodt in Mowbray, who had received her plant from her old charwoman who in turn had been given hers by her former employer fifty years before. I planted the rose against a very tall Pride of India tree, hoping that the large semi-double clear pink flowers would hang from the grey-white stems of the tree when both were in flower. In front of the rose I planted blue plumbago, which grows with so much energy that I periodically have to cut it right back to the ground to save the rose from being engulfed. However, I am rewarded every year by the splendid sight of Pride of India splashing its bright pink high against a cobalt sky, with warm pink 'Bourbon Queen' clinging to its knees and clear blue plumbago echoing the sky at its feet.

The real beauty of the rose can however only be appreciated when one looks right into the heart of the bloom, for then one sees that the petals are shaded and streaked with a deeper pink and then, too, the wonderful fragrance enchants one with its intense sweetness.

1 Stephen Brett Nurseries of Port Elizabeth and Uitenhage included it in their 1905 plant catalogue.

PLANT
A vigorous climber or pillar rose with long sturdy branching stems growing to 9 metres high. The few thorns are slightly curved and scattered.

FOLIAGE
Five oval heart-shaped leaflets with finely serrated edges and dull, almost leathery surfaces. The stems are sturdy, slightly velvety and have a few small prickles on the undersides. Stipules are adnate and have smooth, glandular edges.

FLOWERS
Pointed fat buds with short sepals open to semi-double light-pink flowers 8 cm in diameter; the outside petals are wide and notched, the inner ones small and wavy. The petals are faintly streaked or blotched with a darker pink. Many pistils form a squat bunch half the length of the short stamens. The calyx is truncated and smooth; short triangular sepals with tiny folioles reflex to lie against the corolla. Flowers are most abundant in spring but produce a few odd blooms at other times; they are very fragrant.

INFLORESCENCE
A corymb of three to four flowers on strong upright glandular pedicels; bracts are thin and small.

'Bourbon Queen'.

'Coupe d'Hébé'

'Coupe d'Hébé'.

Laffay in 1840 produced this hybrid from unknown Bourbon and China parents.

The charm of this rose lies in the perfect cup shape of the bloom and the clear, almost shiny pink colour and lovely fragrance. It is a vigorous shrub with many erect stems, sometimes inclined to droop when laden with flowers. 'Coupe d'Hébé' flowers only in spring and early summer.

It was growing in the Cape Town Botanic Garden soon after its introduction, and now, almost one and a half centuries later, is again available and becoming a favourite.

'Blairii No.2'

'Blairii No. 2'.

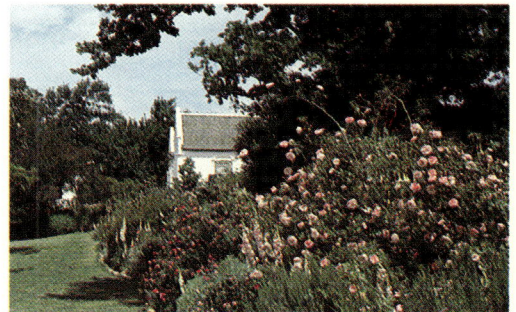

'Blairii No. 2', a Bourbon rose raised in 1845 by a Mr Blair of Stamford Hill, grows in several old rose gardens in the Western Cape, but I have found no record of its first introduction to this country.

The plants grow vigorously, throwing out sturdy shoots two to four metres long which, if unsupported, bend over and eventually form large arching shrubs. At Boschendal I have planted a 'Blairii No. 2' on a sloping bank which gets only morning sun. The 'Old Monthly' and yellow day lilies grow at its front edge; yellow and white datura and pink oleander form a backdrop higher up. In spring all these flowering together create a magnificent spectacle, 'Blairii No. 2' excelling with its hundreds of large clear pink blossoms strung along the many arching branches in light contrast to the heavy yellow and white bells of the 'moonflowers'. The bees love the overpowering fragrance of this garden nook and so do I.

PLANT
A vigorous shrub or climber growing to a height of over 5 metres with many arching branches. There are many brownish hooked thorns.

FOLIAGE
Five light-green oval leaflets with smooth surfaces and medium serrations. The stalks are delicate and have many hooked thornlets on the underside. The young leaves are often a dark reddish-brown. Stipules are adnate and narrow.

FLOWERS
Large round buds open to quite full flowers with broad clear pink petals which roll back a little on the outer edges. The inner petals are small and curly but do not completely cover the yellow stamens on their long filaments, or the short pistil. The calyx is cup-shaped and smooth; the sepals foliated, furry on the underside and have glands on the edges and midrib. The flowers appear only in spring and have a delicious strong fragrance.

INFLORESCENCE
One or two flowers on short glandular stalks along the main branches.

'Louise Odier'

'Louise Odier' is a Bourbon rose of exquisite beauty, particularly attractive when the clear pink flowers are half open with their cupped petals primly overlapping each other and finished at the base with a frill of sepals. I like to plant it with Cape forget-me-nots, aristea or petrea as I love the dark-blue colour of these flowers offsetting the pink of the rose.

Introduced to European gardens by Margottin in 1851, the rose soon made its appearance in the Cape and is recorded in Saul Solomon's garden in Sea Point in 1866 from where eight plants were sent, together with a few hundred other varieties of rose trees, to the newly established Botanic Garden in Durban.[1]

I have been unable to trace existing old plants at the Cape, but was fortunate to obtain slips from an imported plant in the Knox-Shaw's garden in Elgin. Although these slips have grown well and produce flowers throughout the year, they are by no means as vigorous nor do they provide the profusion of blooms that I have noticed in European gardens. I suspect that they enjoy cooler weather conditions and should perhaps be planted in dappled sunlight.

1 Minutes of the Natal Botanic Society, 1865.

PLANT
A lax shrub about 2 metres high, with many long branched stems. The scattered thorns are short, curved and reddish.

FOLIAGE
Five medium-sized heart-shaped leaflets with smooth surfaces. The stalks have a few scattered glands and prickles on the underside; adnate stipules are narrow with free tips and glandular edges.

FLOWERS
The neat oval buds open to clear pink flowers about 8 cm in diameter. The broader outer petals enfold the smaller inner ones in neat rows, retaining a loose cupped shape even when the flower is fully blown. A number of stamens with white filaments surround the loose hairy styles with shiny cream stigmas. The calyx is cup-shaped and smooth; sepals have medium-sized foliations, are glandular on the outer surface and along the edges, and velvety on the underside. The flowers are fragrant and appear sporadically throughout the year, the best show being in spring.

INFLORESCENCE
Two to three flowers in a corymb on short glandular stalks. Bracts are elongated, leaflike and edged with stalked glands.

'Louise Odier'.

PLANT
A sturdy much-branched plant just over 1 metre high with many short, slightly hooked thorns.

FOLIAGE
Five cordate, medium-sized dark-green leaflets with shiny surfaces slightly duller on the underside. The stalk is smooth with no prickles; stipules are adnate, narrow and reddish.

FLOWERS
Large globular buds with short sepals open into large, flat, rosette-like flowers 10–11 cm in diameter. The light clear-

'Souvenir de la Malmaison'

'Of the Bourbon Roses, Souvenir de la Malmaison has a most inexplicable hold on the affections of the Cape gardener—and always with the accent thrown violently on the last syllable', Dorothea Fairbridge wrote in her book on South African gardens in 1925, adding that she had no taste for the flowers which reminded her of inverted mushrooms.

Familiarity obviously made Miss Fairbridge contemptuous of a rose which, soon after its introduction in France by Beluze in 1843, made its debut in the Cape Town Botanic Garden and subsequently became the darling of many a Victorian gentleman's rose garden.[1]

One such garden was Herschell, the family home of Mr H. E. Rutherford in Claremont. When Emma Rutherford left to marry the Revd Andrew Murray junior in 1856, she packed slips of this Bourbon rose, together with other plants, her piano and precious porcelain, in the ox-wagon that was to take her on the long journey to her new home in Bloemfontein, where seven years before, the twenty-year-old Revd Murray had been appointed Colonial Chaplain to the Orange River Sovereignty.[2]

Soon after their arrival at the parsonage, the young couple grouped their Cape Town plants in one round and two corner beds, placing the flower garden in a square plot between the stone boundary wall and their house. To prevent frost destroying their new treasures, branches were laid over the beds and skins covered them at night. Soon Emma was able to write to her family that 'Souvenir de la Malmaison' was flowering in her garden and to tell them how much she and Andrew enjoyed the sweet scent of their roses.

Near the end of his life, when Emma had been dead for over ten years, the old Revd Murray was to be reminded of those happy Bloemfontein days by the fragrance of the 'Malmaison' rose tree in his Wellington garden.

My first meeting with 'Souvenir de la Malmaison' took place one evening at dusk when I was walking in the garden of the late Miss Nita Steyn in Swellendam. This well-loved old lady had bequeathed her home Mayville to the Drostdy Museum and had stipulated in her will that a rose garden in memory of herself and her sister Nina should always be maintained in a corner of the property. I was turning over ideas for this memorial garden (which I had been asked to design), when I was astonished to see, glimmering in the failing light, a large flat bloom the size of a saucer on one of Miss Nita's few remaining old rose bushes. When I bent down for a closer look I was met with the most delicious fragrance of any rose that I had ever experienced. The following morning, when sunlight revealed the silky, light-pink petals beautifully folded layer upon layer into a perfect large rosette, I too became enamoured of this old Cape favourite, and immediately resolved to include a few plants of it in the memorial garden.

In the same garden I have also planted the climbing variety, which was introduced by Bennet fifty years after its parent. It is as beautiful, with flowers as perfectly formed, though of a much paler colour. The wonderful scent of this old Bourbon makes it most desirable for growing over a summer-house, and I can think of no greater contentment than to sit under a bower of 'Souvenir de la Malmaison' on a warm spring evening, perhaps with a cold glass of Twee Jonge Gezellen and a few good friends to share the quiet bliss.

1 Stephen Brett in his 1905–6 *Plant Catalogue* describes 'Souvenir de la Malmaison' as 'one of the grandest roses in cultivation'.
2 Joyce Murray, *Young Mrs Murray Goes to Bloemfontein*, 1954.

pink petals are broad and have a porcelain-like quality. There are many well-formed stamens on long filaments around a bunch of short styles with shiny cream stigmas. The calyx is small, cone-shaped and glandular towards the stalk which is also glandular. Sepals are short, unfoliated, glandular along the midrib and velvety on the underside. Flowers appear throughout the year and have a very strong fragrance.

INFLORESCENCE
From one to thirteen in a corymb at the top of the branches when plants are exceptionally vigorous.

'Souvenir de la Malmaison'.

'Boule de Neige'

The rose hedge in the Grahamstown Botanical Gardens at the turn of the century might have been 'Boule de Neige'.

In a Grahamstown cemetery.

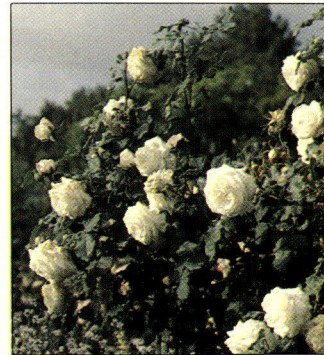

On the outskirts of Grahamstown lie a number of old cemeteries with graves dating to the middle of the 19th century. Here I spent a very happy morning with Professor and Mrs John Rennie who refused to leave me there alone for fear that I should be molested by one of the many vagrants frequenting this desolate area. These two kindly people trailed along with me patiently, growing more and more interested in the old roses that I found and becoming gradually overloaded with the many specimens and cuttings that I was gathering with great fervour. For here was the largest find of old roses that I had come across in any single place in the Cape.

They told me that in the 1930s Judge Victor Sampson's widow took it upon herself to beautify the old graveyards where members of the Anglican, Presbyterian and Dutch Reformed Churches had been buried for almost a century. Mrs Sampson chose the 'queen of flowers' to plant on every grave and along the pathways. Gallicas, Bourbons, Albas, Chinas and Teas were obviously selected for their hardiness, so that after fifty years of declining care, plants were still producing masses of flowers in the spring of 1981. I suspect that the only damage to these old plants had been done by ignorant but well-meaning caretakers who over-zealously prune shrubs which should be left to grow without disturbance, except for a good soaking once a week.

Amongst the dark-green foliage on one of these rose trees I noticed many beautiful buds, but no open flowers. I sketched a bud with long, foliated sepals reflexed in a whorl like a Catherine wheel, but a year passed before I was able to identify the rose as 'Boule de Neige'.

Though I had often picked the fully open white snowball flowers of this lovely Bourbon to arrange in my bedroom for their delicious fragrance, it was only when I started to sketch and describe the details of the whole plant that I recognized the bud and distinctive foliage of the unknown Grahamstown cemetery rose and realized how often one looks without seeing!

A correspondent of the *The Cape Amateur Gardener* of 1913 encouraged gardeners to plant more rose hedges, and recommended 'Boule de Neige' as one of the most eminently suitable varieties for lower hedges. He advised that plants should be 'spaced two and a half feet apart in a double row, with the two rows staggered'. McFarland (in *Roses 8*) also recommends it as a very hardy plant, good for hedging.

Yet at the Cape I have not succeeded in growing 'Boule de Neige' from slips and my friends have had the same experience. I can only suppose that it must have lost some of the vigour which would have made it easy to propagate in large numbers early in the century. Any gardener wanting to plant a hedge of this old rose now, will therefore have to resort to budded or grafted plants.

'Boule de Neige'

PLANT
A dense branching plant 1,5 metres high, having many small straight red thorns.

FOLIAGE
Five oval dark-green leaflets with cone-shaped proximal ends, serrated margins, smooth shiny surfaces on sturdy stalks with no prickles on the undersides. Stipules are adnate, entire and have longish free ends.

FLOWERS
Globular buds, greenish-white tinged red, with blunted tops, open to very full white flowers 7 cm in diameter. The petals are heart-shaped with deep notches on the outer edges. There are very few stamens and the pistil consists of a bunch of long hairy styles with greeny-cream stigmas. The calyx is cup-shaped and smooth; the long foliated sepals are smooth on top and velvety on the undersurfaces. The flowers have a strong fragrance and appear throughout the year with a flush in the spring.

INFLORESCENCE
Single flowers on smooth sturdy pedicels are borne on branchlets at the top of the plant. Bracts are long, thin and leaflike.

'Boule de Neige'.

'Mme Isaac Pereire'

'Mme Isaac Pereire' is a much more recent Bourbon climber than 'Zéphirine Drouhin' (it was introduced by Garcon in 1881) and is even more striking. It grows more vigorously, the flowers are larger, fuller, of a deeper rose colour, and the scent is exquisite. If I had to choose the most spectacular climber of all, this would be my choice, both for its perfection of form and splendid fragrance.

I found one old plant amongst the rose trees in the Mill River garden,[1] but a number of newly imported trees are thriving in the gardens of several old rose enthusiasts. I have recently planted one at Boschendal and, judging by the surprised exclamations that the large flowers evoke from delighted visitors, there should soon be quite a demand for plants of 'Mme Isaac Pereire'.

1 In the Langkloof near Oudtshoorn.

PLANT
A vigorous shrub or climber to 4 metres, also useful as a pillar rose.

FOLIAGE
Five oval, dark-green, well-serrated leaflets on strong stalks with hooked thorns. The stipules are adnate and narrow with smooth edges.

FLOWERS
Large round buds with slightly longer sepals open to large, very full blooms about 10 cm in diameter. The broad, dark-cerise petals are tightly packed in whorls, loosely quartered in the centre. The small flat calyx is cup-shaped and the sepals unfoliated. Flowers appear throughout the year and are wonderfully fragrant.

INFLORESCENCE
One to three flowers on short side branchlets.

'Mme Isaac Pereire'.

'Souvenir d'Alphonse Lavallée'

Although McFarland classifies this richly coloured rose of the late 19th century with the Hybrid Perpetuals, I agree with Graham Thomas that the very full, quartered flower of 'Souvenir d'Alphonse Lavallée' is more characteristic of the Bourbons, and I am therefore including it here.

I remember that this was one of the roses which my cousin Helie van Heerden grew in her rose collection at Moorreesburg in the early 1940s. She had decided to design and plant a rose garden near to the fresh water reservoir so that she would be able to lead the water onto the rose beds. Everyone in the town thought she was slightly touched, for where did she think she would get enough fresh water to keep her roses growing in the long dry summer months? And how long would it last, this precious stuff, if she wasted it on roses? The reservoir was filled from water that ran off the roof of the house and outbuildings in the rainy season, but that water was sparingly used for cooking and washing hair. The windmill clankling away in the backyard brought plenty of water up from the depths of the hard red gravelly soil, but that water was brack and everyone knew that it was totally unfit for all plants, except statice and vygies.[1]

But cousin Helie had an indulgent husband and a determined mind. She had seen the illustrations in the rose catalogue and her imagination was fired. We sat for hours marking all the roses she would order, choosing the most exotic sounding names, for we had no idea what they would look like. 'Souvenir d'Alphonse Lavallée' could not be resisted and though the list had to be shortened repeatedly, this dark red rose stayed, arrived and was planted.

From then on, I looked forward even more eagerly to my holidays with my cousin. As we strolled through the rows of rose trees surrounded by low stone walls, I thought the stone arches which carried her climbers the most beautiful I had ever seen, while she repeated the magical rose names 'Etoile de Hollande', 'Frau Karl Druschki', 'Souvenir de la Malmaison', 'Souvenir d'Alphonse Lavallée'. I cannot remember how she solved her water problem, but her plants were taller than I was, and the flowers that filled her house were the envy of the whole town.

It was more than thirty years later that I saw another 'Souvenir d'Alphonse Lavallée'. Terry Reddick, who was helping me with the Boschendal garden, took me to his cottage to identify a rose which his mother-in-law had brought from her home. When I saw the rose tree full of dark-red velvety flowers, memories of my happy school holidays came rushing back, and as the name 'Souvenir d'Alphonse Lavallée' rolled off my tongue, I remembered my dear cousin's smile as she bent down to savour the sweetly fragrant rose.

The bloom for this portrait was taken from a plant growing in Mrs Walsh's garden in Tweed Street in Newlands. Most of the cottages in this street date back to the early years of this century. How beautiful it would be if the whole street facade could be restored and the gardens planted with shrubs and annuals of the period.

1. Mesembryanthemums.

PLANT
A branched vigorous shrub 1–2 metres high with hooked reddish thorns.

FOLIAGE
Five broad, oval, dark green leaflets with deeply serrated edges and shiny surfaces. Stipules are wide with free tips and are tinged red.

FLOWERS
Pointed round buds open into very full, quartered, dark crimson flowers of about 7 cm in diameter. The petals are broad and lighter towards the loosely folded centre, but darker in the outer rows. A number of short stamens surround a bunch of very short velvety stigmas. The calyx is cup-shaped; the short sepals, velvety on the underside, are unfoliated and slightly glandular. Flowers are produced throughout the year and are very fragrant.

'Souvenir d'Alphonse Lavallée'

'Johnman's Cottage Rose'

'Johnman's Cottage Rose'.

In a Riversdale garden.

Growing at the front door of Schreuder's house in Stellenbosch. This house was built in 1709 and was recently restored.

Two very pretty fragrant pink roses growing at the Cape have completely eluded identification.

One of them grows in Mrs Johnman's Stellenbosch garden, and is called by her 'my Pink Cabbage'. It is a branching shrub of 1–1,5 metres high, with smooth, oval pointed, light-green leaves. The flowers are loosely globular, very full with muddled central petals of a clear salmon pink. They are very fragrant. The calyx is flat and cup-shaped, and the sepals, of which two are quite well branched, reflex right back against the stem. The flower-stalk is bristly.

Members of the American Heritage Rose Society who looked at slides of this rose thought that it might be a Hybrid Bourbon. Searching through old Cape plant lists I came upon a rose called 'Léopold' which grew in Cape Town in 1858. This was probably 'Léopold de Bauffrémont', which William Paul described in 1848 under his Hybrid Noisette group as 'pale rose, large and very double; form cupped . . . A beautiful Rose; grows well in a pot'. Could this be the rose from Mrs Johnman's garden?

I found a similar rose in Peter Beales' collection of old roses in his Norfolk nursery, which I notice in his *Classic Roses* remains unidentified.

'Kaapse Roos'

'Kaapse Roos'.

The farm Hazendal near Bottelary where I found old plants of the 'Kaapse Roos'.

ALICE FAYN TROTTER.

The second unidentified pink rose, generally called 'Die Kaapse Roos' ('The Cape Rose'), is commonly found in old gardens and graveyards. It has many tall-growing lax green branches; the blooms are borne at their tips. The leaves are heart-shaped, have a leathery texture and markedly serrated edges.

The large round bud opens into a globular bloom about 6–7 cm in diameter, which looks like a tight cabbage head. The petals are darker inside, lighter outside and roll back on the edges. The calyx is smooth, oval, taken in at the top and glandular; two of the sepals are longer, foliated and reflex more than the rest. The flower-stalk is sturdy, light green and glandular.

This rose has been growing at the Cape for more than a century.[1] It is mentioned by several writers and seems to have been a great Victorian favourite. Some people call it 'Die Slamse Roos' ('The Malay Rose') because it used to grow on the slopes of the Lion's Rump near the 'Malay Quarter' in Cape Town.

A community of Muslims, descended from the slaves who were largely brought from Malaysia to the Cape by the Dutch in the 17th and early 18th centuries, live together in this part of Cape Town in very pretty terraced houses, some dating back to the 18th century. A number of picturesque mosques are regularly attended by the men, and

the muezzin's call, echoing through the streets of Cape Town like the twelve-o'clock gun from Signal Hill, halts the busy city for a moment before the headlong rush continues.

Roses play an important part in the cultural life of the Muslims. They love to include them in the bouquets for their very colourful wedding ceremonies, during which the bride leaves the reception at her parents' home three times with her bridesmaids, each time changing into a more splendid wedding gown.

At their funerals too, the rose has its use. First the dead man's body is washed with holy water (abdas), then with soap and water, after which clean water is poured three times over his face, arms, head and legs. More water is poured three times down the right side and three times down the left, after which the body is treated with camphorated water and then carefully dried. After this it is wrapped into three linen sheets perfumed with aromatic oils and rose petals. I have been told that the highly scented 'Kaapse Roos' was preferred for this purpose.

The 'Kaapse Roos' has such a distinctive appearance that it should be easy to identify, yet no amount of diligent research has enabled me to give it a more precise name. I wonder whether this rose originated in some Eastern garden and was brought to the Cape directly from there in the early days of the Dutch colony, perhaps by Muslim families?

1 It occurs commonly in old cemeteries, and at the farm Hazendal outside Stellenbosch I have found a hedge said to be almost a century old.
2 Hildagonda Duckitt relates in her diary how her mother planted it at their farm Groote Post in the early 19th century.

Miss M. E. Rothman also mentions this rose in her description of the flower gardens of her youth. She thinks 'Cabbage' might have been translated into 'Kaapse', hence the name 'Kaapse Roos'.
R. F. M. Immelman, in describing the garden of his great-grandmother, Magdalena Johanna Malan (born 1814)

on the farm Vondeling near Bainskloof, mentions a Cabbage rose which grew in a walled garden near the main house: this could have been either of the two roses on these pages. (Unpublished manuscript, U.C.T. Library.)
3 According to Dr I. D. du Plessis, who wrote several books on the customs of the Cape Muslims.

'Zéphirine Drouhin'

'Zéphirine Drouhin'.

'Kathleen Harrop' catching the last rays of the setting sun on Pam Barlow's farm Rustenburg in Ida's Valley.

In many respects this Bourbon rose of unknown parentage, which was introduced by Bizot in 1868, can be regarded as the Perfect Rose. It grows very easily from slips, is thornless, richly coloured, deliciously fragrant, lasts well when cut, produces several crops of abundant blooms in spring and autumn and is comparatively free of disease.

At the Cape, 'Zéphirine Drouhin' soon became a very popular climber. In *The Cape Amateur Gardener* of 1913 it was highly recommended as a hedging plant, supported by stout wooden posts 'let into the ground at intervals and standing six or seven feet out of the ground'. The rose plants were to be tied to galvanized wires strained between the posts and were to be trimmed only where they overhung the walks.

I know of a plant that grows on such a fence in front of the little thatched cottage built for Cecil John Rhodes in the Groot Drakenstein at the beginning of this century. He did not live to see the house completed and the roses were planted by a later occupant. Each spring when the orchards are in full bloom, the shocking-pink rose blooms splash their bright colour against the dark blue Simonsberg, repeating the show in autumn against the mellowing warm colours of the surrounding trees and orchards.

My favourite plant, however, is on the Barlow farm Schoongezicht in Ida's Valley. Here a magnificent specimen covers a large area of brick garden wall, presenting a breathtaking sight when it flowers together with its sport, the light pink 'Kathleen Harrop' growing on the same wall. Sheila Heany, who for many years supervised this wonderful garden, told me that it had become a tradition in their family for the mother to hand down slips of this rose to her daughter on her wedding day so that, after several generations, 'Zéphirine Drouhin' was still treasured and to be found growing in the gardens of her family.

PLANT
A strong climber with many branching thornless stems.

FOLIAGE
Five bright-green, large oval leaflets with matt surfaces and serrated edges. The stalk is sturdy and rough on the underside but without prickles; there are some glands on the proximal end. Stipules are adnate and entire with smooth edges.

FLOWERS
Long, pointed, dark-pink buds open into semi-double, shocking-pink flowers of 9 cm in diameter. The pink petals (about 15–20) are wide with wavy edges and white shanks; the stamens with thin white filaments curve inwards over the shorter column of styles which are joined at the base but carry loose stigmas. The calyx is goblet-shaped and smooth; sepals are smooth on top, velvety below, have short folioles and reflex right back against the glandular flower-stalk. The flowers appear in great abundance in spring and autumn with a few blooms in between. They have a strong pleasant fragrance.

INFLORESCENCE
One flower on a short branchlet along the main and side branches.

118

'Variegata di Bologna'

'Variegata di Bologna'.

Another Bourbon of exquisite colouring is this Italian charmer introduced by Bonfiglioli in 1909. I bought a plant from Ludwig's nurseries and planted it at Boschendal in semi-shade, having seen in the Knox-Shaw garden in Elgin that the best flowers were produced on a plant growing under a tree. In fact, this plant had surprised us all by producing a few flowers which were not striped at all but of an even shade of dark purple — the deepest purple that I have seen on any rose!

When, in 1986, I visited David Rustan's incredibly beautiful rose garden, he showed me his 'Variegata di Bologna' covered with these dark purple blooms. He thinks that the original plant from which she sported was probably 'Victor Emanuel'.

'Mme Pierre Oger'

'Mme Pierre Oger' has the delicate colouring
and refined shape of a pearl.

'Mme Pierre Oger'.

I had often wondered whether the famous pink rose named after Queen Victoria had ever grown at the Cape where she used to have many loyal subjects. How fitting, I thought, it would have been if 'La Reine Victoria' had been planted in the garden around the foot of her statue fronting the Houses of Parliament in Cape Town.

But I could find no record that this rose had ever been introduced here and it was therefore with great excitement that I recognized a plant in full flower growing on a neglected grave when I entered the Kirstenbosch cemetery for the first time a few years ago.

The graves were simple mounds of earth, here and there surrounded by low brick walls, but the terrain was so overgrown with kikuyu grass that one had to walk carefully for fear of collapsing into a grave or falling over a disintegrated headstone. Yet roses in flower everywhere had changed this dreary place into a gay scene full of promise for an old-rose hunter.

I picked many roses, hoping that I would not be confronted by one of the relatives of the departed. For many of the gardeners from the adjacent world-famous Kirstenbosch Botanic Gardens had once lived in cottages near by and had buried parents and children in the small cemetery next to their stone church. During the weekends these labourers used to work in the gardens of surrounding home owners, teaching them the mysteries of cultivating the indigenous treasures that flourished at Kirstenbosch.

In my mother-in-law's veld garden in Bishopscourt, old one-eyed Joey was a wealth of information and eventually became her permanent gardener when his whole community was moved into new homes on the Cape Flats from where they were fetched and delivered daily by bus. Joey knew the names of a few old roses, but as his English was non-existent he pronounced them strangely and was not of much help when it came to identifying them.

I spent many happy hours amongst the roses of this graveyard, identifying *R. roxburghii plena*, 'Félicité et Perpétue', 'Lady Hillingdon', 'Devoniensis', 'Homère,' 'Frau Karl Druschki' and 'La Reine Victoria', but some Tea and China roses remain unidentified to this day. I had resolved to take cuttings in the autumn, but when I returned I was devastated to find a 'cleaned-up' cemetery, with neatly outlined graves, gravel paths and not a sign of green!

Fortunately Basil Bennetts had a good plant of 'La Reine Victoria' in his garden in Wynberg from which I was given slips to plant at Boschendal. Here the lovely clear pink heads of cupped flowers delight me throughout the year.

J. Schwartz introduced this Bourbon rose in 1872. Six years later a rose in every respect similar, except for colour, sported from it and was put on the market by C. Verdier under the name of 'Mme Pierre Oger'.

'Mme Pierre Oger' grows in a few Cape gardens and also on a grave in Paarl's oldest cemetery. In good soil the plant, like its mother, reaches two metres in height with several strong branches covered throughout the year with pretty, smooth, oval pointed leaves. The flowers which appear in groups of four to six at the top of the stems are of a soft pearly-white colour and, like pearls, rounded in form even when fully open. The sun tints the edges and backs of the outer petals with light pink, but I prefer the pale fragile flowers that open in the shade.

Alfred Smee in his book *My Garden* (1872), declared that a standard rose tree was a 'horticultural mistake' and looked like 'a mop with the handle stuck in the ground'. He preferred growing his roses as pyramids. Although standards are still as popular as ever, I find it a pity that pyramids are so seldom seen in modern gardens, for they undoubtedly provide a sculptural quality and give accent to drab borders and monotonous flower-beds. Both 'La Reine Victoria' and 'Mme Pierre Oger' can be grown very successfully in this shape by training the stems (which are inclined to droop) to grow up against three poles tied at the top to form a pyramid, and pruning the shoots to different lengths. In this way a fine display of blooms is produced, especially once the poles are covered with foliage.

Both these Bourbons are deliciously fragrant and last well when brought indoors. A bunch of 'Mme Pierre Oger' and 'La Reine Victoria' should look stunning if arranged together in one of those frilly-mouthed glass vases beloved by the Victorians.

'La Reine Victoria'

PLANT
A many-stemmed slender shrub growing 1 to 1,5 metres high, with scattered red hooked thorns.

FOLIAGE
Seven smallish, oval pointed, dark-green leaves with smooth shiny surfaces, duller on the undersides. The stems are slightly glandular at the proximal ends and have hooks below. Quite large stipules have smooth edges.

FLOWERS
Pointed dark-pink buds with slightly longer sepals open to perfect cup-shaped flowers about 6 cm in diameter. The many petals are silvery pink with paler shanks; the short stamens surround a bunch of equally short styles. The calyx is oval and smooth; sepals are foliated, smooth on the upper side, velvety below. A few strongly fragrant flowers appear throughout the year, but the best show is in spring.

INFLORESCENCE
A corymb of four to six flowers appearing at the tops of the stems.

'La Reine Victoria'.

121

A painting of Fernwood shows a late
19th century garden with arches, pergola,
summer-house and grazing wildebeest
in paddocks.

·Q·

THE NOISETTES

·O·

'Champneys' Pink Cluster' was the name given to the parent of this group of roses. It occurred as the result of a cross between 'Parsons' Pink China' and *Rosa moschata* that arose in the garden of John Champneys, a Charleston rice grower. Champneys gave the hybrid to two nurserymen: his neighbour Philip Noisette and William Prince, of New York. Philip Noisette sent seed of 'Champneys' Pink Cluster' to his brother Louis in France who named the best of his first seedlings 'Le Rosier de Philip Noisette'.[1] These subsequently gave rise to a number of hybrids which became known as Noisette Roses.

One recognizes the Noisettes by their rapidly growing lanky branches, their almost evergreen leaves, and their clusters of delicately coloured flowers produced throughout the year.

William Paul described seventy-four varieties of Noisettes in mid-19th century European gardens, of which the following six grew in the Cape in 1858 (the descriptions are adapted from Paul):

'Phaloé': flowers cream, delicately tinted carmine, large and full; growth moderate.
'Cloth of Gold' ('Chromatella'): flowers creamy white, yellow centres, very large, very double, globular; growth vigorous.
'Lamarque': flowers white, deep straw centres, large, full, cupped; growth vigorous.

'Euphrosyne': flowers pale rose with yellow and fawn, large, full, cupped; growth moderate.

'Céline Forestier', not mentioned by Paul, was also a popular Victorian Noisette in Cape Town, as were 'Maréchal Niel' (1869), 'Mme Alfred Carrière' (1879) and 'Crépuscule' (1904).

The Noisettes grew with such vigour and flowered so profusely at the Cape that most city and country gardeners were soon busy constructing arbours, summer-houses and arches to support these climbers, and verandas everywhere were festooned with roses. 'Céline Forestier', 'Mme Alfred Carrière' and especially 'Crépuscule' are still widely cultivated; less frequently one sees 'Maréchal Niel' and 'Réve d'Or'. 'Jaune Desprez' (introduced by Desprez in 1830) has recently been imported and is fast becoming a favourite, for it is particularly vigorous and the loose, pinkish-yellow flowers have a most charming, although rather unusual form.

Unfortunately most of the mid-19th century Noisettes have been replaced by more brightly coloured modern climbers. Though some of these are indeed very impressive, I think that the Noisettes are not to be ignored, since they remain unexcelled for vigorous growth and massive display; here at the Cape, where the climate obviously suits them so well, they deserve to be more widely grown.

1 Roy E. Shepherd, *History of the Rose*.

123

'Jaune Desprez'

'Jaune Desprez'.

The farmer's wife usually had a walled garden where her precious plants were protected from the livestock. This is the 19th century garden at the farm Mosselbank in the Tygerberg. The rose at the gate is probably 'Céline Forestier'.

While attending the Second International Rose Conference in Adelaide in 1986, I found that there was a lot of uncertainty about the rose known as 'Jaune Desprez'. In David Rustan's garden at Renmark, a rose which I recognised as 'Céline Forestier' was thought to be 'Jaune Desprez'.

At home a 'Jaune Desprez', sent to me by a most reliable nursery, turned out to be 'Paul Transon'. Ludwig Taschner then airmailed a bloom of 'Jaune Desprez' to me, and its photograph appears on this page. He was sure that this time he had imported the correct plant material, but unfortunately it was rather late in the season, so the specimen was not a very good one.

PLANT
Vigorous climber with many hooked thorns.

FOLIAGE
Two to five oval pointed smooth, light-green leaflets on delicate stems with small hooked thorns on the underside. Sepals are thin and entire with loose ends.

FLOWERS
About forty oval pointed petals, opening flat with the smaller ones crumpled untidily in the centre. The flowers are cream, flushed light pink and are 6–7 cm in diameter. A bunch of short cream pistils is surrounded with quite a number of shortish stamens. The small calyx is narrow, goblet-shaped and covered with many short glands which are also on the upper surface of the medium sized sepals. The flowers are fragrant and appear throughout the year.

INFLORESCENCE
Small clusters of flowers on short side branches.

When the present owners of the farm Zanddrift in the Swellendam district decided to donate the old homestead, which they could no longer afford to maintain, to the local Drostdy Museum, the curator asked us to inspect the house to advise on the feasibility of 'moving' the old building.

As we walked through the dimly lit rooms, admiring the solid stinkwood and yellowwood doors and shuttered windows, the fine ceilings and wall cupboards, and marvelled at the thick clay walls, our thoughts turned to Jacobus Botha, the first owner of this farm. In 1734 when Governor Jan de la Fontaine had travelled from the Cape to inspect the damaged ship *Huijs te Marquette* anchored in Mossel Bay, Botha had assisted him with food and water and as a reward was granted the loan farm Jan Harmenz Gat which afterwards became known as Zanddrift. Botha probably built the first part of the house soon after the grant, but after he had ceded his rights to his youngest daughter Elsie in 1769, she (according to legend then estranged from her second husband) came to live at Zanddrift and enlarged the old house by extending it to the rear. Two slaves and her youngest daughters assisted her with the building work.

One hundred years later when the wild country had been considerably tamed, Jacobus van Zyl, a descendant of Jacobus and Elsie Botha, brought his bride Susan, the youngest of thirteen Marquard children, to live in his old family home. Susan had grown up in the elegant Victorian Sea Point society and brought to Zanddrift not only her charming social graces, but many plants amongst which were the roses 'Céline Forestier', 'Devoniensis', the 'Old Monthly', 'La France' ('I can smell them as I think of them', her great-granddaughter told me) and many other roses, the names now forgotten.[1]

As I walked in the old Zanddrift garden, past the hedge of Monthly roses gay with many pink blooms, and stopped to admire the sweet, full, primrose flowers on a tall 'Céline Forestier' still thriving in front of the old house, I thought of the many women who had each in their own way helped to shape this family home; women with intrepid courage and the will to create for their families a safe environment of order and beauty, so far removed from civilization.

When the Zanddrift homestead was eventually demolished and rebuilt at the Swellendam museum, daughter plants of the old 'Céline Forestier' together with a hedge of Monthly roses were planted in the front garden to give visitors a glimpse of the rose fashions of the mid-19th century.

Trouillard had introduced 'Céline Forestier' to European gardens in 1842, and towards the end of the 19th century it become well known at the Cape, appearing in every rose catalogue with glowing accounts of its many virtues. I have found 'Céline Forestier' in many old Cape gardens, but the oldest tree I know of is the one which Susan Marquard planted at Zanddrift in 1876 which still produces flowers as beautiful as it did over one hundred years ago.

1 The Marquard house in Arthur Road at the old bus terminus has today been replaced by a block of flats. The information is from Mrs P. Grobbelaar, Susan Marquard's great-granddaughter.

'Céline Forestier'

PLANT
A tall branched shrub up to 2 metres high or a low climber.

FOLIAGE
Five oval pointed, yellow-green shiny leaflets on sturdy, slightly glandular stalks with prickles on the underside. Stipules are very narrow, adnate with a few sessile glands on the edges.

FLOWERS
Round pointed yellow buds, often flushed with crimson, open into flat, full, quartered blooms about 7 cm in diameter. The broad primrose-yellow petals, sometimes with an apricot sheen, fade to light cream in the ageing flower. Stamens are rudimentary and the slightly hairy styles very short; they none-the-less form a green eye in the centre of the neatly shaped flower. The calyx is cup-shaped and smooth; the sepals oval and short with a few small folioles, the undersurfaces velvety and the edges slightly glandular. Flowers appear throughout the year and are sweetly fragrant.

INFLORESCENCE
One to three flowers at the top of the branches on smooth short stalks. The bracts are short, leaflike and smooth.

'Céline Forestier'.

From left to right:
'Chromatella' or 'Cloth of Gold' was another 'Lamarque' seedling popular in Victorian Cape gardens. Walter Duncan in the Clare valley near Adelaide, with his century-old plant.

'Lamarque' (1830), parent of 'Solfaterre', was growing in Cape Town by 1858, but is now seldom seen.

This century-old 'Chromatella', growing at the farm Newstead in the Balgowan district, Natal, holds up the veranda.

Below:
The front porch of the now demolished Arderne homestead in Claremont was adorned with a large 'Chromatella'. (From a photograph lent by Miss Tredgold, granddaughter of Henry Arderne.)

Growing alongside the water furrow in a Stellenbosch garden is an old rose tree, about four metres high, which bears the most stunning yellow roses that I have ever seen. The scraggy bush leans heavily on an old iron support and regularly throws out young branches. One is sure to find at least one or two of the voluptuous roses on the tree when visiting the garden, but in the spring and autumn the flowers are larger, more abundant and of the deep yellow colour that makes the rose so distinctive.

I often return to this rose tree to contemplate the heavy, globular, fully quartered nodding blooms, hoping sooner or later to find a name for it: 'Solfaterre', 'Perle de Lyon', 'Comtesse de Frigneuse'? Catalogue and book descriptions of old roses are tantalizingly vague, so I can only hope that one day I will meet a lover of old roses who will recognize this beauty and name it with assurance. In the meantime I shall call it 'Solfaterre', the 'Lamarque' seedling which was introduced in 1843 by Boyeau and which was growing in Cape gardens soon after, for this, according to descriptions, seems to be the most likely diagnosis.

I have never seen this rose anywhere else and though I have sent good slides of it to rose friends all over the world it remains unidentified.[1]

1. Subsequent slides were sent to the Sangerhausen Rosarium, whose staff agreed that this was probably 'Solfaterre'.

'Solfaterre'

PLANT
A strong gawky shrub 3—4 metres high, with reddish-brown stems and numerous strong hooked thorns.

FOLIAGE
Five oval pointed, smooth olive-green leaves on strong stalks with hooks on the underside. The stipules are thin and smooth with free tips.

FLOWERS
Large round pointed buds open to globular, quartered golden-yellow flowers 8 cm in diameter. Stamens are very few and the numerous smooth styles have branched stigmas. The calyx is cup-shaped and smooth, the sepals short with insignificant folioles reflexing early. Flowers appear throughout the year and have a fresh Tea fragrance.

INFLORESCENCE
One to three flowers in a corymb on reddish-green stalks which sometimes nod.

'Solfaterre'.

'Maréchal Niel'

ROSES.—GENERAL SELECT LIST.

Price—Our Selection, 12s. per dozen ; Post Free, 16s. ; Packed for Rail, 13s. 6d.
Customers' ,, 20s. ,, ,, 24s. ; ,, ,, 21s. 6d.

Customers' Selection does not include those varieties specially priced ; any Roses not priced at more than 2s. each can be included, if not sold out.

La Boule d'Or (T.)—Flowers golden yellow. Each, 2s.
—— **France** (ex. H.T.)—Bright lilac, the centre silvery white, flowers large, globular, fragrant, distinct and good ; the best of its colour. Each, 2s.
—— **d'89** (H.P.)—Brilliant red, sometimes lined with white, very large, almost like a Pæony ; very free, buds long. Each, 2s.
—— **Marque** (cl. N.)—Sulphur-white, very large and full ; a superb Rose. Each, 2s.
—— **Motte Sanguine** (H.P.)—Reddish carmine. Each, 2s.
—— **Reine** (H.P.)—Satin-pink, very free-flowering variety. Each, 2s.
—— **Rosiere** (ex. H.P.)—Velvety crimson, large, full and superb. Each, 2s.
Leon XIII. (T.)—White, slightly shaded with straw-colour, centre ochre, large and full ; fine petals, buds long like *Niphetos*. Each, 2s. 6d.
Le Soleil (New. T.)—Chrome or canary-yellow, large, full, cupped ; very fine vigorous. A grand new Rose, highly recommended. Each, 2s. 6d.
L'Ideal (ex. cl. N.)—Metallic-red and yellow, shaded golden. Grand buttonhole Rose and companion to *W. A. Richardson*. Each, 2s.
L'INNOCENCE (H.T.)—Flowers large, full and globular, pure white, double, borne on long straight stems ; very few thorns, large bronzy green, handsome foliage. Each, 3s. 6d.
Little Pet (C.)—White, small and double. Each, 2s. 6d.
Lord Raglan (H.P.)—Scarlet-crimson ; a grand old Rose. Each, 2s.
Louis Leveque T.)—Reddish yellow, shaded with bright chamois-yellow and vermilion. Each, 2s. 6d.
—— **Van Houtte** (ex. H.P.)—Very dark blackish maroon. Each, 2s.
Mabel Morrison (H.P.)—Similar to *Baroness Rothschild*, differing from that variety in the flowers being nearly white. Each, 2s.
Ma Capucine (T.)—Flowers copper shaded. Each, 2s. 6d.
MADAME ALFRED CARRIERE—Flesh colour, shaded salmon, large and full ; a beautiful climbing Tea Rose. Each, 2s.
—— **Berard** (ex. T.)—Beautiful salmon-coloured, shaded with a deeper colour. Each, 2s.
—— **Boll** (H.P.)—Deep rose, very large and full. Each, 2s.
—— **Bravy** (T.)—White centre, flushed with pink, and the best of the tinted white Tea Roses. Each, 2s.
—— **Bruel** T.)—Called the *White Dijon*. Each, 2s.
—— **Camille** (T.)—Delicate rose, veined yellow, reflexed white. Each, 2s.
—— **CHARLES CRAPELET** (H.P.)—Rosy scarlet, large smooth petals, flowers beautifully formed ; a superb Rose. Each, 2s.
—— **C. Joigneaux** (H.P.)—Red, shaded lilac, very double. Each, 2s.
—— **CUSIN** (T.)—Purplish rose, slightly tinted with yellowish white ; full and distinct. Each, 2s.
—— **de Rougemont** (H.P.)—White, shaded pink. Each, 2s.
—— **DE WATTEVILLE** (T.)—Salmon-white, each petal bordered with bright rose, like a Tulip ; large and full, buds long ; a truly grand Rose. Each, 2s. 6d.
—— **E. Helfenbein** (T.)—Chamois leather, shaded and veined with apricot and carmine-rose. Each, 2s.
—— **E. Michel** (New) (H.P.)—Deep pink, flowers of exquisite shape, free-flowering. Each, 2s. 6d.
—— **Eugene Verdier** (T.)—Deep chamois-leather, large, finely formed, very sweet ; one of the best Roses ever offered. Each, 3s. 6d.
—— **Falcot** (T.)—Deep rich orange-yellow, petals large ; a superb Rose, producing lovely buds. Each, 2s.
—— **F. de la Forrest** (H.P.)—Colour delicate rose, very pretty, growth vigorous. Each, 2s.
—— **GABRIEL LUIZET** (H.P.)—Pale pink, a delicate and beautiful tint of colour ; large and full ; cupped, very sweet, quite first-rate. Each, 2s.
—— **H. DE POTWOROWSKA** (T.)—Long oval carmine buds, open flowers amaranth, shaded with rose and reflexed with a paler shade. Each, 3s. 6d.
—— **Hippolyte Jamain** (H.P.)—Delicate flesh, passing to white ; globular. Each, 2s.
—— **Hoste** (ex. T.)—Each, 3s. 6d.
—— **JACQUES CHARRETON** (T.)—White, centre coppery salmon, flowers globular, very free. Each, 2s. 6d.

MARÉCHAL NIEL (The Best Yellow Climbing Rose).
Each, 2s. 6d. and 3s. 6d.

Madame Joseph Combet (H.T.)—Creamy white shaded with rose, centre yellowish rose, large, full. Each, 2s.
—— **Lambard** (T.)—Flowers salmon-pink, shaded rose and yellow ; a very fine Rose. Each, 2s.
—— **Margottin** (T.)—Citron-yellow, centre rosy peach. Each, 2s.
—— **Marie Cirodde** (H.P.)—Clear rosy peach. Each, 2s.
—— **M. Lavalley** (T.)—Bright rose, shaded and reflexed with white, large and double. Each, 2s.
—— **Moreau** (H.P.)—Flowers red, shaded violet. Each, 2s.
—— **Morren** (T.)—Creamy white, shaded salmon. Each, 2s.
—— **Norma** (T.)—Perpetual-flowering, beautiful yellow. Each, 2s.
—— **Rivers** (H.P.)—Clear flesh, changing to blush. Each, 2s.
—— **Verrier Cachet** (H.P.)—Bright rose shaded with vermilion, very large, full. Each, 2s.
—— **Victor Verdier** (H.P.)—Brilliant rosy carmine of great substance. Each, 2s.
Mademoiselle Germaine Raud (T.)—Creamy white with deeper centre. Each, 2s.
—— **Helena Cambier** (H.T.)—Variable from salmon-rose to coppery rose. Each, 2s.
MAGNA CHARTA (H.P.)—Bright pink, suffused carmine, very large and full. This Rose still holds its own, and should be in every collection. Each, 2s.
Maiden's Blush (T.)—Lovely colour, beautifully scented. Each, 2s. 6d.
Mai Fleuri (T.)—Pure satiny white, very large and full. Each, 2s.

Collection No. 60.—100 choice Roses, in 100 choice sorts. Price £10. Post Free £12. Packed for Rail £10 10s.

37

'Maréchal Niel' in
Smith Bros. Nursery
Catalogue, 1906.

'Beautiful deep yellow, the handsomest rose in cultivation.'
'Rich in brilliant yellow, full and globular, very sweet, magnificent.'
'A bright rich golden yellow, splendid.'
'Peerless in colour, unexampled for size, perfect in form; after more than a quarter century it still remains the ideal climbing Tea rose.'

These glowing accounts from Cape nurserymen reflect the unsurpassed popularity of 'Maréchal Niel' in the early part of this century. I remember seeing the canary-yellow blooms of this climber in almost every Stellenbosch rose garden of the 1930s and 1940s. The outer petals, rolling back to form points, give the flower a starlike appearance which, together with its nodding head and light-green shiny foliage, distinguish this rose from all other yellow ones.

As a young girl, I used to conjure up romantic visions of the French general after whom this rose was named, and learnt only much later that Adolphe Niel had been one of Napoleon III's marshals, who won his title in 1859 after he had distinguished himself in the battle of Solferino. Marshal Niel became French minister of war in 1867, three years after the nurseryman Pradel had commemorated him by giving this yellow Tea rose his name.

'Maréchal Niel' was a forgotten memory until I recognized it again one day in Margaret Lawder's garden at Leliefontein in the Klein Drakenstein. She had obtained a slip from an old plant growing on the mountain-top farm Moutonsvlei belonging to Walter Versfeld, and very generously gave me a few slips for the Boschendal garden. Now that she is no more with us, the light yellow roses are a constant reminder of this keen gardener's sunny nature.

Walter's father John Versfeld was the first member of the family to establish himself on the plateau on top of the Piquetberg mountains. Here he started farming with merinos more than a hundred years ago when the ascent to the mountain top through the kloof above the mission station, Goedeverwagting, was almost impossible. Undaunted, Versfeld built his own five-mile long pass which was so steep and nar-row that vehicles could only pass where loops had been provided in the road. As a child, the happy holidays I spent on top of the mountain were always marred by the thought of the descent down this hazardous road.

John Versfeld's two sons, Frank and Walter, inherited their father's drive and inventiveness. They started growing *boegoe* (an aromatic shrub), tobacco and summer fruit during the Second World War and were so successful that many newcomers followed suit. Today hardly a corner of the plateau remains uncultivated, and a brand new tar road provides easy access to the top. Moutonsvlei no longer belongs to the Versfelds and the 'Maréchal Niel' planted by John Versfeld over a hundred years ago and tended by his sons afterwards, recently disappeared when the old rose garden was changed.

Slips of the Moutonsvlei rose had, however, been handed down to various Versfeld children by Hildagonda Duckitt (whose mother was a Versfeld). One was planted at her home, Groote Post, and another at Waylands, the farm near Darling belonging to Mr Fred Duckitt. Mr Duckitt is well known for the wonderfully rich piece of veld that he has preserved and made accessible for the enjoyment of wild-flower lovers every spring. He told me that the old 'Maréchal Niel' plant in his garden had died a few years ago when someone left the tap on, since the very brack water was more than the old rose could withstand.

I am happy that a descendant of one of these Versfeld roses should still be growing in the Boschendal garden, commemorating a pioneering family of fine agriculturists and gardeners.

The flowers are at their best when fully open.

'Maréchal Niel'

Lourensford, one of the most famous 19th century Cape gardens, where Noisettes over the pergolas probably featured prominently.

PLANT
A vigorous climber to 4 metres with many large strong reddish-green thorns.

FOLIAGE
Five oval pointed, light-green leaflets with smooth, shiny surfaces, lighter below. The sturdy, smooth, reddish-green leaf-stalks have small red hooks on the underside. Stipules are adnate and maroon.

FLOWERS
As soon as the large oval pointed greenish-yellow buds open, the outer petals reflex and curl back to form points, while the central petals, their edges rolling back, crowd into four quarters. The open flowers are about 9 cm in diameter and because of their heavyness, inclined to nod from a rather weak stalk. Stamens are insignificant and the pistils very short. The cup-shaped calyx is smooth and shiny; the sepals have a few small folioles, are shiny on the upper side and velvety below. They reflex right back against the stem as the bud opens. The flowers appear throughout the year and have a sweet fragrance, not very marked.

INFLORESCENCE
There is usually only one flower on a short, nodding, reddish stem.

'Maréchal Niel'.

'Crépuscule'

'Crépuscule'.

Over an arch at Salomonsvlei.

'Crépuscule', introduced by Dubreuil in 1904, soon became even more popular at the Cape than any of its predecessors, for the trusses of buff-yellow blooms are produced at regular intervals throughout the year and are often so numerous that they cover the entire plant in a cloak of golden colour.

It grows quickly and easily from slips, producing flowers when scarcely one metre high, and if the plant is allowed to ramble unpruned over its arch or pergola, it eventually builds up into a large mass of growth. 'Crépuscule' grows best in full sun, and sunlight fills the golden blooms with a radiance which is reflected throughout the garden.

I love this rose so much that I find a place for it in every garden that I plan, and then wait for the delighted acclaim which never fails to come from clients at the first surprising burst of colour.

Being of an apricot-buff colour, the blooms tone in very well with lighter pink and brilliant blue flowers; I have seen 'Crépuscule' looking particularly effective in a garden where it has been planted with 'Francois Juranville' and petria on the same pergola.

'Rêve d'Or'

Towards the end of the 19th century, old varieties of Noisette roses were among the most prized plants of Cape cottage gardens. 'Rose clad houses are the glory of many rural districts, those particularly popular being Rêve d'Or, Aimée Vibert, Maréchal Niel and Mme Alfred Carrière. These roses have outlasted their contemporaries thus proving their hardiness and their own intrinsic merits', wrote an enthusiastic gardener in the *Cape Garden* of 1909, who then went on to describe how effectively these Noisettes could be used over pergolas, arches, pillars and walls.

How sad that these once common supports, usually made of wood or iron, have long since perished or been demolished, taking with them the lovely old climbers which are now hard to find. 'Rêve d'Or' is the only one which has obstinately refused to be wiped out and I have pleasant memories of many old trees which surprised me with their vigour and health. One was draping streamers of yellow blooms amongst the white blossoms of an old pear tree, another cascading in yellow profusion from the top of a Victorian veranda, and yet another spouting yellow fountains of roses over a large shrub which had collapsed in the middle of a lawn, all vestiges of its original support long vanished.

On a farm in the Camdeboo, the owner had constructed a new arch for an old tree which he had pruned back heavily a few years before. He was subsequently rewarded with the most exuberant display of roses on the vigorous new shoots which sprang from the gnarled old stump. I arrived on this farm late one afternoon and had the good fortune to see the mass of buff-yellow flowers, alive with crinkled and quilled petals, caught in the golden light of the setting sun.

Ducher in 1869 developed this gorgeous climber in his Lyon nursery from 'Mme Schultz', an earlier pale yellow Noisette. It subsequently became one of the finest climbers of its day, thriving especially in the milder climates of the French Riviera, California and also in the Cape of Good Hope.

It is a most rewarding rose to grow because of its vigour and disease resistance. Since the flowers are produced on the well-ripened laterals of the previous year, it also needs little pruning. Furthermore, the yellow-green shiny foliage always makes the plant look fresh and cheerful even during the few intervals when there are no flowers. In all this it compares most favourably with the modern climbers. Its buff-yellow flowers mix particularly well with the pink ones of 'Zéphirine Drouhin' and 'Mme Isaac Pereire', two later Bourbons.

I planted 'Rêve d'Or' and 'Crépuscule' over the four entrance arches to a miniature rose garden which I had planned around a fountain at Salomonsvlei in the Klein Drakenstein. A hedge of crimson 'Fellemberg' cuts off this area from the rest of the rose garden. When the yellow arches and crimson hedge flower together, my friend Mildy Malan knows that it is time to invite me to tea, and I am never sure whether I am more delighted with the welcome greeting of her small children (here is the 'auntie' who works in our garden!) or the wonderful profusion of rose colour.

Left: An old 'Rêve d'Or' climber on the veranda of Captain van der Merwe's house in Rondebosch.
Right: 'Rêve d'Or' over an arch in the Camdeboo.

PLANT
This is a vigorous climber with strong branching stems which will grow 6–7 metres high. It has large red hooked thorns.

FOLIAGE
Five oval pointed yellow-green leaflets, 8 cm long, with smooth shiny upper and slightly duller lower surfaces and evenly serrated margins. The sturdy leaf-stalk has a reddish tinge and small red hooks on the undersurface. Stipules are smooth and narrow.

FLOWERS
Large well-formed dark ochre-pink buds with short sepals, open into full frilly flowers about 10 cm in diameter. The larger outer petals roll back and the smaller central ones, tinted pink on the outer surface, are folded on themselves or curl inwards towards the many delicate yellow stamens. The smooth sepals have no folioles. The rose has a lovely strong Tea fragrance and flowers throughout the year with special shows in November and May.

INFLORESCENCE
One to three roses in trusses along the length of the branches.

'Rêve d'Or'.

131

Rosa x noisettiana manettii

Rosa x noisettiana manettii.

A ccording to Roy Shepherd in his *History of the Rose* (1954), this dark pink semi-double rose was first cultivated from seed by a Dr Manetti of the Monza Botanical Garden near Milan in about 1835. Thomas Rivers, who introduced it to England soon after, started using it as an understock from 1850.

At the Cape this rose is very vigorous and healthy (unlike Roy Shepherd's plants which were badly susceptible to black spot) and makes a very pretty shrub in the garden. The many long reddish smooth stems bend over gracefully; the small deeply serrated leaves have a purple-reddish tinge; and the dark-pink flowers, which appear in several bursts throughout the year, also have the same purplish tinge which makes the whole shrub quite distinctive.

Hips.

'Mme Alfred Carrière'

Whenever I see 'Mme Alfred Carrière', I think of the garden of Dorothy Johnman in Stellenbosch, for it was there that I was first introduced to this most charming Noisette late on a warm spring evening when the fading light had lent an urgency to our progress through her garden. We stopped before the trellis from which many pale roses hung in masses and felt no need to walk any further. 'And this, is Mme Alfred Carrière.' Enchantress! I thought, and saw her oyster glow slowly fading as she yielded to the darkening night, leaving only her sweet musk fragrance to remind us of her presence, while Mrs Johnman told me the tale of her garden.

In the early 19th century this garden was attached to the property of Dr George Schroeder who lived at 52 Dorp Street. The house and garden of Mrs Johnman's grandfather, the Revd John Hahn, were at that time like a small island surrounded by the old doctor's estate. The Schroeders lived in grand style in their beautiful home and marvellous garden which extended from Dorp Street to the present-day Schroeder Street. Their only daughter Anna was beautiful, clever and musical, an excellent pianist and the belle of Stellenbosch, but she never married, for it was believed that there was insanity in the family. When the old doctor died and she inherited his estate, she continued to live in 52 Dorp Street until in 1930 the lonely old lady died deep in her nineties.

She had been a good friend to the Revd Hahn until the Boer War made enemies of them and then, to spite the old minister it is thought, she built a house right in front of his home, cutting out his view to the mountains. Ironically enough, the minister's granddaughter today owns this Schroeder house, as well as the property of her grandfather which includes a row of cottages and gardens in Herte Street. These had been constructed by the old missionary in the 1840s to house emancipated slaves.

These old gardens, planted by two of the minister's daughters and lovingly tended today by their niece, become a magical world of colour and scent every year in the spring. Forgotten varieties of plum and pear white with blossom, pink crab apple, tender green mulberry buds, bluebells, irises, violets, primulas and heavy swags of jasmine swinging from one tree to the next together with rambler roses of every colour and description on old oak, camphor and wild olive trees, delight the visitor where no straight path or organized bed curbs the profusion of growth or tapestry of colour.

Mrs Johnman picks with generous abandon for weddings, funerals, birthdays and other special occasions and when I went home that evening, my car was filled with the fragrance of my new discovery, 'Mme Alfred Carrière', the rose that was in 1908 proclaimed the 'best white climber' by 62 out of 83 voters of the National Rose Society. No other variety belonging to any other class had received so many votes. By then she had already been available for twenty-nine years in Europe and a Cape favourite for many years.

Caught in her spell, I resolved to multiply this old Noisette and make her a favourite once again in the gardens that I plant, and this promise I have diligently carried out with no trouble at all. For she grows easily from cuttings and within two years will cover a large trellis with her disease-free shiny foliage and fragile pink blooms.

'Mme Alfred Carrière'.

PLANT
A climber with many arching branches of medium vigour, growing 3–6 metres high. There are a few scattered brown hooked thorns.

FOLIAGE
Five large droopy oval leaflets with finely serrated edges and shiny smooth surfaces. The stalk is sturdy and short with a few glands and prickles on the underside. Stipules are short and thin with smooth edges.

FLOWERS
The oval bud with its long sepals opens into a full flower 8 cm in diameter. The larger outer petals are flesh-coloured but the shorter curly central petals are flushed a soft oyster that soon fades to white. There are a few short stamens and the pistil is light green, short and delicate. The goblet-shaped calyx is smooth, the sepals long and tapering with short folioles. They reflex only to hold the corolla. The flower-stalk is short, glandular, and inclined to nod; the bracts are small and thin. The flowers appear throughout the year with a flush in spring and have a wonderful fragrance.

INFLORESCENCE
One to three flowers in trusses along the main and side branches.

The old manor house at Jonkershoek before
it was Victorianized.
Below: Purple bougainvillea with golden roses
at Muratie, Stellenbosch.

The Department of Forestry, which bought the farm Jonkershoek in 1934 for use as an experimental station, had asked our office to make an inspection of the old buildings to assess their historical value and to report on the feasibility of restoring them. It was while we were busy measuring and taking notes on site that this somewhat tedious task was considerably brightened for me by the discovery of a golden-yellow Noisette rose growing alongside the 'Bachelors' home'. The forestry officials living in these old quarters knew only that the rose tree had 'always been there' and that it flowered throughout the year, but could not say how old it was nor who had planted it.

The farm Jonkershoek lies on the banks of the Eerste River in a narrow valley east of Stellenbosch. The first owner, a German named Jan Andriessen (also known as Jan de Jonker) received his grant of land in 1683 from Governor Simon van der Stel a year before he married the slave girl Lysbeth Jansen. Though we know that he and his family lived for fifteen years on the farm that still bears his name, and that he farmed sheep and cattle and produced wine, there is no record of any flowers that he might have cultivated.

We were, however, able to ascertain that the unknown yellow rose had been planted by F. G. Watermeyer who took transfer of Jonkershoek almost two hundred years after the first owner. Watermeyer had Victorianized the old manor house, slave quarters and cellar and, retaining the magnificent oak grove on the slope in front of the old home, had created a terraced Victorian garden with tiered fountains, brick steps and garden walls decorated with ornate urns. In a nearby dell he planted a rose garden with all the magnificent varieties of the early 20th century. The one rose tree, two defunct fountains, and remnants of walls and steps were the only features to remind us sadly of the garden's past grandeur.

Peter Beales was able to identify the Jonkershoek rose for me as 'Duchesse d'Auerstädt', a Noisette introduced in 1888 by A. Bernaix. In the early 20th century Gowie's Nurseries sold this rose from their branches in Grahamstown, Bulawayo, Bloemfontein and Johannesburg. They called it a 'Tea, bright deep yellow, fine form, strong grower; one of the best yellow roses'. Stephen Brett of Port Elizabeth and Uitenhage at the same time sold it as a 'climbing tea, pure yellow in bud, with the slightest tint of nankeen yellow when open, 2/6 each'.

'Duchesse d'Auerstädt' obviously flourished in the warm Cape climate and stole the hearts of Cape gardeners because of its vigorous growth, disease-free foliage and masses of deep-yellow cupped blooms produced abundantly throughout the year. No wonder that Mr Watermeyer chose to plant it in his new rose garden at Jonkershoek and that no one has had the heart to remove the fine old shrub since.

'Duchesse d'Auerstädt'

'Duchesse d'Auerstädt'.

PLANT
A vigorous climber to 8 metres with many branching stems. Thorns are sparse, small and hooked.

FOLIAGE
Five round to oval large leaflets with smooth shiny surfaces and finely serrated edges. The stalk is sturdy with very few prickles on the underside; stipules are adnate and narrow with smooth, slightly glandular edges.

FLOWERS
The large, round pointed, lime-yellow bud opens into a globular full flower about 9 cm in diameter, with very bright butter-yellow petals grouped into four loose quarters. The central petals are flushed apricot and the intense yellow colour is retained in the fading flower. Stamens are numerous, pistils loose; the calyx is large, cup-shaped and smooth; the sepals are long and tapering with tiny folioles, glandular margins and velvety undersides. The fragrant flowers appear throughout the year with good shows in spring and autumn.

INFLORESCENCE
One to three flowers on long, sturdy, smooth flower-stalks. The small leaf-shaped bracts have glandular edges.

'Général Galliéni' shows the typical colour variation characteristic of the Tea Roses.

THE TEA ROSES

Two ancient Chinese garden roses (one pink and one creamy buff) which were sent to England at the beginning of the 19th century gave rise to a new class that came to be known as the 'Tea Roses'. This name came about not because the parents had formed part of the cargo of spices and tea on board the East India traders which transported them, but because they introduced to the Western rose breeders the exciting new fragrance of fresh Ceylon tea.

Tea fragrance was not the only novelty which they were to transmit to their progeny, however; for apart from their constant flowering habit, there was in these roses a delicacy of colour and refinement of form that appealed strongly to the Victorian gardener. Unfortunately the Tea roses did not thrive in the cold northern European climates where they had to be grown under glass.

'It is curious to look back on one's childhood and recall the awe with which Tea roses were regarded — things too delicate and precious for any place but the conservatory', wrote Rose G. Kingsley in her book *Eversley Gardens and Others*.

Nor did the seed ripen satisfactorily in the cold. It was only in the warmth of southern French nurseries that the first famous Tea roses were bred and introduced to the world, mainly by Pernet Ducher, Robert and Moreau, and the Guillots.

William Paul advised gardeners to grow these new roses against a south or east wall or in pots that could be brought in during the cold English weather. He even recommended placing beehives on tripods over standard Teas during the colder months! In 1848 he described 145 varieties of Tea rose of which the following were recorded in Cape Town ten years later:

'Comte de Paris': flesh coloured shaded rose, large, full, cupped;
'Hyménée': white with yellowish buff centres, large, very double;
'Malton' ('Josephine Malton'?): rich cream with buff centres, tops of petals sometimes tinged lake, large and very double, cupped, exquisite;
'Devoniensis': creamy white with buff or yellowish centres, very large, full, cupped.

In the Cape the Teas thrived and did so well that a third of the roses listed in catalogues at the turn of the century belonged to this class. The colours described were chiefly creams, yellows and pinks, for the scarlets and dark crimsons seemed to be confined to the Hybrid Perpetuals.

Now, eighty years later, I have found only fourteen of the seventy varieties offered for sale in 1905. Of these 'Lady Hillingdon' and 'Archimedes' occur most commonly with 'Général Galliéni' close on their heels.

I planted my small collection of Teas at Boschendal one by one as I acquired them, and as the bushes have hardly ever been pruned, a surprising mixture of ever-changing colours is produced as the intertwining branches flower throughout the year.

In a well-planned garden, however, Tea roses need to be more carefully placed for their distinctive qualities to be fully appreciated: their shiny oval leaves with finely serrated edges, dark maroon when new; the sharply hooked thorns on smooth reddish stems; and the delicate full flowers which change amazingly from the rich colours of the warm summer to the paler blooms of midwinter.

I like to group 'Lady Hillingdon' with berberis and white rock-rose; 'Général Galliéni' on its own as a specimen against a dark green hedge; 'Madame Lambard' in a shrubbery with grey *Rhogodia hastata* and white hibiscus; 'Archimedes' three together, surrounded by miniature agapanthus; 'Smith's Yellow' on its own leaning against the garden steps; pale pink 'Odorata' with dark blue Cape forget-me-not; 'Catherine Mermet' before a light green myrtle hedge, and 'Marie van Houtte' by itself, where it can build up into a large rounded shrub.

Perhaps Tea roses should have a garden of their own, very sunny, with gravel paths edged by *Hebe speciosa multiflora* or grey lavender cotton set off against warmer-coloured irises. Then I would provide summer shade over the pathways with many arches, and cover these with 'Maman Cochet' or 'Souvenir de Madame Léonie Viennot', adding perhaps a few Noisettes like 'Rêve d'Or', 'Jaune Desprez', or 'Crépuscule'. I would not spray my Tea roses, for they are healthy plants if grown in full sun, and when I walk in my Tea rose garden (where I will always find many blooms) I would like to be aware of numerous bees going about their happy work and sharing my contentment.

'Devoniensis'

'Devoniensis' was a very popular Victorian rose
but is now rarely found at the Cape.

When I visited Petersen's old rose nursery near Copenhagen and asked the new owner Mr Thim whether he knew 'Devoniensis', he delightedly took me to his hothouse where, on a scraggly plant, a pale flower had just opened into the characteristic magnolia shape. I think that in cold climates the fully blown rose which we know so well at the Cape is probably seldom seen.

In our warm Cape sun this rose needs no protection, and it used to be found in many old gardens. It seems that the English settlers, appreciating its love of warmth, took it with them to their colonies. It is recorded from the Cape Town Botanic Gardens in 1858 and I have found a few old plants in gardens and cemeteries of the Eastern Cape where British settlers established new farms from 1820 onwards.

I noticed that the Revd William Ellis also saw 'Devoniensis' growing in several private gardens as well as in the Governor's garden in Mauritius when he visited the island in 1853.[1]

Roy Shepherd believes that 'Devoniensis' was the first English Tea rose. According to him it was raised in 1838 by Mr Foster of Plymouth, Devon, from 'Smith's Yellow' and 'Park's Yellow Tea-scented China'.[2] McFarland, on the other hand, suggests that the parentage is uncertain, and may be 'Elinthii' x a yellow China.[3]

The warm cream colour of the China parent has certainly been retained to glow in the centre of this lovely, loosely quartered rose, and the delicious Tea fragrance is there too. 'Devoniensis' is undoubtedly one of the most beautiful climbers that has ever been grown at the Cape and deserves to be re-introduced into the landscape where it was once so popular. I do not know of any modern climber that could compete with its delicate colour, fragrance and mass of recurrent blooms.

1 W. Ellis, *Three Visits to Madagascar, 1853-1854-1856,* New York, 1859. 'Devoniensis appeared with long slender shoots and thin-petalled, pale flowers' (p. 99).

2 *History of the Rose,* 1954.
3 *Roses 8,* 1980.

'Archimedes'

'Archimedes'.

'Dr Grill' resembles 'Archimedes' in many respects.

W hen I first saw the lifeless stump of the Tea rose called 'Archimedes' draped over an arch in a Stellenbosch garden, I thought that the old plant was dying.

Lots of manure, regular watering and words of encouragement, however, seemed to awaken a new vigour and one day the owner, Mrs Johnman, phoned me to say that a young shoot had appeared at the base of the plant.

I was relieved, for nowhere overseas had I seen another specimen of this old variety. Though its name appears regularly in South African Victorian nursery catalogues, 'the most beautiful of all Tea roses' is strangely absent from rose literature and gardens outside this country.

I have a strong suspicion that 'Archimedes' might be one of those many roses that arrived at the Cape directly from the East in the mid-19th century when officials of the English East India Company sent regular presents of rose plants to relatives and friends living at the Cape. But although Victorian biographers mention the fact that the roses growing at the Cape were mostly introduced from the East, no lists have survived which could help identify the specific varieties involved. It is however recorded that 'Archimedes' had found its way into the Botanic Garden in Cape Town by 1858.

Like most of the Teas, this rose often disguises herself by painting her face pale blush or even a dark pink. Such a flower was brought to me for identification by Leslie Whileman of the Worcester Museum, and caused some confusion until he produced more blooms showing the rose in her true colours. This rose had come from the garden of Mrs Shore in Russel Street; when in 1930 Mrs Shore moved into the house (which previously served as a 'nagmaal huisie' for her parents who farmed in Goudini)[1] the rose tree was already well established.

The parentage, originator and date of introduction of this Tea rose remain a mystery for the present.

PLANT
A vigorous plant with sturdy branched growth to 5 metres.

FOLIAGE
Five oval pointed leaflets with medium serrations and smooth, shiny surfaces. The stalk is sturdy and reddish with prickles on the underside. Stipules are smooth, shiny, reddish and eglandular.

FLOWERS
The well-shaped round bud with short sepals opens to a flat, fully quartered, heavy flower about 9 cm in diameter. The silky petals are fawn-white with a pink flush on the outer reflexing petals. Stamens are rudimentary and the pistil hardly visible below the disc. The smooth calyx is shallow and cup-shaped; the sepals smooth, short and without folioles, velvety on the underside. The flowers appear in spring and autumn flushes and sporadically in between. They have a pleasant Tea fragrance.

INFLORESCENCE
A truss of one to three flowers appears along the main stems on flower-stalks which are smooth, reddish and have a few short bristles. There are one to two short leaf-like bracts.

---

1 Nagmaal huisie – literally 'communion house'. Most farmers till quite recently owned small townhouses where they stayed when they came to town for the communion church service once a month. This was a time for shopping and meeting old friends and relatives so that 'nagmaal' become a very important social occasion.

'Triomphe du Luxembourg'

'Triomphe du Luxembourg'.

'Triomphe du Luxembourg', showing open flower. Half size.

Several very beautiful Tea roses growing at the Cape have remained unidentified. Two are illustrated here in the hope that someone will recognize them and perhaps confirm my guesses at their identities.

The rose reproduced in full scale on the opposite page grows in Mrs Johnman's garden in Stellenbosch and is probably at least sixty to eighty years old. I found a second plant, guarded by a small marble angel, in the Mowbray cemetery where lack of regular watering had stunted its growth but not curbed the steady production of blooms. I sent slides to rose friends all over the world but could find no name for it.

Another darker orange Tea rose, with a much looser flower, grows on several Langkloof farms where friends had passed on slips to each other, but again no one could name it. I found the same variety in the Graaff-Reinet district on the farm Klipfontein where the whole plant was a lively mass of bright orange.

'Triomphe du Luxembourg' was sold by most late 19th century Cape nurseries, and the photograph above taken of a flower picked in a Stellenbosch cottage garden from a shrub almost a century old, fits in well with an old catalogue description: 'perpetual flowering Tea, salmon-buff with a flush of pink in the centre; beautiful in bud'.

'Adam' was the first 'distinctive horticultural variety' of Tea Rose, according to Shepherd in his *History of the Rose*. It dates back to 1833 but gained popularity in the Cape only towards the end of the century. The photograph below, taken in Dean Ross's beautiful garden near Adelaide in S.W. Australia, shows the loose cupped form and warm colours. Unfortunately I have not found any remaining Cape plants.

'Safrano', said to be the first yellow Tea. has a warm yellow buff colour and two to three rows of petals. However, in Trevor Nottle's garden in Adelaide, I was shown a much fuller 'Safrano' as well as 'Isabella Sprunt', its yellow sport. In Petersen's nursery in Denmark, 'Safrano' matched the official description and so does our Cape one, but who can be quite sure and who is guessing?

'Adam'.

'Safrano' in the Petersen nursery, Denmark.

'Safrano' and its sport, 'Isabella Sprunt', in Trevor Nottle's garden.

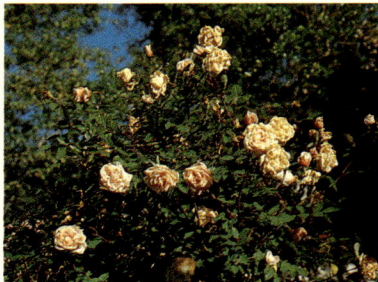

Mrs Johnman's Tea Rose.

Unknown Tea Rose

'Emily Dupuy' and 'Bouquet d'Or' (right)
painted by Moon in the late 19th century.
Both these Tea Roses show similar colouring
to Mrs Johnman's unknown rose.

PHOTOGRAPHS BY TREVOR NOTTLE

Mrs Johnman's unknown Tea Rose.

'Homère'

Right: 'Duchesse de Brabant' used to be a favourite Tea Rose at the Cape.
Below left to right:
'Souvenir d'un Ami' (1846), grown in Cape gardens at the turn of the century, is now rarely seen.
'Homère' in all its stages.
'Jean Ducher', described in Gowie's 1904 catalogue as 'Varying from pale lemon to salmon yellow, shaded peach', has disappeared from Cape gardens. This photograph was taken in the Nancy Steen Memorial Garden in Auckland, New Zealand.

On a nameless grave in the old French Hoek Huguenot cemetery, a stunted 'Homère' with a gnarled old stem sends out short shoots to bear perfect flowers at regular intervals throughout the year, even when the season is hot and dry. Tiny slips taken from this tree in the autumn grew with surprising vigour to form, within a year, strong thriving plants far larger than the mother plant.

A second plant in a Stellenbosch cottage garden was identified by the owner as 'Homer, at least sixty years old'. It looked just as miserable and deceived me into thinking that it was a miniature rose until slips grown on my kitchen window sill under a glass jam jar shot out with the same vigour to form large plants which soon produced crops of fine roses.

I realized that the will to survive in the face of old age, neglect and adverse weather conditions was obviously firmly embedded in the genes of this old Tea rose, and that it needed only a little loving care for the hidden vigour to be released into a fury of exuberant growth.

Bertram Park states that some of the oldest existing rose trees in England belong to this variety. I was therefore interested to read an article by Stewart Deas in the 1962 *Rose Annual* in which he describes a 'Homère' rose tree, a hundred years old, growing against a wall of the Church of St. Mark at Staplefield in Sussex. At that time the plant was 'somewhat in decline' and the author suggested that it should be renewed from cuttings. The old tree had been grafted and it was at the union of the rose with the stock that the deterioration was most evident. Perhaps if the Staplefield rose tree and those at French Hoek and Stellenbosch had grown on their own roots, they might have maintained their initial vigour.

Apart from its carefree growth and disease-resistant foliage, 'Homère' was much beloved in Victorian times for its exquisite, neatly shaped, small pink buds which were ideally suited for buttonholes.

At the Cape, where it became known as the 'Buttonhole Rose', it was advertised by Charles Ayres in 1888 as 'rose, centre Salmon, variable'. Twenty years later, Gowie's Nurseries (and its branches in Grahamstown, Bulawayo, Bloemfontein and Johannesburg) were still selling it as a 'Salmon tea rose, beautiful in bud'.

The flowers are indeed very variable both in shape and colour, sometimes remaining cup-shaped or opening flatly quartered; sometimes cream, rosy-cream flushed pink, or bespeckled all over with crimson spots and splashes.

However, the pretty buds with their pink pouting lips flushed darker crimson, and the silky textured frilly-edged petals of the open flower are always easily recognized together with the delicious Tea fragrance that makes this rose such a delight.

The Bourbon rose 'Mrs Bousanquet' could be mistaken for 'Homère', as both roses have the same shape and delicate colouring. However the latter has more rounded buds and the flower is slightly looser and a little more blush.

Other creamy-salmon Tea roses are shown on this page.

'Homère'

'Homère'.

PLANT
This is a vigorous shrub, angularly branched, growing to
1 metre or higher. It has large, slightly curved, red thorns.

FOLIAGE
Five round-oval pointed leaflets with small serrations on
the reddish-tinged edges. Leaf surfaces are smooth on top,
matt below and the reddish leaf-stalk has a few small glands
and quite large hooked prickles on the underside. The
stipules are thin and have glands along the straight margins.

FLOWERS
The neat, round buds with scrolled tips and short, quickly-
reflecting sepals, open into fully quartered flowers 7 cm in
diameter. The petals are crinkly and of a very light creamy-
blush colour flushed darker pink towards the outer edges.
Sometimes the flower is more cream, sometimes more blush
and sometimes it is splattered with crimson blotches on the
petal edges. There is a mass of short stamens around a short
style but these are not visible amongst the many petals. The
calyx is cup-shaped and smooth; the sepals oval-pointed
with tiny folioles, velvety on the undersurface and with
glands along the edges. Flowers appear throughout the year
and have a fresh Tea fragrance.

INFLORESCENCE
One to four flowers in a panicle at the top of the branches.

143

'Catherine Mermet'

'Catherine Mermet' in the
front garden of the old wine farm
Muratie, near Stellenbosch.

The Humansdorp rose. (Half size)

This is one of Jean-Baptiste Guillot's most famous roses. Introduced in 1869, its fine form soon earned it many a prize on the rose shows and thirty years later Miss Jekyll still thought it had 'the most perfectly formed flower of all Teas'.[1] It also became one of the most popular cut-flowers, 'esteemed by those who force roses for the market as one of the most valuable'.[2]

Nurserymen at the Cape, no doubt influenced by its European and American success, soon brought 'Catherine Mermet' to the notice of local gardeners; 'this flesh coloured rose of exquisite form' was widely advertised as an exhibition rose.[3] I have found a number of old plants in late 19th century gardens, but have been disappointed by their untidy growth, the weak nodding stems which make the flowers unsuitable for arrangements, and the fragrance which is not as strong as in some of the other Teas. I am sure that regular pruning would soon eliminate all these weaknesses, for some blooms that I have picked on firm long stalks have indeed been impressive, and given me an insight into its former popularity.

I always stop to chat to the owner of a very large plant growing in a street garden in Humansdorp, for the old gentleman who lives there has become quite a good friend and loves to talk about his unique rose tree. He is quite sure that it carries two kinds of roses, the one yellow, the other pink; and one day he picked one of each colour for me to photograph together so that people would not think him a liar. I told him the rose might be 'Franziska Krüger' ('Catherine Mermet' x 'Général Schablikine') but that I was not sure of the name. 'No what', he said 'all I care about is that it should go on flowering all the year. That's why I don't cut the tree back either.'

1 G. Jekyll and E. Mawley, *Roses for English Gardens.* 1902.
2 Samuel B. Parsons, *Parsons on the Rose.*
3 Gowie's *Catalogue 1905–6.*

'Catherine Mermet'

PLANT
A sturdy bush up to 2 metres high with many branching stems and strong reddish thorns.

FOLIAGE
Large oval leaflets with medium serrations and smooth shiny surfaces. Stipules are adnate; young leaves coppery brown.

FLOWERS
Large pointed buds with slightly longer sepals open to cup-shaped heavy flowers of a warm light-pink colour. They later expand to reveal a very fully quartered bloom about 9 cm in diameter. Stamens and styles are short and rudimentary; the calyx is large, smooth and cup-shaped; the long, tapering sepals with a few folioles, velvety on the underside, reflex right back against the stem. The flowers are borne throughout the year and have a sweet Tea fragrance.

INFLORESCENCE
One to three flowers on long stems.

From Gowie's *Seed and Plant Catalogue, 1904-1905.*

'Catherine Mermet'.

'Marie van Houtte' in Dean
Ross' garden, S.W. Australia.

'Marie van Houtte' with dark red
flowers, in a Riversdale garden.

The Riversdale rose later in the season.
All the flowers are light yellow.

'Marie van Houtte'.

One of the most hardy Tea roses commonly found in the drier southern Cape country towns is 'Marie van Houtte'.

In Riversdale, a friend who had been searching through the older part of the town for old roses, took me to a garden which had obviously been neglected for many years. Kikuyu grass had smothered everything except a rose tree which had somehow held its branches on high and was covered with hundreds of ochre-yellow blooms.

The old Victorian house was painted that deep cream colour so often seen on the buildings of our smaller towns, which is easy on the eye in glaring sunlight and indeed a practical colour for roughly plastered walls which catch the flying dust from untarred streets on windy summer days. The roses were of the same ochre colour, but the thick petals were prettily washed with dark pink towards their edges, appearing almost maroon in the older flowers. Nobody could identify this two-toned rose and from all the descriptions of yellow Teas, the name that seemed to fit it best was 'Marie van Houtte'. At Mottisfont, 'Marie van Houtte' seemed slightly paler than my Riversdale rose but in other respects was very much the same.

A photograph of a half-open 'Rosette Delizy' in *Old Garden Roses in Bermuda* is reminiscent of the Riversdale rose.[1] It is a Nabonnand Tea of 1922 and a cross between 'Général Galliéni' and 'Comtesse Bardi'.

When Leslie Whileman, horticulturist of the Worcester Farm Museum, brought a specimen for identification, the same flowers were of a much more even tone of yellow — the tips only slightly flushed.

But he had also noted the change of colour with the seasons and I have subsequently come to learn that this Tea rose, like so many of its class, varies a great deal in the depth of its colour and the extent of the pink shading which sometimes flushes the whole face of the flower with dark crimson. I suspect that the intensity of the sunlight has a lot to do with this, for blooms growing in shade seem to be of a lighter cream.

This delightful colour combination of yellow and crimson was achieved by Ducher in 1871 when he crossed the yellow 'Mme Falcot' with the rose-coloured 'Mme de Tartas'. The attention of Cape gardeners was soon attracted to 'Marie van Houtte', which appears in all late 19th century and early 20th century catalogues throughout the Cape Colony. In King Williams Town it was still being advertised by James Leighton in his 1940 catalogue.

In Mauritius and Réunion, 'Marie van Houtte' apparently also made a home for herself early this century, for I saw numbers of old trees in Creole country gardens and in the formal forecourts of St. Denis mansions where, out of the rose season, the trees were dotted with yellow and pink blooms. In one of these gardens I was almost devoured by a furious black dog when in my excitement to get a photograph, I crept into the garden without noticing the 'Chien Mechant' notice on the gate.

The Australian author, A. S. Thomas, found in 1975 that 'Marie van Houtte' was still being grown in the Grasse district near Nice for making perfume. Together with 'Ulrich Brunner Fils' and 'Louis van Houtte' it had replaced earlier varieties because of its resistance to disease, its continuous flowering and its excellent scent.

All these admirable qualities, together with its distinctive colouring, should earn a place for this old French Tea rose in any modern garden. The slips I took from the Riversdale garden have grown well and are already brightening up the gardens of many friends.

1 Published by the Bermuda Rose Society, 1984.

'Marie van Houtte'

'Marie van Houtte'.

'Marie van Houtte'
from Brett's *Catalogue*,
1904.

PLANT
A vigorous, branching shrub 1 to 1,5 metres high, with few thorns.

FOLIAGE
Five oval-pointed leaflets with shiny upper and duller lower surfaces; the edges are shallowly serrated. The stalk is sturdy and has prickles on the underside. Stipules are narrow and adnate.

FLOWERS
The large globular bud is cream flushed with crimson, and opens to a very full quartered rose 8–9 cm in diameter. The colour varies from pale to dark cream and the edges of the petals are flushed a darker pink to crimson. There is a short bunch of pistils and very few stamens. The calyx is cup-shaped and smooth; sepals are short, unfoliated, reflexing, velvety on the underside. The flowers appear throughout the year and have a strong Tea fragrance.

INFLORESCENCE
Usually one flower on a short reddish stalk which is inclined to nod.

'Mme Lambard'

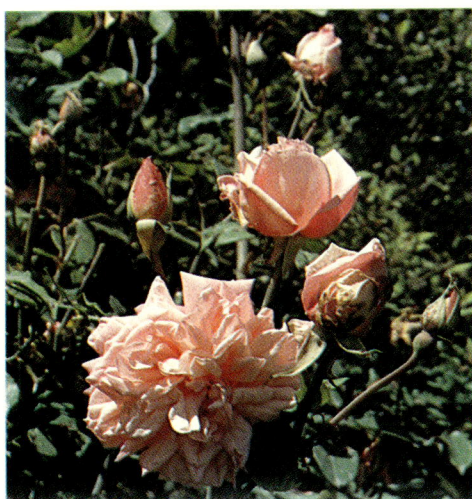

1.2 'Mme Lambard'.
  3 Like all Tea Roses the colour
    of 'Mme Lambard' varies from
    light yellow-brick to dark
    maroon-red, as seen here in
    a Cape cemetery.
  4 Smith's catalogue indicates
    the popularity of Tea Roses at
    the Cape in 1906.

Madam Cabriel Luizet (H.P.), light, silvery-pink.

Madam Honore Defresne (T.), deep yellow, reflexed
  copper, large and full, 2/6 each.

Madam Hoste (T.), flowers yellowish-white, with
  deep yellow centre, large and full.

Madam Isaac Perreire (H.P.), rose-carmine, large
  and full.

Madam Lambard (T.), flowers salmon-pink, shaded
  rose and yellow, a very fine rose, 2/6 each.

Madam Margottin (T.), citron-yellow, centre rosy-
  peach.

Madam Norma (T.), perpetual flowering, beautiful
  yellow.

Madam Victor Verdier (H.P.), brilliant rosy-carmine,
  of great substance.

Madame Camille (T.), delicate rose, veined yellow,
  reflexed white.

Madame Cusin (T.), violet-rose with lighter centre,
  good form, distinct, very pretty in bud, 3/6 each.

Madame C. Kuster (T.), pale yellow, distinct.

Madame Eugene Verdier (T.), deep chamois-yellow,
  large, finely formed, very sweet, one of the best
  roses ever offered, 2/6 each.

Madame Falcot (T.), deep rich orange-yellow petals,
  large, a superb rose, producing lovely buds, 2/6.

Magna Charta (H.P.), rose-pink, suffused with carmine, very large, full, of good form, habit erect,
  magnificent foliage, flowers produced in more
  than usual abundance for so fine a variety, 2/6.

'Mme Lambard' appeared in Cape catalogues very soon after its introduction in France by Lacharme in 1878. It was variously described as 'salmon-pink shaded rose and yellow; a very fine rose',[1] or 'bright rose, paler at times; very variable in colour; blooms large; fine form and splendid habit of growth; being a very profuse blooming variety makes it an ideal rose for any garden', along with the advice, 'prune moderately and give plenty of rich manures'.[2]

The variation in colour seems to be related to the seasons. The flowers are pink and yellow in the spring, but a darker maroon in the autumn.[3] It is a most rewarding rose, for even in the heart of winter 'Mme Lambard' will be bright with flowers, looking for all the world like bunches of gaily tied taffeta bows on a Victorian bustle.

In Professor Rennie's old cottage garden in Grahamstown I found a large 'Mme Lambard' happily sprawling over a high street wall. Always covered with flowers, it cheers up the neighbourhood throughout the year.

The tallest trees I have seen at the Cape, however, are growing in the small west-coast town of Darling. They were proudly shown to me by John Duckitt after we had spent a wonderful spring afternoon looking at the veld on his farm Waylands, where three hundred different species of indigenous plants were flowering in fabulous profusion. I thought that roses in his aunt's Victorian garden would be a bit of an anticlimax, but when I saw the four spreading trees, each one about four metres high, covered in pink blossoms, I changed my mind. How happy I felt and how contented as I drove home that evening after a tea with freshly baked brown bread and veld honey and a mind filled with 'kelkiewyn',[4] white arums, red babianas and pink roses!

'Mme Lambard' grows not only in old Cape gardens but is also the Tea rose most often found in cemeteries. While I was photographing the many large specimens cheering up the old Mowbray cemetery just below Professor Chris Barnard's office and cardiac research laboratories, I was reminded of the impressive opening speech which this world-famous heart surgeon had made at the sixth international rose conference in Pretoria. The only rose he knew, he said, was the beautiful red one which had been named after him, so he guessed that he had been invited to open the conference not because of his knowledge of roses but because the heart and the rose were both the symbol of love. And only through love would all the countries of the world find peace!

1 Smith's catalogue, 1906.
2 Hugh Manson, Rose Culture (Adapted to South African Conditions).
3 In June 1983 I saw very beautiful specimens of this rose in Mauritius cottage gardens where they appeared to be of a darker pink than usual. In Australia and New Zealand 'Mme Lambard' is also well known although there appears to have been some confusion at one stage with the looser 'Bishop Darlington'.
4 'Winecups' Geissorhiza mathewsii var. eurystigma.

'Mme Lambard' ('Mme Lombard')

PLANT
A vigorous shrub with angular growth, from 1,5 to 3 metres high. There are many hooked, wide-based red thorns.

FOLIAGE
Five oval pointed medium-sized shiny leaflets, tinged red when young. The stalk is sturdy, reddish-green, glandular at the proximal end with many sharp hooked thornlets on the underside. Stipules are adnate, smooth and narrow with glandular edges.

FLOWERS
Oval pointed buds with slightly longer sepals open into quartered blooms which expand into flat quilled rosettes about 8 cm in diameter. Newly opened blooms are creamy-yellow to apricot in colour but the petals turn darker as they age, so that an older bloom will be shaded dark pink to maroon, the shanks only remaining yellow. Stamens are thin and remain on the fruit together with the bunch of short red styles after the petals have dropped. The smooth calyx is oval to round; sepals large with leaflike points, smooth on the upper side, velvety below, persistent on the fruit. Flowers appear throughout the year and have a positive Tea fragrance.

INFLORESCENCE
One to three flowers in a corymb at the ends of new shoots on smooth sturdy stalks with narrow, reddish bracts.

'Mme Lambard'.

149

'Perle des Jardins'

'Perle des Jardins'.

'Perle des Jardins' in an
antique copper warming pan.

This rose was brought to my attention by Mrs Margaret Lawder of the
farm Leliefontein in the Klein Drakenstein. She had collected a
slip from a friend and was generous in passing on cuttings which I
grew and planted at Boschendal.

The compact shrub grows one to two metres high. It has pointed
light-green leaves which are always healthy and shiny; the flowers are
carried on sturdy stems and appear throughout the year. Very often
I have been able to pick a bunch of these yellow roses when no other
shrub has even a bud to offer.

This Tea rose was introduced in 1874 by F. Levet and is, according
to McFarland, a seedling of another yellow Tea rose, 'Mme Falcot'.

It appeared in Cape plant catalogues soon after its European introduction and was described by S. Brett in his 1905 catalogue as 'flowers
deep yellow, strong, healthy constitution, exceedingly free flowering,
very sweet, growth vigorous, 2/6 each'.

Although I have not identified this rose with certainty, Brett's description (apart from 'deep yellow' colouring) seems very apt, and
McFarland's 'Perle des Jardins' is 'straw-coloured' like mine.

In the booklet *Old Garden Roses in Bermuda* published by the Bermuda Rose Society, there is a fully open rose which looks exactly like my
'Perle des Jardins' on p. 25, but named 'Anna Olivier'. The clear yellow
colour seems to be closer to my 'Perle des Jardins' than to 'Anna Olivier'
whose petal shanks are inclined to have an orange-bronze tinge, especially in the bud stage.

At the second International Heritage Rose Conference in November
1986 in Adelaide, it became clear to me how little certainty there is
among international rosarians in the identification of Tea roses so I am
confidently calling this rose 'Perle des Jardins' until someone proves
me wrong![1]

1 Slides recently sent to the Sangerhausen Rosarium were
   identified as 'Perle des Jardins'.

'Etoile de Lyon'

About 1 metre high with reddish stems and many hooked thorns.

FOLIAGE
Three to five dark-green oval leaflets with shiny smooth surfaces and shallowly serrated edges. Young leaves are a coppery red and the leaf-stalk is reddish, smooth and shiny. Stipules are of the same colouring, and are narrow and smooth. Leaves are very prone to mildew.

FLOWERS
Large, fat, pointed, greenish-yellow buds open to very full, quartered, light primrose-yellow roses 9–10 cm in diameter. The central petals are crinkled or crumpled, the outer cup-shaped ones are tinged red on the back. The few stamens have short yellow filaments; stigmas are short and pale yellow. The large calyx is cup-shaped, smooth and light-green tinged red. Sepals are long, with small folioles, light-green tinged red; they reflex right back against the stem. The flowers appear throughout the year and have a distinct Tea fragrance.

INFLORESCENCE
One to three flowers in a cyme on strong, reddish, smooth stalks which sometimes bend under the weight of the flower.

'Etoile de Lyon'.
Below: An old 'Etoile de Lyon'
in the French Hoek cemetery.

When all conditions are entirely to her taste, 'Etoile de Lyon' is one of the most exquisite of all yellow Tea roses. She reminds me of the little girl who

When she was good
She was very, very good
But when she was bad, she was horrid.

'Etoile de Lyon' insists on warm sunshine, good ventilation, plenty of manure, and regular water on her roots, but never on her leaves and most definitely not on her flowers. Given these circumstances, one will be rewarded by the beautiful form of her smiling face, filled with numerous crinkled deep-lemon petals in starry array. Shyly aware of her striking looks and sweet fragrance, she droops her head slightly on a pedicel suffused with red. New leaves sport lustily around her in copper-coloured contrast. Then she is very, very good.

But when conditions are not to her liking, she will refuse to expand and remain sullenly pouting in a fat round bud until eventually the ball of petals will turn brown, rot and drop, while the leaves will curl and be come white with fungus. The whole plant will then look wilted and utterly horrid.

How frustrated I have been with this rose, for I always seem to miss the specimen where both leaves and bloom are in spotless condition for a portrait. In the Boschendal garden where she grows, well-meaning labourers insist on overhead spraying when days are dismally hot; and no amount of explaining will convince them that roses, and especially this one, do not appreciate such refreshment.

It is fortunate for her that the first bloom I found, which grew from a stump over a grave in the old cemetery at French Hoek, was the rose at her best. I wonder whether I would have lavished such very special care on my small slip, had she presented her sulky face to me at our first meeting.

Yet 'Etoile de Lyon', despite her weaknesses, must have been quite a belle in her day, for Cape nurseries imported her soon after her introduction by P. Guillot in 1881 and she was advertised by all with great enthusiasm.[1] I will say this for her that there is hardly a time of the year that she is without flowers.

1 Stephen Brett's *Catalogue,* 1905: 'Fine saffron-yellow, brighter in centre, large and full'.
Smith Bros., Uitenhage, *Catalogue,* 1906: 'Fine saffron-yellow, brighter in centre; very large and full; a grand Rose'.

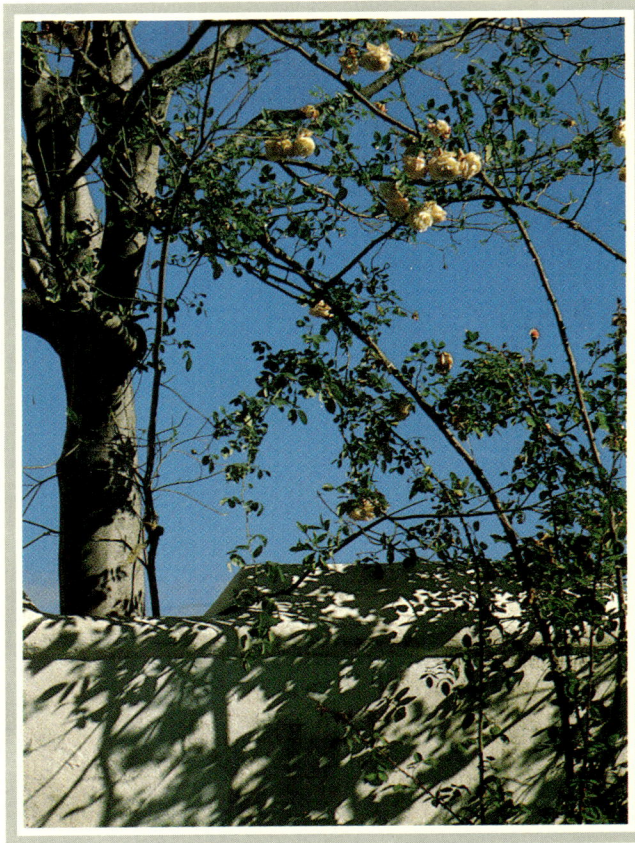

'Maman Cochet' climbing
up a saffron pear tree.
Right: The white 'Mme Cochet' was
regarded as the best of all white roses
when it was first introduced.

'Hugo Roller' (W. Paul Tea, 1907)
was still popular at the Cape in
the 1940s. It can easily be mistaken
for 'Maman Cochet' especially at
the bud stage.

This beautiful Tea rose, introduced by Cochet in 1893, is commonly seen in old Cape gardens straggling along walls or fences or sprawling untidily over large areas, its angular branches densely intertwined. The very large flowers are somewhat reminiscent of 'Peace', with the same cream-flushed-pink colouring, but they are smaller, more globular and inclined to nod when fully blown. She receives her beautiful colouring from her parents, 'Marie van Houtte' and 'Madame Lambard', both of which were popular Victorian Tea roses at the Cape.

Nancy Steen considered 'Maman Cochet' to be one of the best-loved old Tea roses in New Zealand,[1] and here at the Cape, nurserymen early this century also regarded it as an excellent rose, which could be highly recommended.[2]

A few years ago, when I visited Druid Lodge, the late 19th century home of the English family in Robertson,[3] I was shown 'Mrs English's favourite rose' growing amongst a number of other Tea roses in the back garden. The surrounding trees had become so large that they cast a shadow over the rose trees and consequently I was unimpressed with the few blooms which Mrs English's favourite rose tree had produced. Since then, however, I have had the good fortune to see many healthy old trees growing in the sunshine which they love, producing flowers as praiseworthy as those described by the old nurserymen.

From 'Maman Cochet' a white sport was introduced three years later which also became well known in the Cape, but Miss Fairbridge found it unsatisfactory as a white rose, since it turned pink in the sun. A writer in *The Cape Amateur Gardener* of 1913, however, found it charming for table decoration 'if blended with other pale-tinted roses', as white roses alone were 'too cold and colourless against a white tablecloth, and have a very artificial look unless coloured candles are used'.

A second sport, introduced in the early 1900s, was a climber in all other respects similar to the mother plant; it too was widely cultivated at the Cape. I once saw a very beautiful specimen of this rose growing high up into an old Kalbas pear tree, where the heavy round flowers, hanging like pale pink Chinese lanterns among the trusses of white pear blossom, looked particularly beautiful against a bright blue sky.

All these varieties of 'Maman Cochet' are carefree disease-resistant plants which require very little pruning, but ask only for plenty of sun to produce their abundance of flowers throughout the year.

1 In *The Charm Of Old Roses* Nancy Steen called it 'a real old garden stalwart and a great favourite in old gardens'.

2 Smith Bros. of Uitenhage listed it in 1905 as 'an excellent Rose, and one we can highly recommend . . . Each, 3s.6d.' Gowie's *Seeds and Plants, 1904-5* described it as 'Large and fine, one of the best teas'.

3 This house today serves as a local town museum.

'Maman Cochet'

'Maman Cochet'.

PLANT
Vigorous angularly branched shrub growing to about 3 metres high with many stout hooked thorns. There is also a climbing variety.

FOLIAGE
Five medium-sized oval pointed leaflets, dark olive in colour with shiny smooth surfaces, duller below. Leaf-stalks are delicate, slightly glandular and have white hooked prickles on the underside. Stipules are reddish-green and narrow with slightly glandular edges.

FLOWERS
The large, oval pointed buds with short sepals open to globular flowers 8–9 cm in diameter. The cream petals are broad, thick and have wavy edges. The central petals are tightly packed into quarters, but the outer ones are looser, rolled back on the edges and sometimes flushed or streaked pink. Flowers are heavy and inclined to nod. The calyx is smooth, large and cup-shaped. Sepals are short, glandular along the margins and velvety on the underside; they reflex right back as soon as the bud opens. Stamens are rudimentary. The flowers appear throughout the year and have a fresh Tea fragrance.

INFLORESCENCE
One to three flowers on a corymb on sturdy smooth pedicels; leaflike bracts are small and reddish.

153

1 The bizarre colours of
  'Général Galliéni'.
2 Général Galliéni.
3 In a Tamboerskloof garden.
4 *Rosa chinensis mutabilis*. (½ size)
  I have often wondered whether the
  Tea Roses are not perhaps derived from
  this single China which so vividly
  displays the typical colour change from
  yellow in the newly opened flower
  to crimson in the fading one.
5 On an old property in Oudtshoorn.
  This Tea rose produces flowers ranging
  in colour from yellow to dark maroon
  throughout the year. I have not been
  able to identify it.

4
3 5

'Général Galliéni', one of the most spectacular and distinctive of Tea roses, was very much 'in the mode' in late Victorian Cape Town. It still makes its appearance in derelict country cemeteries and here and there in the small street gardens of Oranjezicht and Tamboerskloof.

A particularly dilapidated house in this area one day caught my attention. In front of its bedraggled veranda, where remnants of pretty wrought-iron indicated grander days, was an unkempt garden in which some unusual dark maroon roses were flowering amongst the tall weeds. Hearing that the house might be sold and fearing that the garden might be 'renovated', I knocked at the front door to ask permission to pick a rose and procure a few slips.

An old lady, as neglected as her home, opening the door a few centimetres, spoke through her pouting blood-red lipsticked mouth, 'No! You can't pick any of my roses!' and slammed the door. Now I seldom take people at their face value, and knowing that she hadn't really meant to be mean, I returned a few evenings later and in the darkness helped myself to a few blooms and slips by torchlight. The three resultant rose trees have grown beautifully and in turn provided slips for many friends' gardens.

The rose was easily identified by several gardeners older than myself as 'Général Galliéni'. M. Nabonnand when he introduced this new Tea rose in 1899, three years after the Indian Ocean island of Madagascar had become part of the French Empire, named it in honour of the first Governor-General of that colony. I often wonder whether plants of the rose were sent from Nabonnand's Mediterranean nurseries to the General's home in Madagascar and if so, how they would have fared in that very hot climate.

I have noticed that variations in the Cape climate have a peculiar influence on the General's colour, which varies from a coppery yellow in the cooler autumn months to dull maroon in the hotter weather. Sometimes all the colours appear together simultaneously as if the rose wished to display its parentage quite clearly — the dark red of 'Souvenir de Thérèse Levet' and the coppery yellow tones of 'Reine Emma des Pays-Bas'.

I like to arrange full-blown 'Général Galliéni' blooms in an old copper vase with brass bandy-legged feet, for the tousselled flowers on their angular stalks seem to lie comfortably in the flattish vase and the wonderful range of rich colours picks up the glowing tints of polished copper and brass.

These dark red roses often remind me of the unhappy red lips and dull eyes of my Tamboerskloof acquaintance whose house and garden still look the same, and I wonder whether the owner ever picks any of the roses still flowering gallantly in her garden to arrange in some old vase, to bring warmth into her dreary days.

'Général Galliéni'

PLANT
This branched angular shrub grows to 1,5 metres high. It has many hooked red thorns.

FOLIAGE
Five large, oval pointed, dark-green leaflets with wavy edges, shallowly serrated. The surfaces are shiny and often tinted red especially when young. The stalk is sturdy with small pale hooks on the underside. Stipules are adnate, very narrow and have smooth edges.

FLOWERS
Pointed maroon buds open to very full flowers about 10 cm in diameter. The outer petals reflex and the inner ones are folded and quartered untidily. The young flowers are sometimes apricot-pink to yellow and the older ones blood-red or maroon, but the colour varies a great deal. Stamens are poorly developed and form a ring around the short red bristly styles. The calyx is round and smooth; sepals are short with small folioles, velvety below, edges microscopically glandular. They reflex right back against the stem. Flowers have a fresh Tea fragrance and appear throughout the year.

INFLORESCENCE
One to three flowers on the ends of young branches.

'Général Galliéni'.

Unknown Tea roses
in the Langkloof.

'Lady Roberts' (1902); a sport
from 'Anna Olivier', also with
apricot colouring.

'Lady Hillingdon' at Vredenburg.

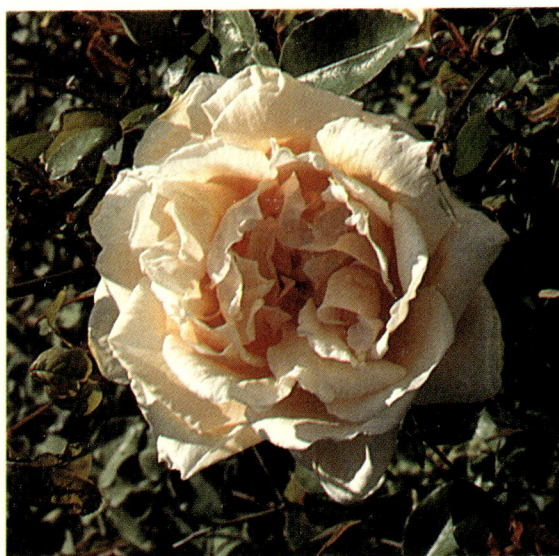

'Laurette Messimy' (1887),
another apricot-coloured Tea
rose; derived from 'Rival de
Paestum' and 'Mme Falcot'.

The winter had been long, cold and very wet, so that the beautiful spring sunshine infused a gaiety into the morning, inspiring Margaret Cairns and myself with a light-heartedness as we went driving through Mowbray, Rosebank, Rondebosch, Wynberg and Newlands to look for old roses.

Margaret had grown up in these suburbs and knew every old cottage and mansion, every graveyard, hedge and alley, every sad story of decimated estates and vanished gardens. But even she was surprised at the extent of the changes in her old haunts and at the paucity of our finds. Gone was the yellow Banksia hedge, pride of Pillans Road; gone too were the old rose gardens at Alphen, Hohenort and Mont Rose. The wealth of old roses had been 'cleared out' of the small graveyard adjoining the Kirstenbosch stone church, and we looked in vain for all Dorothea Fairbridge's hedges which had turned the southern suburbs into a fairyland in the springtime.

The human spirit strives to forget what is painful and so the sadness of that spring morning is a half-forgotten memory. What I do remember clearly, however, is that it was the right time for 'Lady Hillingdon', who showed herself to us on that day in all her splendour.

A huge Erythrina was aflame with flowers when we arrived in the secluded front garden of the old thatched manor house of Vredenburg in Mowbray.[1] The garden was in shade but for many cups of sunlight held in the open blooms of a rose tree whose fresh young leaves formed a delightful coppery contrast.

We were enchanted with the clear apricot-yellow, fragrant roses which proved to be 'Lady Hillingdon', and could imagine the pride with which Lowe, the originator of this rose, must have greeted the distinctive new colour he obtained by crossing the creamy-pink 'Papa Gontier' with the pale-yellow 'Madame Hosta' in 1910.

Having received our hearty ovation. 'Lady Hillingdon' thought she would give us an encore, so when we walked into the garden of the mill-house next to Josephine's Mill, there she was again with young red leaves and golden flowers shining in a streak of sunlight which fell through the high green trees framing this old rose garden, which had once provided Mrs van der Byl, her previous mistress, with many prize-winning roses for the local shows.

But the grand finale was still to come, for on turning from Weltevreden Road into Heseldon Street, a most glorious sight met our eyes in the corner cottage garden where a 'Lady Hillingdon' two metres high, and as much across, was one solid mass of yellow roses. Suddenly I was filled with warmth and a feeling of great goodwill as I recognised the rose tree which Leonie Hofmeyr had asked me to identify a year before. She had been given a large bunch of yellow Tea roses, picked from this garden, by the young man of the house as a token of appreciation for the well-loved teacher of his early school days.

1 This house has since been acquired and restored by the
  Cape Town architect, Dirk Visser, who has preserved the
  old rose trees in the garden.

'Lady Hillingdon'

PLANT
Delicate branched shrub 1–1,5 metres high with light greeny-red stems and sparse red-grey hooked thorns.

FOLIAGE
Three or five medium-sized oval pointed leaflets, dark coppery-red when young, olive-green tinged red later. Edges are finely serrated; surfaces smooth and shiny on top, greyer on the underside. Stipules are narrow, smooth and greeny-red.

FLOWERS
Long pointed buds with slightly longer sepals open to loose semi-double flowers 8 cm in diameter. Petals are broad, of a silky texture, apricot in colour, darker towards the centre, paler in the older flowers. The many stamens have quite long thin yellow filaments; the pistil is short with a bunch of yellow-green stigmas. The calyx is cup-shaped and smooth; foliated sepals are velvety on the underside and reflex right back as the bud opens. The flowers appear throughout the year and have a marked Tea fragrance.

INFLORESCENCE
A cyme of one to four flowers on reddish-green stalks, smooth but for a few glands.

'Lady Hillingdon'.

157

Welgelegen, an old Dutch farm in Mowbray,
still has remnants of a beautiful late 19th century
garden, which is now being restored.

THE HYBRID PERPETUALS

A varied group of roses were developed from the old garden roses and the newer Chinese hybrid roses towards the end of the 1830s. With so many different parents, one can expect quite a variety of form; yet certain habits of growth, foliage, flower shape, and the fact that they all were remontant to a certain degree, made it possible to place them in one group.

An extraordinary number of these roses were to flood the market over the last fifty years of the 19th century. As the fashion for bedding roses was then in its prime, new varieties were greeted with great enthusiasm to plant in the oval, kidney-shaped, heart-shaped or simple round or square beds cut into lawns.

At the Cape, gardeners were no less anxious to have the very latest introductions for garden display or for the rose shows which followed in the wake of newly established botanic gardens in most of the larger towns.

'Crimson shaded scarlet' seems to cover the descriptions of nearly all the Hybrid Perpetuals listed in rose catalogues of the early 1900s, when most pink, white or pale yellow roses were either Teas or Hybrid Teas. And when one comes across a large rose tree in an old garden with 'superb glowing scarlet' flowers, how shall one know whether it is 'The Shah', 'Ulrich Brunner', 'Xavier Olibo', 'Sir Joseph Paxton', 'Richard Wallace', 'Pierre Notting', 'Sir Camet Wolseley' or the Dukes of Edinburgh, Teck or Wellington? For all of these were described in the same glowing terms in Cape plant catalogues.

As thatched cottages acquired frilly striped verandas and old Dutch casements made way for the smarter English sash windows, the Hybrid Perpetuals crept into Cape gardens one after the other. And though their blooms were sometimes floppy and lacked substance for indoor arrangements, their sweet fragrance and graceful charm were as welcome as the few flowers which appeared after their summer flush had passed.

But as thatch made way for the more practical galvanized iron and gables were demolished or severely clipped to fit under the new streamlined roofing materials, so the casually planted Hybrid Perpetuals made way for the more practical Hybrid Teas. Gardens became more contrived and the charm and romance of our great-grandparents' gardens became only a memory or a pretty picture on a postcard or old photograph.

Hybrid Perpetuals that grew in Cape Town in the early 1900s:

ABLE CARRIERE	Purple crimson
ALFRED COLOMB	Fiery cherry-red
ANNA ALEXIEFF	Pretty rose colour
BARON DE BONSTETTEN	Rich velvety purple
BARON SHUARAND	Velvety crimson
BARONESS ROTHSCHILD	Beautiful light rose
BLACK PRINCE	Fine dark rose
CHARLES DARWIN	Deep crimson
CHARLES DICKENS	Rose
CHARLES LAMB	Clear bright red
CHARLES LEFÈBVRE	Brilliant velvet-crimson
COQUETTES DES BLANCHES	Pure white
DR ANDRY	Brilliant crimson
DR HOGG	Deep violet
DUKE OF EDINBURGH	Rich velvety crimson
EARL DUFFERIN	Rich velvety red, shaded maroon
EMPEREUR DU MAROC	Rich velvety maroon
FISHER HOLMES	Shaded crimson scarlet
FRAU KARL DRUSCHKI	Snow-white
GÉANT DES BATAILLES	Crimson
GÉNÉRAL JACQUEMINOT	Superb glowing scarlet and crimson
GLOIRE DE MARGOTTIN	Bright cherry red
GRAND MOGUL	Crimson shaded scarlet and black
JOHN HOPPER	Brilliant rose
JOHN STUART MILLS	Light clear red
JULES MARGOTTIN	Cherry pink
LORD ROGLAN	Scarlet crimson
MABEL MORRISON	Nearly white
MADAM CHARLES WOOD	Crimson shaded purple
MADAME GABRIEL LUIZET	Light silvery pink
MAGNA CHARTER	Rose-pink with carmine
MARGARET DICKSON	White with pale flesh centre
MARIE BAUMANN	Soft carmine red
MONSIEUR BONCENNE	Blackish crimson
MRS BAKER	Light crimson red
PAUL NEYRON	Dark rose
PIERRE NOTTING	Deep crimson
RICHARD WALLACE	Bright rose
ROBERT DUNKIN	Light rosy-lake
SIR CARNET WOLSELEY	Glowing crimson
SIR JOSEPH PAXTON	Bright rose
THE SHAH	Scarlet crimson
ULRICH BRUNNER	Red
WHITE BARONESS	White
XAVIER OLIBO	Velvety black

I found 'Baronne Prévost' in the garden of the magistrate's residence in Oudtshoorn.

'Baronne Prévost' together with 'The Bishop' in a Paarl garden.

The heavy flowers are carried on sturdy stems.

An avenue of cypress trees in an Aberdeen street.

A few years ago I drove through the small town of Aberdeen, craning my neck this way and that in search of old roses. The magnificent cypress trees along the gravel streets indicated that the townsfolk there had been horticulturally very active in the early part of this century. On the street boundaries furrows still carried water to the erven gardens, and snatches of quince hedges showed how these boundaries had been demarcated before the arrival of the barbed wire fences which were now everywhere in evidence.

Entangled in one of these hedges was a rose bush with a few pink buds reminiscent of 'Baronne Prévost', but the friendly owner sitting on the stoep under his veranda could not give me the name. 'The hedges here were all of quince and pink roses when I was a boy,' he said, 'but they are all gone now. They smelt so sweet, especially in the early mornings', he added nostalgically.

Further down the street I peered into a backyard where years of diligent sweeping had smoothed the yellow earth to a hard surface. Next to a wire chicken-run, growing out of the dry ground was a large rose tree, upright, lusciously green and full of blooms! Not a soul was to be seen anywhere, so I crept guiltily up to the roses, relieved that my husband was not there to scold me for trespassing.

The flowers were huge, of a clear strong pink colour, petals perfectly arranged into large flat quartered rosettes with inner smaller ones neatly rolled into a central ring around the half-visible styles. The scent was

exquisite, the calyx large and cone-shaped and I knew that I was looking at 'Baronne Prévost' — the hedge rose of Aberdeen.

From the Botanic Garden in Graaff Reinet, established in 1872, numerous trees and garden plants were distributed to the surrounding villages and farms of the semi-desert Karoo until the early 20th century. Aberdeen, scarcely 50 kilometres from this garden, would have benefited from its work in propagating and acclimatizing new plants, and most probably received trees for its streets and roses for its hedges from that source.

Perhaps the original Graaff Reinet plants had in turn come from the Cape Town Botanic Garden where over a hundred different rose varieties, including 'Baronne Prévost', were recorded in 1858, only ten years after Governor Sir Harry Smith had turned the neglected old Dutch East India Company's garden into a 'Botanical Institution'.

When the obvious advantages of satellite gardens became apparent in the Cape (as elsewhere in the British colonies), Graaff Reinet was one of the first to be established. The widespread interchange of plants and knowledge was manifest late that spring afternoon more than a century later in the little Karoo village of Aberdeen.

I looked at the beautiful pink blooms on the single 'Baronne Prévost' plant growing from the hard earth next to the chicken-run and thought how incongruous it looked six thousand miles and a hundred years removed from its ancestor.

160

'Baronne Prévost'

'Baronne Prévost'.

PLANT
A strong growing upright shrub about 2,5 metres high with many slightly hooked thorns of different sizes.

FOLIAGE
Five large oval pointed leaflets up to 7 cm long with clear, light-green matt surfaces and medium serrations, sometimes bidentate. The stalks are strong, round, light green and glandular with short bristles on the underside. Stipules are adnate and have entire edges with some glands.

FLOWERS
Large oval pink buds with short sepals open to very full flat quartered flowers up to 10 cm in diameter. The outer petals are broad and recurving; the inner smaller ones are usually arranged in a rosette around the central button-eye, but sometimes they present a more muddled appearance. Stamens are rudimentary and the styles just visible. The calyx is large, cone-shaped and glandular; sepals are small compared to the size of the flower, slightly foliated and glandular on the outer surface and edges, velvety inside. The flowers appear mostly in spring with fewer blooms throughout the year. They are deliciously fragrant.

INFLORESCENCE
One to three flowers on rough, sticky, very glandular stalks.

Manie de Waal's house in 1899.

Graham Thomas, who in his *Shrub Roses of Today* said 'It is sad and inexplicable to me how such a famous pink rose as 'La Reine' (1842) can have disappeared', will no doubt be overjoyed to know that this early Hybrid Perpetual has been found again at the Cape and, as it grows easily from cuttings, has been planted in a number of gardens.

I well remember the first time I saw the masses of pink roses on a shrub which had grown, unpruned, into a large untidy tangle. The garden in which it stood was as remarkable as the house and its owner.

Dwarfed by tall surrounding buildings in Andringa Street in the oldest part of Stellenbosch, the small house looked from the outside like many others which had been so common in my youth. But when Marius le Roux, curator of the Stellenbosch museum, took me inside to meet the owner, Manie de Waal, I stepped back almost a century in time.

The old man greeted us in a very friendly manner and took me out to see his garden which, like his house, had remained unchanged since his birth in 1895. Mr de Waal had inherited the property from his father and lived there with his sister, keeping everything as his parents had left it: the original paint and paper on the walls, the oil lamps in all the rooms (for electricity had been steadily refused), and the old black Dover stove in the kitchen from where the wooden fire sent up daily columns of smoke to the surrounding flat dwellers. In an adjoining barn were preserved all the trappings of a smithy[1] and cartwright.

Like Alice, I walked into a magic garden. Earthen paths, shaded by unpruned fruit trees, were edged with round river stones which also formed the paving for the water furrows. The rose trees had been planted with total abandon cheek by jowl with gardenia, oleander, rosemary, myrtle, and that indispensible Cape cottage herb known as 'wilde-als' with which housewives treated all ailments from festering toe-nails to

pneumonia. (I well remember the gall-like bitterness of the infusion which my grandmother made me swallow for any complaint, and to this day the taste returns when I bite into an orange-peel, which was given to neutralize the bitterness.)[2]

Sprawling over this grey shrub, I saw a large rose tree covered in many rich pink blooms which I did not recognize but which enchanted me with a wonderful fragrance. For some time afterwards I was unable to identify the globular rose which I fortunately found later growing in several other Cape gardens, for Manie de Waal's property has long since been demolished to make way for modern developments. Then one day I read Mrs Keays' excellent description of 'La Reine' once again,[3] and it dawned on me that Manie de Waal's unknown rose was none other than that most famous of all French Hybrid Perpetuals, which Laffay in 1842 acclaimed as the 'Queen of France'.[4]

For many years this queen was to reign supreme in Europe[5] as well as in the Cape, where she was introduced soon after her first appearance. But writing in 1888, Parsons virtually deposed her: 'When our first edition was issued (1847) this variety was unequalled. Others have now surpassed it. However it is still valuable for its glossy rose colour and large semi-globular form.'[6]

As a specimen plant I believe 'La Reine' is still unequalled in many respects. It needs support when young, but will eventually build up into a most handsome shrub with large, deep-pink globular blooms along the entire length of the graceful bending branches, appearing several times a year. It is a healthy vigorous plant, needing almost no pruning. If picked at the half-open stage, the flowers will last for several days indoors, spreading their delicious fragrance for everyone's enjoyment.

---

1 The workshops next to the house were let by his father.
2 This indigenous plant belonging to the Compositae family is related to the European *Artemisia absinthum*, also known as 'absinth' or 'wormwood'. It was traditionally used for colds, fevers, rheumatism and indigestion. It is also considered to be an anthelmintic, an antiseptic, an antiflatulent as well as a general tonic. In France it forms the main

ingredient of the liqueur, absinthe, and at the Cape, too, it was often put into brandy to form a crude type of liqueur. With its grey-green foliage 'wilde-als' makes as pretty a garden plant as its European counterpart.
3 E. E. Keays, *Old Roses*, 1935, reprinted New York, 1978.
4 'Reine des Francais'. It was also known as 'Rose de la Reine'.

5 In William Paul's *The Rose Garden*, a coloured plate of 'La Reine' shows all the typical features, but the colour is too pale. According to him it was a magnificent rose, but varied in quality.
6 Samuel B. Parsons, *Parsons on the Rose*, 1888, reprinted New York, 1979.

'La Reine'

PLANT
Shrub 1,5–2 metres high with many long arching branches.

FOLIAGE
Five oval pointed dark-green leaflets with dull surfaces and serrated edges, on sturdy stalks which are slightly glandular. Stipules are adnate and narrow and have small sessile glands on the edges.

FLOWERS
Fat pointed buds with long foliated sepals expand into large, rich pink, globular blooms. The broad petals have wavy edges and are beautifully overlapped so that the half-expanded flower resembles some exotic underwater anemone. The inner petals are darker than the outer ones. The large calyx is cone-shaped and has a few stalked glands towards the pedicel which is also slightly glandular. The sepals are branched and velvety on the lower surface, glandular on the upper surface. The flowers make a fine show in spring, and appear in lesser numbers throughout the year. They are deliciously fragrant.

INFLORESCENCE
Flowers are borne at the tops of the branches or on many side branchlets along the reflexing stems.

'La Reine'

'Géant des Batailles'

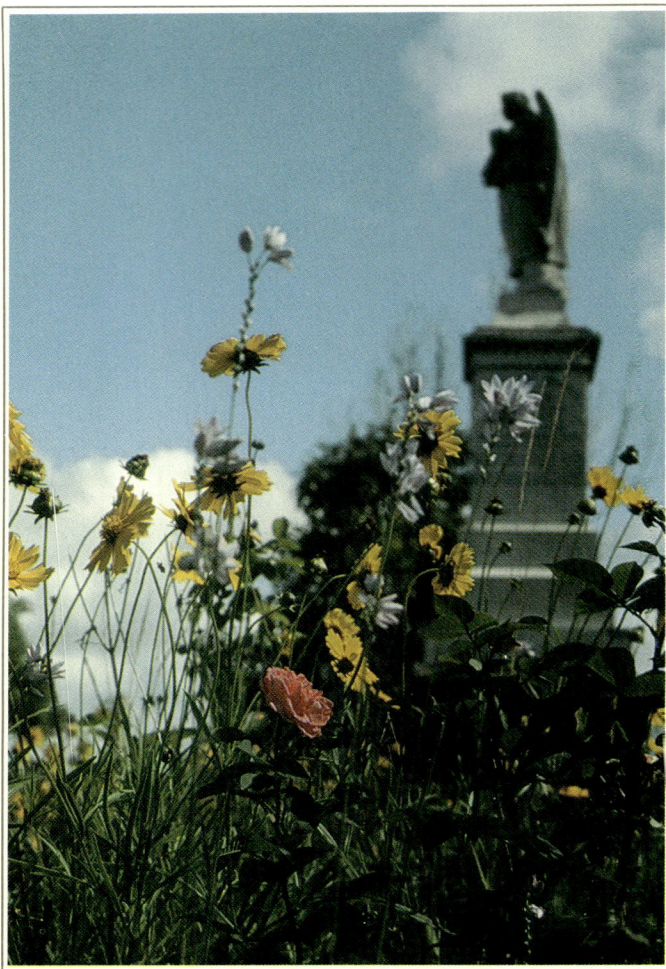

Right: 'Géant des Batailles' seems to have been a popular cemetery rose in Australia as well. Here it is seen in the Rookwood cemetery in Sydney.

Below left: Over an old wall with a *Rosa multiflora* hybrid.

Below right: Minutes of the Durban Botanic Society 1865, noting the arrival of four dead 'Géant des Batailles' plants.

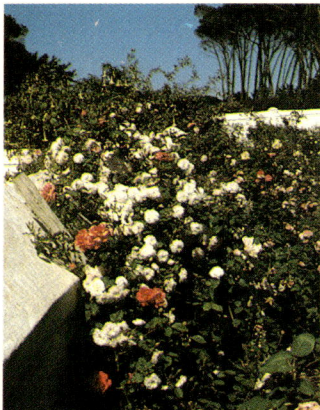

When in the early 19th century Josephine Bonaparte started collecting roses from the various corners of Europe to create the first *Roseraie* at Malmaison, she inspired French breeders with an ardent fervour that was to lead to the introduction of many beautiful new varieties. Thus in 1828 Vibert developed from the wild *Rosa sempervirens* the famous climber which he dedicated to his daughter, 'Aimée Vibert'; Jacotot in 1853 created the buff-pink Bourbon 'Gloire de Dijon'; Prodal in 1864 produced the famous yellow Noisette 'Maréchal Niel'; Laffay in 1842 the first Hybrid Perpetual, 'La Reine'; J. B. Guillot in 1867 the first Hybrid Tea, 'La France', as well as the first dwarf Polyantha, 'Pacquerette' in 1875, and Pernet-Ducher, surpassing all these in 1898, produced the supreme triumph of hybridization with his first Pernetian rose, 'Soleil d'Or'. All these roses became world famous and their impact was felt at the Cape too.

From France came also the first fiery crimson roses, which were greeted with even more excitement, for they added an entirely new dimension of colour to the existing rose scene. 'Gloire des Rosomanes', introduced by Vibert in 1825, and its offspring, 'Géant des Batailles' from Nerard and the older Guillot in 1846, were highly esteemed by nurserymen. William Paul considered them to be 'a stride in the right direction' of rose breeding.[1] They were both prolific seed-bearers and the vigorous 'Géant des Batailles' in particular became a popular pollen parent, transmitting through its numerous descendants the brilliant crimson which is still prevalent in many of our most modern roses.

Ten years after its appearance in France, 'Géant des Batailles' was growing in the private and public gardens of Cape Town and from there was probably distributed to the many botanic gardens of the Colony. The Durban Botanic Society for instance, recorded in 1865 that it had received four plants of this rose from Saul Solomon's garden in Sea Point, but that they had arrived dead![2]

In 1888 Charles Ayres' *Seed Catalogue and Garden Guide* still included 'Géant des Batailles' ('crimson shaded purple' at 2s each) in his list of Hybrid Perpetuals. The old trees which I have seen growing against Victorian verandas in the Gardens area of Cape Town and in the 'Malay Quarter' at the foot of Lion's Hill probably came from there. I have also found 'Giant of Battles' on several late 19th century country graves and along farm boundaries where it had obviously been planted as hedges in the dim past.

For several years I had been unable to identify this vigorous tall rose which flowers several times a year, and no amount of paging through books was of any help. Once again I projected the numerous slides taken in overseas rose gardens, when suddenly it dawned on me that the 'Giant of Battles' taken at Petersen's old rose nursery near Copenhagen was identical to my mystery rose. There was the same smooth, rather small cup-shaped calyx with half-reflexed sepals; young dull green leaves tinged puce on the edges; the same inflorescence and the same bright cerise-red full flowers. William Paul had included a painting by Andrews in his *Rose Garden*, but how much more beautiful the live flower was, I could now appreciate for the first time.

1 *The Rose Garden*, 1848.
2 *Minutes of the Natal Botanic Society* from 1865 onwards. The Killie Campbell Collection, University of Natal.

'Géant des Batailles'

Hip.

PLANT
A vigorous shrub from 3–5 metres high, useful as a pillar rose or as a high hedge. It has many sharp hooked thorns of various sizes.

FOLIAGE
Five large oval leaflets with smooth dull green surfaces inclining to puce along the shallowly serrated edges of young leaves. The stalk is sturdy, glandular, tinged reddish and has small hooked thorns on the underside. Stipules are adnate and glandular with smooth edges.

FLOWERS
The dark crimson round pointed buds with shortish sepals open into very full flat flowers of about 7–8 cm in diameter. They are a brilliant crimson-red colour, turning maroon as they age. The outer petals are broad; the inner ones smaller and folded on themselves, indefinitely quartered around a twisted bunch of protruding hairy styles and a few short stamens in the centre. The calyx is cup-shaped and smooth; the slightly foliated sepals are glandular on the outer surface, velvety on the inside and reflex only to hold the corolla. The flowers make a marvellous show in spring and have further smaller flushes during the summer and autumn. They have a marked fresh fragrance.

INFLORESCENCE
Groups of three or more flowers at the ends of branches on sturdy glandular pedicels. Two green bracts have glandular edges.

'Géant des Batailles'.

165

'Anna de Diesbach'

Mrs Bowles' hedge of 'Anna de Diesbach' with the old-age home in the background.

Along the stream at Orange Grove, the Barkhuisen farm in the Langkloof.

'Tourists come to Oudtshoorn for two reasons only: to see the Cango caves and to visit an ostrich farm', the town clerk of this well-known Karoo town confidently asserted. We were trying to convince him that the demolition of old stone buildings and street gardens demanded by his road-widening programme would be a disastrous loss for the town. Having spent two days photographing and making notes on the threatened buildings and their surroundings, we could understand the helpless frustration of those citizens who were objecting to the ambitions of their town leaders.

The town we saw was a beautiful one. We noticed a shopfront with delicately moulded teak woodwork and solid brass door handles; a fine stone church with an arched door and windows opening onto the pavement; 'ostrich feather palaces' built in the heyday of the feather craze when local inhabitants became rich overnight; ornate houses with bay windows and elaborate turrets, curved verandas and garden walls richly decorated with ornamental cast-iron balustrades brought from foundries in Cape Town, or imported from Britain at the turn of the century.

There were also remnants of 19th century rose gardens, planted when it was fashionable to win prizes at the local rose exhibitions and have one's name published in the *Oudtshoorn Courant.*

'Mr Nils Johnson, a professional gardener was the judge and gave the First award to Mrs C. M. Lind, and the Second to Dr Russell and the Third to Miss Ann Stegman' the *Courant* announced on Monday 22 October 1894, when nine enthusiasts exhibited their roses at the first Oudtshoorn rose show in the newspaper's office, earning 30/- for the Ladies Benevolent Society. The *Courant* was of the opinion that chrysanthemums and roses grew to such perfection in Oudtshoorn that the Agricultural Society should organize shows of fruit and flowers periodically, adding 'The education of a good show is invaluable!'

Roses really do excel themselves in this dry hot Karoo town. The red clay soil, when flooded with the clear cool water from the irrigation channels criss-crossing the town, seems to liberate magical vigour in young rose shoots. When short people like myself walk through an established Oudtshoorn garden, we have to stretch up to see the large blooms crowning the rose trees.

I thought of all these things as I listened to the town clerk, but sensed his complete lack of interest in my answer: 'Your Cango caves have lost their wonder and mystery under multicoloured neon lights, and your ostrich farm is over-commercialized. But if you were to retain your oldest town streets, restore the old avenues, water furrows and rose gardens, then you would really have an invaluable asset for discriminating future tourists!'

There would be no problem in filling the small street gardens with Victorian rose favourites from mother trees in the town. 'Lady Hilling-don' could nod its apricot-yellow heads with the dark maroon of 'Général Galliéni'; 'Mrs Herbert Stevens' and 'Géant des Batailles' could splash the green veranda fretwork with white and crimson; and the sunken beds along the paths could provide colour throughout the year with 'Old Monthly', 'Catherine Mermet', 'Gloire des Rosomanes', 'Maman Cochet', 'Marie van Houtte' and several hitherto unidentified pink roses at present growing in Oudtshoorn gardens.

One of these unknowns, which I have tentatively identified as 'Anna de Diesbach'[1] from a description by Ethelyn Keays (*Old Roses*, 1935), provided me with the most unforgettable sight of my Oudtshoorn visit when I was introduced to the back garden of Mrs Bowles. By transplanting the runners of one plant, this ardent gardener had formed a short hedge which was so successful that the procedure was repeated until she had screened off a boundary 8 metres long. When I saw this hedge it was a sheet of pink blooms splendidly contrasted against a bed of yellow and blue irises. Mrs Bowles was so pleased with the result that she had decided to turn the corner of her boundary and proceed with the hedge down the next, much to the delight of the old people living in a home on the other side who would pick the blooms to bring colour and fragrance to their rooms.

How I would like to extend Mrs Bowles' hedge to fill the ugly corners of Oudtshoorn's main streets with 'Anna de Diesbach'. Once the 'Glory of Paris', it could soon become the 'Glory of Oudtshoorn'! But I know that even this floral glory would not stop bulldozers from 'improving' the town. Soon the few remaining street gardens with their old-fashioned roses will disappear, and tourists who are not lucky enough to be invited into the hidden back gardens will never experience the delight of an 'Anna de Diesbach' hedge in flower as I did that spring morning in Mrs Bowles' garden.

This rose has been sent to me for identification from gardens throughout the Cape. It is usually called a 'Cabbage rose', although it is clearly not a Centifolia. One of these arrived with the post one morning, wrapped in straw, sacking, a plastic bag and brown paper. It was labelled 'Ouma Mietjie's Cabbage', and was accompanied with a long family history:

Ouma Mietjie (Maria Johanna Albertina Meeding), just turned sixteen, married the nineteen-year-old Antonie Michael Ferreira in 1827. These two settled at Kabeljouwsrivier, a large farm near Humansdorp, where Ouma Mietjie was soon kept busy with a family of sixteen children and a large garden. Her great-granddaughter, Mrs C. Wait of Uitenhage who sent me the rose parcel, told me that Ouma Mietjie had a passion for plants and used to collect them from far and wide; this rose was found on a visit to her daughter who lived in Mossel Bay.

Ouma Mietjie's husband died when she was forty and her youngest child was six months old ('fortunately', says Mrs Wait, 'or there would have been many more children'). But continuous pregnancies had not affected her health, for she lived another forty years — perhaps kept sprightly by her gardening activities. The cycad she planted on her husband's grave is now a huge tree and her 'Anna de Diesbach' has provided numerous offspring for distribution among her descendants who remember their Ouma Mietjie by the 'cabbage rose' in their gardens.

1 M. Lacharme introduced this 'La Reine' derivative in 1858 ('La Reine' x an unknown seedling) and it must have reached the Cape soon afterwards.

166

'Anna de Diesbach'

PLANT
A vigorous shrub with many upright shoots to 1,5 metres, with small light-brown hooked thorns spaced evenly over the stems.

FOLIAGE
Five oval leaflets with matt upper and velvety lower surfaces, the margins finely serrated. The stalk is sturdy, rough and glandular on the underside but has no prickles. Stipules are adnate, entire and glandular.

FLOWERS
Round buds with short sepals open to full, globular, deep pink flowers about 7 cm in diameter. The petals are broad and have wavy edges. The stamens have large anthers and thin filaments; the hairy pistils are in a loose column, longer than the stamens. The calyx is smooth, pyriform and taken in slightly at the top; the foliated sepals have glands on the upper surface and are velvety below, reflexing halfway. Flowers appear throughout the year and are very fragrant.

INFLORESCENCE
One to five flowers on a head; the central one is on the shortest stalk and is the first to flower. The flower stems are glandular and slightly bristly.

'Anna de Diesbach'.

167

'Général Jacqueminot' in front of a Genadendal cottage.

'Crimson Glory'. Half size.

In 1858, only five years after Roussel had introduced 'Général Jacqueminot' to Europe, this brilliant scarlet rose was listed amongst the roses growing in the Botanic Garden in Cape Town. There seems to be some uncertainty as to its parentage. Some say that it was a seedling of 'Gloire des Rosomanes', others that it was a hybrid between that and 'Géant des Batailles'. It certainly has the same scarlet colouring, occasional white streaking and delicious fragrance of 'Gloire des Rosomanes', and as the flowers age they display the darker purple hues of the 'Giant'.

After one and a quarter centuries all three of these scarlet roses are still to be found in old gardens at the Cape, though 'Général Jacqueminot' is the least common. According to Roy Shepherd its bright red colour and intense fragrance 'were used as a basis by which other roses were judged' for more than fifty years. He regards it as one of the greatest rose parents of all time — it gave rise to more than five hundred seedlings and sixty sports.

Two of its best-known descendants, 'Crimson Glory' and 'Etoile de Hollande', were to be found in almost every Cape rose garden when I was a schoolgirl, and they still occur frequently in older gardens. 'General Jack' itself, however, is a scarce rose and I had searched far and wide without tracing a single plant, when I was told of a very old red rose growing in Grace Taute's garden in the Langkloof. This turned out indeed to be 'Général Jacqueminot'.

No one knew which of the Taute ancestors had planted the rose nor what it was called. Grace was pleased that I took cuttings, for she and her brother Clive had sold the old family farm in order to move to Oudtshoorn where they would be closer to medical attention. Disaster had struck this fifth generation of Tautes when all four sons were born with haemophilia and died one after another, leaving eventually only Clive as a bedridden invalid tended by his sister Grace, who never married. A visit to Clive was an enriching experience, for despite his disability he was an entertaining host and as cheerful and bright as the crimson roses in his garden.

Fortunately the Langkloof slips grew well and have been multiplied at Boschendal for distribution to other gardens. 'Crimson Glory' and 'Etoile de Hollande' have also been grown on their own roots and planted in a bed together with their crimson ancestor.

PLANT
Strong growing shrub with many stout stems having slightly hooked thorns of different sizes.

FOLIAGE
Five oval-round pointed leaflets with marked serrations and dark-green matt surfaces. Stalks are sturdy and have prickles; stipules are adnate, narrow, and light green.

FLOWERS
Round red buds open to half-full flowers about 8 cm in diameter. Petals are broad with wavy edges, crimson turning purple-maroon as they age. There are numerous short stamens around a bunch of hairy pistils. The calyx is cup-shaped and smooth. The sepals are long, pointed and unfoliated; they are slightly glandular on top and velvety on the underside. The very fragrant flowers appear in a flush in spring and autumn with fewer blooms in between.

INFLORESCENCE
Two or three flowers at the end of short side shoots at the top of the stems. Flower-stalks are glandular and the leaf-like bracts light green.

'Général Jacqueminot'

'Général Jacqueminot'.

'Black Prince' was a popular rose in Jan
Gysbert Hugo's garden at 'Non Pareille' in the
late 1800s when this photograph was taken.

The spectacular Hybrid Perpetual 'Souvenir du Dr Jamain' (1865), seen here at
Mottisfont, still grows at the Cape.

Babette Taute and the author
making notes about the old roses
in her garden.

'**B**lack Prince' was identified for me by Leonie and Isabel Hofmeyr.
It was one of the thousand roses that grew in their father's parsonage garden in Somerset East, and according to them, among the
most beautiful, and in its time a very popular Cape rose.

'Black Prince' was introduced by William Paul in 1866, twenty years
after he had written *The Rose Garden*, so I do not have his description
of this remarkably dark crimson rose with the delicious fragrance.

The one plant I was fortunate to see, from which I took cuttings, grew
in the garden of Mill River Farm where so many other old varieties
have survived. As my friend Babette Taute has a great love and appreciation for our cultural heritage, I am confident that her old tree
is being well cared for.

Another dear friend of mine, the late Choppie Botha, once told me
of a 'Black Prince' which used to grow in the garden belonging to her
grandmother, Hanna le Roux, on the farm Middelpos near De Rust.
The old lady was so fond of Choppie that after her husband's death
the little girl went to live with her and kept her Ouma warm at night
by sleeping behind her back.

Mrs le Roux adored the 'black rose' and often picked bunches to arrange indoors. At her husband's funeral 'Black Prince' was no doubt
prominent in the wreaths covering the coffin when the long funeral
procession moved down the silent street of De Rust for the memorial
church service. Choppie remembered the many flowers and the long
procession but was otherwise very much preoccupied in wiping off
the black shoe polish which was streaming down her face on that boiling hot afternoon. She and Bêdjie, her nursemaid, had thought that
her white panama hat would be unsuitable for her darling Oupa's funeral and had therefore improved the colour with black Nugget!

Choppie eventually became my neighbour and grew fields of roses
to pick for the Pretoria market. The favourite red rose then was 'Happiness' which she sold by the hundred, always complaining that red
roses lacked the fragrance of those she knew in her youth.

It is indeed a pity that the many dark-maroon roses which used to
fill Victorian gardens are now so rare. I have taken photographs of two
which were mentioned in almost all late 19th century Cape catalogues.
One is 'Francis Dubreuil' which I saw in David Rustan's magnificent
rose garden in South Australia, and the other is the lovely 'Dr Jamain'
which produced a marvellous show in the old rose garden at Mottisfont when I visited it in 1981.

'Francis Dubreuil' (1894), one of the very few
dark crimson Tea Roses, was a much-loved Victorian
rose at the Cape, but the only plant I could find
to photograph was in David Rustan's magnificent
rose nursery in S.W. Australia.

'Black Prince'

PLANT
*Branching shrub 1,5–2 metres high with robust smooth
stems and scattered strong hooked thorns.*

FOLIAGE
*Five oval dark-green shiny leaflets on strong stems with
small hooks on the underside. The stipules are smooth,
narrow and dark.*

FLOWERS
*Large well-formed buds open to full, very dark red flowers
with central petals in a loose whorl. Stamens are insignificant. The flowers on short side stems are usually solitary.
They are very fragrant and the shrub has blooms most of
the year.*

'Black Prince'.

Paradise garden
of my youth.

The double bed where my aunt and uncle slept was empty and through the window above my small iron bed the morning light was streaming into the room. I dressed quickly and ran through the long dining-room where the sun's rays through the opened top door lit up the shiny black peach-pip floor. 'Be careful of the poisonous Things.' Involuntarily I curled up my toes as the oft-repeated warning flashed through my mind, conjuring up hairy spiders and black scorpions which from time to time scurried past my feet in the dark.[1]

From the kitchen came the soft monotonous hum of my aunt's high voice; she sang without words but I recognized her favourite hymn, 'O goedheid Gods hier nooit volprese'.[2] The fire from the wooden stove picked out her slow movements as she poured coffee and sat down at the table, quietly.

Out on the back stoep, where large figs hung from their green arbour, I shuddered as I ran past the place where my cot used to stand when I was a baby. 'As we walked out of the door,' my mother had told me, 'this big female baboon was sitting next to your head — she wanted to steal you!' The baboons were not afraid of women and the troop would descend on the garden as soon as the men went out to the fields.

Down the stone steps, past the giant oak tree I ran, over the water furrow where we raced our boats made from the maroon-coloured bracts of the banana flowers. Past the orange grove where no ray of sunlight penetrated the dark-green leafy canopy and onto the gravel path I followed the water furrow. And there I saw him, with open-necked white shirt, black trousers and black waistcoat — my uncle!

He stretched out his hand and from the gnarled rough fingers the strength that dispelled all apprehension flowed through my small freckled hand, bringing peace and contentment.

'Gwendoline', he said, 'see how wonderful are God's creations; remember this beautiful morning and cherish it in your heart.' The pure white shasta daisies, tall blue agapanthus, clouds of white michaelmas daisies and enormous pink roses covering a tree next to him seemed to dwarf both of us: the magic moment gelled in my mind.

Now, some sixty years later, I can still recall that crisp summer morning, the singing birds, the water rushing down the stone furrow, the long border of flowers against the stone garden wall and the sweet fragrance of orange blossom and roses. Were the huge pink rose blooms a distortion of childish perception? I think not, for when I first saw 'Paul Neyron' flowering in Peter Beales' Norfolk garden in 1985 I was astounded at the size of the flowers. Could this be the rose of my uncle's garden? All the nurseries in Cape Town were, after all, selling this popular rose in the 1920s.

I have often been surprised to find or hear of solitary rare roses in

---

1 Outside doors in old Cape Dutch houses were often divided horizontally so that the upper leaf could be opened while the lower part remained shut to keep out stray animals. Mud floors were often inlaid with peach pips and finished with aloe juice which turned them black. The hairy 'Baboon spider', though more frightening, was not as poisonous as the 'Black Widow' which was also common in that district.

2 God's goodness and grace can never be fully appreciated here on earth.

'Paul Neyron'

'Paul Neyron' with the common
South African butterfly, *Acraea horta*.

The author admiring 'Paul Neyron' in
Peter Beales' garden in Norfolk.

the most unexpected places in the Cape: Eve Palmer was sent a plant
of 'Paul Neyron' from Mrs King's farm near Belfast; she also found a
second plant almost two thousand kilometres away in the Transvaal,
in the garden of a 19th century house near Dulstroom. I have not been
lucky enough to find even a single shrub of a rose which must have
been quite common early this century.

My uncle never travelled further from his farm in Moorreesburg than
a day's ride on his favourite horse would take him. However, once a
year his red Willys Overland was taken out of the wagon-house for
the trek to his fruit farm behind the Piquetberg mountains. For three
months all our relatives would gather there to process the fruit: the
women cooked jam, preserves and chutney in big black pots over open
fires under the ancient pear trees; they peeled peaches for drying in
the sun and boiled the must for *moskonfyt*. They made raisins and
gathered nuts, while the men distilled and tasted *witblits*.[3] All the
while we children swam, played and ate mulberries and watermelon
to our heart's content — and kept out of the way of the grown-ups.

My mother who taught singing in Stellenbosch joined us in her holidays and brought presents for everyone: 'Cape Sweets' and bananas
for my aunt; dolls and pretty new dresses for me. Did she bring slips
of 'Paul Neyron' for her brother's garden?

3 Clear white alcohol distilled from fermented fruit. Literally 'white lightning'.

PLANT
*The shrub is 1–1,5 metres high with many upright light-
green stems and thorns.*
FOLIAGE
*Five oval pointed light-green leaflets with smooth surfaces
on sturdy stalks; the underside is rough but has no thorns.
Stipules smooth, light green, entire.*
FLOWERS
*Large round pointed buds with longer foliated sepals open
to very full, very large dark-pink blooms 9–10 cm in diameter. As the flower opens the petals (of which there are
at least a hundred) form four dense untidy groups. The outer
petals are broad and the inner ones oval with long white
shanks. There are many stamens on white filaments and
branched styles with many cream stigmas. The calyx is a
shallow cone; the sepals quite long and leafy in the open
flower. Flowers appear throughout the year and are fragrant.*
INFLORESCENCE
*Single flowers at the tops of the branches on sturdy, slightly
rough stalks.*

A more sophisticated Victorian rose garden,
planned for the Cape Town Gardens, shows geometric
rose beds, trellis work and arched entrances to an
enclosed garden.

Bloemendal in Mowbray, taken in the late 19th
century. The garden shows round beds in the lawn
filled with Hybrid Perpetuals as well as a metal
arch in Eastern style, probably intended for Noisettes.
Devil's Peak rises in the background.

Posy from Stephen Brett's 1905 catalogue.

As I drove past the Pniel graveyard one day I thought I saw a bouquet of pink roses on a grave and stopped quickly to have a closer look. The graves were dappled with sunlight falling through overhanging oak branches already half bare and yellow-leaved in their autumn dress. The gravel on the paths and ground was dried out and baked hard by the long hot summer, yet as I approached the object of my curiosity I saw not the expected bouquet of roses in an old glass bottle, but a growing plant. It had many upright stems which were covered in luxuriant green foliage and topped with clear-pink cupped blooms neatly shaped and surrounded by long green foliated sepals. I was delighted by such an unexpected display of roses at that time of the year, and on bending down I was further rewarded with the most delicious scent. Nearby some labourers were digging a new grave with great difficulty, and I marvelled at the strength of soft rose roots, capable of extracting from the hard soil what was needed to produce such delicacy of flower and exquisite fragrance. Not wishing to disturb the pretty sight, I picked one flower to photograph and afterwards to plant as a slip. This was fortunate, for when I visited the grave again a few months later, the whole plant had disappeared.

Since its introduction by Bennett in 1857, 'Mrs John Laing' has been a popular rose in the Cape and highly praised by nurserymen and gardeners alike for its beautiful rosy-pink colouring, its ease of growth in the poorest of soils and its abundant blooms throughout the year. I have come across several old plants still flowering profusely in old cottage and farm gardens in the Boland, and it is one of the few old roses still stocked by rose nurseries.

As a picking flower it is most rewarding, for the long straight stems have few thorns, the strong blooms are easy to arrange and last long, while the fragrance permeates a room without being overwhelming. No wonder Dean Hole called it 'Beauty's Queen'!

'Mrs John Laing'

PLANT
A strong shrub growing up to 1,5 metres high, with many upright stems. It is practically thornless.

FOLIAGE
Five dark-green, long oval leaflets pointed at both ends. The surfaces are smooth and shiny above, velvety below, and the edges are serrated and glandular. The sturdy stalks have small hooks on the underside and the stipules are narrow with glandular edges.

FLOWERS
The large deep-pink globular buds with long foliated sepals open into very full cup-shaped flowers of about 8 cm in diameter. The firm, oval petals are clear pink, paler towards the shanks. Stamens of unequal length are haphazardly arranged around the short clump of white pistils. The narrow calyx is cone-shaped, glandular and has short bristles; sepals are large, much foliated, glandular above and velvety below. The main flush is in early spring but the plant has blooms for most of the year; the flowers are very fragrant.

INFLORESCENCE
Usually one per head on a sturdy glandular stalk.

'Mrs John Laing'.

175

God is
ons eene
Toevlugt.

'God is our only refuge'.

THE HYBRID TEAS

Roy Shepherd in his *History of the Rose* gives a very detailed account of how the first Hybrid Teas came to be grown and recognized as a separate class after 'La France' was introduced in 1867 by the Guillot nursery in Lyons.

According to him the earliest Hybrid Teas were mostly derived from the Tea roses 'Adam', 'Dr Grill' and 'Mme Bravy', which were used as open-pollinated seed parents. It was only after 1873, when Lacharme introduced 'Captain Christy', that breeders started to use Hybrid Perpetuals as seed parents.

For many years the earliest of these roses were classified either as Teas or Hybrid Perpetuals. In 1880 when the English breeder Henry Bennett visited Lyons, it was decided at a conference with the leading French nurserymen to call this new class 'Hybrid Teas'. The name took a while to catch on, however.

In 1898 for the first time the Hybrid Teas were separated by the Na-

tional Rose Society and judged as a class on their own. After this their reputation spread quickly through Europe and the Cape. By 1904 ten to fifteen per cent of roses offered in nursery catalogues were classified as Hybrid Teas (some still incorrectly), about thirty per cent were still Teas, and thirty per cent were Hybrid Perpetuals.

Their exciting colours as well as their new shape — tightly pointed central petals and reflexing outer petals — stimulated tremendous enthusiasm for the Hybrid Teas. At the Cape, new varieties were offered for sale very often within a year of their European introduction. This new class soon ousted all others, and the older roses were often saved solely by domestic workers for their cottage gardens or graveyards, where the rose-hunter may often be lucky still to find them.

But of the numerous Hybrid Teas introduced before 1910, very few are still in cultivation except where they are now being treasured in the gardens of old rose specialists.

Wedding photograph of Emily Olivier of Oudtshoorn who married Dr Heyns in April 1912. The bouquets of maidenhair and roses most probably contained 'La France', the most fashionable rose at that time.

OUDTSHOORN MUSEUM.

In 1867 the newly formed Society of Horticulture of Lyon appointed a panel of fifty judges to select a French rose which would be worthy of the name 'La France'. Out of more than one thousand entrants, they selected a pink rose that had been raised by Jean-Baptiste Guillot. It was their opinion that this rose might be the first of a new class — a cross between Tea and Hybrid Perpetual, and therefore, eventually to be called the Hybrid Teas. Although it is often stated that the parents of 'La France' were the full, creamy-white, fragrant Tea, 'Mme Bravy', and the bright crimson, globular, fragrant Hybrid Perpetual, 'Victor Verdier', M. Guillot himself did not know the parentage of his unique seedling.[1]

Not long after its European debut, 'La France' became immensely popular at the Cape. From Cape Town to the Karoo, from the coast to Namaqualand, wherever a garden contained roses, one of them was sure to be 'La France'; wherever an amateur artist painted roses, 'La France' would take the place of honour! How often I have listened to the praises of the beautiful pointed buds, the clear-pink reflexing petals flushed darker on the outside, the many blooms throughout the year, but above all, the exquisite fragrance. My mother-in-law insisted that, as she walked along a pavement, she could tell by its fragrance in which gardens 'La France' was blooming.

I have been told of how 'La Mode' de Villiers, a man who owned a fashion shop in Paarl, adored 'La France' roses. He married an Ameri-

can heiress and for many years owned the Klein Constantia estate where he entertained in grand style, after he had added a tennis-court, swimming-pool with summer-house, croquet lawn, music gallery, chapel, swan-filled lake, Japanese bridge and many terraces with pergolas, to the simple old farm complex. Many tales are told about this flamboyant personality, but best of all is the account of the burial which he arranged for his brother. On reaching the open grave, the mourners found that the earthen walls had been covered with chicken-mesh, and in the wire hundreds of 'La France' blooms had been secured to form a solid pink and very fragrant lining!

Today 'La France' rose trees are difficult to find in old Cape gardens and slips do not grow vigorously, but fortunately Ludwig's Nurseries in Pretoria are selling very healthy trees which are producing, throughout the year, copious blooms probably as beautiful and fragrant as those which grew in bygone Victorian gardens.

Eve Palmer told me that Ludwig's 'La France' roses were grown from bud-wood obtained from the garden at Cranemere, her family farm in the Camdeboo. I visited that garden a few years ago to try and identify 'Aunt Fanny's old roses' that Eve had described to me. Unfortunately on the afternoon when I arrived no 'La France' roses were in flower, but some 'Ophelia's and a large pink 'Sachsen Gruss' cast their spell over me and I dawdled in the beautiful old garden till the dark stormy sky had stolen all the light from the blooms.

---

1 J. Harkness, *The Makers of Heavenly Roses.*

'La France'

From Gowie's 1904 catalogue.

PLANT
A branching shrub 3–4 metres high with many hooked thorns.

FOLIAGE
Five or seven shiny oval leaflets on sturdy stalks with prickles on the undersurfaces.

FLOWERS
Pointed buds open to light-pink flowers of about 8 cm in diameter. The outer petals, curling back on their edges, reflex away from the inner, slightly pointed ball of unfolded petals. 'La France' can be distinguished from other pink roses by the darker pink colour on the back of the petals. The cup-shaped calyx is smooth and the quickly reflexing sepals are velvety on the undersurfaces. Many stamens surround the mass of hairy pistils which have thin branched styles. Flowers appear throughout the year and are exceptionally fragrant.

INFLORESCENCE
One to three flowers in a corymb at the tops of the branches.

'La France'.

'Irish Elegance'

At the beginning of the 20th century a number of single-flowered Hybrid Teas were raised mainly in the Northern Irish nurseries of A. Dickson and Sam McGredy. They were an instant success and even attained a certain amount of snob value. 'All these Irish roses', H. McFarland observed, 'belong in the gardens of those who appreciate simple beauty.' They bloomed freely over a long time and so produced a constant show throughout the summer months.

From Ireland they were quickly brought to the Cape, for in those days there were no import restrictions. So, soon after their introduction in 1900, arrived the pinky-crimson 'Irish Glory' and pure white 'Irish Beauty' from A. Dickson, followed by his scarlet 'Engineer' four years later, and then in 1905 came 'Irish Elegance' and 'Irish Fireflame' in 1914, both in apricot-yellowy colours.

I was fortunate to find a plant of 'Irish Elegance' in a Stellenbosch garden recently and was immediately charmed with the long pointed orange buds and lovely colouring of the large single flowers. The cuttings I took grew very easily and the plants are healthy and quite vigorous. All early 20th century writers agree that these plants should hardly be pruned and that 'Irish Elegance' will eventually grow into a very pretty shrub. H. R. Darlington in his *Roses* (1911) believed it to be 'the most decorative rose we have'.

I remember an occasion when we as senior prefects of the Rhenish Girls High School had been invited to tea with the principal in her private sitting-room before leaving the school. I could not keep my eyes off a silver vase in which only two single roses had been arranged. We were in great awe of Miss Siggs, so it was with some hesitation that I asked her the names of the two roses. She looked at me with her penetrating blue eyes and said, 'It is strange how few people see the beauty around them. I know that you do, and so your life should be filled with happiness.' I never forgot her words nor the two roses in the silver vase. The one was 'Dainty Bess', the other 'Irish Elegance'.

'Irish Elegance'.

'Dainty Bess' and 'Cécile Brunner' in an old castor oil bottle.

'Gruss an Teplitz'

PLANT
A branched shrub 1–2 metres high with many hooked thorns.

FOLIAGE
Five oval dark-green leaflets with shiny surfaces and deeply serrated edges. New leaves have a reddish-bronze colour. Stipules are adnate and smooth.

FLOWERS
Round buds with longer foliated sepals open to full cupped flowers. The petals are of a wine-red colour and have white shanks. There are many stamens which have long filaments. The hairy styles are bunched together, each one having two small red stigmas. The calyx is cup-shaped and has a few glands. The flowers appear throughout the year and are very fragrant.

INFLORESCENCE
Solitary flowers appear on short side branchlets at the tops of the stems.

'Gruss an Teplitz'.

This is another very fragrant crimson rose which is directly descended from 'Fellemberg'. 'Gruss an Teplitz' shows many characteristics of the China roses, but is now more commonly classed with the Hybrid Teas. It was introduced by P. Lambert in 1897 and grown in Cape Town gardens shortly afterwards.

A writer in the *Cape Amateur Garden* of 1913 recommended that a double row of 'Gruss an Teplitz' plants set just under a metre apart with positions alternating in the two rows, made an excellent hedge. As the growth is not as angular as that of 'Fellemberg', less pruning is required to keep the hedge in shape.

The flowers are fuller and larger than those of 'Fellemberg', the heads less inclined to nod, and the deep crimson of the petals more colourful. The wonderful spicy fragrance of its ancestor has fortunately been inherited. A hedge of this rose is almost evergreen and seldom without flowers.

This was one of the roses I found growing at the 'Auld House', ancestral home of the Barrys in Swellendam, when I first started looking for old roses. Slips made from the Barry plants grew as easily as most China roses usually do, so that 'Gruss an Teplitz' now brings fragrance to the gardens of many friends. In the meantime my youngest daughter had married the present owner of the 'Auld House' (no longer a Barry), and as the mother plant has disappeared from the garden we are making enough plants for a new hedge. This is undoubtedly one of the most invaluable roses for bringing fragrance into the garden and home.

'Sachsen Gruss'

'Frau Karl Druschki' in the autumn.

'Sachsen Gruss'.

'Sachsen Gruss', introduced in 1912 as a cross between 'Frau Karl Druschki' and 'Mme Jules Gravereaux', possesses all the admirable qualities of her mother and was as popular in the Cape. I have found beautiful plants surviving on many old graves, where the clear icing-sugar pink flowers attract one from afar.

Before it was damaged by fire, a particularly fine tree in the old Muslim cemetery below Groote Schuur Hospital gave pleasure to many passers-by. I nearly landed in serious trouble for snipping slips off this tree, but later realized that the justifiably irate caretaker had been more upset by the exuberant antics of my two small poodles for desecrating the dishevelled graves of the Muslim ancestors, than by my assault on the rose tree. I apologised profusely and we parted on very good terms.

'Frau Karl Druschki'

PLANT

A very vigorous branched shrub sometimes growing to 3 metres high, with many short grey-brown hooked thorns.

FOLIAGE

Five large oval dark-green leaflets with glossy smooth surfaces and finely serrated margins. The sturdy stalk has a few tiny glands and many sharp hooked thorns on the underside. Stipules are adnate, shiny and narrow.

FLOWERS

Large pointed white buds tinged crimson open to full cupped flowers about 10 cm in diameter, with large white petals. When fully opened, the many stamens on very fine white filaments and the short creamy green stigmas are visible in the centre of the loose flower. The calyx, small for the flower, is cup-shaped and smooth; the sepals with leafy tips and a few small folioles are large and glandular along the edges. The flowers appear throughout the year and are entirely scentless.

INFLORESCENCE

Groups of one to three flowers on short strong glandular stalks which have short red bristles.

Hip.   'Frau Karl Druschki'.

Introduced in 1901 by Lambert, this rose is the result of a cross between 'Merveille de Lyon' and 'Mme Caroline Testout'. It appeared only a few years later in the Cape, where gardeners greeted it with great enthusiasm. 'Frau Karl Druschki' was soon sold by every nursery throughout the Colony. So we read in the 1905 catalogue of Smith Bros from Uitenhage that this was 'still the finest white rose' — perhaps their reason for selling it at five times the price of other rose plants! Their claims were certainly extravagant: 'We have no hesitation in recommending it with confidence, not only as a first class exhibition rose, but as a garden variety of great merit. In fact, we must add that we consider this Rose the "FINEST IN THE WORLD". Hugh Manson in his *Rose Culture* was still enthusiastic in 1910: 'This beautiful creation may be grown to the highest possible perfection for exhibition.'

Wherever one finds remains of early 20th century gardens, this is the rose which inevitably survives, for it is extremely tough, disease-resistant and no amount of neglect seems to discourage its flow of large white blooms throughout spring, summer and autumn. It is one of the few old roses which is still sold by nurseries. Amateur gardeners would do well to buy it, as they will soon have a large tree with many flowers most of the year.

For flower arrangements the large white roses have proved to be extremely useful because of their long stems and sturdy flowers which last well when brought indoors. What a tragedy that the 'White American Beauty' or 'Snow Queen', as non-Germans once called this rose,[1] should have not the slightest whiff of fragrance.

1 J. P. Duminee remembers in his book *Twilight over the Tygerberg* that the name was changed to 'Snow Queen' 'during the Kaiser's war'. There were many of these 'aery white roses' in his father's garden at 'Sea View', their home in Tygerberg near Cape Town.

From left to right:
Against the Drakenstein mountains.
At Genadendal.
With 'Giant of Battles' at Boschendal.

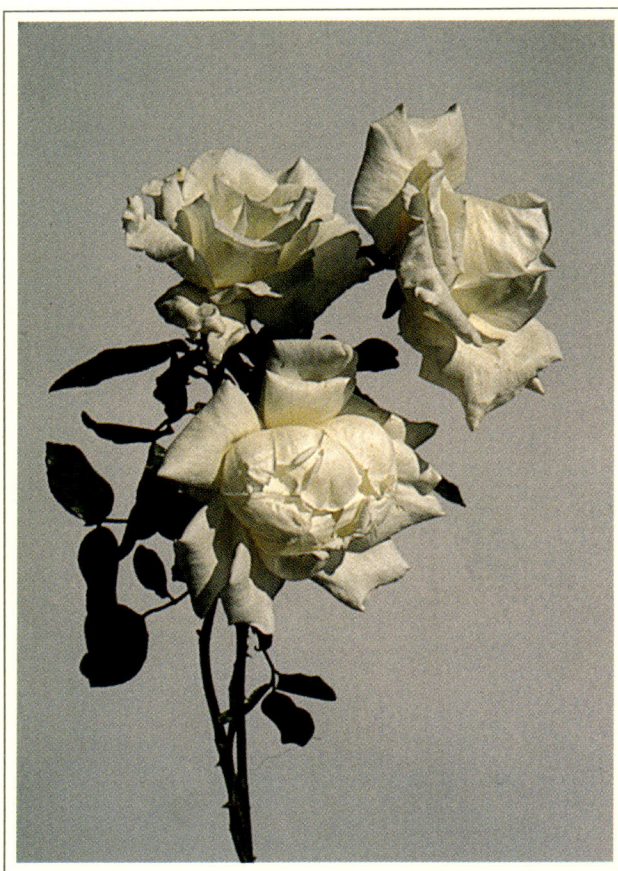

Just as snow transforms the most dismal European landscape into a breathtaking spectacle, so the Cape spring covers untidy old graveyards with a multicoloured carpet of indigenous flowers and sheets of white roses, changing them into havens of delight. 'White Banksia', *Rosa laevigata*, *R. fortuniana* and 'Mrs Herbert Stevens' were the favourite roses to plant on Victorian graves, though the pink 'Blush Damask' was not frowned upon, especially as this was such a drought-resisting rose. Too soon however, the spring annuals and ramblers drop their flowers and then the two shrub roses have to fight the dreariness with occasional bursts of white flowers on untrimmed lanky branches.

This was how I first came across 'Mrs Herbert Stevens', McGredy's 1910 white Hybrid Tea, in the old Stellenbosch cemetery. The sturdy long branches of a shrub two metres high were bending down over broken cast-iron railings under the weight of many large white roses. I asked the caretaker whether I might pick a rose and he generously handed me several large sprays, at the same time hacking back most of the remaining bush to impress upon the plant that its allotted terri-

tory was behind the bars.

The slips made from these branches have grown into vigorous plants so that in many Cape gardens 'Mrs Herbert Stevens' is as much appreciated as it used to be at the beginning of this century.

This rose is much more graceful than its parent 'Frau Karl Druschki', and also retains a great deal of the charm of its other parent, the Tea rose 'Niphetos'. The bud is delicate, though not by far as fine as the long foliated bud of 'Niphetos' which was much in demand for buttonholes in the early 1900s. Fortunately 'Mrs Stevens' inherited the sweet fragrance of its Tea parent, which makes it a most superior rose for me.

When I visited Nancy Steen's garden in Auckland in November 1986, I noticed that she had used the climbing form in her white garden. Hanging from the trees next to a simple white bench, the flowers lit up the evening shadows like Chinese lanterns, and I thought how pleasant it would have been if I could have sat on the little white bench with this pioneer of heritage roses in New Zealand, talking about her garden and telling her about the old roses growing at the Cape.

'Mrs Herbert Stevens'

'Mrs Herbert Stevens' (slightly enlarged)

'Niphetos' buds from Gowie's 1905 catalogue.

PLANT
A lanky shrub 1,5–2 metres high, with many brown hooked thorns. There is also a climbing form.

FOLIAGE
Five oval acuminate, light-green leaflets with smooth shiny surfaces and finely serrated edges. The stalk is sturdy with tiny glands but no thorns. Stipules are wide and short, entire with tiny glands on the edges.

FLOWERS
Long pointed white buds with shortish sepals open to full flowers of about 8 cm in diameter. When the broad outer satiny white petals with 'torn-off' edges open, the inner ones remain folded over each other to the centre; these finally open to form a loose flower, revealing the many thin white stamens and short fleshy pistils. The calyx is cup-shaped and smooth. The sepals have many small folioles and reflex quickly; they have small glands on the outer surfaces but are velvety on the inside. The flowers appear throughout the year and are sweetly fragrant.

INFLORESCENCE
One flower on a short stalk which has small glands and a few soft bristles.

'Mrs Herbert Stevens' in Nancy Steen's garden.

185

Species roses and their hybrids at Ida's Valley.

THE SPECIES ROSES

Over an enormous variety of climate and terrain, stretching from the icy waters of Alaska to the hot sands of Ethiopia, in habitats as diverse as the Sacramento Mountains of New Mexico, the hot beaches of Bengal or the vast plains of Siberia, in all these places the ancestors of our modern garden roses — the wild roses of the world — have been growing for centuries untold.

Almost two hundred varieties of these species roses have been described, some only knee height, others climbing to incredible heights, yet all have the simple flower pattern of five petals surrounding a crown of golden stamens and central pistil, except for *Rosa sericea* which alone has four petals.

Despite its modest size, this simple flower has through the ages entwined itself in the hearts and minds of men, and assumed an importance far above all other flowers — symbol of passionate love, of virginity, of innocence and of re-awakening.

In spring, the Eskimo crowns himself with *Rosa eglanteria* as it appears through the melting snow, while in England children once danced around their maypoles wearing chaplets of the same rose.

And if we look at *Rosa willmottiae*, wild rose of the cold Tibetan heights, we must bow in reverence to a little flower which has been on the earth many millions of years before man made his appearance.

Although the wild roses for so long and in so many places have formed a part of the natural environment, for some strange reason they have never felt at home south of the equator. And so the first roses that were picked at the point of Africa were garden roses brought from their northern homes along with the many other commodities that were to ease the lives of the 17th century Dutch settlers at the foot of Table Mountain.

Soon after the Dutch established their victualling station at the Cape of Good Hope to supply ships bound for the East with fresh produce, they began to import European species roses, no doubt for their medicinal value. For rose hips are rich in Vitamin C, the specific substance that heals scurvy and builds up resistance to the debilitating diseases that in those times took such a heavy toll of ships' crews.

'Arrival of the long-expected *Ghyn* in a most miserable condition. All the men were suffering from scurvy, 80 were laid up, 21 had died . . . In the latitude of the Cape they were becalmed 50 days, and were sadly distressed with their sick', reads a typical entry in the governor's diary, made on 16 May 1710.

Chinese and Japanese wild roses arrived from the East at the turn of the 18th century; around this time the so-called Cape 'dog rose' *(Rosa laevigata)* was widely used for boundary hedges.

In the 19th century, after the Cape had become a British colony, the new settlers brought the rose of their country lanes — *Rosa eglanteria* — to use for hedging material where they settled on Eastern Province farms. Away from their natural enemies, these hedges eventually ran wild and today the Eglantine is a noxious weed in certain areas.

Then, towards the end of the 19th century, as plant collectors such as Ernest Wilson introduced new Eastern species to Western gardens, Cape gardeners eagerly imported these newly discovered plants for their gardens, or for landscape work on larger estates.

As properties were subdivided and gardens became smaller, however, the species roses have had to make way for more compact shrubs, and now one seldom sees the scrambling hedges, or large specimens which were once so picturesque a part of the Cape countryside.

Rosa eglanteria

'Meg Merrilies'.

From left to right:
Some of Mary Lawrence's Sweet Briers:
'Semi-double Sweet Brier'.
'Manning's Blush Sweet Brier'.
'Double Red Sweet Brier'.

'Common Sweet Brier'.
'Royal Sweet Brier'.
'Double Mossy Sweet Brier'.

Since Elizabethan times or perhaps even further back in English history, this insignificant little pink rose, with thorny branches and sweetly scented leaves, has been the most loved and favoured of all the wild roses growing in the English countryside.

In the mid-16th century Rembertus Dodoneus, Professor of Botany at Leyden, described how the Eglantine was planted together with 'tame' roses in Western gardens even though 'It is like to the wild rose plant, [*Rosa canina*] in sharpe and cruell shootes . . . but with greener leaves of a pleasanter smell'.[1] By 1581 Mathias de Lobel mentions that both single and double Eglantines were being grown as garden plants.[2]

John Gerard in his famous herbal provides more detail on the 17th century Eglantines: 'the fruit is long, of colour somewhat red, like a little olive stone, and like the little heads or berries of the others, but lesser than those of the garden: in which is contained rough cotton, or hairie downe and seed, folded and wrapped up in the same, which is small and hard.' He too describes a double garden form: 'We have in our London gardens another Sweet Brier, having greater leaves, and much sweeter: the flowers likewise are greater, and somewhat doubled, exceeding sweet of smell, wherein it differeth from the former.'

Towards the end of the 17th century the Eglantine was still the only wild rose grown together with 'tame roses' in Dutch gardens: 'de Eglantier worden hier te Lande in de Hoven geoeffent en onderhouden' wrote Petrus Nylandt in his *Kruytboek* of 1680, warning gardeners that all roses should be planted from suckers in the full moon if they were to produce an abundance of flowers.

Nylandt was a doctor of medicine and his herbal contained remedies for every conceivable disease: a potion prepared from a handful of rose hips boiled up in a pint of wine was his cure for excessive menstruation, white vaginal discharge and 'Druppel-pisse' (difficulty with passing water). No wonder that the Eglantine with its generous hip production should have been such a popular garden plant in 17th century gardens!

Linnaeus named the Sweet Brier *Rosa eglanteria*[3] but in later publications caused considerable confusion by using this name for *rosa foetida* and calling the Sweet Brier *Rosa rubiginosa*, which alludes to the rust-coloured glands below the leaves. *Rosa rubiginosa* was subsequently used by botanists until it was decided to retain Linnaeus' original name, and so *Rosa eglanteria* with its literary associations is today the accepted botanical name.

Mutation and spontaneous hybridization with other roses produced further double forms of Eglantine, and by 1799 Mary Lawrance could illustrate five kinds.[4]

The most interesting of all these early cultivars was *Rosa rubiginosa zabeth* (as it was then known) named after Queen Elizabeth I. It was believed that the essential oil of this rose formed an ingredient of an extract which the queen herself made up. Its virtues were described as follows: 'It wonderfully strengthens the head — the heart and other parts of the human body, it restores the spirit, restores the memory and remarkably improves the power of procreation.'[5]

By 1848 William Paul could describe fifteen double varieties of the favourite 'Rose of the Poets', with imaginative names such as 'Celestial', 'Elvira', 'Hessoise', 'La Belle Distinguée' and 'Clementine'.[6] The latter, which was found growing alongside a country lane in Cheshire far from habitation, had probably arisen as a spontaneous hybrid between *Rosa eglanteria* and a *Rosa damascena* hybrid. This old rose, which is so beautifully depicted by Ellen Willmott,[7] was reintroduced by Wil-

liam Paul in 1892 under the name of 'Janet's Pride', and was being advertised in Cape nurseries as a 'new' rose in 1906![8]

It was apparently this natural hybrid that inspired Lord Penzance to work with Sweet Briers on a hybridizing program between 1890 and 1895. He produced sixteen new varieties that were distributed by the English nursery, Keynes Williams & Co. of Salisbury. Some of these roses were named after characters from Sir Walter Scott's novels such as 'Meg Merrilies' (1894), gay, single, crimson, with very fragrant foliage; or 'Rose Bradwardine' (1894), a vigorous plant with clusters of warm pink flowers. Both these roses grew at the Cape in the early 1900s together with the coppery 'Lady Penzance', but according to Dorothea Fairbridge these Penzance hybrids were not as vigorous in the Western Cape as one would have expected.[9]

Recently 'Meg Merrilies' has been planted with great success in the Swellendam Drostdy gardens and in Maisie Knox-Shaw's garden in Elgin where it grows very well, giving a wonderful show in the spring and again in the autumn when the numerous hips turn a bright cherry-red. But the Sweet Brier itself is noticeably absent from plant lists and records of the Western Cape after its first introduction by Commander Jan van Riebeeck in 1657, although one sometimes sees scraps of old hedges lingering along forgotten farm tracks this side of the Hexriver mountains. I have also noticed very old bushes on the Kromrivier farm in the Koue Bokkeveld.

It is as one travels up the east coast, however, that the Eglantine becomes much more common, growing wild alongside the road between Joubertina and Avontuur, on farm werfs in the Graaff-Reinet district or in graveyards of the Langkloof. By the time one reaches Barkley East, 'dog rose' hedges are to be seen everywhere, and in the Stormberg and the Katberg it has found a habitat so much to its liking that it has gone romping across the veld to make a pest of itself.[10]

These are the parts of the Cape Colony which were settled by almost four thousand British immigrants in the 1820s, when the British Governor, Lord Charles Somerset, decided that considerable expense could be avoided by replacing the military troops in this war-ridden frontier with a denser civil population. On arrival, the settlers (who had not been told where they were to be granted land) had to adapt themselves to an inhospitable environment where wild animals abounded and local tribes burnt down their homes, took their cattle and threatened their daily lives. How they must have longed for the tranquil, landscaped English countryside! Sweet Brier was imported at an early date to the Eastern Province for use as hedging material, and perhaps the fragrance of rose foliage after a hectic rainstorm might have assisted at times to calm jagged nerves and to 'strengthen the spirit' of those brave pioneers.

On the old family farm Wheatlands in the Graaff-Reinet district, I found remnants of *R. eglanteria* hedges probably planted by Thomas Parkes soon after he had acquired the 3 000 morgen in 1849. At that time there were well-established vineyards, fruit orchards and lucerne fields. Quince hedges already surrounded the vineyards and pomegranates bordered the homestead garden, but Parkes added Sweet Brier hedges around his new vineyards. 'Limy soil', said Hazel Short, the present owner, 'produces the best brandy, and as Wheatlands' brandy was considered to be of the finest in the country, it was always to be found on the Governor's table!' When ostrich and sheep farming became more lucrative at the turn of the 19th century, brandy-making was stopped at Wheatlands and the vines removed, leaving only parts of the old Eglantine hedges as a reminder of her forefather's brandy prowess.

1 R. Dodoneus, *Cruijdeboeck*, first published Antwerp, 1554. The English translation is by Henry Lyte.
2 M. Lobelius, *Cruydtboeck*, London, 1580, reprinted 1605.
3 In his *Hortus Cliffortianus*, 1737.
4 In her *'Collection of Roses'.*

5 From Rosenberg's *Rhodologia*.
6 *The Rose Garden*, 1848.
7 *The Genus Rosa*, Vol. 2.
8 Smith Brothers of Uitenhage, 1906 plant catalogue.
9 *Gardens of South Africa*, 1925.

10 In 1986 I noticed remnants of Eglantine hedging along many country roads in the Clare valley in South Australia and was told that there too it has become a noxious weed.

Rosa eglanteria

SWEET BRIER, EGLANTINE

'Janet's Pride' from Ellen
Willmott's *The Genus Rosa.*

Rosa eglanteria.

PLANT
*Graceful arching shrub to 2 metres high with many grey
hooked thorns often in pairs just below the branchlets.*

FOLIAGE
*Five small oval leaflets about 20 mm long with evenly ser-
rated glandular edges, matt top surfaces and slightly velvety
undersides. The leaf-stalk is short and glandular with small
prickles underneath. Stipules are short and wide with
glandular edges. Leaves have an apple fragrance.*

FLOWERS
*From small oval buds with long foliated sepals emerge
single light-pink flowers, each with five broad heart-
shaped petals around a neat circle of yellow stamens on
cream filaments and a short knob of pistils in the centre.
The flower-stalk is short and has many stalked glands and
bristles, and two short, green, glandular bracts at the base.
The calyx is goblet-shaped and glandular with many spines;
sepals are elongated, daintily foliated, glandular and velvety
on the inside.*

INFLORESCENCE
*Flowers appear only in spring, usually in threes on the ends
of small branchlets. The hips are a bright shiny red with
bristles at the proximal end.*

Hips.

Rosa canina

Parkinson's sketch of the beduduar caused by a wasp sting on the stem of *Rosa canina*.

This is the true Dog Rose, which occurs so frequently along the English country lanes that Gerard in 1597 found it too common to describe: 'it were too small purpose to use many words in the description thereof: for even children with delight eat the berries thereof when they be ripe, make chaines and other prettie gewgawes of the fruit; cookes and gentlewomen make tarts and such like dishes for pleasure thereof, and therefore this shall suffice for the description.'[1]

In the Cape any single rose, whether large, small, white, pink or yellow will be called a 'Dog Rose', and few people realize that the brier with small pink flowers, which is the best-known of all British roses, received its canine association from Pliny who believed that its root contained a remedy 'against the biting of a mad dog', which might explain why the Greeks called it *Cynosbatos* or 'Dog Berry'.[2]

Rosa canina grows naturally in Western Europe and South West Asia and was consequently well known in Holland in the early days of the Cape Colony, yet I could find no record of its presence in early Dutch gardens at the Cape. Perhaps here too there was no mention of it because it was too common! As it grew so easily from seed or slips one can hardly imagine that the Dutch would not have planted a rose with so many virtues at the Cape, either as hedges in city gardens or along farm boundaries.

I have seen remnants of such *Rosa canina* hedging growing on the river banks of 'The Oaks', a beautiful old farm near Greyton, and fifty years ago there were still hedges of *R. canina* growing in the old Company's Garden in the centre of Cape Town, but these have now disappeared.

In the days when import control was not so strictly applied, many Cape gardeners acquired their roses directly from European nurseries. As *Rosa canina* was the understock most commonly used from 1820 onwards, large shrubs of it are often to be seen in the midst of old rose gardens, where they have shot up from the roots of some favourite Hybrid Perpetual and have been allowed to remain perhaps for the sweetly fragrant flowers or the numerous cheerful bunches of shiny red hips in the autumn.

These hips, which in John Parkinson's days were still 'much devoured by the poorer sort of women and children that eat them gladly,'[3] are rich in vitamin C, and the earliest herbalists prescribed them for scurvy, for spitting of blood (tuberculosis) and for all kinds of coughs and other chest complaints. The seeds were also found valuable for treating kidney stones. The pulp is pleasantly acid and was best preserved, according to Culpeper, by beating it up with sugar to form a conserve.[4]

In the 17th and 18th centuries rose conserve was exported annually by the Dutch from the Cape to the East, but it is not clear which rose was used for this purpose, though it might very well have been *Rosa canina*.

A peculiarity of *Rosa canina* that applies also to *Rosa eglanteria* is that they are both susceptible to the attack of a wasp which causes an exudation of a spongy material on the stem 'rough hayred and of a green colour turning towards red'. This so-called 'brier-ball', also known as 'Beduduar' by the early apothecaries, was thought to cure baldness: 'Stamped with honey and ashes [it] causeth haires to grow which are fallen through the disease called alopecia'.[5] Like the seeds, it was also used for kidney stones and difficulty in passing water.

A row of *Rosa canina* which I planted at Boschendal has grown into a graceful arching hedge 2 metres high within two years and while I write is covered with red hips. I have a good mind to take my vitamin C in coming winters in the form of a rose conserve which should be far tastier than the white synthetic pills of the modern apothecary.[6]

White *Rosa canina*.

1 Gerard's *Herball*, 1633 edition. Chapter 3: 'Of the Wilde Roses'.
2 Pliny, *Natural History*, Book XXV.
3 John Parkinson, *The Theatre of Plants*, 1640, Chapter 26.
4 Culpeper's *Complete Herbal and English Physician*, 1826, facsimile reprint 1981.

5 Dodoneus in the sixth part of his *History of Plants*, translated by Henry Lyte, 1619.
6 According to Miller's *Gardener's Dictionary*, 1807, the hips were 'agreeable enough when ripe and mellowed by frost: Beaten up with sugar it makes a pleasant conserve, more used as a vehicle for other medicines than any virtue of its own'.

190

Rosa canina

Hips.

Pink *Rosa canina.*

PLANT

A graceful, arching shrub to 5 metres high with many small brownish-grey hooked thorns, all of the same size.

FOLIAGE

Five pointed leaflets with mid-green dull surfaces and bidentate finely serrated edges. Stalks thin and dainty, rough below, but with no hooks. Stipules are wide like little wings with two loose points, edges smooth.

FLOWERS

Tiny oval buds with long foliated sepals open to single pink or white flowers 5 cm in diameter, with heart-shaped petals and a single ring of many stamens on thin long filaments around a short club-shaped bunch of pistils. The calyx is goblet-shaped, with a smooth shiny surface like the short flower-stalk. Much-branched sepals are very dainty, long and tapering, rough on the outer surface and velvety on the inside. The flowers appear only in late spring and are sweetly fragrant.

INFLORESCENCE

One to three flowers on small branchlets at the top of the shrub.

FRUIT

Many oval, shiny, smooth, cherry-red hips appear in the autumn.

Rosa glauca

Jacquin's painting in *Fragmenta Botanica*.

Hips.

O ver the last ten years this rose, formerly known as *Rosa rubrifolia*, has been made available through the few South African nurseries that are prepared to import old shrub and species roses. I think they have chosen this wild European rose because the distinctive reddish tinge of the dainty leaves has made it famous for flower arrangements, at present a very popular art form amongst South African housewives. I myself find not only the leafy branches, but the light-pink flowers and smooth shiny calyces with persistent long expanded sepals particularly charming for miniature arrangements.

According to Loudon the plant, which is indigenous to Dauphine, Savoy, the Pyrenees and Austria, was first described by Villars at whose funeral branches of these rose-coloured flowers were strewn over the grave.[1]

Jacquin's *Fragmenta Botanica* has a particularly fine illustration of this rose which is reproduced here.[2]

Rosa glauca may have been growing at the Cape since the early 19th century, but there is unfortunately no record of when it was first introduced. In 1940 it was still being recommended for use as 'specimens in the herbaceous and ornamental borders or as hedges on boundaries and open woodland estates'.[3]

I have found it a difficult plant to grow and other gardening friends have the same complaint, for although it does not die, the plant is slow to push out new shoots. Perhaps we should try adding more lime to the Cape soil which is probably too acid for its liking.

1 *An Encyclopaedia of Plants*, 1836. Loudon called it 'The red
   leaved Dog Rose'.
2 1800–1809, T. 106.
3 *The S.A. Rose Book*, by 'The Vicar', 1940.

Rosa glauca

Rosa glauca.

PLANT
A dainty shrub 2 metres high, with many thin arching stems and a few scattered thorns.

FOLIAGE
Five oval puce-grey leaflets with edges markedly serrated; surfaces matt on top, greyer below. Very dainty leaf-stalks have a few scattered glands on the underside but no thorns. Stipules are short with smooth edges, free tips and are puce-coloured along the central axes.

FLOWERS
Quite a large bud opens to a small, very dainty, single, light-pink flower of 4 cm in diameter. The petals are flushed darker towards the tips and have deeply indented edges. The flower-stalk is short, straight and has many stalked glands. Many yellow stamens on short filaments surround a number of short pistils with small cream stigmas. The calyx is smooth, puce-coloured and has long, thin, very dainty, tapering, unfoliated sepals edged with glands. The flowers, not markedly fragrant, appear in spring on short side branch-lets at the top of the stems.

INFLORESCENCE
Consists of a corymb of two to three flowers, usually one open at a time.

'Williams' Double Yellow'

The original wild rose, *Rosa pimpinellifolia*,[1] was well known to Dutch 16th and 17th century herbalists who called it the 'dune rose'.[2] According to Dodoneus, it was not highly regarded: 'The whole plant is base and low, and the least of all both of the garden and wild kind of roses,' he wrote.[3] This may be the reason why this rose does not appear in the records of the Cape Colony.

A variety of *Rosa pimpinellifolia* which I believe to be 'Grandiflora' (known in Europe since the early 19th century) was however grown in the Cape, but I have no knowledge of when it was first introduced. In the *S.A. Rose Book* by 'The Vicar' (1940) it is mentioned as one of the best-known species roses to be used as a shrub.

I have seen a tall hedge of *Rosa pimpinellifolia* 'Grandiflora' in Oudtshoorn growing together with 'Albéric Barbier', the single and fully quartered flowers, both cream, making a very pretty sight against the dark-green foliage. It is now sold by a few nurseries as *R. altaica* and is therefore once again appearing in rose gardens.

Another Scotch rose at present growing in Cape gardens was sent out from Kew in 1968 in a collection of 18th century roses intended for the restoration of the garden at Government House. This small yellow rose was labelled '*Rosa spinosissima lutea plena*',[4] and is also known as 'Williams' Double Yellow'.

As these Kew roses were turned down by the chief Public Works gardener, who was responsible for executing our plan, they eventually found a home in the restored Boschendal garden where they formed the core of what was later to become an extensive old rose collection.

The initial two 'Williams' Double Yellow' plants have in a few years multiplied and spread to cover a large area on a bank planted with Damask roses from the same Kew collection. As both these roses flower for only a few weeks in spring and early summer, I have underplanted them with *Amaryllis belladonna* to give a show in autumn, with tall and low-growing pink fuchsias, with santolina to provide patches of grey, with heliotrope and rosemary for their fragrance, and with a scattering of Monthly Roses and the miniature *Rosa lawranceana* to give colour throughout the year.

'Williams' Double Yellow' resulted from a cross between *Rosa foetida* and *Rosa pimpinellifolia* and was first introduced as a garden variety by John Williams from Lancaster in 1828. It is also known as the 'Old Double Yellow Scots Rose' or 'Prince Charlie's Rose'.

I have since discovered that this little rose is quite difficult to control, for it sends out runners in all directions to form a thick undergrowth of very prickly shoots. Fortunately I have enough room on the Boschendal bank, and in spring the numerous bright yellow flowers never fail to delight visitors, so that many of them have gone home with the gift of a small prickly plant. The miniature leaflets, tiny blooms and dark maroon hips are so different from other roses that most gardeners are fascinated by them.

'Williams' Double Yellow'.

From Parkinson's *Theatre of Plants.*

PLANT
A suckering shrublet 0,5 metres high with many upright brown stemmed shoots covered in numerous straight thorns and bristles.

FOLIAGE
Five or seven very small, finely serrated sessile leaflets 10–15 mm long on dark-green, very dainty stems, bristly on the underside. Stipules are large in proportion.

FLOWERS
Small light-yellow buds with longer sepals open to semi-double yellow flowers with cordate petals. The few rows of stamens have yellow filaments and anthers crowding in towards a bunch of pale greeny-cream stigmas. The calyx is smooth but the flower-stalk has a few thin bristles. Sepals are long and narrow, unfoliated, velvety on the under-surface and stretch upwards after the petals have fallen. The flowers appear in spring and early summer and have a very sweet faint fragrance.

INFLORESCENCE
Single flowers on short side branchlets at intervals along the main shoots.

FRUIT
The hips are round and have the dark-puce colour of all Burnet roses.

1 Formerly *Rosa spinosissima*. This class is also known as the Scotch or Burnet roses.
2 Petrus Nylandt, *Kruydtboeck*, 1680: 'De Duynerooskens worden aan de zeekant in de Duynen gevonden.'
3 *Cruijdeboeck* (1554). From Henry Lyte's translation (1619).
4 It is no longer known by this name.

Rosa pimpinellifolia 'Grandiflora'

'Stanwell Perpetual' has been growing at the Cape since shortly after its introduction in 1838. It was found to be especially useful as a hedge rose. (Half size)

PLANT
Many erect stems up to 1,5 metres high with numerous straight grey thorns of varying lengths.

FOLIAGE
Seven or nine sessile leaflets 2 cm long with markedly serrated edges, on dainty, stiff leaf-stalks. The stipules are narrow and loose from the stalk for more than half their length.

FLOWERS
The round buds with longish sepals open to semi-double creamy white flowers about 7 cm in diameter. Petals in the outer row are oblong with notched edges, the inner ones much smaller and curling inwards. There are many short yellow stamens around a bunch of short styles. The calyx is round, shiny and smooth, like the flower-stalk. Sepals are smooth, entire, long and tapering, reflexing outwards in the open flower, folding upwards when the petals fall. The flowers appear in spring and sometimes produce a few blooms again in autumn. There is a fresh spicy fragrance.

INFLORESCENCE
Solitary flowers on short branchlets along the many branches.

FRUIT
Round dark-puce shiny berries.

Rosa pimpinellifolia 'Grandiflora'.

The Musk Roses

Mary Lawrance's *Rosa moschata* 'Single Musk Rose'.

Mary Lawrance's *Rosa moschata* 'Double Musk Rose'.

Rosa arvensis from the *Botanical Magazine* (No 2054).

The most fascinating of all the old roses is undoubtedly the Musk, for from its small white flowers was produced, according to legend, the first attar or oil of roses — the most exquisite, delicate and prized perfume of the East.

A story from a Mogul History translated by Langles in 1804 is quoted by Thory in Redouté's *Les Roses* to accompany his fine painting of the double musk rose, and runs as follows:[1]

Nur Jahan, the Mogul empress, in preparing a special fête for her husband, Jahangir, had caused a water canal in their garden to be filled with roses. The heat of the sun drew from the rose-water the essential oil which floated on the surface, spreading its perfume to the delight of the royal pair, who gathered the substance by soaking it up with cotton. After this, Kashmir became famous for the attar which was produced in a similar fashion, though other roses besides the Musk were subsequently used as well.

Perhaps the Musk rose growing in Nur Jahan's garden came originally from the fields of Kashmir or the mountain plains of Nepal or even from the Himalayas. Perhaps it was brought from Central Asia by Babur, first of the Mogul emperors, or by his succeeding sons who were all renowned for the fabulous gardens they created wherever their conquests took them, and for their intense interest in unusual plants which they collected to plant in these gardens.

But long before the Moguls had established themselves in Hindustan, early European writers were aware of the Musk rose. Aristotle's most faithful student, Theophrastus (around 300 B.C.), in his classification of plants described the Musk roses *Rosa moschata multiplex* (minor and major) growing in Greece, and in Roman gardens at the time of Christ a small white rose, named *coroneola* (little chaplet) which had a wonderful perfume and flowered only in autumn, was described by Pliny. In the seventeenth century this rose was identified by Parkinson as the double Musk rose.[2]

One cannot help wondering whether these Musks of ancient Greece and Italy had also arrived from Persia, and whether they were the same roses which later herbalists of the 16th and 17th century were to describe

in more detail:

Muske roses hath slender springs and shootes, the leaves and floures be smaller than the other Roses, yet they grow by almost as high as the Damaske or Province. The Floures be small and single and sometimes double, of a white colour, and pleasant savour. The five first kinds of garden roses doe floure in May and June, and so doe the wild Roses and the Eglantine; but the muske roses doe floure in May and again in September, or thereabouts.

Dodoens, when describing the European Musk roses in 1554, also mentions that these were the same as Pliny's 'coroneola'.[3]

Further information comes from later Dutch herbalists such as Te Groen, gardener to the Prince of Orange: 'All these [roses] one can plant as shrubs or hedges, but the double Musk rose must be planted in pots to be taken indoors in winter.'[4]

This confirmed what Petrus Nylandt had written in his *Kruydtboeck* six years before, and since the Dutch were excellent gardeners, it is clear that the Musk rose they describe must have originated in a warm country and could therefore have thrived only in Western countries with warm climates or in gardens where it could receive special winter protection.

John Lindley also mentions that the Musk flowered in August–September and found that in his time the Musk rose had made its home 'in Spain, the coast of Barbary to the North of Africa extending across the continent from Egypt to Mogadore and thence to Madeira'.[5] Lindley also noted that English winters were 'too rigorous' for it, although it was generally cultivated because of its 'fine musky perfume'.

In France, too, the Musk rose proved to be not altogether hardy. The herbalist Lemery found that the best Musk roses grew in warm areas such as Languedoc or Provence,[6] and Thory stated that plants should be sheltered in winter.

What made the rose so desirable in spite of its tenderness was of course its strong musk fragrance. During these early times musk was highly valued as a perfume in Europe and was being imported from the East at great cost. The Abbé Alexis Rochon, a member of the Acade-

1 Vol. I (1817), pp. 33, 99.
2 J. Parkinson, *Theatrum Botanicum*, 1640.
3 Rembertus Dodoneus, (1517–1585), *The History of Plants*, translated by Henry Lyte in 1619.
4 *Den Nederlandtsen Hovenier*.
5 *Rosarum Monographia*, 1820, p. 122.
6 *Traité des Drogues*, 1698, Dutch translation 1743.

Welvanpas Musk Rose

The Musk rose at Welvanpas.

Hips.

PLANT
Angular sprawling shrub to 4 metres with many thorns, some straight, some hooked.
FOLIAGE
Five or seven oval pointed leaflets about 3 cm long, with marked serrations and slightly downy surfaces. The very short leaf-stalk is eglandular and slightly velvety with short hooked prickles on the underside. Stipules are adnate, the edges entire and smooth.
FLOWERS
Small, pointed, pale pink buds, with sepals of the same length, open to very pale blush flowers of about 4,5 cm in diameter. The broad oval petals bend back from the many dainty yellow stamens and shortish green pistil. The tiny oval calyx is slightly hairy like the sepals and flower-stalk. Sepals, which have a few short folioles, reflex right back. The flowers are very fragrant and flower in spring, producing a lesser show in the autumn.
INFLORESCENCE
Three or more flowers in a widespread corymb.

my of Science in Paris who made a voyage to the East Indies in 1727, subsequently published his experiences and a memoir on the Chinese trade.

Reading his description of how musk was obtained, one wonders at the human mind's ability to draw the fine lines of distinction between what it regards as enjoyable and what it finds distasteful through unpleasant association — in the realm of the senses the mind often becomes totally illogical in its obsession with sensual fulfilment. Here one has a substance 'a kind of bilious, fermented, curdled, and almost corrupted blood, taken from a bag under the belly of a species of roe-buck . . . When the animal is killed, this bag is cut off; and the curdled blood being separated from it, is hung up to dry in the sun'. To facilitate transport the musk was put back into the bag and the Abbé warns traders to search the bags for signs of tampering, for the Chinese often added small stones or lead to them! This curdled, corrupted blood contained the perfume which was so highly prized and to which the rose perfume was likened when it received its name.

The musk-deer is found in Kashmir, the Himalayas, Siberia and China, and perhaps its home may in some areas have coincided with that of the wild Musk rose, although the habitat of this wildling has not yet been established for certain.

Apart from its fragrance, the Musk rose had its medicinal value: it was thought to 'purge very mightily waterish humors yet safely and without all danger taken in the quantitie of an ounce in weight'. So Gerard wrote in 1597, adding however that the Damask was more commonly used for this purpose.[7] Parkinson confirms this, adding that the Arabs knew about such remedies. Lemery gives a more drastic dosage: 'three or four of these roses from a warm climate taken in a conserve or decoction will cause strong purging even to blood'.[8]

John Gerard writes of a third 'vertue' of the Musk rose not mentioned by other herbalists, that the white petals stamped in a wooden dish with a piece of alum would produce a juice which could be used to colour pictures in books or, for that matter, meats or sauces!

While Gerard was writing his *Herball*, Shakespeare was painting the

scene of a midsummer night:

> I know a bank whereon the wild thyme blows,
> Where oxlips and the nodding violet grows
> Quite over-canopied with luscious woodbine,
> With sweet musk-roses, and with eglantine.[9]

Not only Shakespeare, but other poets over the next three hundred years were to extol the virtues of the Musk rose. Thus Milton in 1637 was to write of:

> The tufted crowtoe, and pale jessamine,
> The white pink, and the pansy freaked with jet,
> The glowing violet,
> The musk-rose and the well-attired woodbine.[10]

Keats, in the early 19th century, dwells on its intoxicating richness:

> Fast fading violets cover'd up in leaves;
> And mid-May's eldest child,
> The coming musk-rose, full of dewy wine,
> The murmurous haunt of flies on summer eves.[11]

And to its deeply evocative scent Tennyson was to return later in the century:

> Come into the garden, Maude,
> I am here at the gate alone;
> And the woodbine spices are wafted abroad,
> And the musk of the rose is blown.[12]

But while there is no problem in identifying the eglantine of the English countryside, the Musk roses forming part of Titania's flowery canopy cause some confusion, for how could the herbalist's garden Musk rose, being tender, have thrived among the wild flowers of the English woodland? Graham Thomas suggests that Shakespeare was probably referring to the only trailing British wild rose, *R. arvensis*, which also has small white flowers but unfortunately not enough fragrance to justify

7 In his *Herball*.
8 Nicolas Lemery, *Algemeene Verhandeling der Enkele Droogeryen*, 1743.
9 *A Midsummer Night's Dream*.
10 'Lycidas'.
11 'Ode to a Nightingale'.
12 'Maud'.

Ellen Wilmott's 'Musk Rose'
was probably *Rosa brunonii*.

'Rosier moschata', painted
by Redouté.

Redouté's 'Rosier moschata
flore semi-plena'.

even a poet calling it 'Musk'. Moreover, if Hakluyt is right in giving 1582 as the date of its introduction to England from Italy it could hardly have naturalized itself in the decade before Shakespeare wrote his play. Shakespeare's Musk rose therefore remains an enigma.

Another mystery which remains unsolved is how the old single and double Musk roses described by almost every English, French and Dutch herbalist up to the beginning of the 19th century, came to be replaced by *Rosa brunonii*, introduced in 1820 and grown from then onwards under the name of 'Musk rose'. Was this relative from the Himalayas more resistant to the cold European winters? Then why is the old Musk not still thriving in the warm Mediterranean countries where it used to grow wild in Lindley's time?

In his search for the old Musk rose, Graham Thomas discovered, in the autumn of 1963, a plant that he believed was a genuine old Musk rose growing in E. A. Bowles' garden at Myddelton House: 'on a cold north-west facing wall of the house was a rose just coming into flower'. These rose blooms were single but plants from the old bush produced double flowers in Mr Thomas' garden, both of which he illustrates most beautifully in his book on climbing roses.

But let me leave the mysteries of the poets' wild Musk rose and Graham Thomas' old Musk growing in the cold, for others to solve and describe instead the Musk roses I have found growing at the Cape.

High up in the topmost corner of the Bovlei valley, on the way to Bainskloof, lies the old Retief family farm of Welvanpas where I found my first Musk rose.

It was a sunny spring morning, and in the side court of the old thatched house, shocking-pink oleander and Pride of India made a fine sight as I was taken to see the 'very rare and precious Musk Rose' growing over a fence about 4 metres high. Nobody could tell how long it had been a part of the family scene or where it had originally come from. I was disappointed at my first encounter with such a famous rose, for the sprays of small double creamy pink flowers were unimpressive and totally scentless.

I took a branch of flowers home together with other old roses and it was in the dead of night that I woke with a wonderful feeling of excitement. From the container of roses on a table near my bed a strong perfume emanated which I immediately recognized as musk. I sent fresh flowers to Kew and Mr Thomas' answer came back, 'Probably a Musk'.

I planted a slip in the Boschendal garden and was surprised after two years with a few flowers in spring and again in autumn exactly as described by the old herbalists.

Two years later I discovered a second Musk rose on the farm Klipfontein in the Graaff Reinet district. It was early evening when we drove into the farmyard, having hastened all afternoon through the dry autumn countryside along a road crawling with numerous large centipedes after a snatch of rain the previous week. As I opened the wooden gate into the old garden, I sensed a whiff of musk, and to my utter joy discovered a large truss of dainty white flowers hanging from the shadow of a very old pear tree. It was a much daintier flower than the Welvanpas one, for the outer petals rolled back while the many small odd-shaped inner ones were curled and mixed up with the yellow stamens. In the older flowers the central petals had turned brown with the stamens, though the outer petals were still white.

Looking again at all the old illustrations of Musk roses I could find, I was intrigued to see how similar Jacquin's Musk rose was to my newly discovered one, where even the central small petals of his older flowers are tinted light brown![13] This rose bush has probably been growing in the Klipfontein garden for more than a century.

In the Western Cape the Musk roses are obviously very happy and even in 1940 they were still being highly recommended. Though my searches have revealed no other than the ancient Welvanpas and Klipfontein trees, I am sure that there are many plants hidden away 'to blush unseen' in the byways of the Cape, waiting to be found and appreciated.

13 *Rosa moschata* in his *Fragmenta Botanica*, 1800–1809.

'Klipfontein Musk Rose'

The Musk rose at Klipfontein.

PLANT
Rambler to 4 metres, with smooth stems and angular growth.

FOLIAGE
Five to seven narrow pointed leaflets about 4 cm long bending down from the stem attachments. They have well-serrated edges, dull-green surfaces, grey on the underside. Stipules are adnate, thin and have slightly fringed glandular edges.

FLOWERS
Small pointed buds open to semi-double white flowers of 4 cm in diameter; the outer row of petals reflexes, rolling back at the outer edges soon after the flower has opened. The inner smaller petals are curled and crumpled into a bunch together with the stamens, turning light-brown soon after the flower has opened. The light-green pistil forms a column in the centre. The tiny oval calyx is smooth, narrowing at the top and tapering into the delicate flower stem which is glandular. Seen magnified, the small light green bracts have a velvety surface. The sepals have a few small folioles, are velvety especially on the undersurface, and reflex quickly. Flowers are very fragrant and appear in spring and autumn.

INFLORESCENCE
A corymb of five to seven flowers.

Jacquin's Musk rose.

199

Rosa brunonii

Rosa brunonii in the Stellenbosch
University Botanical Garden.

A tall Robinia tree in the Stellenbosch Botanic Garden is a wonderful sight each spring when thousands of dainty white flower trusses cascade from its topmost branches, casting a most delicious fragrance over the whole garden. The tree grows next to a small stone pond which the curator, Wim Tijmens, has created at its feet, no doubt to reflect the pretty picture, for the garden gives much pleasure not only to the people of the town, but also to the thousands of university students who often stroll through to admire the many interesting plants.

Only when I picked a small bunch of flowers did I discover that the blooms did not belong to the tree at all, but to a climbing rose. Then I was filled with excitement, for I realized that the climber was none other than *Rosa brunonii* or the Himalayan Musk Rose, introduced to England in the 19th century.

Apparently this climber had originally been procured by Mr Herre of the Stellenbosch Herbarium in the early 1930s for his newly planned biological garden which consisted of small beds each planted with shrubs to illustrate specific plant characteristics.

Mr Herre had many friends in Hamburg, East Africa and also in India with whom he corresponded and exchanged plants, and though he left no record, it seems very likely that this rose came directly from the East. It is very similar to those illustrated in the 1981 *Rose Annual* which are identified by Graham Thomas as *Rosa brunonii*. This rose was first sent from Nepal to England in 1820 by Dr Wallich and was described and named by Lindley after the botanist Robert Brown.

Rosa brunonii became known in the 19th century as *Rosa moschata nepalensis* or the 'Himalayan Musk Rose', and perhaps because of its hardier constitution, usurped the place of the earlier Musk roses.

Rosa brunonii is not mentioned in any old Cape plant list and Mr Herre's climber, probably unique in the 1930s, is still the only old plant which I have found. But as this vigorous climber is now available from Ludwig's Nursery, I have been able to plant several specimens around the modern wine cellar that our office has just completed on the old farm, Klein Constantia.

For Mr Herre's plant left an indelible impression on my 'inner eye', and already I can visualize the fragrant clouds of white roses in Dougie Jooste's tall oaks, or the gravel bank behind his cellar covered in luscious green foliage and masses of white spring blossom. Perhaps in a few years the roses will seed themselves, as they love to do, and provide surprise displays in unexpected corners on the rest of the farm.

Rosa brunonii

Rosa brunonii as illustrated in
the *Botanical Magazine*,
1843 (Vol. 69, T 4030).

Rosa brunonii.

PLANT
Climber 10–12 metres high.

FOLIAGE
*Five or seven narrow pointed leaflets 3–4 cm long, with
well-serrated edges and furry surfaces, the lower surface
more markedly so. The stalk is covered in soft hairs and
scattered glands. The stipules are narrow, short, hairy, adnate and have free tips.*

FLOWERS
*Tiny round pointed buds with longer sepals open to single
half-cupped white flowers 2,5–3 cm in diameter; the cordate petals have slightly wavy edges (not notched). The
flower-stalks are hairy and covered in very many stalked
glands. The calyx is oval, round and very glandular; the
sepals long and thin with small folioles, hairy on both sides
and glandular. The style forms a column and is surrounded by many stamens. The flowers appear in spring and
are very fragrant.*

INFLORESCENCE
*A panicle with many flowers in groups of one to three on
thin longish stalks with small leaflike bracts at the com-
mencement and at branching points of the stalk.*

Gillian Batchen in her
Sydney garden with a
seedling *R. brunonii.*

Rosa foetida lutea

AUSTRIAN BRIER

Yellow and copper Austrian Brier roses
in Miss Otto's tortoise-yard.

Mary Lawrance's 'Single Yellow Rose'.

Rosa foetida from the Botanical
Magazine, Vol. II, p. 363.

When one drives through the village of De Rust on the way to Oudtshoorn from Beaufort West, one is not aware of all the pretty houses tucked away in the few side streets of this sleepy little Karoo town. My good friend Anne le Roux, who had been scouting around in the district for old roses before my arrival, guided me to the Victorian cottage with a frilly wooden decorated veranda where Miss Maggie Otto lived.

This retired schoolteacher, though physically frail, was still very perky in spite of her eighty-five years and could give a very good account of the roses and other plants that used to grow in the district during her childhood.

'Cabbage roses, Sweet Brier, Jupiter's Lightning, La France, Souvenir de la Malmaison — we used to exchange cuttings of all these, so that the same roses were in all the gardens', she recalled.

When she guided us through the kitchen door into her backyard, numerous large tortoises suddenly stuck out their scaly heads and waddled towards us on their bandy legs, begging for something to nibble. Miss Maggie told us how worried she was about the fate of these old friends when she should no longer be there to care for them.

My fascination with the tortoises was, however, soon cut short when I observed a thicket of roses flowering in the middle of this rather bare yard. Large single bright-orange flowers formed a mass of brilliant colour like some French impressionist painting.

I had admired Redouté's paintings of these Asian roses[1] and also those in Ellen Willmott's monograph,[2] but now I could understand for the first time why Pernet-Ducher, that avid French rose breeder of the late 19th century, had worked so hard to introduce these bright colours into his new roses. The golden yellow and bronze that lit up Miss Maggie's tortoise yard was quite unlike the soft pastel shades and mauve

reds of the old garden roses. In the fully quartered 'Soleil d'Or' which Pernet-Ducher introduced in 1900 by crossing the 'Persian Double Yellow' with his previously created Hybrid Perpetual, 'Antoine Ducher', he captured the colours which to this day startle one with their brilliance in Hybrid Teas like 'Radio', 'Sutter's Gold' and 'Super Star'.

Gerard in his herbal describes Rosa foetida (then known as Rosa lutea) as it grew in England in 1596 and tells how he disproved the theory that it was derived from a wild rose grafted onto a Broom![3] He mentions that Clusius, director of the Botanic Garden at Leyden,[4] had brought the yellow rose from Austria (where it was growing wild) to Holland in 1560. Because Gerard described its leaves as being scented like the Sweet Brier, it was for a long time classified with the Eglantines and consequently was known as the 'Austrian Brier'.

How this Persian rose reached Austria does not seem to be recorded, but a very interesting series of articles by David Hooper in the Kew Bulletins of 1930 and 1931 throws some light on the original habitat of the rose. It was found growing wild from the Crimea to Asia Minor, through Persia to Turkestan, Afghanistan, Punjab and Eastern Tibet. In the Hari-rud Valley it was known as 'Gul-i-raman-zeba' (lovely flower), and in Teheran, 'Gul-i-zara' (yellow flower). It was noted that this widespread yellow rose sometimes produced a variety with copper-coloured petals.

Parkinson in 1629 also believed that the copper rose was a variety of the yellow and this I could see for myself on that spring day at De Rust, for when I dug up some plants which Miss Maggie had kindly offered me, I found both the yellow and copper roses flowering on the same bush.

Two doctors who collected drugs from the bazaars of Teheran, Hamadah and Kirmandshah during the 1930s found that a confection

1 Les Roses, Vol. II, p. 71.
2 The Genus Rosa, plates 90 & 91.
3 Gerard, Of the History of Plants, 1633 edition.
4 Charles de l'Ecluse (1526–1609).

Rosa foetida bicolor

AUSTRIAN COPPER ROSE

Jacquin's illustration of the copper Austrian Brier in his *Hortus Botanicus Vindobonensis*, 1770.

PLANT
This is a thin, fragile-looking plant with many brownish-green stems forming a large clump by suckering. The many thorns of different lengths are thin and straight, of a light-brown colour and often in pairs.

FOLIAGE
There are five small oval sessile leaflets about 2 cm long with well-marked serrations. They are medium to light green with a matt upper surface, slightly lighter below. The petiole is short and delicate with small prickles on the underside. The stipules are tiny, thin and smooth with loose tips.

FLOWERS
The fat round buds with short sepals open into cup-shaped single flowers 5–6 cm in diameter with golden-yellow petals curving inwards over the stamens which have long thin filaments and bright yellow anthers. The calyx is smooth and quite large for the size of the flower; sepals are short-ish and oval with tiny folioles, dull on the outer surface and velvety on the inside. There is no scent to speak of and that which is present is not as unpleasant as the name signifies. The flowers appear from spring to midsummer.

INFLORESCENCE
The flowers appear one or sometimes two at a time on short side branchlets along the main stem.

Rosa foetida bicolor.

203

'Soleil d'Or'.

Rosa foetida persiana
is a profuse bloomer.

Mary Lawrance's *Rosa sulphurea*
or 'Double Yellow Rose'.

called 'Gulangabin', made from honey and the petals of the Persian Yellow rose, was used to alleviate colic and diarrhoea. The seeds were also used for stomach ailments. According to them, this drug was referred to by Abu Man Sur over a thousand years ago, which prompts them to remark that 'the drug supplies of this country, like the laws of the Medes and Persian, are unchangeable'.[5]

How these Persian roses arrived on several Karoo farms during the 19th century can only be guessed at. According to Curtis, both colours were growing 'almost universally in British gardens' in the early 1800s,[6] and it is quite likely that the British pioneers who settled in the Eastern Cape from 1820 onwards had plants sent out 'from home' once the threat of indigenous tribes had been dispelled and ornamental gardens became the symbol of their security.

Perhaps rose plants were obtained from the Cape Town garden of Baron von Ludwig, for in 1831 both the yellow and copper roses were growing there and von Ludwig was generous with his plants. It was also about this time that the *Cape Almanac* advised gardeners not to prune their yellow roses if they wanted them to produce flowers, so its seems as if *Rosa foetida* was a well-known Cape rose by the early part of the 19th century.

In 1906 at Uitenhage, the nursery Smith Bros were still offering three varieties of *Rosa foetida* with the proud announcement: 'Of all the Roses the Austrian Copper is the greatest novelty; it is quite unlike a Rose in appearance, being more like a single Dahlia or Begonia, . . . for table decoration they are exquisite.' It is probably from this nursery that the ancient Persian wild roses found their way into the tortoise yard of Miss Maggie Otto's Victorian cottage garden in De Rust.

I wonder whether the 'old people' at the Cape ever used the yellow petals to stop diarrhoea or colic?

5 Drs J.M. Cowan and C. Darlington in the *Kew Bulletin*,
   1931.
6 *Botanical Magazine* no. 1077.

Rosa foetida persiana

PERSIAN YELLOW ROSE

The Reeves illustration
of *Rosa foetida persiana*.
(Lindley Library)

Rosa foetida persiana differs
from *Rosa foetida lutea* only in the
greater number of its petals.

Rosa rugosa

Rosa rugosa.

PLANT

A shrub 1–1,5 metres high, covered with numerous slightly hooked thin grey downy thorns of different lengths spread all along the stems and flower-stalks. The plant multiplies quickly by suckering to form a large dense mass of growth.

FOLIAGE

Five or seven leaflets, oval with blunted distal ends, roughly serrated edges and deeply veined rugose surfaces. There are many light-green hooks on the underside of the leaf-stalk. Stipules are wider than usual, with free tips and smooth edges.

FLOWERS AND FRUIT

The large round buds open into white or mauve-pink floppy single flowers 8 cm in diameter, with crinkled petals surrounding a mass of prominent yellow stamens. The sepals are much branched and sometimes quite long, persisting for a long time after the petals have dropped. The flowers are borne continuously from spring to autumn and have a sweet scent. Very often a shrub will produce flowers and ripe hips at the same time, making a very pretty show, for the shiny round hips are large and of a bright cherry-red colour.

INFLORESCENCE

One to three flowers are borne on the top of the branches in a head, rather hidden by surrounding leaves.

Rosa rugosa

'Mme Georges Bruant' (1887),
a Rugosa hybrid, has pure
white recurrent blooms.

Mary Lawrance's
'Hedge-hog Rose'
or *Rosa ferox*.

Carl Thunberg in 1784 was the first botanist to describe this rose which is a native of N.E. Asia, North China, Korea, and Japan where Thunberg collected it. According to him it was known as the 'Ramanas rose' by the Japanese.[1]

Roy Shepherd describes how the first plants were distributed in Europe from 1796 onwards by the nursery Lee and Kennedy of Hammersmith, but it is not clear how the plants were obtained from Japan.[2] *Rosa rugosa* at that time was not a popular garden plant nor much used for hybridizing although it sets seed easily. It was only after its introduction by Thomas Hogg into America in 1872 that various breeders started working with it, producing there as well as in Europe a number of varieties, some of which are still favourite garden shrubs in the Cape.[3]

The dark purplish-mauve and white single Rugosas were popular in the early 1900s as specimen plants and for hedges, especially in the Eastern Cape where they were sold by Smith Bros of Uitenhage.[4] This nursery also sold the first European hybrid Rugosa, 'Madame Georges Bruant',[5] which had large white semi-double flowers, and was described by them as a 'novelty' for which they charged two shillings a plant in 1905.

Visitors to gardens where Rugosas grow are always surprised to be told that these suckering shrubs are indeed rose trees, for their mint-like wrinkled leaves and large fleshy hips are most atypical.

These showy hips, like bunches of small red tomatoes, occur abundantly throughout the year often simultaneously with the flowers, so that though the fast-fading flowers are not popular for home decoration, the plants are always a gay sight in the garden and therefore well worth planting. The hips attract a variety of small birds who seem to love the fleshy pulp. My friends who like to pick the hips for making jelly have to do so as soon as they start reddening, or else they are faced with only the empty husks left by the birds.

The one disadvantage of *Rosa rugosa* is its propensity for suckering which can be a nuisance in a small garden, but in large gardens or public places its rampant growth can be advantageously used to cover large areas of poor soil.

I was pleasantly surprised to see hedges of Rugosas mixed with *Rosa canina* at the large camping site on the dunes of The Hague, where the dense green growth effectively separates individual campers, cutting off visual and sound intrusion with the extra bonus of fragrance from the abundance of brightly coloured flowers.

A few years ago I found a large number of the single Rugosas in the Provincial Roads Nursery at Paarl where somebody had planted them in containers, obviously with the idea of using them for landscaping the reserves along the highways. Although they would have done well in the dry sandy soil and windy climate of the Cape Flats, the decision to use indigenous plants like proteas and leucospermums had made these plants redundant so that I was able to buy them for museum gardens.

At the Cape we have an abundance of beautiful wind-resistant indigenous shrubs suitable for growing in poor or sandy soil along road reserves, so that sensible landscape architects are making less use of imported material which holds neither surprise nor excitement for overseas tourists. Lovers of old roses will still be able to see them in public parks and museum gardens.

1 Thunberg, *Flora Japonica*, 1784. A specimen of *Rosa rugosa* (no. 12202) is preserved in his Herbarium. (Microfiche copy in the Bolus Herbarium.)
2 *History of the Rose*, 1954.
3 The pink 'Grootendorst' (1918) is to be found in quite a number of Cape gardens. 'Blanc Double de Coubert' (1892) is sold by Ludwig's Nurseries in Pretoria.
4 They were advertised in their 1905 catalogue as 'Japanese Roses' with an illustration of the flowers and hips.
5 Introduced by Bruant in 1887.

Rosa laevigata

This is said to be the first Chinese rose which was described in the West and the original specimen, collected by Plukenet in 1696, can be seen in the Sloane collection at the Natural History Museum in London. It has been given many names by the various botanists through the ages: *Rosa sinica* by Aiton, *Rosa nivea* by Candolle, *Rosa triphylla* by Roxburgh, and in Georgia, where it has become naturalized and is now the State flower, it is known as the 'Cherokee rose'. In 1933 G. A. Stevens wrote, 'It is a weed along the irrigation banks of the South West, but a very handsome and beautiful thing',[1] but no one knows when or by whom the first plant was introduced from China to America.

At the Cape where *Rosa laevigata* is commonly found in old gardens, people call it the 'Dog rose' and those who 'know better' mistakenly call it 'the Macartney rose' as both these roses have single large white flowers and glossy foliage.

Since my girlhood this rose has had a special meaning for me, for it starts flowering in early September when Stellenbosch country ditches and the banks on which the roses grow are covered in pink and yellow oxalis and white arum. I used to cycle out a day before my birthday to pick large trailing branches of the white roses for arranging in all the rooms of our flat. My mother's singing studio, furnished with dark-green velvet divan cover and apple-green curtains, was particularly cheered by the bowl of white roses on the old Fritz Kuhla piano, which was reflected in the large gilt-edged mirror together with pupils singing their Mah-meh-mee-moh-moos. My mother loved to have lots of flowers in our home and confided to me that the roses helped her to have greater patience with the more untalented pupils.

Later, in my student days, when we were allowed to wander through the Groote Schuur grounds at our leisure to pick white violets in the oak grove or 'wild dog roses' from the hedges, my birthdays never lacked their roses.

Nowadays my birthday rose is not quite so common and I am delighted when I sometimes come across a remnant of old hedge with light-green glossy foliage spilling over a grassy bank; or a vigorous shrub climbing high up into an old oak, leaping in bright green swags from one branch to the other, throwing out long trailers of shiny white flowers. I noted with pleasure that the tangle of roses that in my young days had turned a kloof on the farm Deze Hoek near Piketberg into a snow-white dell each spring, had not been cleared; and that the *Rosa laevigata* growing over the old Drostdy garden wall at Swellendam was still being lovingly trimmed.

One evening when we were working late in Dal Josafat, where *Rosa laevigata* used to demarcate many boundaries in the 1930s, I suddenly became aware of a glimmer of white roses on a huge plant growing from the mud walls of an old farm ruin, long arms of white blossom making strange patterns against the cloudy dull-red evening sky.

I have often wondered how, and from where, this Chinese rose was first brought to the Cape.

Roxburgh, who called it *R. triphylla* (the leaflets are usually arranged in groups of three), records that it grew in the British East India Botanic Garden in Calcutta before 1794; and Captain John Barnes, who lived for twelve years on St. Helena, noted that *R. triphylla* existed on that island before 1814.

But whether it had arrived from the West, the Far East or St. Helena, Cape farmers obviously appreciated a rose which could be propagated so easily from cuttings to form an impenetrable, hardy and very beautiful hedge within a year or two. It is certain that *R. laevigata* hedges were already in general use during the first decade of the 19th century, either to enclose kitchen and flower gardens in the towns, or to bound vineyards, orchards and farm 'werfs' of the surrounding countryside.[2] In the *Cape Almanac* of 1820 farmers and gardeners were advised that in August 'cuttings of the common white 'Macartney' rose may be put in for future budding' and this same advice is repeated annually in the *Almanac* for the rest of the century, but it is not clear whether this reference is to *Rosa laevigata* or the real Macartney Rose.[3]

I have noticed with great pleasure that farmers are starting to propagate this rose again for planting against the lifeless wire fences that dominate our present country landscape and perhaps the fields of spring arum lilies will once again be enhanced with banks of white *R. laevigata* along our country lanes.

The pink counterpart of *R. laevigata* is believed to be derived from a cross with the first Tea rose, *Rosa x odorata*. It is not often seen at the Cape, but I have noticed very old shrubs in Stellenbosch and Paarl growing over boundary walls of Victorian cottages. As most of the older generation remember the 'Pink Dog Rose' quite clearly, it must have been popular in the early 1900s, shortly after it was first introduced to European gardens by J. C. Schmidt in 1896.

'Anemone', as it is now called, is similar to its white parent in most respects except that the plant is more gawky, the shiny foliage less profuse and unlike *R. laevigata* it flowers throughout the year, the large clear pink roses making a very pretty sight indeed, especially in the spring when the whole plant is covered in flowers.

The 'Yellow Dog Rose' which most laymen regard as a variety of *R. laevigata* is actually derived from *R. bracteata* and is described under 'Mermaid' in that section.

1 G. A. Stevens, *Climbing Roses*, New York, 1933.
2 The author of *Life at the Cape 100 years ago by 'A Lady'* describes an old Cape Dutch house in the Gardens: in the kitchen garden, myrtle and the 'prickly white roses' were the guardians of the strawberries and the lettuce (p. 24).
3 January, April, June, August and December are all mentioned as months suitable for making cuttings of the 'Macartney' rose. I think this was probably a reference to *Rosa laevigata*.

PLANT
This rose grows into a graceful sprawling shrub or climbs into trees 6–10 metres high, hanging down from the top branches in long trailing shoots. It has numerous very sharp hooked thorns.

FOLIAGE
Three yellow-green, oval pointed leaflets with small serrated edges and shiny upper and lower surfaces. The leaf-stalk is reddish with tiny prickles on the underside; stipules are very narrow and deciduous.

FLOWERS
Well-formed white buds with longish sepals open to large, white, slightly cup-shaped flowers, about 9 cm in diameter. Numerous dainty light-yellow stamens crowd around the short pistil. The calyx is oval and covered with soft bristles which appear also on the flower-stalk. The smooth, long, tapering sepals with small folioles are shiny on the upper surface and velvety underneath. They reflex only halfway. There is a slight fragrance and the blooming time is very early spring although flowers do appear at other times of the year during hot spells.

INFLORESCENCE
One or sometimes two flowers appear on short branchlets along the main stems.

Rosa laevigata

Rosa laevigata.

Rosa roxburghii

1 Mrs Johnman's veranda in Stellenbosch.
2 Reeves' illustration of *R. roxburghii*.
   (Lindley Library)
3 *Rosa microphylla* in the *Botanical Magazine*
   (Vol 63, T 3490).
4 Calyx and sepals (magnified).

1 3
2 4

When I saw this beautiful Chinese rose growing for the first time in Mrs Johnman's garden in Stellenbosch, she assured me that her father, the Revd Hahn, had had it in his garden at least since the beginning of this century. She called it 'an old Moss Rose', but on closer examination it proved to be nothing of the kind, the prickly outgrowths on the calyx being hard and rough like a chestnut and unlike the soft green down of a mossy calyx.

I was intrigued with the grey flaky stems, the pretty fern-like foliage and the charming two-toned pink flowers half hidden amongst the green leaves. I picked several sprays and found that in a flat China bowl, the angular leafy branchlets arranged themselves in their own ornate fashion and the sweetly scented open roses lasted for almost a week.

I have since found *Rosa roxburghii* in many cottage gardens and cemeteries in the Cape Peninsula and also in small towns further inland. In Knysna a well-established hedge along a street boundary on the hill looked particularly charming with the many pink flowers set against the blue lagoon below the small village.

Wherever it appeared, owners were proud of their 'Old Rose' but no one had a name for it and not even the name 'Chestnut Rose', commonly used in Europe, had been heard of. As no record exists of its first introduction to the Cape, I suspect that *Rosa roxburghii* was one of those roses which arrived directly from the East in the early 19th century when British families in India and the Cape were exchanging plants freely.

W. Roxburgh, after whom the rose was named, called it *Rosa microphylla* and included it in the list of plants growing in the Calcutta Botanic Garden in 1814.[1] He noted that it had been introduced to these gardens two years before from China by W. Kerr and that the Chinese called it 'Hai-tong-hong'.

R. roxburghii was introduced to England about ten years later, flowering for the first time in Colvill's nursery in 1826 and after that also at Glazenwood, the garden of William Curtis, founder of the *Botanical Magazine*. The rose was illustrated and described in this magazine in 1836.[2] Mr Curtis thought at the time that it would be hardy enough to withstand only mild winters, but that sharp frosts would destroy it. Perhaps this is the reason why it is rare in English gardens today and does so well at the sunny Cape.

The single form of the 'Chestnut Rose', *Rosa roxburghii hirtula*, became known only around 1880. I have never had the opportunity of seeing it in flower although plants have recently been imported by Ludwig's Nurseries in Pretoria.

1 *Hortus Bengalensis*, 1814, reprinted 1980.
2 T. 3490.

Rosa roxburghii

'THE CHESTNUT ROSE'

PLANT
A spreading, branched shrub to 3 metres high with light-grey stems and papery bark. There are many straight grey to reddish upward-pointing thorns, often two at the base of each leaf-stalk.

FOLIAGE
Nine small, dainty, oval pointed, bright green leaflets with finely serrated edges and smooth surfaces. The leaf-stalk is flattish and thin but strong, and has no prickles. Stipules are very narrow with smooth edges.

FLOWERS
The large cup-shaped buds are covered with fat green prickles. The flowers are about 8 cm in diameter and are very full. The many dark-pink, central wavy petals are surrounded by broader mauve-pink petals; there are very few stamens around the slightly hairy short pistils in the centre. The calyx is remarkable for its flat cup shape and the numerous green prickles which extend onto the oval pointed sepals and down onto the flower-stalk.

INFLORESCENCE
One to two flowers on short leafy branchlets on the main stems. The flowers are borne from early spring through summer to autumn and have a sweet fragrance.

Rosa roxburghii.

211

Left: *Rosa bracteata* from the *Botanical Magazine*, Vol. 34, T 1377.
Right: *Rosa bracteata* from Jacquin's *Fragmenta Botanica* (1800–1809).
Below: His Excellency the Earl of Macartney: Ambassador Extraordinary from the King of Great Britain to the Emperor of China (1796).

China had closed her doors to all foreign traders in 1755, allowing only limited concessions in Canton and Macao, but even there local officials made it so difficult particularly for British merchants, that it was decided to send an embassy to the Emperor at his court in Peking to negotiate improved trading conditions.

On the 26th September, 1792 Lord George Macartney, previously Governor of Madras, left Portsmouth as leader with Sir George Staunton, a keen botanist, as second-in-command. Staunton's eleven-year old son was Macartney's page and, learning Chinese more quickly than the adults, was of considerable service as interpreter. He was later to act as official interpreter on a second embassy under Lord Amherst, for Macartney's embassy was unsuccessful, largely because the Englishmen refused to 'kow-tow' — to prostrate themselves nine times before the Emperor — unless the ceremony were repeated by equally high-ranking Chinese officials before a portrait of George III!

These two embassies have long been forgotten, but Macartney's name is remembered to this day by a Chinese rose which Staunton collected on their first expedition and which became known in Europe as the 'Macartney Rose', or *Rosa bracteata*.

Perhaps plants of this rose were left at the Cape on the embassy's return journey, or perhaps they were brought out from England during the eighteen months of Macartney's subsequent term of office as governor of the Cape after the British occupation in 1795.

Whatever the date of its first appearance at the Cape, it appears that by the mid-19th century it was growing everywhere in the countryside with such vigour and ease that it was generally used as budding stock.[1]

In the 1920s Dorothea Fairbridge still mentions its frequent occurrence in the Paarl and Stellenbosch districts where it bordered vineyards and roads and climbed into many trees. She thought it to be 'the most beautiful hedge in the world when odium can be kept at bay'.[2]

The most mysterious disappearance of this rose from the Cape landscape could perhaps be ascribed to this disease, or possibly it never has been common at the Cape at all; for *Rosa laevigata*, which is still to be seen everywhere, is often erroneously referred to as 'Macartney's rose'.[3]

Dorothea Fairbridge however mentions both these Chinese roses and as it is most unlikely that she would have confused the two, the disappearance of *Rosa bracteata* remains unsolved.

While trying to pick a flower from a vigorous climber in the Knox-Shaw garden in Elgin, I was made to appreciate why the Macartney Rose was such a successful hedge, for it has the most vicious thorns of any rose I know.

1 'Cuttings of the common white or Macartney rose may now be put in to form stock for future budding': 'The Gardener's Calendar' in *The Cape Almanac*, August 1868. Curtis, in his description of this rose (*Botanical Magazine*, t. 1377), also finds that it 'is easily propagated by layers or cuttings'.

2 D. Fairbridge, *South African Gardens*, Cape Town, 1925, p. 76. 'Probably the first climbing Rose grown at the Cape was the white Macartney, brought here from China many generations ago . . . It resembles *Rosa sinica alba* very closely, but the petals are flatter.'

3 Ella and Florence du Cane in their *Flowers and Gardens of Madeira* (1909) also mention that *Rosa laevigata* was often mistaken for the Macartney Rose on that island.

Rosa bracteata

'MACARTNEY ROSE'

A hedge of 'Mermaid' at Elgin.

Rosa bracteata.

PLANT
Vigorous climber to 5 metres with very many large, curved, sharp thorns.

FOLIAGE
Five to seven dark-green smooth oval leaflets; they have rounded points, deeply serrated edges and sturdy stalks with thorns on the undersides. The stipules are much fringed.

FLOWERS
The oval buds with longer sepals, surrounded by five to seven fringed bracts, open to single flat blooms 10 cm in diameter. The thick large white petals are notched on the edges; numerous bright yellow stamens and a short bunch of pistils fill the centre. Flowers appear throughout the year and have a sweet fragrance.

INFLORESCENCE
Solitary flowers at the tips of side branchlets.

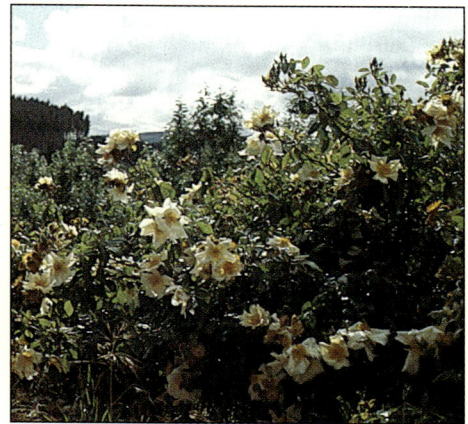

'Mermaid', the hybrid of *R. bracteata* and an unknown yellow Tea rose.

Rosa sericea pteracantha

Hip of *Rosa sericea pteracantha*.

This interesting form of *Rosa sericea* was collected in Yunnan by the French missionary, Delavay, who sent seed to Maurice de Vilmorin in France in 1890. Plants were distributed in England soon afterwards and probably reached the Cape in the early 20th century. In 1940 'The Vicar' still regarded it as useful for ornamental shrubberies or in a more practical way for hedges.[1]

The particular interest of *R. sericea* lies in the fact that it is the only rose species whose flowers usually have four rather than five petals. In the form *pteracantha*, the numerous thorns have particularly wide bases that appear reddish and almost translucent with backlighting, giving the plant an even more remarkable appearance. This is the only variety now to be found in Cape gardens, and probably the one to which the 'Vicar' was referring forty years ago.

A plant I obtained for the Boschendal garden has grown extremely well to form a shrub four metres high in three years. The tiny white flowers are insignificant, but the fern-like foliage contrasted with the large red thorns creates a great deal of interest among visitors, especially those who are keen on 'floral arrangements'. I have noticed that the small round dark-red shiny hips which, according to Faber, are eaten by the Chinese,[2] are also a favourite item in the diet of many small birds.

This is an excellent shrub for using in semi-shade where a large area needs to be covered quickly, and where trespassers are to be kept out effectively.

1 'The Vicar', *The South African Rose Book,* Cape Town, 1940.
2 *Botanical Magazine,* t. 8471 (1912).

PLANT
Very large vigorous sprawling shrub over 5 metres high and as much across. New young shoots, straight and stiff, grow several metres in one season. The numerous thorns have broad flat bases which are tinted red and appear transparent especially on the young stems.

FOLIAGE
Eleven to thirteen small oval pointed leaflets 2−3 cm long. The matt dark-green surfaces are duller on the underside and have evenly serrated edges. The stalk is thin and dainty with small hooked prickles on the underside; the stipules are adnate and narrow.

FLOWERS
The tiny white flowers, 3−4 cm in diameter, open flat. Each has only four petals around the short pistil and yellow stamens which are not as numerous as in other species. The calyx is oval and smooth, the sepals short and unfoliated. The small white flowers, never profuse, are sprinkled over the shrub in early summer, the petals dropping quickly. There is not much scent.

INFLORESCENCE
The flowers appear singly on lateral branchlets along the main stems.

Rosa sericea is the only species rose with four petals.

A young twig of *Rosa sericea pteracantha*.

Rosa hugonis

SHRUB
Many graceful stems up to 2 metres high with numerous strong broadly based thorns.
FOLIAGE
Seven to nine tiny, oval, matt leaflets 7 mm long, on very dainty, thin, smooth stalks without prickles. The smooth stipules are narrow and adnate.
FLOWERS AND FRUIT
Tiny round yellow buds open into small, single, clear-yellow flowers 2,5 cm in diameter. The petals open flat around numerous stamens on thin longish filaments. Pistils form a short bunch in the centre. The calyx is round and flattened; the sepals, half reflexed, are thin, smooth and tapering. The flowers have a faint fragrance and appear in profusion in spring although a few come out again in autumn together with the pretty small round cherry-red berries.
INFLORESCENCE
A solitary flower on a smooth dainty stem.

Rosa hugonis.

In the *Botanical Magazine* of 1905 W. Botting Hemsley records how seeds of *Rosa hugonis* were collected by Father Hugo Scallan, a Roman Catholic missionary in West China, probably in the province of Shensi or Szechwan. Plants were raised from the seeds in 1899 at Kew where they proved to be fairly hardy.[1]

I had seen illustrations of this lovely shrub with its light-green fern-like foliage and small yellow single flowers, so immediately recognized a plant on the farm Klipfontein near Graaff-Reinet. Mrs Parkes, the owner's wife, told me that she had brought slips from her parents' home in the Aliwal North district where the rose had been established before 1921, but she did not know how it had arrived at a destination so far inland.

Rosa hugonis, like other species roses, especially those newly introduced from the East, were popular garden plants at the Cape in the early part of this century and are still to be seen growing luxuriantly in a number of old gardens. In the Kirstenbosch cemetery a large shrub made a very pretty sight against the old stone church when I first saw it one spring scattered all over with yellow flowers, but it was cleaned out with the other old roses in the following year.

Last year I came upon a well-grown shrub on the farm Dwarsrivier in Banhoek near Stellenbosch. It had probably been planted there some years before when the land belonged to Professor Rycroft, then curator of the Kirstenbosch Botanical Gardens, who had imported rose seed from all over the world for his garden. What surprised me about this plant was that it was flowering in autumn which seemed rather strange for a species rose, but on driving around to check on other plants in the Western Cape I found them all flowering, though not with the profusion of spring.

In the *American Rose Annual* of 1937 a Judge James Lowell of Boston commented on the fact that his *R. hugonis* plant had flowered profusely in spring and produced a few blooms again in September. I have therefore come to the conclusion that this behaviour is not confined to the sunny Cape with its variable weather as I had first supposed, and have since noticed a few autumn flowers on other species roses.[2]

1 T. 8004.
2 A *Rosa laevigata* in a Rondebosch garden flowers regularly in autumn, sometimes quite profusely.

Rosa banksiae banksiae

PLANT
Vigorous climber to 10 metres throwing out long straight rods with very few thorns.

FOLIAGE
Three to five dark-green shiny leaflets 2–3 cm long with shallowly serrated edges. The stalk is thin, delicate and thornless. Stipules are thin, attached only at the bases, and deciduous.

FLOWERS
Tiny round buds with short sepals open to very double round balls of small oval white petals. There are a few longish yellow stamens and a pistil consisting of short green threads. The small calyx is cup-shaped, smooth and shiny; the pedicel thin and smooth, inclined to droop. The sepals are smooth, unfoliated and reflex partially. Flowers appear in August and have a sweet fragrance in both varieties.

INFLORESCENCE
Ten to fifteen flowers in an umbel.

Rosa banksiae banksiae.

216

Rosa banksiae banksiae

A five-year-old *Rosa banksiae banksiae* at Boschendal.

The first of the Banksia roses to reach Europe from China was the small double white one which William Kerr sent out to Sir Joseph Banks in 1807. The rose was appropriately named the 'Banks' or 'Lady Banks Rose', for at that time Joseph Banks was the royal horticultural adviser at Kew and it was he who had arranged for Kerr, a gardener there, to be sent to China to collect plants for the garden.

Curtis described and illustrated a specimen from Lady Banks' garden at Spring Grove in his *Botanical Magazine* (t. 1954). He remarked that even if planted in a warm place in the open garden it was susceptible to frosts and therefore better off in a 'border of the conservatory'. The yellow Banksia, introduced to Europe in 1824 by G. D. Parkes (who also introduced the first aspidistra) probably fared no better when unprotected.

At the Cape, on the other hand, many vigorous specimens of great age testify to the happy growth of Banksias in our congenial climate. I myself have watched a slip of the white Banksia, planted in the Boschendal garden, develop a trunk of 10 cm in diameter and branches trailing from the top of a Pride of India tree 12 metres high in less than five years.

Perhaps it is this vigorous growth which has endeared the Banksias

to Cape gardeners for more than a century, for although the date of their introduction is not known, it is certain that both the yellow and white varieties were growing in the Botanic Garden in Cape Town in 1858.

Three years later on the 13 February 1861 Mrs Dale, the wife of the Superintendent-General of Education in the Cape Colony, recorded in her diary that she had planted a Banksia in her garden at Montague House in Woodstock, but she did not mention its colour. By the end of the 19th century large trees of both the white and yellow varieties were to be found in gardens throughout the Colony.

The oldest surviving white Banksia may be the one which was planted from a slip in the 1870s by Walter Edwards at the house he built for his first wife on the farm Klipfontein in the Graaff Reinet district. This rose, which now covers a pergola nine metres long by two metres wide, is still a vigorous and healthy plant, producing thousands of flowers every spring. Douglas Parkes, the present owner who is the grandson of Walter Edwards on his mother's side, replaced a broken wooden pergola with the present new one made of concrete pillars and wire meshing in 1938. He told me that the plant was then as big as it is now.

Rosa banksiae lutea

The Yellow Banksia at Tokai.

CAPE ARCHIVES E641

Another Banksia, this time a yellow one which is almost as old, grows on the Malherbe farm Ezelfontein near Ceres. It was planted as a slip by Maria Johanna Malherbe when she and her husband, Philippus Bernardus, moved from Paarl to Ezelfontein in 1883. It grows by itself over the werf wall on the side of the old Cape Dutch mansion. Each spring grandchildren and great-grandchildren are pleasantly reminded of their forbear, but the beautiful mass of yellow blossoms does not reveal the fact that she was quite a formidable old lady!

Dorothea Fairbridge was enchanted with a yellow Banksia, 'a mass of soft rich colour', that had grown to the top of the front stoep wall at Tokai. One does not know how old this tree might have been, for it no longer decorates the entrance to this famous old home. Would it perhaps have witnessed the tragedy of the horseman who, for a wager, rode his steed up the steep stoep steps, falling to his death on the descent?

While we were restoring the houses in Church Street, Tulbagh, after the 1969 earthquake, we noticed several Banksias growing in the town's oldest streets. A most spectacular yellow one grew at the entrance to a Victorianized house in Van der Stel Street, spreading its welcoming branches from the cast-iron entrance gate to the veranda over the front door. It was just as well that we took a photograph of the wonderful spring show in 1970, for the old climber was chopped down soon afterwards. How does one understand such behaviour?

Victorian Capetonians were also fond of planting Banksia roses over verandas or arches leading to their front entrances. Some have survived, such as the white one planted in 1905 by Charles Logan at the front stoep of his new house in Thornhill Road, Rondebosch. But many have had to make way for development: the yellow and white Banksias on arches that Gertrude Ordman knew in her father's Tamboerskloof garden which pre-dated 1893; or the yellow Banksia hedge which gave Banksia Street in Rondebosch its name. I remember the many white and yellow Banksias adorning the Victorian villas of Tamboerskloof in the 1930s when I used to spend happy holidays in a double-storied house on the corner of Kloofnek and Warren Streets. How I long for the beautiful rose gardens which one saw from the rattling tram on its way up to Kloofnek!

Miss M. E. Rothman, reminiscing on the plants and gardens of her youth, describes her love for the yellow and white Banksias, 'the rose without thorns', her sweet and fragrant old friends who asked for little and appreciated the slightest attention. In Swellendam, her home town, where she died a few days after her hundredth birthday, many yellow Banksias on pavements and in backyard gardens still herald the spring with a burst of colour when all other roses are still dormant. The white variety, on the other hand, which together with the Macartney Rose and 'Seven Sisters' were for many years regarded as the supreme climbers, is scarce. However, one plant over an archway in the Mayville museum garden is growing with such speed that it should soon provide a magnificent spectacle.

As the Banksias have proved their vigour and longevity at the Cape, grandparents should perhaps once again plant these old stalwarts and in this way link themselves with the generations to come.

Rosa banksiae lutea

'Who doubts success is lost before he starts.'

A century-old plant of *R. banksiae lutea.*

Rosa banksiae lutea differs
from *R. banksiae banksiae*
only in colour.

219

Rosa x fortuniana

'My Banksia is out', said Mrs Johnman as we walked through her garden in Stellenbosch, pointing towards a cloud of white flowers festooning several large fruit trees. I picked some long sprays of these pretty white roses and thought how much larger they were than the Banksias I had seen elsewhere, noticing also that the flower-stalks were covered with soft prickles very much like *Rosa laevigata*.

At home I arranged the 'Banksia' in an apple-green wall-vase together with some jasmine which was still pink in bud. The light-green shiny sprays with posies of white roses along their thin stems, cast frivolous shadows on the wall against a background of jasmine lacework. The rose was scentless, but the sweet jasmine penetrated the whole house.

When I started making notes about this rose, I was delighted to find Parsons' beautiful illustration in Ellen Willmott's book of roses,[1] and it became clear to me why *Rosa x fortuniana*, which is the correct name for this variety, had both Banksian and Laevigata characteristics, as these two roses are the parents of Mrs Johnman's 'large Banksia'.

In the *Garden Chronicle* of 1860, Robert Fortune, after whom this rose is named, describes how he found it growing in gardens around Ningpo and Shanghai and how the Chinese revered this white climber. They frequently used it in trellis-work, over garden walls, or to cover alcoves — a purpose for which it is admirably suited because it is such a luxuriant grower and profuse bloomer. Fortune, who had been commissioned in 1842 to collect plants in China for the London Horticultural Society, regarded this rose (which was one of the first he sent to England) as a very beautiful variety, having 'some advantages peculiar to itself'.

There is no record of when *Rosa x fortuniana* was first introduced to the Cape, but judging by the many old trees I have found in mid-19th century cemeteries and unexpected corners of the Groot Drakenstein Valley, I would guess that it reached us not long after Fortune's plants reached England.

I like to plant this climber in corners of the garden which other roses would find too shady, for it grows fast and, once established, seems insensitive to neglect. Looking only for a willing tree to support its long lax branches, it will spread quickly to a height of 10 metres and from there shake out its papery rosettes to hang like little white bells all along the main branches in the early spring when most other roses are still completely dormant.

Apart from this virtue I discovered that *Rosa x fortuniana* had another even more precious use:

In Swellendam Anna Rothman showed me one of her family heirlooms — a small black iron skillet containing a note written by her mother, the well-loved Afrikaans writer, whom every schoolchild in the Cape knows as 'M.E.R.'. It stated that Anna's grandmother had used the little pot exclusively for preparing rose syrup to cure gripe in babies by boiling sugar, water and the fresh young flowers of the small white 'medicine rose'. This 'medicine rose' was *Rosa x fortuniana* and used to be gathered regularly from a straggling shrub on the Rothman boundary fence by the 'old women' of the town.

Knowing full well that 'gripe' in babies remains the most unexplained of all paediatric phenomena and persistently defeats the most modern medicines, I am all for using this harmless syrup again which is, after all, more useful in soothing the mother than the screaming infant. So let all newly-weds take heed and plant this white Chinese rambler in their gardens before their firstborn arrives!

1 *The Genus Rosa*, 1911, Vol. I, p. 109.

Rosa x fortuniana

The skillet in which Miss Rothman's mother used to boil her rose-water. (Now in the Swellendam museum.)

PLANT
This is a very vigorous climber 6–10 metres high.

FOLIAGE
Three light-green narrow pointed leaflets, shiny and smooth on both surfaces with finely serrated edges. The stalk is delicate and smooth with no prickles. Stipules are small, attached only at their bases, and deciduous.

FLOWERS
The fat round buds with short sepals open into very full small flowers 4–5 cm in diameter. The outer petals roll back, the smaller central ones are crumpled together in a tight bundle till the flower unfolds fully. Flower-stalks are long and thin; they hang down and are covered with many soft prickles. The calyx is truncated and smooth; the short triangular-shaped sepals are smooth on top, velvety below and have smooth edges. The scentless flowers are the first roses to appear in spring but do not recur.

INFLORESCENCE
An umbel with two to three florets hanging down from side branchlets along the length of the young stems.

Rosa x fortuniana.

221

Rosa moyesii

Rosa moyesii as illustrated
in the *Botanical Magazine*
(Vol. 136, T 8338).

The showy hips of *R. moyesii*.

In the *Botanical Magazine* of 1910 this species rose is illustrated and described as a 'strikingly beautiful rose' coming from the high mountains of Szechwan between Mt. Omi and Tatsien-lu at 2 500 – 3 000 metres. The rose was first collected in 1893 by A. E. Pratt who supplied seed to Veitch & Sons. The plants raised in their nursery at Coombe Wood first flowered in June 1908.

It is not certain when and by whom *Rosa moyesii* was first introduced to the Cape. By 1940 it was, however, well known and one of the newer species roses often used for hedge boundaries, as specimen plants on lawns, in herbaceous or ornamental borders, or in open woodland spaces 'on estates and pleasure grounds where there is room for the garden to run into and mix with nature's planning'.[1]

I have planted a *Rosa moyesii*, got from a local nursery, at Boschendal where it does not appear to be very happy though I know of a plant doing very well in Elgin where the cooler climate might be more to its liking.

This tall plant with its fern-like foliage is an asset to any garden even when not in flower, but the blood-red blooms which appear in spring and the very ornamental cherry-red hips of autumn make this an even more desirable plant, justifying the popularity that it enjoyed fifty years ago.

1 *The S.A. Rose Book*, by 'The Vicar', 1940.

222

Rosa moyesii

Rosa moyesii.

PLANT
The sturdy upright branches grow 3–4 metres high with strong straight thorns which have wide attachments.

FOLIAGE
Seven or nine small roundish-oval, bright-green leaflets with sharply toothed edges and matt upper surfaces, slightly greyer below. The stalk is thin but straight and covered with many stalked glands and small straight thorns on the underside. Stipules are wide with loose ends.

FLOWERS AND FRUIT
Rounded pointed buds, with slightly longer dainty sepals, open to single bright even-red flowers of 5 cm in diameter with a ring of many stamens surrounding a short green pistil. The small calyx is bottle-shaped and is covered with stalked glands like the flower-stalk. The slightly hairy glandular sepals with leaf-like tips reflex to hold the open flower, then curl upwards when the petals drop, covering the persistent dry stamens of the orange-red hips. The flowers appear in spring and do not have much fragrance.

INFLORESCENCE
One to two flowers on short branchlets along the main stems.

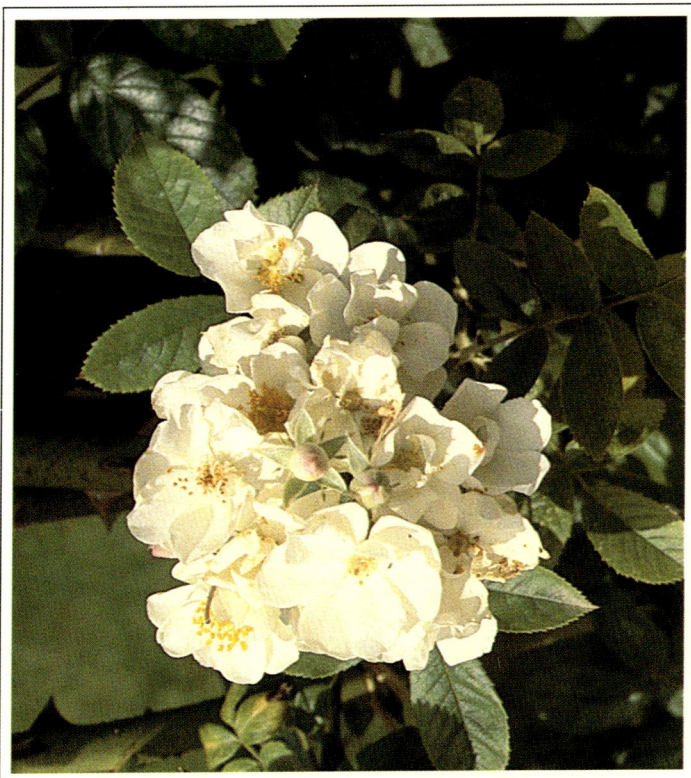

Right: 'Thalia' (1895), a pretty white rambler derived from *Rosa multiflora* and 'Paquerette'.
Below: C. P. Thunberg from *Travels in Europe, Africa and Asia* (1770–1779).

Carl Peter Thunberg was the first European to collect and describe specimens of this wild rambler which occurs naturally in Japan, Korea and North China.

In South Africa, Thunberg is a well-known and much respected botanist for it was he who first systematically explored, collected and described our indigenous flora during his stay in the Cape from April 1772 to March 1775.[1]

A pupil of the celebrated Linnaeus, he joined the Dutch East India Company as a medical officer with the help of the botanist Burman in Amsterdam, who arranged for him to go to Japan. Because the Dutch alone were at that time allowed limited trading rights in China and Japan, Thunberg had to spend some time at the Cape to learn to speak Dutch so that he could pass as a Dutchman in the East! He collected plants and seed from Japan, Java and Ceylon; and on his return to Europe in 1778 broke his journey for two months at the Cape, where he may well have given some of his finds to old friends and keen gardeners, though no record of this exists.

Thunberg presented his herbarium of 23 510 specimens to Uppsala University where he had become professor of Botany after Linnaeus. One of these specimens (no. 214) is *Rosa multiflora* which he collected in Japan and described in his *Flora Japonica*.[2]

As *Rosa multiflora* seed germinates easily, one wonders why Thunberg did not bring seed of this very useful plant with him to Europe. It seems to be generally agreed that the first person to do so was Mr Coignet, a French engineer in the employ of the Japanese government, who in 1862 sent seed to his father-in-law M. Henon, Mayor of Lyon, who distributed it to M. Guillot, from whose nurseries the rose eventually reached the rest of Europe and America.

The cross-breeding of *Rosa multiflora* with larger roses soon gave rise to many new ramblers at a time when few were available. By the end of the 19th century the many varieties of new Multiflora ramblers that were being introduced annually caused great excitement among gardening folk so that arches, pergolas and summer houses sprang up in every garden.

At the Cape, too, Multiflora hybrids became extremely popular and garden photographs of the period show tall hedges, arches, pergolas or verandas covered in these blooms. Catalogues and garden journals of the early 1900s fire the imagination with glowing descriptions: 'Thalia, masses of small white flowers'; 'Aglaia, very showy'; 'Euphrosine, bright red, very pretty'; 'Psyche, pale rosy pink, very vigorous and good', and romantic-sounding rose names appear in captions written in white ink in family photo-albums under stiffly posed groups: 'Aunt Katy and Uncle John with Tausendschön' or 'Suzy and Rachel under the Veilchenblau arch'.

Whenever I see the bleak wires around modern tennis courts I think of those delightful courts where I used to play as a schoolgirl. The wires then were tall green walls of ivy and ramblers which provided a kaleidoscope of colour in the spring. From their wild parent, all these hybrids inherited a freedom of growth and disease resistance which made them easy to cultivate and quick to provide a show, so that they became as popular as modern petunias for providing 'colour in the garden'. Today these old-timers are still evident in cottage gardens throughout the Cape.

The only place where one sees the original species rose, however, is in neglected old gardens where the stock has survived long after the grafted roses have died, for *Rosa multiflora* was at one time a common understock at the Cape before 'Indica Major', more tolerant to heat, drought and alkaline soil, came into use.[3]

Roy Shepherd writes enthusiastically about the virtues of this species in America where it has been planted to beautify industrial areas and parks, to stabilize contours, to act as windbreaks, snow fences, road barriers and to hold embankments.[4] Perhaps farmers in the cooler parts of the Western Cape might consider brightening up their estates by using these lower hedges instead of the ubiquitous pine which cuts out sunlight and sooner or later keels over to damage valuable orchards.

1 3100 species were described in his *Flora Capensis* (1807–1820).
2 Published in Leipzig in 1784.
3 Geo. Carter, in his *South African Home Garden* (Maritzburg, 1914) maintains that 'most of the stocks used in Europe are unsuitable for the South African climate and soil'. He states that grafting stock was mostly *Rosa multiflora*, which was propagated by planting cuttings 10-12 inches long in May, leaving only 2 inches above the ground.
4 Roy Shepherd, *History of the Rose*, 1954. In *Garden and Forest* (New York, 1890) the introducer is said to have been Andre Leroy of Anger. Gisele de la Roche, on the other hand, in the 1975 reprint of Redouté's *Les Roses* states that the single-flowered variety of *R. multiflora* was introduced by Robert Fortune.

Rosa multiflora

Hips.

Rosa multiflora.

PLANT
A vigorous arching shrub growing 3−4,5 metres high or climbing to a height of 6 metres. The hooked thorns are sparse or absent altogether.

FOLIAGE
Seven or nine small leaflets, oval with blunt to pointed tips, medium serrations, matt dark-green upper and greyer velvety lower surfaces; no glands, but prickles on the back of sturdy reddish leaf-stalks; stipules markedly fringed with glands on the edges.

FLOWERS
Tiny, neat, cream-coloured buds with short sepals, opening to small single white flowers 4 cm in diameter. Petals are heart-shaped and slightly cupped. The light-green pistil is prominent and club-shaped; it stands free in the centre of many short dainty yellow stamens which curve over the style in the older flowers. The tiny round calyx is smooth; the sepals are foliated and velvety on the undersurface, reflexing right back against the glandular flower-stalks as the flower opens. There is a sweet fragrance but this is not marked. The flowers appear in the last two weeks of October.

INFLORESCENCE
A dense panicle with many flowers.

225

Rosa multiflora nana with pink nicotiana and arums.
'Little White Pet'.
A miniature hedge of *R. multiflora nana* with blue petunias.

R. *multiflora nana* resembles *R. multiflora* in all respects except that it is very much smaller in all its parts, it does not climb and it flowers throughout the year.

I have found this rose in several cottage gardens in Stellenbosch and Somerset West where owners cherish their dainty plants, not only because they are so easy to multiply from cuttings or seed, but also because the tiny white or rose-coloured flowers make a pretty show throughout the spring and summer even when the plants are scarcely 15 cm high. When the leaves fall in the autumn, the miniature cherry-red round hips covering the light-green branching twigs are a delight to pick for arranging with the small flowers in miniature displays.

Its dainty growth makes *R. multiflora nana* a valuable plant for small gardens. I have clipped mine into formal low hedges to surround beds of St. Joseph lilies, and shaped a plant into a round ball to centre a bed of thyme or petunias. I have also used them as an informal edging to a bed of 'Old Monthly' roses. It makes a good pot plant too, trimmed to a formal shape or left as a small shrub with mauve alyssum at its feet.

The origin of *Rosa multiflora nana* seems to be obscure, and I do not know how long it has been growing at the Cape. In the *African Court Calendar and Directory* of 1830, the 'Gardener's Almanac' advises that in January all Chinese roses should have the flowering branches cut down 'to a few eyes to ensure a regular succession of fine trusses of blossoms'. 'China roses' at that time might have included *Rosa multiflora nana*, which was perhaps imported directly from the East, for it is recorded in 1852 that most of the roses being introduced at the Cape were from China.[1]

In the autumn of 1859 Mr Dale, Superintendent-General of Education at the Cape and a keen gardener, planted out 'some hundreds of the small cluster roses' received from Wellington,[2] at his home 'Montagu Cottage' beyond Salt River. Could these have been *Rosa multiflora nana*?

Unfortunately vague references are all we have to go by, but whatever its date of introduction, the many useful qualities of this little rose justify its continued cultivation here. If ever I were to breed new miniature roses, this is the parent plant with which I would start.

It is in fact thought that *Rosa multiflora nana* is itself a natural garden hybrid derived from *Rosa chinensis* and *Rosa multiflora* — the same two parents used by Guillot Fils in 1875 to produce the first known Polyantha rose, 'Pâquerette'.

I have not had the good fortune to see this rose, but 'Little White Pet', a small Polyantha probably very similar to 'Pâquerette', was introduced by Henderson in 1897 and sold at the Cape soon afterwards; it is still available from Ludwig's nurseries in Pretoria. I have used this sweet white miniature in the same way as I do *Rosa multiflora nana*. The plant is not as compact, but the dense trusses of small white double flowers throughout the year make it as valuable for edging beds or massing together with other carpeting flowers in confined gardens.

1 *Mrs Dale's Diary.* Edited by J. Murray, Cape Town, 1966.
2 In the Cape Colony.

Rosa multiflora nana

Hips.

Rosa multiflora nana.

PLANT
Small dainty plant up to 1 metre high; its branched stems have many light-brown hooked thorns.

FOLIAGE
Five or seven small, oval pointed, coarsely serrated leaflets, with dull mid-green surfaces slightly lighter on the undersurface; dainty slightly furry petioles with many hooks and a few scattered glands on the underside. Stipules are adnate, fringed with glands on the edges.

FLOWERS
Tiny round buds with short sepals open to single white, slightly cupped flowers 1–2 cm in diameter; petals are heart-shaped, sometimes flushed rose, with many short yellow stamens around a columnar light-green pistil. The calyces are tiny, globular and have microscopic furring but no glands; the sepals have tiny folioles. The flower-stalk is glandular and has tiny bracts with fringed edges. Flowers appear throughout the year, and have a fresh fragrance.

INFLORESCENCE
Panicles with numerous flowers borne at the tops of the branches.

The Rubidge family at Wellwood, 1927.

When we started restoring the old Cape farmstead and outbuildings at Boschendal in the Groot Drakenstein,[1] the old flower garden below the house had become a dense mass of tangled growth: dark-purple bougainvillea, white acacia, Pride of India, *Rosa laevigata*, *R. multiflora carnea* and 'Indica Major' had become so interlocked that neither man nor animal could penetrate the thicket. Only with a bulldozer could the area be cleared and the gentle slope restored so that the two large Pride of India trees could be trimmed into presentable shapes.

At the lower edge of the garden the old irrigation furrow was reinstated, and on its banks we planted a hedge of *R. multiflora carnea* by inserting slips cut from the demolished growth at sixty cm intervals. After five years the hundred-metre-long hedge was twice my height. When in springtime the solid bank of soft pink rose clusters is seen against the cobalt blue Drakenstein mountains, turning this garden into an exquisite fairyland, I know of no more breathtaking spectacle.

This rose has probably been growing in the Western Cape since the early 19th century, for one sees remnants of hedges along many farm roads, in cemeteries, on railway banks and in the gardens of old homesteads, often growing together with 'Russelliana' or *R. fortuniana*.

In the Eastern Cape I found that it was just as widespread, and especially plentiful on those farms associated with the Rubidge family in the Graaff Reinet district.

In 1821 at the age of thirty-five, Captain Robert Henry Rubidge retired to the Cape from the British navy after fighting in the Napoleonic Wars since his fourteenth birthday. When the Eastern Province was

in turmoil after the Sixth Frontier War and Dutch farmers were 'trekking' further inland, abandoning their burnt-down derelict farms, Rubidge was able to buy a large farm at a low price in the deserted area. He called it Glattwyn after his town of birth and in 1838 he moved into the small three-roomed stone cottage where the water furrow ran through the middle of his bedroom floor.

Though the cottage had altered by the time I visited it, a strong stream of water was still running in the old stone furrow past an ancient willow tree and a large scrambling rose bush with a thick gnarled stem in front of the cottage.[2] The present owners, Anne and Walter Murray, both descended from the first Rubidge, told me that a slip of this rose bush had been taken to the farm Klipfontein in 1840, which meant that the plant was at least a hundred and fifty years old and had probably been planted by Captain Robert Rubidge or his wife. As it was not flowering during my visit, Anne sent me a spray of flowers the next spring, when I was able to identify it as *R. multiflora carnea*.

Slips from this old tree grew as vigorously on Wellwood, another Rubidge farm nearby. In the black and white photographs taken in 1927 (which were kindly sent to me by the present owner, Richard) the tall hedges, heavily laden with a mass of blossom, completely dwarf the admiring Rubidge family and their friends.

I have found no records to indicate when *R. multiflora carnea* was first introduced to the Cape and for all I know it might have been offloaded here by passing ships long before it reached Europe. Loudon described it as the 'Bramble Flowered rose' in the *Botanical Magazine* in 1807,[3] stating that a Mr Evans of East India House had introduced it to England in 1804 from China, believing that it would have yellow flowers. When it flowered for the first time in Colvill's nursery, however, it turned out to be a double pink form of the species described by Thunberg in 1778, but which had not yet been introduced to Europe. Though the new pink rambler grew easily from slips and was distributed to many gardeners, it did not flower successfully in England.

To accompany the very beautiful painting in Redouté's *Les Roses*,

---

1 This work was begun in 1973. Boschendal is one of a group of farms in the Groot Drakenstein known as the Rhodes Fruit Farms, belonging to the Anglo-American Corporation.

2 In the 1847 *Eastern Province Almanac* 'gigantic willows' are described on this farm.

3 T. 1059.

4 Vol. II, pp. 67–8.

5 Palacio de Seteais, where the Treaty of Sintra was signed in 1809.

Rosa multiflora carnea

Rosa multiflora carnea.

Thory describes how this rose was brought from Colvill's nursery to France by M. Boursault in 1808, flowering in Dr Cartier's garden four years later. Thory goes on to say that the cold winter of 1812 destroyed all the plants in the vicinity of Paris.[4] Perhaps this lack of hardiness explains why I have not seen it in English or Parisian gardens.

In Portugal, on the other hand, the warmer climate is obviously conducive to its growth. I have seen it flowering profusely at Sintra against a wall of the old Castle of the Seven Sighs[5] and also at the Quinta da Bacalhoa which was built in the 16th century by the son of Alfonso Albuquerque, the first Portuguese to establish a fortress in the East.[6]

One wonders how long this rose has been growing in Portugal? For almost a century before the Dutch and English ships even rounded the Cape, the Portuguese had opened the trade routes to the East and maintained a fortress at the Japanese port of Nagasaki. Perhaps they brought rose plants home from the East, but perhaps the ships were too heavily laden with all the other riches to leave space for such useless luxuries.

There are indications that *R. multiflora carnea* has been growing in the Portuguese colony of Madeira at least since the beginning of the 19th century. In 1857 Lowe noticed that the species and the double pink variety were both to be seen 'in fences, by roadsides and near cottages and houses everywhere, growing without culture, as if wild'.[7]

Unlike the Portuguese, the English did not seem to grow this rose in their colonies at an early date, for by 1814 (when it had already been known to English gardeners for seven years) it had not yet made an appearance in the Calcutta Botanic Garden nor on the British island of St. Helena where it was listed only twenty-two years later.[8] I saw very few trees in Australian and New Zealand heritage rose gardens during my visit in 1986.

Though plentiful at the Cape, it was not listed in Baron von Ludwig's garden in 1831 nor in the Company's Botanic Garden in 1858. The origin of Captain Rubidge's 150-year-old *Rosa multiflora carnea* in the Graaff Reinet district therefore remains an unsolved mystery.

6 This was the Dom Manuel Fort at Cochin.
7 *Manual of the Flora of Madeira.*
8 See Roxburgh's plant lists for the Botanic Gardens at Calcutta and St. Helena, both dating to 1814.

PLANT
Large arching shrub 5–6 metres high, or climber to 10 metres. Many hooked reddish thorns.

FOLIAGE
Five oblong, pointed, medium-green leaflets with dull upper and grey lower surfaces. The leaf-stalk is sturdy with many prickles on the underside. Stipules are fringed.

FLOWERS
Small oval buds with slightly longer velvety sepals open to very full flat flowers 3,5 cm in diameter. Petals are heart-shaped, icing-sugar pink, paler to the centre; they fade to white. The hairy pistils are twisted together to form a green central point. Flower-stalk and cup-shaped calyx are glandular and velvety. The flowers are sweetly fragrant and appear only in spring.

INFLORESCENCE
Dense panicle with very many flowers.

229

'Tausendschön'

An unknown *Rosa multiflora* hybrid.

The Cape 'Seven Sisters' in a Pniel garden.

'Tausendschön'.

A rose which resembles 'Seven Sisters' very closely is 'Tausendschön' (Schmidt, 1906). It is also descended from *R. multiflora* through 'Weisser Herumstreicher', in its turn descended from 'Pâquerette'. 'Tausendschön' is a most apt name for a rose which will ramble over six metres up into a tree, to cover it in spring with a 'thousand beauties'. The clear pink flowers with lighter shanks fade to paler pink, but there is never the same colour variation as in 'Seven Sisters'; and then, of course, it flowers only once a year. The stems are thornless.

Rosa multiflora (*variety unknown*)

'SEVEN SISTERS'

This garden variety of *Rosa multiflora* produces a continuous spectacle of flowers throughout the year, and is commonly known at the Cape as 'Seven Sisters', a rose which had long been cultivated in Japanese and Chinese gardens before it was introduced to Britain at the start of the 19th century.

One finds this rose quite often in older Cape gardens. It seems to enjoy a great deal of popularity especially amongst the poorer people, perhaps because of its carefree growth and generous production of flowers. I found several plants in the small gardens of the mission town of Pniel.

As the newly opened flowers are dark shocking-pink and the older ones almost white, there is always a variety of shades on the shrub, especially as the flowers are long-lived. Sprays when picked are a joy to arrange indoors, for the dainty branches with fern-like foliage are very effective in softening up arrangements of stiff Hybrid Tea roses. I have often used the bright flowers and buds in wedding bouquets and chaplets because the blooms are remarkably tough and long-lasting.

Although this rose is usually planted to cover fences or walls, I have seen it looking very charming when used as a large sprawling shrub in front of an evergreen hedge along an entrance driveway. But this can only be achieved where there is no shortage of space, for if allowed to grow unpruned, it eventually builds up into a tall shrub with many graceful arching branches.

When I showed slides of the Cape 'Seven Sisters' at the International Heritage Rose Conference in Adelaide in 1986, Peter Beales pointed out to me that it was not the same as the 'Seven Sisters' known to British nurseries, and therefore this rose must for the moment remain an unidentified form of *Rosa multiflora*.

The Cape 'Seven Sisters'.

1 A boundary hedge at Salomonsvlei.
2 'Blush Rambler', another similar but non-recurrent rose.
3 'Rambling Rector' resembles this unidentified Multiflora, but its flowers are paler and occur only in spring.
4 Could this illustration, done by Reeves during his stay in China in the early 19th century, be of the same rose?
5 I have planted this rose at the Boland Farm Museum.

This very pretty rambler was found growing in the tangled under-growth where Boschendal's old garden used to be. Many slips were taken which grew quickly into large bushes that now adorn the white wall of the werf, as well as pergolas in the restored garden, with masses of sweetly fragrant pink rose trusses almost throughout the year.

I have found that this rose is widespread throughout South Africa and especially plentiful in old Cape gardens, but no one knows its name. Some have thought it might be 'Blush Noisette' (the 'Rosa noiset-tiana' portrayed by Redouté)[1] but its vigorous growth is against this. 'Blush Rambler' was considered, but flowers only once a year. 'Champ-ney's Pink Cluster' was discarded after reading 'The Two Roses of Charleston' by Leonie Bell in the *Rose Annual* 1983, in which her sketch shows a completely different inflorescence.

The slightly fringed stipules indicate the possibility of Multiflora parentage, and when flowers were sent to Kew for identification this opinion was upheld, so that I am now simply calling it the 'Everflower-ing Multiflora' until it can be more definitely identified.

Its remontancy, very sweet fragrance and ease with which it grows from slips make this rose particularly valuable as a decorative garden shrub. The vigorous healthy plants are most useful for tall hedges or where quick coverage of unsightly banks or structures is required. This winter I planted many three-month-old rooted cuttings against the road banks on the approach to Dougie Jooste's new wine-cellar at Klein Con-stantia, and if these all grow into the large sprawling shrubs which I expect, future wine-tasters will certainly have more to enjoy than Dou-gie's good wine!

1 Vol. II, p. 27.

'Everflowering Multiflora'

'Everflowering Multiflora'.

PLANT
A vigorous rambler 3–5 metres high with numerous light-brown smallish hooked thorns often grouped in pairs below the nodes.

FOLIAGE
Five or seven oval pointed dark-green leaflets with serrated edges and matt surfaces, velvety on the underside. The stalk is furry and has sharp hooked prickles below. Stipules are short, wide and have fringed edges.

FLOWERS
Round pointed buds with short sepals open to semi-double flowers of about 5 cm in diameter. The clear pink petals (about twenty-five to thirty) are slightly cupped, so that the flower never opens quite flat. Many stamens curl inwards over the green column of the pistil as the flower ages. The calyx is oval and velvety like the thin flower-stalks; the short sepals with tiny folioles, velvety on both surfaces, reflex quickly right back against the stems. The large trusses of flowers make a fine show in spring but appear again in lesser flushes throughout the summer and autumn. They are very fragrant.

INFLORESCENCE
A cyme of many flowers (from three to thirty and more) arranged in groups of three to four.

'Hiawatha'

'Hiawatha'.

'Philadelphia'

'Philadelphia'.

This very attractive Multiflora rambler, with its large trusses of tiny crimson flowers that look very much like miniature 'American Pillar' roses, had formed a thick green carpet in a corner of the Pniel graveyard where small unmarked graves consisted only of earth mounds. On a sunny spring morning I thought how much more appropriate it was to commemorate the tiny departed with these cheerful small flowers than with grey granite stones or pink marble angels.

Slips I took grew easily, and I planted them against a white wall next to 'American Pillar' for the fun of confusing visitors in the springtime when the large and tiny flowers would bloom together as from one plant, both having single dark-pink flowers with white centres and a mass of bright yellow stamens.

Closer inspection will soon distinguish the vigorous Wichuraiana hybrid, with its small shiny leaflets and larger panicle of flowers, from the more delicate Multiflora which is a daintier plant in all its parts with softer, duller leaves and fringed stipules.

'Hiawatha' is one of the numerous descendants of 'Crimson Rambler', the other parent being 'Paul's Carmine Pillar'. After its introduction by Walsh in 1904, it was soon found in South African gardens where it became a popular pergola rose until the more robust and showy Wichuraiana hybrids surpassed it. One rarely sees 'Hiawatha' in gardens of today, but the slips I took at Pniel have thrived and found homes in gardens of several friends who love old roses.

Peter Knox-Shaw, my rose-collecting ally, had heard with dismay that the old thatched cottage named Forenaughts in Wynberg was to be levelled to make way for a new block of flats. Miss Wolfe, his neighbour who had been living in the cottage since her childhood, was delighted to hear that we were interested to save some of her old rose trees and gave us a running commentary on all the varieties we encountered as we crept through the tangled mass of uncontrolled growth which had once been a splendid garden.

Honeysuckle and myrtle, white Banksia entwined with wisteria, 'Maman Cochet' and a maroon pompon-like rose which was introduced as 'Philadelphia', all clutched at our clothes and limbs, their thorny branches barring the once neat pathways and scratching viciously as we took cuttings and dug out plants. How desperate, helpless and sad we felt, knowing that whatever we left would be destroyed within the week.

Fortunately most of my cuttings grew and within one year 'Philadelphia' flowered. The trusses were not as large and impressive as those I had seen against the thatched roof of Forenaughts, but the ruby pompons on their delicate stalks were healthy, and vigorous young shoots raised expectations of a fine show the following spring.

'Philadelphia' was introduced by Van Fleet in 1904 from 'Crimson Rambler' and 'Victor Hugo'. It never achieved the popularity of 'Dorothy Perkins' or 'Excelsa' at the Cape, but was quite often used and was still being advertised by Leighton Nurseries in King William's Town in the early 1940s as 'superior to Turner's Crimson Climber' which had been regarded as one of the best Victorian climbers.

This rose's charm for me lies in the small flowers, their rich colouring and the long lax sprays which I like to use for softening stiff rose arrangements.

PLANT
A very vigorous climber to 7 m with dark-green lanky stems and many light-brown hooked thorns.
FOLIAGE
Five or seven light-green oval leaflets with serrated edges, matt surfaces and prickles on the leaf-stalk. Stipules are fringed and have slightly glandular edges.
FLOWERS
Tiny round buds with short sepals open to single cup-shaped flowers 3 cm in diameter; the dark-pink to crimson petals are white towards the centre. There are many light-yellow very dainty stamens around a bunch of short furry styles. The calyx is small, round and smooth; sepals are short, unfoliated, furry on both surfaces and have a few sessile glands on the edges. Flowers are slightly fragrant and appear only in November for a few weeks.
INFLORESCENCE
Large panicles usually of six to twelve flowers, in groups of three.

PLANT
A rambler capable of scrambling 6 metres high, with straggly growth and small light-brown hooked thorns.
LEAVES
Five or seven oval pointed, very delicate, light-green, finely serrated leaflets with many small hooked prickles on the thin stalk. The fringed stipules are edged with a few glands.
FLOWERS
Small oval buds with sepals slightly longer open to very full, dull maroon, pompon flowers 4–5 cm in diameter on dainty, slightly glandular stalks. Stamens are short and inconspicuous, the styles loose and slightly longer. The calyx is cup-shaped and smooth; sepals are smooth and narrow with a few very small folioles, reflexing only half way. Flowers have very little fragrance and appear only for a few weeks in November.
INFLORESCENCE
A dense panicle of very many flowers.

'Goldfinch'

Alongside the road that runs through the small mission village of Pniel near Stellenbosch, there is a green bank where the 'Goldfinch' rambler grows. From the confines of its small cottage garden it has thrown out long branches over a decrepit fence, weighing the rusted wires to the ground and spilling over into the roadside, gathering armfuls of morning glory along its way to form a tangle of light-green foliage.

When the time approaches for this rose to flower, I drive through Pniel whenever I can, for suddenly one day the green bank will be a mass of primrose yellow trusses festooned with purple-blue morning glory trumpets. Fortunately the overhanging oaks cast a dappled shadow over this spectacle, preserving the bright yellow which otherwise soon fades in the strong sunlight.

Inspired by this charming colour scheme, no doubt, my friend Basil Bennetts decided to plant his slips of the Pniel 'Goldfinch' next to a 'Veilchenblau' which had entwined itself around a statuette in his cottage garden at Wynberg. Here in the early spring, the large dainty trusses of the two ramblers splash their yellow and mauve against a wall of shiny dark-green ivy for the delight of visitors to the nearby tea-nook.

I visited the garden early one morning before the sun had had a chance to fade the yellow or dispel the fragrance of the roses, and finding it difficult among the vicious thorns to reach an unblemished spray to photograph, I snipped off a truss which had quaintly perched itself on the statuette's head.

Paul and Sons developed 'Goldfinch' in their Cheshunt nursery in 1907 from the rambler 'Hélène' and an unknown rose.[1] It was introduced to the Cape soon afterwards but its demure colouring could not compete against 'Alister Stella Gray', which flowered twice a year and was considered by some to be the best yellow cluster rose at that time.[2] Yet I have not been able to trace a single plant of the latter, whereas 'Goldfinch' is quite commonly seen in early 20th century Western Cape gardens.

'Goldfinch'.

PLANT
A rambler of angular growth, 4–5 metres high, with very many short red hooked thorns.

FOLIAGE
Five or seven oval pointed matt leaflets with finely serrated edges; stalks are strong, straight and have small hooks on the undersurface; stipules slightly fringed on the edges.

FLOWERS
Small oval fat buds with short sepals open to semi-double flowers 5 cm in diameter, primrose yellow when freshly open, fading later to cream. There are many stamens with long thin filaments and small anthers around a shorter pistil. Calyces are smooth and cup-shaped; flower-stalks are delicate and slightly glandular. The sepals have small folioles and are slightly rough and glandular on the outside. Flowers appear in October only for two to three weeks and have a fresh fruity fragrance.

INFLORESCENCE
A large panicle with many clusters of three flowers per stalk.

1 According to McFarland *(Modern Roses 8)*.
2 *The Cape Garden,* 1909.

Mill River cottage garden.

Multiflora ramblers at Boschendal.

Rosa helenae, a Chinese species introduced to the Cape in the early 1900s, was often planted with other ramblers.

'Mrs F. W. Flight', a climbing cluster-rose found in the Cape soon after its European introduction in 1905.

'Veilchenblau' was introduced by J. C. Schmidt in 1909, and is a grandchild of *Rosa multiflora* through 'Crimson Rambler' which reached the West directly from a Tokyo garden in 1878. The other parent seems to be unknown although some authors think that it might be the fragrant crimson-purple 'Erinnerung an Brod'.[1]

When I visited the Roseraie de l'Hay-les-Roses near Paris in July 1980, the ramblers were in full bloom and truly an incredible sight: avenues of arches festooned with masses of rose blooms enchanted the eye wherever one walked. Pale pink 'New Dawn', crisp white *Rosa helenae*, rose-pink 'Mrs F. W. Flight', 'White Dorothy', cream-pink 'Lady Godiva', yellow 'Paul Noël' — these had all been mere names up till that time, but how much more beautiful they were than I had ever imagined! Old friends like 'Dorothy Perkins' and 'Excelsa' assumed a new magnificence, but most impressive of all these was 'Veilchenblau' in a dense mass of rich mauve blossom, the colour and fragrance more exquisite than I had ever experienced at the Cape, where it is still to be found in many gardens.

This rambler has always been a special favourite of mine ever since I first encountered it, when as a shy young girl I was invited to spend a holiday at my husband's family home in Newlands, many years before we were married. Mrs Jessie (Queenie) Fagan was an ardent gardener and though the grounds were not large, her grouping of plants, colour combinations and choice of plant material were all excitingly new to me. What impressed me most were the climbers covering the high tennis court fence where Virginia creeper, wisteria, 'Dorothy Perkins' and 'Veilchenblau' grew right up to the top of the wire. 'Veilchenblau' was in full bloom that first holiday and I remember how surprised I was at the extraordinary colour.

For months afterwards I would repeat the strange name to myself and see in my mind's eye the trusses of mauve-blue flowers against a bright blue sky, or a small blue-green vase filled with the same sweetly scented semi-double flowers placed next to my bed in the guest room, welcoming me to the home of the family which was eventually to become my own.

With my daughter Jessie and her fiancé Ian, who were with me that summer day at Roseraie de l'Hayes-les-Roses, I ambled up and down beneath the rose bowers clicking away happily with my camera to record some of the beauty which was giving us so much pleasure. As we stopped once again before 'Veilchenblau', the girl who bore her grandmother's name, suddenly said 'How I wish Ouma could have been here today to share with us this beautiful garden', and the cheerful mauve flowers suddenly filled us with sadness and longing for the grandmother who had become only a memory.

'Veilchenblau'

'Coronation', darker and more
crimson than 'Veilchenblau'.

PLANT
*Vigorous rambler growing 4–5 metres high. The stems are
usually smooth and thornless although there may be a few
hooked thorns.*

LEAVES
*Five or seven large, oval pointed, light-green leaflets with
smooth shiny surfaces and deeply serrated edges; sturdy,
slightly glandular stalks. Stipules are widish, very finely
fringed and glandular.*

FLOWERS
*The small round buds, with short sepals, open into
semi-double flowers 3 cm in diameter, with many
prominent yellow stamens in the centre.
Flower-stalks are densely glandular as are the
sepals and bracts, though the small round calyx
is smooth. Flowers appear mostly in early
November and have a strong fresh fruity
fragrance.*

INFLORESCENCE
*Loose panicles up to 20 cm long with
many clusters of flowers.*

'Veilchenblau'.

237

Ellen Willmott's
Rosa wichuraiana.

*R*osa luciae was first described by Crépin in 1871. (At this time it included the species *R. wichuraiana* which Crépin was later to name separately.) It occurs very commonly in Japan but also in Korea, Manchuria and parts of Eastern China, extending as far south as Hong Kong, Whampoa, the Quantung Provinces and Formosa. It is not clear to me who first introduced plants to the West, but it appears to have been growing in German botanic gardens when Crépin first saw it. The rose commemorates Lucy Savatier, the wife of a French naval doctor who, together with her husband, botanized in Japan from 1866 to 1875.

In 1886 Crépin decided that some specimens of *R. luciae* differed to such an extent that they should be distinguished as a separate species. He named this new group after the botanist Max Ernst Wichura, who had collected plants in Japan during his travels in the Far East as part of a Prussian diplomatic mission in 1861. According to Krussman, Wichura sent living plants of *R. wichuraiana* to Germany in that year but they died soon afterwards. 'In 1880', continues Dr Krussman, 'he sent a second batch of plants to the Botanic Gardens of Munich and Brussels',[1] but this is obviously a mistake, for Wichura had been dead for fourteen years by then.

In 1888 plants *(R. wichuraiana?)* were sent by Mr Louis Spath of Berlin from Germany to the Harvard Arboretum in America. Here they flourished and were widely distributed, soon becoming popular because of their vigorous growth and suitability as a ground cover. Hooker describes how the Parks Department of Boston used this rose for covering rocky slopes 'where its remarkable habit, hardiness, the brilliance of its lustrous foliage and the beauty of its flowers which appear when most shrubs are out of bloom, certainly recommend it to the attention of the cultivars of hardy plants.'[2] It later became known as the 'Memorial Rose' because of its usefulness as a ground cover for cemeteries.

From America the rose reached Kew in 1891. In the previous year Barbier, who had obtained stock from Michael Horvath of the Newport Nursery in Rhode Island, started using it in his Orléans nursery as a seed parent for hybridizing new varieties of climbers.

Soon the so-called 'Wichuraiana hybrids' were being introduced to the market both from America and from the Orléans nurseries in France. Every year new champion climbers and ramblers were ac-claimed by gardeners for their exuberant growth, their luscious, shiny foliage and the profusion and sweet fragrance of their colourful flowers.

The literature on these two species roses is most confusing and it is not clear to me which of these many rambler hybrids are descended from *R. luciae* and which from *R. wichuraiana.* Some writers think that the group with larger flowers like 'Albertine', Albéric Barbier' and 'Francois Juranville' (which were introduced by Barbier), are derived from *R. luciae,* whereas the smaller-flowered roses like 'Dorothy Perkins' and 'Excelsa', introduced from America, are hybrids of *R. wichuraiana.*[3] Yet Bean doubts that *R. luciae* was ever introduced to Europe, or that it entered into the parentage of these ramblers.[4]

Hooker describes and illustrates a rose that flowered at Kew which he calls *R. luciae* in the 1895 edition of *Curtis' Botanical Magazine.* When this is compared with the illustration of *R. wichuraiana* in Ellen Willmott's monograph (1914) it is clear that these are two different species, for although the foliage of both is very similar, the flowers of *R. luciae* are slightly cupped, have oval-cordate petals and seven loose hairy styles whereas those of *R. wichuraiana* are larger with elongated petals curling back and containing only one club-shaped style. It is, however, puzzling to find that both belong to the Synstylae group.

The rose known at the Cape as *R. wichuraiana* is probably *R. luciae* for its resembles the illustration in the *Botanical Magazine* very closely and has, like Hooker's *R. luciae,* seven loose styles in the centre of the prominent mass of yellow stamens.

This rose was popularly grown at the Cape in the early 1900s, trained over fences, clipped neatly into hedges, or used to cover open banks and pergolas. In 1924 Dorothea Fairbridge observed that 'the parent Wichuraiana has not been surpassed by any of its more showy children'.[5]

When I was a child *R. luciae* was commonly used for hedges but now is seldom seen. At the farm Ida's Valley near Stellenbosch, there is still a particularly fine specimen, trimmed into a hedge and forming an arch at the entrance to the rose garden. My photograph was taken of a flower obtained at the Swellendam Museum, where the horticulturist is, like the Americans, using *R. luciae* as a ground cover, the thorny branches being most effective in keeping visitors to the paths!

1 *Roses,* 1982 translation.
2 In the *Botanical Magazine,* 1895, t. 7421.
3 Gerd Krussman, *Roses,* 1982 translation.
4 *Trees & Shrubs Hardy in the British Isles,* 8th revised edition.
5 *Gardens of South Africa.*

Rosa luciae

PLANT
A prostrate shrub with long, trailing, somewhat angular branches that form a thick mat when allowed to straggle over the ground. It can, however, be trained to climb to 6 metres or to form a neatly clipped hedge. Fawn-coloured hooked thorns are situated at the base of every leaf and branchlet.

FOLIAGE
Five or seven oval pointed leaflets on short stems with tiny hooks on the back. Leaf edges are coarsely toothed and the surfaces glossy on both sides. Stipules are short with dentated edges which have very tiny glands.

FLOWERS
Small round buds with short sepals open to single white flowers 2,5 cm in diameter with shiny heart-shaped petals, slightly cupped when open, and with prominent yellow stamens in the centre. There are seven hairy free-standing styles. The calyx is elongated and oval; the sepals have tiny folioles, velvety on the inside and slightly glandular on the outside. The flower-stalks have many stalked glands and an oval bract at the base. The flowers are sweetly fragrant and appear only in spring.

INFLORESCENCE
Panicles of seven to ten florets along the main branches.

Rosa luciae.

Hips.

Rosa luciae from the *Botanical Magazine* (Vol 121, T 7421).

'Albéric Barbier'

PLANT
This is a vigorous scrambler, growing to 3 metres or much higher if given support. It has long angular branches and many sharp hooked thorns.

FOLIAGE
Five or seven dark-green shiny oval leaflets with medium-sized well-marked serrations. The petiole is sturdy and has many small hooks. Stipules are broad, smooth and shiny with longish loose tips and slightly glandular edges.

FLOWERS
The fat round cream buds have slightly longer sepals and open to very full flat quartered flowers of 8 cm in diameter. Petals are cream, fading to white, club-shaped and slightly crumpled, giving the flower a crinkled appearance. The inner petals hide the few short stamens but not the small bunch of creamy green, slightly hairy stigmas. The dark-green calyx is cup-shaped, taken in at the top, very smooth and shiny; the sepals are shiny on the outside and downy inside. The flowers appear in late spring but odd ones occur now and again throughout the summer. They have a marked fresh fragrance.

INFLORESCENCE
Small bunches of two to four flowers along the main branches.

'Albéric Barbier'.

The dark-green glossy foliage of this vigorous sprawling rambler creates a luscious background for any flower-bed or herbaceous border throughout the year. Fortunately there are many large specimens of this rose still to be seen in the southern suburbs of Cape Town along street boundaries where the ubiquitous vibracrete fencing has not yet been installed. For even when not in flower, 'Albéric Barbier' makes a most attractive informal hedge. How much more pleasant is a living green wall like this, through which the passer-by is allowed glimpses of the garden within, than the unsmiling face of dull grey concrete. And then in spring when the many quartered white flowers are scattered like stars over the shiny green background, the hedge becomes a joyful spectacle which the whole neighbourhood can share, perhaps to pick a small twig with flowers to take indoors, or just to savour the fresh fragrance apparent even from across the street.

I know a garden where this climber, together with 'Géant des Batailles', has found its way high up into an old cypress tree, and when the rich cream and brilliant crimson flowers are out together, speckled against dark green foliage and bright blue sky, a more beautiful sight can hardly be imagined.

A small yellow Tea rose called 'Shirley Hibberd' was the one parent of 'Albéric Barbier' and *Rosa wichuraiana* the other. From the former it probably inherited its thick creamy white petals, and from the species rose its shiny leaves and vigour. 'Albéric Barbier' was the result of a successful experiment conducted by the French hybridist Rene Barbier of Orléans on a young Wichuraiana plant which he had received from America in 1899. A small cluster of flowers on this plant was pollinated and yielded ten seeds of which five produced plants, one of them being 'Albéric Barbier'.[1]

This rambler became popular at the Cape chiefly as a hedging plant only in the late 1920s and many of the hedges which still flourish in the southern suburbs probably date from this period. Notwithstanding its many good qualities, however, there is at present no South African nursery that sells 'Albéric Barbier', and those wishing to establish new hedges will have to obtain cuttings from existing old bushes.

1 *The American Rose Journal*, 1926, p. 175.

'Silver Moon'

'Silver Moon'.

Roses like 'Silver Moon' were often used for hedges in the early 1900s. This hedge in full bloom was in the garden of the Superintendent of the leper colony on Robben Island in the late 19th century.

Along the dusty road that bounds Willie Krause's rose nursery in Daljosafat, 'Silver Moon' throws out its long vigorous shoots over the crumpled wire fence and sprawls into the weedy stormwater furrows. In late spring the first clusters of pointed buds appear along the branches and soon afterwards the whole glossy shrub is covered in a profusion of large milk-white blooms.

When I first noticed the rose, I thought it was *Rosa laevigata* which is plentiful in that old Huguenot dale, but the dark-green leaves invited closer inspection and I found that the semi-double white flowers had six large outer petals and four to five incurving smaller ones in the centre, all much more frilly and informally arranged than the single blooms of *Rosa laevigata*.

It was Wendy Pickstone who identified the rose for me as 'Silver Moon', a hybrid of *R. wichuraiana* and *Rosa laevigata*. She knew it well, for this rambler grew to perfection in the front garden of her old family home at Lekkerwyn in Groot Drakenstein where her father had planted a rose garden in the early 1900s.[1] At that time this Van Fleet rose, introduced in 1910 by P. Henderson, was fresh off the shelf and probably caused quite a stir among the Drakenstein farmers when it started flowering. Old Mr Pickstone cleverly planted it together with 'Souvenir de Madame Léonie Viennot' which continues to supply splashes of shocking-pink colour in the glossy green rose hedge throughout the year, long after the brilliant white spring display and fresh fragrance of 'Silver Moon' have disappeared.

1 H.E. Pickstone later owned a rose nursery at the farm Klein Constantia.

PLANT
This is a very vigorous climber which will grow up to 8 metres on a support or otherwise form a large sprawling shrub. It has smallish brown hooked thorns.

FOLIAGE
Five dark-green oval-pointed leaflets have shiny smooth surfaces and flat evenly serrated edges. The leaf-stalks are sturdy, tinged red and have many hooked prickles. Stipules are narrow with smooth edges.

FLOWERS
Large oval buds with slightly longer sepals open to semi-double, slightly cup-shaped, milk-white flowers 9 cm in diameter. The petals have uneven edges as if torn off at the top, giving the flower a frilly look. The large yellow anthers have long, pale, thin filaments. The calyx is goblet-shaped, smooth and dark green; the sepals, with a few short folioles, are shiny smooth on the upper surface, velvety below. The flower-stalk is slightly rough. Flowers appear only in spring and have a lovely fresh fragrance.

INFLORESCENCE
Two to four flowers appear together on short side branchlets along the main stems.

CAPE ARCHIVE 688

'Dorothy Perkins' hedge at
Boschendal in the early 1900s.

'Dorothy Perkins' over an old wall.

'Dorothy Perkins' ground-cover at Knysna.

'First Love' at the Parc de la Grange, Geneva.

'Dorothy Perkins'

'Dorothy Perkins'.

PLANT
This is a vigorous rambler with lax trailing stems which, when supported, will climb to 7 metres high. The stems are somewhat angular and are covered with many curved small hooked thorns.

FOLIAGE
Five small oval shiny leaflets about 2,5 cm long have deeply serrated edges and stiff thin stalks with prickles on the lower surface. The stipules have serrated edges.

FLOWERS
Small round buds with short sepals open to full round baby-pink florets of 3–4 cm in diameter. There are many longish bright yellow stamens and a light-green shorter pistil somewhat hidden by a muddle of petals. The shiny smooth calyx is cup-shaped; the oval sepals, slightly velvety on both sides, reflex half-way. The rose has a faint sweet fragrance and flowers only for a short time in late spring.

INFLORESCENCE
A corymb of twelve to thirty flowers usually in groups of two to four.

When as children we played at make-believe weddings, 'Dorothy Perkins' was chosen for the bridesmaids' bouquets, and 'Excelsa' (which we thought more beautiful) for the bride. One spray of bright crimson flowers embellished with a few bits of trailing fern transformed the ugliest little freckle-face into the most exquisite bride in the world, so there was usually a great deal of argument as to who should be bride. But as the pergolas were always laden with these flowers, the grown-ups did not mind how many we picked, so that each child had a turn to be bride. We were sad that our favourite roses should flower for such a short period of the year.

Soon after its introduction in 1901, 'Dorothy Perkins' became the sweetheart of Cape gardeners. In spring flower-laden arches, verandas, summer-houses and boundary fences transformed the poorest cottage gardens into spectacles of colour, turning village streets into delightful havens for Sunday afternoon drivers and strollers. During the first few years nursery catalogues enthusiastically displayed full-page illustrations, selling plants at double the price of any other rose.

In 1908 'Excelsa' ('Red Dorothy') and 'White Dorothy', were welcomed with as much fervour as their pink sister and these three ramblers retained their popularity at the Cape well into the 1940s.

243

Rambler roses on arches and pillars
at Roseraie de l'Hay-les-Roses.

However, familiarity breeds contempt, and eventually the Dorothies became as 'common' as painted cement gnomes, so that snobbish passers-by would smirk even at the most wonderful spring display of these old favourites while 'Chapman's Crimson Rambler' and 'Etoile de Hollande' stole the show. 'Dorothy Perkins' can still be seen here and there on the fences of labourers' cottages or covering the banks of railway reserves, but 'Excelsa' and 'White Dorothy' are rare in the Western Cape today. Perhaps their previous glory has lingered on in the minds of some, for I have noticed new plantings of the red and pink Dorothies along the highway in Knysna and along the boundary fence of a farm in the Klein Drakenstein.

In one of the most charming rose gardens that I have seen — La Roseraie du Parc de la Grange, which lies on the banks of Lake Geneva — 'Excelsa' is used to perfection. Large trusses of flowers, entirely covering their umbrella supports, drooped down in crimson garlands to contrast vividly with the beds of white Floribundas at their feet. 'Paul's Scarlet Climber' and 'American Pillar' were used in the same way. These dark-red umbrellas of roses were dotted throughout the garden in pools of neatly trimmed Floribundas against the backdrop of stretching lawns and dark-green conifers. In this garden I saw many of the roses which were in fashion when I was a teenager: 'President Hoover', 'Crimson Glory' and 'First Love'.

My daughter sitting with her first love on a bench among the roses, holding hands and talking happily, took my thoughts back many years as I fell into a sentimental reverie:

I was back in a darkened little room in the students' quarters of the Somerset Maternity Hospital adjoining the Cape Town docks. I had woken up confused and disorientated after a day's heavy sleep following on a night's 'baby catching'. In the darkness I became aware of the fragrance of roses and when a colleague opened the door with a cup of coffee, I saw next to my bed a milk jug filled with a large bright pink bunch of 'Dorothy Perkins'. 'Gawie brought it while you were sleeping', she said, smiling at the unusual bouquet, not realizing that with that cheerful bunch my 'First Love' had stolen my heart for good.

I was glad that I had taken Jessie and her fiancé with me to the rose garden, for the enchantment of that fairyland day in the Parc de la Grange will be a precious memory for us to share in the years to come.

Now that they are married, I have planted an 'Excelsa' and a 'Dorothy Perkins' in their garden together with many other old-time ramblers, for I would like my granddaughters to experience many happy hours of playing with flowers as their grandmother used to do.

'Excelsa'

'Excelsa'.

'Excelsa' at Boschendal
in the early morning.

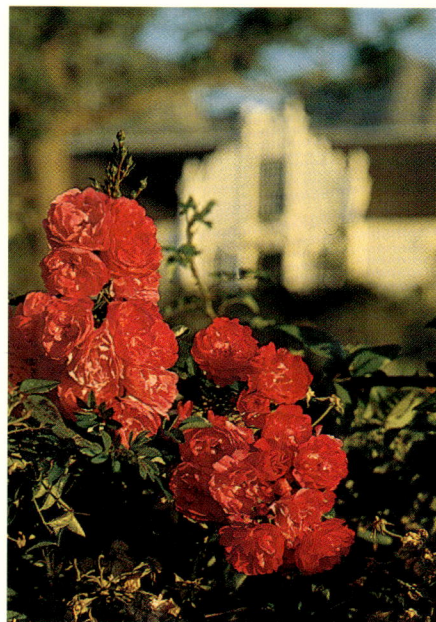

The plant is in all respects similar to 'Dorothy Per-kins' except for the deep crimson of the flowers which has earned it the name of 'Red Dorothy Perkins'. It starts flowering two weeks before 'Dorothy Perkins'.

'Francois Juranville'

In Basil Bennetts' garden.

PLANT
A vigorous climber with many long thin shoots and numerous hooked thorns.

FOLIAGE
Five or seven leaflets, 2–3 cm long with dark-green shiny surfaces, medium serrations and prickles on the underside of the leaf-stalk.

FLOWERS
Pretty, round buds with short sepals open to very full light-pink flat flowers 7 cm in diameter. The short stamens and pistils are of the same length. The cup-shaped calyx is smooth and the broad unfoliated sepals velvety on the underside. The flowers appear in a flush in spring and a few blooms appear sporadically during the rest of the summer and in autumn. There is a strong apple fragrance.

INFLORESCENCE
A corymb of three to five flowers.

'Francois Juranville'.

This is one of the many ramblers bred by Barbier in Orléans in the early 1900s, probably from *Rosa luciae*. 'Francois Juranville' was introduced in 1906, having as its other parent the pinkish-yellow China rose, 'Mme Laurette Messimy'. Early 20th century rose catalogues at the Cape do not mention this rose, but as I have seen it growing over many old arches and verandas of houses dating back to that period, I know that it must have arrived here soon after its European introduction.

The first plant I saw was growing at Leeuwenhof, official residence of the Administrator of the Cape. We had been asked to investigate the possibility of restoring a rather worn down building in the backyard of this three-century-old homestead.[1] While we were examining the mouldings and plastered decorations on the front facade, I became entangled in the long shoots of a thorny rambler which had once been supported against the wall, but was now flung across the foot of the building.

The limp branches with dark-green glossy foliage were covered with large, clear pink rosette-like flowers that spread a delicious fragrance like sweet ripe apples around them. Fortunately I took a few slips with the flowers that I picked to identify, for when next we arrived on site, the builder had conscientiously cleared the area around the building.

In Maisie Knox-Shaw's garden in Elgin, 'Francois Juranville' transforms a quiet shady corner into a vibrant mass of exuberant pink in the spring. Not content with covering a gazebo, she has thrown out long arms into a nearby petria and sprawling 'Crépuscule', mingling her pink with yellow and dark mauve to form a very pretty picture indeed. The surrounding apple orchards would find it difficult to compete with the intensity of apple fragrance diffused by this French charmer.

1 This later turned out to be a slave lodge built in 1786.

'Paul Transon'

From Ludwig's Pretoria nursery I received with great expectation a rose tree named 'Jaune Desprez'. The plant settled down quickly and soon revealed its true character by throwing out long shoots in all directions, and when the first large orange-pink semi-double flowers appeared, it was quite clear that there had been a mix-up with the name-tags. Mr Taschner phoned to apologize and told me that the imposter was none other than 'Paul Transon'.

This proved, however, to be a very happy mistake. For apart from the vigour, health and pretty shiny foliage which it obviously inherited from its Wichuraiana parent, the fragrant, warmly coloured flowers which light up the plant most of the year are a real joy in the garden.

This rambler was introduced by Barbier in 1900, and its other parent (according to McFarland's *Modern Roses 8*) was the Noisette 'L'Idéal'. It needs a lot of space and is most useful for covering unsightly garden structures or for growing over a summer-house, or for shading a patio. It strikes quickly from cuttings and can therefore easily be multiplied.

'Paul Transon'.

'American Pillar'

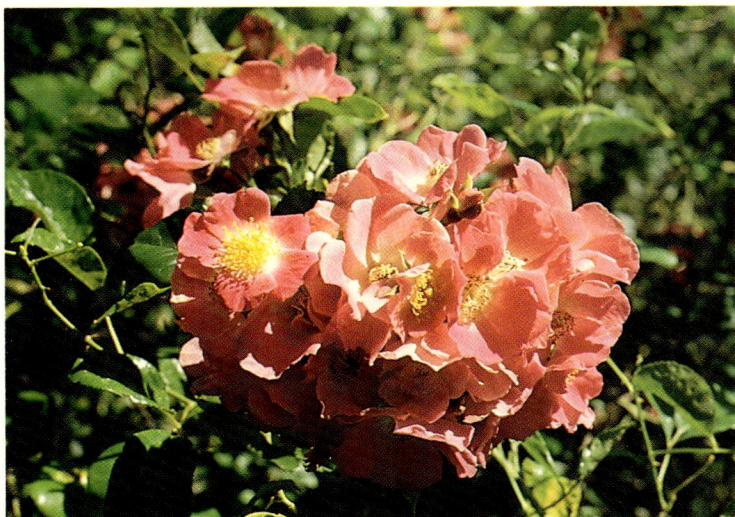

'American Pillar'.

Unknown Wichuraiana hybrid

Unknown Wichuraiana hybrid.

'American Pillar' is probably the most vigorous of all the Wichuraiana hybrids, and is in all respects a very showy plant if one has the space for it to develop to its full potential. I would say that no large garden or public park should be without this rose, for there is nothing as spectacular as a fully grown 'American Pillar' garlanding the branches of a large tree with massive trusses of dainty crimson florets, each with its own small white face and bunch of bright yellow stamens.

I once picked a few sprays to arrange in a tall glass vase in my sitting-room, and this enchanted the family with its vivid colour and sweet fragrance for a week before the flowers eventually dropped.

The American breeder, Van Fleet, produced this superb rose in 1902 by crossing a seedling of the two species *Rosa wichuraiana* and *Rosa setigera* with an unknown Hybrid Perpetual, but the new rose was introduced only six years later by Conrad and Jones.

From America it soon reached the Cape where its vigour gained it a great deal of favour in the gardens of the 1920s. However, as gardens became smaller with successive sub-divisions of erven, its very vigour disqualified the once popular rambler so that it is now seldom seen.

PLANT
An extremely vigorous climber capable of sending out straight shoots 3–4 metres long in one season. The plant has numerous strong hooked thorns.

FOLIAGE
Five or seven small oval leaflets with shiny, dark-green surfaces and well-serrated edges. Stems are short, sturdy and have many sharp hooked prickles on the undersides. Stipules are wide and glandular on the edges.

FLOWERS
The tiny round dark-pink buds with short sepals open to single florets of 5 cm in diameter. The five petals are heart-shaped and slightly curly on the edges, of a bright pink to red colour with white centres. Many stamens with prominent yellow anthers on long white filaments curl inwards over pale green stigmas on short loose styles bunched together in the centre. The calyx is oval, taken in at the top and covered with glands on short stalks. These are also noticeable on the flower-stalk. The sepals are short, unfoliated and glandular with velvety lower surfaces. Flowers appear only in spring and have a sweet fresh fragrance.

INFLORESCENCE
A panicle which can be up to 30 cm long, containing numerous flowers usually grouped in clusters of three or four.

When I was looking for old roses on Dan Retief's family farm Welvanpas at the top end of the Bovlei outside Wellington, I discovered a large shrub covered with trusses of small wine-coloured roses growing in the kitchen garden on the south side of the old H-shaped manor house.

This was a rose I had never seen before. I was intrigued with the remarkable dark wine colour of the petals and the intense delicious fragrance which was noticeable on approaching the shrub. Closer by I saw that the petals of the small flowers had white shanks that formed a circle in the centre of the rose. Where petals had dropped away, the small bottle-like calyces still carried a mass of stamens on long thin filaments and even where these had become desiccated and brittle, the wonderful fragrance had been retained.

The Welvanpas shrub had been regularly trimmed into a round bush and therefore looked quite different from the plant I saw a few weeks later growing over a high wall in Weltevreden Street in Mowbray. It was only then that I could appreciate the true vigour of the rose and guess at a Wichuraiana parentage, for here were those prickly branches 3–4 metres long, shooting up from the base of the plant and growing vigorously in all directions to cover the entire length of the wall.

I sent a spray of fresh flowers to Kew for identification, and the answer came back 'possibly Dr Huey'.

'Dr Huey' was introduced in 1920 by B. and A. and A. N. Pierson, having been raised by Captain George Thomas Jun. at Beverly Hills, California in 1914. The parents were a 'Dorothy Perkins' seedling called 'Ethel' and the red China rose 'Gruss an Teplitz'. The rose I had found could well have inherited its vigorous growth from the former, and its delicious scent from the latter.

My slips rooted easily which reminded me that 'Dr Huey' used to be a very desirable stock rose fifty years ago when it was known as 'Shafter'. According to G. A. Stevens this was 'probably the finest dark red variety for garden effect' in the 1930s.[1]

I found it strange, however, that the most distinctive feature of my 'Dr Huey' — its intense scent — was not mentioned by rosarians, although McFarland concedes 'slightly fragrant' in his description,[2] and I presumed that the soil and warm climate had imbued it with special fragrance here at the Cape.

Having thus satisfied myself that another unknown rose had been nicely tied up, I was most surprised to find the real 'Dr Huey' in Walter Duncan's and David Rustan's nurseries in South Australia, still used as stock and not at all like my rose. No white eye in the centre and much larger double flowers with very little fragrance convinced me that I had been on the wrong track, and once again impressed on me that the only way to know a rose is to grow it and get to know all its guises. It is most unfair to expect anyone to identify an old rose by looking at one specimen of the flower.

Now I am left without a name for this intensely fragrant dark-maroon rose which must date back at least to the early 20th century. Could the fragrance indicate Musk parentage? Perhaps somewhere someone will be sufficiently familiar with this rose to come forward with its correct name, but in the meantime I shall carry on multiplying it to share its fragrance and wonderful spring show with other gardeners.

1 G.A. Stevens, *Climbing Roses*, 1933.
2 *Roses* 8.

Unknown Wichuraiana hybrid.

'Dr Huey'.

Hips.

PLANT
A vigorous rambler with long trailing stems which grow 6–8 metres high. It has many hooked thorns.

FOLIAGE
Five oval pointed leaflets with dark-green glossy surfaces and even, medium serrations. Stipules are wide and long, light-green with smooth edges.

FLOWERS
The small elongated buds have sepals just beyond the tip, and open to semi-double flowers 3–4 cm in diameter, deep wine in colour with white eyes and bright yellow stamens on long delicate filaments which persist long after the petals have fallen. The smooth calyx is small and oval; the sepals have smooth edges and are slightly velvety on the inner surface. There are a few glands only on the flower-stalk. The flowers are very fragrant, and appear only in spring.

INFLORESCENCE
This is a cyme with four or more trusses, each with two or four florets.

Erfurt House, Stellenbosch, C. C.

LARGE CLIMBERS

A number of very vigorous roses which do not fit into any of the classes listed earlier have been grouped together under this heading.

Except for 'La Folette', they are among the most common old roses at the Cape and I would still recommend them for use where carefree, vigorous growth is required.

'Souvenir de Mme Léonie Viennot' flowers most of the year and the other three, 'Félicité et Perpétue', 'La Folette' and 'Beauty of Glazenwood' produce such a magnificent spring show that they are forgiven the lack of flowers during the rest of the year.

Rosa sempervirens,
Mary Lawrance, 1799.

'Félicité et Perpétue'
at McGregor.

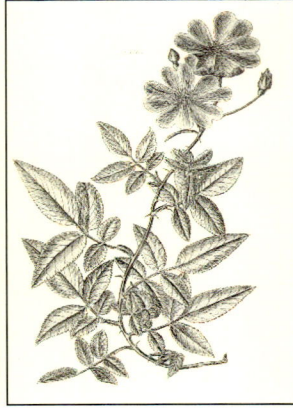

Rosa sempervirens, from
Hortus Elthamensis,
Dillenius, 1737.

'Princesse Marie'.

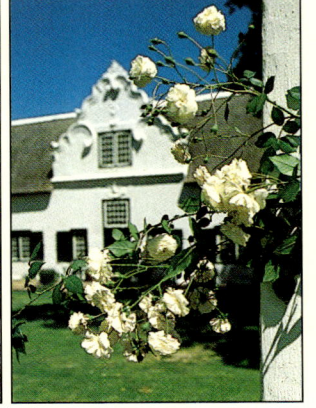

Ida's Valley, near Stellenbosch.

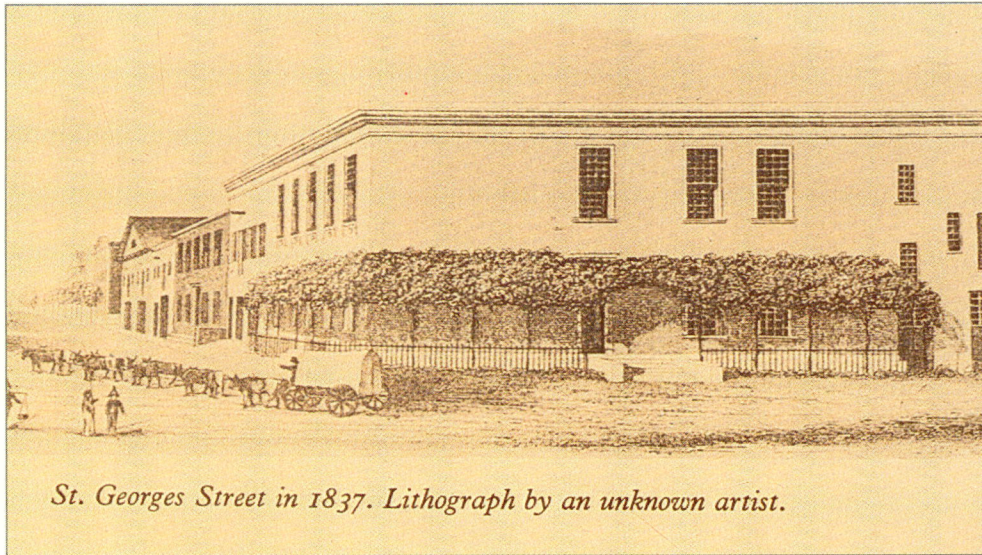

St. Georges Street in 1837. Lithograph by an unknown artist.

The old woman sitting on her bentwood chair on the stoep of her small thatched cottage peered over the rose hedge rather suspiciously at us as our Moto Guzzi came to a stop and I swung off the pillion and opened her garden gate to start a conversation. I was soon greeted politely with the amused smile which is always forthcoming when my helmet comes off to reveal a mop of grey hair.

I asked her how old the rose tree in front of her home was, and was assured that her mother had planted it as a young bride shortly after moving into the cottage 'more than a hundred years ago'.

I then asked her what she called the rose and was thrilled to hear that I was looking at 'Seven Sisters, because the small flowers appear in bunches of seven'.

In the graveyard of the neighbouring old Dutch Reformed Church where we had been asked to inspect a leaking roof, I discovered the same rose straggling across many fallen graves, bravely flowering despite obvious neglect. I admired the gay bouquets of perfect rosette-like florets and neat round crimson-tinged buds, but counted many more than seven flowers to a spray.

At home, my books confirmed that this rambler, sometimes mistakenly called 'Seven Sisters', was actually none other than 'Félicité et Perpétue'[1] – a *Rosa sempervirens* hybrid raised by M. Jacques, gardener to Louis Philippe, Duke of Orléans (and later King of France), at Château Neuilly in 1827.

Rosa sempervirens, a wild rose of Southern Europe and North Africa, had been drawn and described for more than two hundred years when Jacques began to develop garden varieties from it, naming the new roses after members of the Duke's family.[2]

I was fortunate to see three of these early 19th century Sempervirens ramblers flowering simultaneously in the old rose garden at Mottisfont Abbey when I toured through English heritage gardens in July 1983. There was 'Adélaïde D'Orléans'[3] hanging in creamy-rose mass-

es from an arch over a gravel path, its flowers slightly larger and with fewer petals than 'Félicité et Perpétue' and the small buds a clear pale pink. Further down the path was 'Princesse Marie', very much like her sisters, in huge clusters of light pink flowers fading to white, which covered the plant so that hardly a green leaf could be seen. For profusion of flowers and massive display there is obviously nothing to beat these old Sempervirens hybrids.

Since that afternoon when I caught my first glimpse of 'Félicité et Perpétue' at Somerset West, I have found it to be a very common rose not only in the Boland but much further afield throughout the Cape Province, for it seems to be well adapted to all types of climate and soil. In the Koue Bokkeveld I found a large plant growing together with avenues of saffron pear trees on the old farm werf of Langfontein where regular winter snowfalls had not affected its vigorous growth or magnificent display of spring flowers.

From Kuruman in the Northern Cape, where temperatures soar to 40°C and the only source of water is a miraculous fountain producing 18 million litres of water a day, a 'Félicité et Perpétue' plant in flower was sent to me for identification by Dr R. Liversedge of the Kimberley Museum. This plant had come from the original tree growing in the garden next to the mission church built by Robert Moffat in 1838. It had been taken by car by the Revd Alan Butler to Kimberley and flown from there to Cape Town.

My Sunday after-dinner nap was interrupted by Dr Liversedge's excited telephone call, for we were all eager to know what rose Moffat had planted in his garden together with his imported walnut and syringa trees. But by 11 p.m. on Sunday a tired official at the air-freight office assured me patiently that no parcel had arrived for me and that he had been unable to contact the only official in charge of Kimberley's airport.

By Tuesday morning the parcel was eventually traced in Johannes-

1 Named after the Duke of Orléans' two daughters who in turn commemorated the Carthaginian martyrs St. Felicitas and St. Perpetua.
2 R. Shepherd, *History of the Rose*, 1954, p. 42.
3 Named after the sister of the Duke of Orléans.

'Félicité et Perpétue'

Rosa sempervirens major? Half size.   'Félicité et Perpétue'

burg and flown to Cape Town, where officials were not at all impressed with the miserable small white roses which had caused them so much trouble! The shrub was planted in the new garden at Rust en Vreugd which houses part of the William Fehr art collection in Cape Town, and there it has happily established itself.

Though this rose is so common at the Cape, I have found no plants of the other Sempervirens varieties I saw at Mottisfont, and do not know whether they were ever brought here. The Revd W. Ellis also noticed only 'Félicité et Perpétue' on his visit to Mauritius, Réunion and Madagascar in 1855.[4]

There is, however, a very pretty white climber, whose leaves and growth show all the features of the Sempervirens group, which Colin Cochrane and Molly de Villiers from the Swellendam Museum found at the small mission town of Zuurbraak when we were out there one spring looking for old roses. This might very well be the rose which Roy Shepherd describes as 'Sempervirens Major' or 'Double White Noisette'. The flowers are larger, less full and of the same colouring as 'Félicité et Perpétue', but they appear throughout the year. It is thought that this rose may have been a parent of both 'Félicité et Perpétue' and the fuller 'Aimée Vibert'.[5]

Towards the end of the 19th century, when the newly established botanic gardens in the more distant country towns were setting a new style for the Victorian gardener and were distributing information on new economic and useful plants, these Semperflorens ramblers (together with *Rosa multiflora carnea*) were the first to appear on pergolas, arches, trellises and summer-houses everywhere. They established the popularity of ramblers and set the stage for the arrival of the numerous new varieties which were to flood the Cape market of the early 20th century.

PLANT
A very vigorous rambler with long thin branches which will climb to 6 metres high but scrambles over the ground if not given support. It has numerous straight red thorns.
FOLIAGE
Five or seven small oval pointed leaflets with finely serrated edges and dark-green shiny surfaces duller on the underside. Leaf-stalks are delicate, have glands at the proximal ends and prickles on the underside. Stipules are thin with glands on the edges.
FLOWERS
Small round buds with short sepals, tinted pink to crimson, open to perfect little white pompons 4 cm in diameter, which retain a light-pink flush on the outer petals. The central petals are small and curly; they fill the middle of the floret in an untidy fashion, hiding the rather insignificant stamens on their thin white filaments and the column of hairy styles with shiny cream stigmas. The small calyx is cup-shaped and smooth but the flower-stalk has a few stalked glands. The short oval sepals with a few short folioles are furry on the undersurface and glandular on the outer surface as well as on the edges. The flowers occur only in spring and are slightly fragrant.
INFLORESCENCE
A panicle with eight to twelve flowers.

4 In his *Three Visits to Madagascar 1853–1854–1856* (New York, 1859) the Revd Ellis describes the roses he found growing along the boundaries of a Mr Kittery's garden in Mauritius, of which 'The pretty little noisette rose, *félicité perpetuelle* was conspicuous among them' (p. 112).   5 Shepherd, as above.

Rosa x odorata pseudindica

A seedling of *Rosa x odorata pseudindica*. Half size.

'Beauty of Glazenwood was undoubtedly the most beautiful rose in our garden', said Miss Isobel Hofmeyr, and her sister Leonie agreed enthusiastically.[1]

The two sisters, daughters of the last Dutch Reformed minister to live in the old parsonage at Somerset East, were describing the famous garden which had been created by their grandfather, John Murray Hofmeyr.

When a Dutch Reformed congregation was established in Somerset East in 1825 by the Scottish minister G. Morgan, the existing Wesleyan Church building was acquired, together with the surrounding six hectares of land, and refurbished as a parsonage. The next minister, the Revd Pears, also a Scotsman, started a small garden and to this day remnants of an 'Old Monthly' rose hedge which he planted are to be seen in front of the parsonage.

Perhaps it was these gay pink roses flowering throughout the year that inspired the next young parson, Jan Hendrik Hofmeyr, to lay out a rose garden soon after he moved into the parsonage in 1866. Every year this keen gardener extended his rose terraces, importing new varieties from England together with violets, snowdrops, daffodils and eventually peonies to plant beside the rose beds. This was the first time that peonies had been grown in the Cape with success and the first flowers caused quite a stir in the community.

What a paradise the parsonage garden was and how the whole community benefited from its abundance of flowers, fruit, and vegetables! For the sick, the aged, and the bereaved, whether at christenings, weddings and birthdays, the appropriate bouquets, baskets, posies, wreathes, buttonholes or bunches of flowers would be beautifully arranged by the parsonage women and lovingly distributed. No wonder the parson was described as 'a man with a great heart wonderfully gifted by God'. His wife, a Miss Murray from the Graaff Reinet parsonage, also stemmed from a family dedicated to community service.

Their third son, also Jan Hendrik, was the first resident missionary in Nyasaland and, following in his father's footsteps, moved into the parsonage in 1908 after his father's death as the new parson. He loved gardening as much as his father so that the rose garden continued to grow from approximately six hundred roses in 1900 to almost one thousand in 1947 when the property was sold. Today this parsonage is a National Monument and a museum, and the old garden, which had been largely destroyed, is being replanted with as many of the old varieties as can be found, including 'Beauty of Glazenwood'.

I had never seen this lovely rose growing in the Western Cape, but was told by Eve Palmer where to find some old plants when I went on a search for old roses in the Eastern Province.

Robert Fortune himself, who first set eyes on this famous rose a hundred and forty years ago in a Mandarin's garden in Ningpo,[2] could not have been more excited than I was when I caught my first glimpse of the golden crimson rambler in a profusion of colour, completely covering a cottage gable and wall. From the top of the ten-metre-high roof to the ground, long green branchlets festooned with yellow and crimson roses swung down like gaily coloured streamers at a child's party.

Walter and Anne Murray, present owners of the farm Bloemhof near Graaff Reinet, knew that this cottage had been built before 1838 but there was no record of when and by whom the rose had been planted. The cottage now is desolate, for the family lives in a new home near by, but year after year for a few weeks in the spring everyone comes to admire the spectacle of 'Beauty of Glazenwood' in full bloom.

Several farms in the Graaff Reinet and Somerset East districts boast large old plants probably dating to the early part of this century, which leads one to think that slips must have been generously handed out from the first owners, for I have not found it listed in nursery catalogues of that period.

The furthest south where I have found 'Beauty of Glazenwood' is at Mill River Farm in the Langkloof, but slips I have now planted at the Cape seem to be growing quite happily although not as vigorously as I would have liked.

It was at Mill River Farm that I found a very interesting plant three metres high, growing near to an old 'Beauty of Glazenwood'. The same lax, angular habit of growth, the same brownish-green stems with almost straight thorns, and the same small shiny green leaves betrayed its evident parentage, but the flowers were slightly larger and virtually single, although sometimes a few tiny petals curled in over the stamens. The golden-yellow loose petals shaded crimson at the edges were of the same colouring as 'Beauty of Glazenwood' and the texture of the petals and setting of the flowers on small side shoots along the young branches were identical.

I looked once again at Ellen Willmott's Plate 29 which seemed to me to be identical to the Mill River seedling. Miss Willmott states that 'all attempts to trace the origin of this beautiful Rose have failed — and it has not been figured'. She knew of only one specimen, which was growing in Canon Ellacombe's garden at Bitton in Gloucestershire. I suspect that the rose which she called 'Rosa chinensis var. Grandiflora Hort' could be the single form of 'Beauty of Glazenwood'.

I do not know where the name of this rose originated, but Glazenwood (near Coggeshall in Essex) was the home of Samuel Curtis, editor of the *Botanical Magazine* from 1827 to 1846, and I suppose the rose grew well there. It was illustrated in the *Botanical Magazine* in 1852 (T. 4679).

However, no illustration can do justice to the magnificent sight of a fully grown plant in flower. Unlike other ramblers which are smothered in trusses of flowers, this rose tree impresses one with the daintiness of its foliage and the long garlands of coppery yellow flowers. I can now understand why the two Misses Hofmeyr regarded 'Beauty of Glazenwood' as their favourite amongst all the roses in the Somerset East parsonage garden.

1 Eve Palmer, too, told me that she considered this rose, which used to grow at her family farm Cranemere in the Camdeboo, to be the most beautiful of all.

2 Fortune describes his discovery of the rose in the *Journal of the Horticultural Society*, Vol. 1, p. 218 (1846): 'I immediately ran up to the place, and to my surprise and delight found that I had discovered a most beautiful yellow climbing rose.'

Rosa x odorata pseudindica

'BEAUTY OF GLAZENWOOD'
'FORTUNE'S DOUBLE YELLOW'

PLANT
A vigorous climber to 10 metres, covering an area of the same width. From the rather angular main stems, delicate young shoots hang down to give the plant a very airy, dainty appearance. There are many very sharp brown hooked thorns.

FOLIAGE
Five to seven small oval pointed, light-green leaflets with shiny surfaces and finely serrated edges. The stalks are greeny-brown and delicate; they have small sharp hooks on the underside. Stipules are narrow, long and have smooth edges.

FLOWERS
Short fat round buds with longish sepals open into loose flowers about 8 cm in diameter. As the flower ages the broad outer petals reflex and the centre of the flower is filled with shorter very wavy petals. The petals vary in colour from yellow to orange and are flushed with crimson. Stamens are few and the short pistils are bunched together in the centre. The calyx is cup-shaped, smooth and shiny, the sepals long, tapering and unfoliated. The flowers appear in spring only and are very fragrant.

INFLORESCENCE
The flowers are arranged in twos or threes on short branch-lets along the side branches.

Rosa x odorata pseudindica.

255

'Belle Portugaise', another *R. gigantea* hybrid (also 1903), flowering in Trevor Griffith's garden in New Zealand.

'There is a Kirstenbosch rose, you know' Dr John Rourke informed me one day when I arrived at the herbarium of the Kirstenbosch National Botanic Garden where he is curator.

We drove through the fields of yellow, white and blue 'daisies', sweet-scented mauve podalyria, drifts of white arums and buddleias with branches drooping heavily under their load of fragrant lilac blossom. I wondered to myself how I could be so involved with old roses when the beauty of our own floral wealth was at my doorstep.

But when we stopped at the cottage that had been built for Dr Pearson, founder of this world-famous garden, the old-rose fever gripped me once again: a forty foot high oak growing next to the cottage, dressed up in lime green spring garb, presented an incredible spectacle. As if she were Botticelli's *Primavera*, wreaths of bright pink roses were entwined around her neck, spilling out over bosom, arms, lap, and falling in profusion right down onto the green grass at her feet. The large flowers, poised on short side branchlets, seemed to dance along the astonishingly long shoots. Closer inspection of the translucent petals, warm pink on the inside, shocking pink on the outer surface, streaked here and there with white, together with the long oval slightly drooping leaves, suggested that this might be a hybrid of the *Rosa odorata gigantea* which I had seen a year before in the Chelsea Physic Garden in London.

John told me that the plant was at least seventy years old, from which I concluded that it might have been planted by Dr Pearson himself when he moved into the newly completed cottage in 1915.

We found that this rose had not only made itself at home in the Pearson garden, but had spread along a stream adjoining another staff cottage nearby, where it romped happily down the banks in great strides, much to the delight of the cottage inhabitants who appreciated the wonderful show of roses which occurs at least twice a year.

Many months later, while a friend was giving me an account of the magnificent climbing rose 'La Follette' which she had seen flowering in great profusion on the French Riviera, I suddenly realized that this was surely the same as the Kirstenbosch rose.

Unlike the other *Rosa gigantea* hybrids which were bred by a Frenchman in the Botanic Gardens of Lisbon from 1898 onwards, 'La Follette' is an English rose raised in the garden of Lord Brougham by his gardener Busby in 1903. This brilliant climber (whose other parent is unknown) is seldom seen in England, however, for it grows best in a sunny, warm climate.

I am surprised that 'La Follette' should not be more widespread in the Cape where the weather seems to be ideally suited to it, judging by the luxuriant growth of the 'Kirstenbosch Rose'. The American Heritage Rose Society, who helped me to confirm the identity of this rose from slides, were puzzled that it should flower more than once a year. In the 1926 *American Rose Journal*, however, I noticed a letter by H. Nabonnand, who had also used *Rosa gigantea* to breed new hybrids, in which he raises this matter. He said: 'I have never seen my Giganteas remontant, but I believe that as they get older they become remontant, as I have now (December 25) 'Fiametta', 'Countesse Prozor' and 'Lady Johnstone' covered with buds and blooms.' Our aged 'La Follette' at Kirstenbosch is proving the accuracy of Nabonnand's observations.

'La Follette'

'La Follette'.

PLANT
This is an extremely vigorous climber which will send out 3–4 metre shoots to cover an entire tree up to 10 metres high in a few years. It has many sharply hooked thorns.

FOLIAGE
Five or seven long oval pointed leaflets of a light olive-green, shiny on the upper surfaces, duller below. The leaf-stalk with hooked thorns on the underside, as well as the smooth narrow stipules, are tinged red.

FLOWERS
Very pretty large buds with sepals stretching just beyond the shocking-pink point, open into semi-double flowers 8–9 cm in diameter with four or five rows of large petals, the outer ones curving outwards as soon as the flower unfolds, the inner ones filling the centre in a muddled, curly fashion. The inner petals are a warm pink and the outer ones a shocking-pink colour sometimes with odd white streaks, all fading to a cream pink when older. The many stamens are twice the length of the pistils which are short and hairy. The calyx is round, bright green, smooth and shiny, the sepals long and tapering with no folioles, reflexing as soon as the bud starts swelling. The flower-stalk is reddish and glandular, sometimes arched. The flowers make a show several times a year and have a slight Tea fragrance.

INFLORESCENCE
Single flowers are produced along the main stems on short branchlets.

257

'Souvenir de Madame Léonie Viennot'

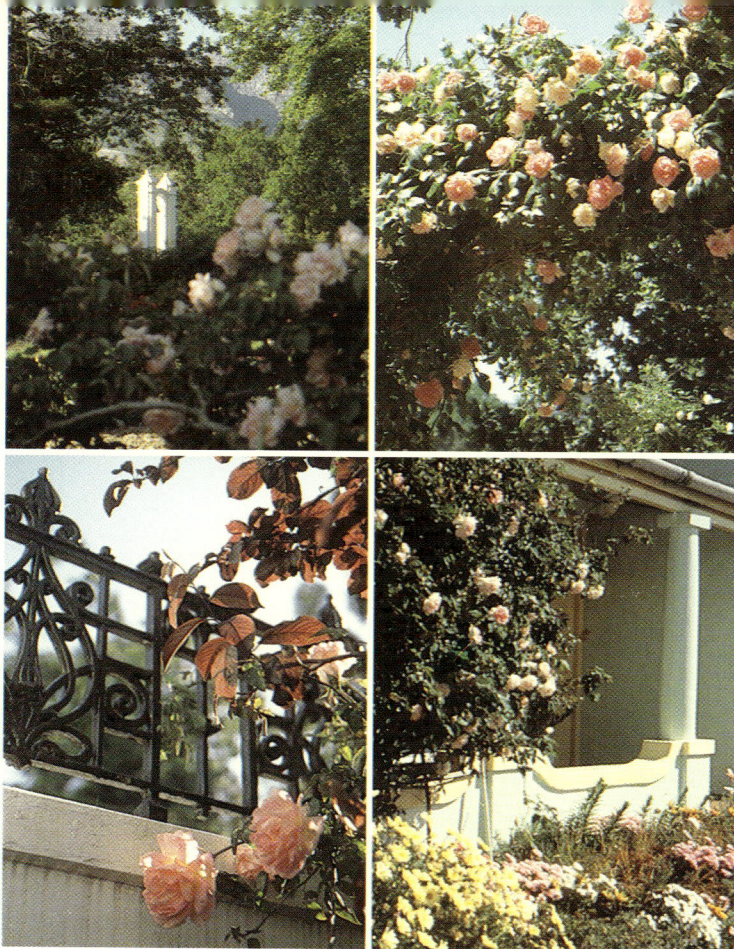

1 In the Groot Paardevlei garden.
2 A two-year-old plant covering an arch.
3 Over a cast-iron trellis in Capt. van der Merwe's garden in Rondebosch.
4 In a Riversdale street garden.

This is another of those Tea roses which presents one with copious flowers throughout the year. It is commonly found in the older gardens of Cape Town's suburbs, and folk in the countryside very proudly take one to admire their old rose, always 'at least a hundred years old' growing over a wall, trellis, pergola, arch or summer-house.[1] It grows so easily from cuttings that even today gardeners love passing on plants to neighbours and friends.

In Mrs Johnman's garden in Stellenbosch an old plant of this rose, allowed to go its own way, had formed a six metre high tangle with 'Tausendschön'. In spring the thousand small bright-pink trusses of the rambler and larger yellow-pink blooms of the climber, with not a green leaf showing, tumble down from their tower to the grass at one's feet in an incredible feast of colour.

'Mme Viennot' hates to be pruned, for flowers are produced on the mature wood and I have seen flowerless plants being thrown out of gardens in which all the roses are severely cut back every year for the sake of 'tidiness'.

In Port Elizabeth a 'Souvenir de Mme Léonie Viennot', which had festooned the gravestones and sprawled over the Jones' family grave in the St. George's cemetery, one year flowered so profusely that it caused a great deal of speculation in the local *Eastern Province Herald* as to its identity. I had fortunately photographed it the previous year and could wisely identify the rose for 'Babiana' in his column 'Growing Things'. That was lucky, for identifying old roses can be a very difficult task. Even those that one knows well are sometimes presented in completely atypical garb and appear strangers.

'Mme Viennot' is especially elusive, hiding herself in a variety of shapes and colours: semi-double or very double; rich creamy-yellow tinted pink, bright shocking-pink tinted yellow, or light faded rose and cream in the older flowers. Yet the porcelain quality of the pink petals, the rich Tea fragrance and shiny foliage, maroon when first emerging, are a great help in identifying this climber.

A. Bernaix in 1898 first introduced 'Souvenir de Mme Léonie Viennot', raised in his Lyon nursery from unknown parents. In that same year another Frenchman, Henri Cayeux, the technical director of the Botanic Garden at Lisbon, began experimenting with the hybridization of *Rosa gigantea*, the wild Tea rose from China, by crossing it with other Teas. From 'Souvenir de Mme Léonie Viennot' x *R. gigantea* he produced the pale rose-pink 'Bela Portuguesa' with large semi-double flowers, 'Lusitania' with smaller semi-double flowers and 'Palmira Feifas' with pale rose, medium-sized flowers.[2] All these climbers were extremely vigorous and floriferous in the warm climate of Lisbon and the Riviera where 'Bela Portuguesa' especially still grows to perfection.

I have not been able to find any of these hybrids growing at the Cape,[3] but the mother herself is obviously very happy in our mild climate. She is still much respected by gardeners and will, I hope, be cherished and preserved especially by owners of Victorian houses as a fitting period plant in their gardens for many years to come.

1 *Gowie's Seed and Plant Catalogue* for 1904–5 states that 'Souvenir de Madame Viennot is classed as a Tea rose and is recommended as a very fine rose'.

2 *American Rose Annual*, 1931, p. 214. Dr Ruy Palhinha, Director of the Lisbon Botanic Garden, describes the roses bred there from 'Souvenir de Mme Léonie Viennot'.

3 Dorothea Fairbridge in *The Gardens of South Africa* (1924) describes it as 'one of the best allround roses that we have'.

'Souvenir de Madame Léonie Viennot'

PLANT
*A vigorous climber with branched, rather angular growth,
excellent for growing over arches, screens, pergolas, verandas and summer-houses. It has many hooked thorns and
the young stems and leaves are of a puce-red colour.*

FOLIAGE
*Five large oval leaflets, olive-green flushed red when young,
with shiny upper, duller lower surfaces. The stalk is tinged
red and has hooked thornlets on the underside. Stipules
are short, tinged red and have smooth edges.*

FLOWERS
*Dark-pink pointed buds with slightly longer sepals open
into cup-shaped loose flowers with five to six rows of petals, pale cream at their attachments, strong pink towards
the edges. They are all of the same length but the inner
ones are narrower. The stamens have thin filaments and
small anthers; they are slightly longer than the bunch of
short, straight, reddish styles with yellow stigmas. The calyx is cup-shaped, taken in slightly at the top, and smooth.
Sepals are tapering, have few folioles and are velvety on
the undersurface and edges. The flowers appear throughout the year and have a lovely fruity fragrance.*

INFLORESCENCE
*Groups of two to three flowers on short branchlets along
the main stems.*

'Souvenir de Mme Léonie Viennot'.

259

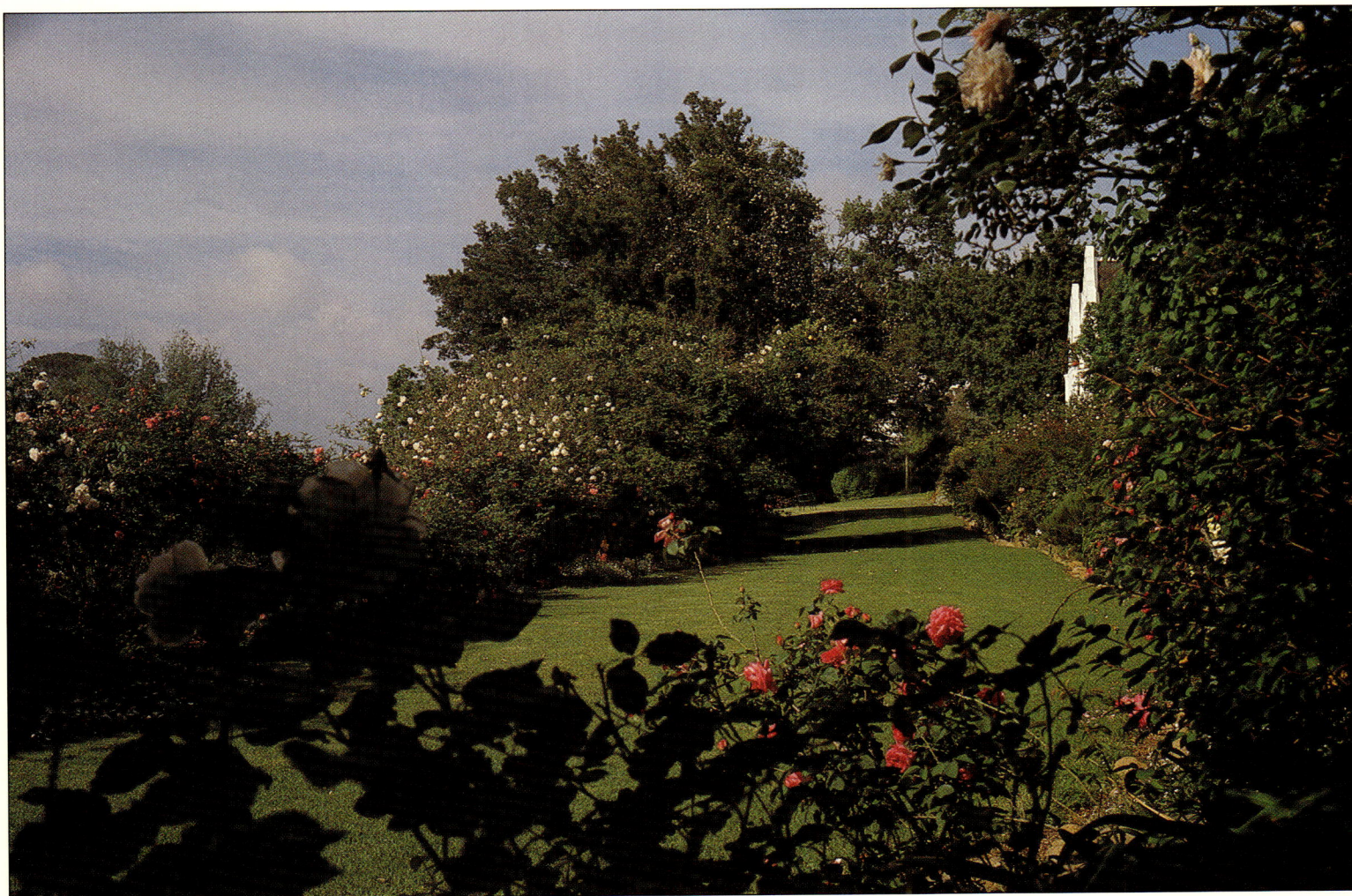

The Boschendal rose garden: a long grass walk with banks of roses on either side.
Below: The blue mountains are an important part of the garden.

Old roses for historic and modern gardens

As rising walls and shrinking spaces eliminate more and more sunlight from people's lives, the need to find plants that will thrive in the remaining sunny corners of the built environment becomes increasingly important. For although in his boundless arrogance man has created simulated plants to fulfil his need for natural beauty, no amount of greenery will satisfy this need unless it displays the element of growth which is the essence of life. For it is his perception of the progression of leaves from stems, of buds from growing tips and of unfolding flowers which really intrigues and humbles the most self-assured of human beings and which provides a perspective of his own significance.

Whether for the small pot on the sunny window-sill of the flat-dweller, or the enclosed courtyard of the city businessman, or the patio pergola of the suburban gardener; or whether it is for the public park, children's playground, factory entrance, or highway bank — there is a shrub, rambling or climbing rose that will suit the purpose perfectly.

The more I work with roses, the more indispensable they have become for me in solving the numerous problems that arise when planning a landscape. I refer, of course, to the group of roses that has become known as the 'Heritage Roses'.

The value of these roses was well known to our ancestors who used them abundantly, often because they had nothing else that would solve a particular problem so effectively. It is sad to reflect that new fashions and new gardening materials have displaced these plants to the detriment of our whole environment. We might do well to review these old favourites and through judicious choice and by appropriate use bring back the charm, colour, and above all, the fragrance of bygone days.

261

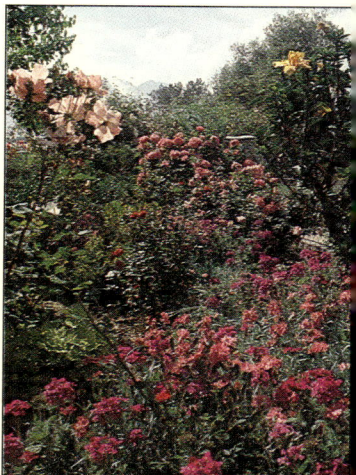

1 2 3 4 5

Though few of them flower for more than one month in a year, the shrub roses are the most useful of all garden plants, needing little pruning or spraying and a minimum of care once established. Their forms are so multifarious that it is no exaggeration to say that a shrub rose can be found for every situation in the garden, whether the soil is loam, clay or sand, acid or alkaline.

Some of the different ways in which I have used heritage roses in modern and historic landscapes are listed below to indicate their value and to inspire landscape planners who have not yet had the pleasure of working with these old-fashioned favourites.

HEDGES

Before wire fencing came into general use, boundaries were often demarcated with the most readily available plant material.

In the Cape Peninsula, oaks planted one metre apart formed tall and handsome hedges, but these were naturally not impenetrable. Thorny pomegranate and pleached quince were more effective, but best of all the hedging materials were roses. Planted at close intervals they intertwined their prickly branches, allowing passage neither to animal nor man. From the earliest history of the Cape Colony roses were planted to mark boundaries and to enclose vineyards and orchards so as to protect the precious fruit from thieves.

TALL HEDGES

These were the roses most often used in the countryside:

'ALBÉRIC BARBIER'
'GÉANT DES BATAILLES'
'INDICA MAJOR'
'MACARTNEY ROSE'
'MERMAID'
R. LAEVIGATA
R. MULTIFLORA VARIETIES
'RUSSELIANA'
'SILVER MOON'

MEDIUM-SIZED HEDGES

These are useful for marking suburban boundaries:

'BOULE DE NEIGE'
'CHÉNÉDOLE'
'FELLEMBERG'
'GLOIRE DES ROSOMANES'
'OLD MONTHLY'
RUGOSAS

SMALL HEDGES FOR EDGING PATHS OR LAWNS

These could be clipped for formal effect:

'CRAMOISI SUPÉRIEUR'
'LOUIS PHILIPPE'
R. CHINENSIS MINIMA
R. LUCIAE
R. MULTIFLORA NANA

GROUND COVERS

These are useful along boundaries where the view is not to be obstructed:

'DOROTHY PERKINS'
'EXCELSA'
R. LUCIAE
'ROSE DE MEAUX'
'WILLIAMS' DOUBLE YELLOW'

ALONG ROADS

For stabilizing banks and as barriers:

'ALBÉRIC BARBIER'
'MERMAID'
R. LAEVIGATA
R. MULTIFLORA AND ITS HYBRIDS
R. ROXBURGHII
'RUSSELIANA'
THE MUSK ROSE AND ITS HYBRIDS

TO COVER UNSIGHTLY STRUCTURES

Species roses and the large climbers come into their own here:

THE BANKSIAS
'FÉLICITÉ ET PERPÉTUE'
'MERMAID'
R. LUCIAE HYBRIDS
R. MULTIFLORA HYBRIDS
'SOUVENIR DE MME LÉONIE VIENNOT'

1 A low hedge of *Rosa multiflora nana* with mauve petunias.

2 Rose arches at Mayville.

3 Santolina hedges bordering beds of Bourbon roses at Mayville.

4 'Anna de Diesbach' backing a bed of yellow irises.

5 Dark pink dianthus and verbena planted with 'Baronne Prévost'.

6 'The Bishop' and *R. multiflora carnea* together make a lovely spring show.

7 'Chénédole' is a good specimen plant for a wide herbaceous border.

8 Sweet William, 'Blush Damask' and Tea roses in a colourful combination.

9 Three-metre-high *R. multiflora carnea* hedge at Boschendal.

10 'Anna de Diesbach' planted next to cascading pools at the entrance to the new wine cellar at Klein Constantia.

FOR CREATING SHADE

Roses can be trained over arches, pergolas and gazebos made from rough poles or sophisticated wooden trellis-work, or from more costly (but more permanent) galvanized iron supports:

'AIMÉE VIBERT'
BANKSIAS
'BEAUTY OF GLAZENWOOD'
'CRÉPUSCULE'
'FÉLICITÉ ET PERPÉTUE'
HYBRID MUSKS
'LA FOLLETTE'
'MARÉCHAL NIEL'
'RÊVE D'OR'
R. BRUNONII
R. LUCIAE HYBRIDS
R. MULTIFLORA HYBRIDS
'SOUVENIR DE MME LÉONIE VIENNOT'

ROSES FOR SEMI-SHADED AREAS

Some European roses are unhappy in the hot South African sun and need to be planted in a shaded position to thrive:

THE ALBAS
THE BOURBONS E.G. 'VARIEGATA DI BOLOGNA'
  AND 'HONORINE DE BRABANT'

SPECIMEN PLANTS FOR FOCAL POINTS

Species roses create a fine spring show and build up into large plants, becoming more beautiful every year. My favourites are:

R. HUGONIS
R. MOYESII

PILLAR ROSES

Bourbons and Noisettes grown on wooden tripods or pillars can look spectacular. Those that are especially showy are:

'CRÉPUSCULE'
'LA REINE VICTORIA'
'MME ISAAC PEREIRE'
'ZÉPHIRINE DROUHIN'

GROUPS OF ROSES PLANTED FOR EFFECT

Rose shrubs and climbers grouped together in endless different combinations can be used to accentuate an entrance, to form a picture through a window, to colour a harsh wall, soften worn steps, form colourful posies on a dull lawn or to create reflections in a quiet pool:

BUFF-PINK 'CRÉPUSCULE' WITH CLEAR PINK
  'FRANCOIS JURANVILLE'
CERISE 'CHARLES DE MILLS' WITH SNOW-WHITE
  'BOULE DE NEIGE'
PRIMROSE 'CÉLINE FORESTIER' WITH SHELL-
  PINK 'RAUBRITTER'
STRIPED PURPLE AND WHITE 'VARIEGATA DI
  BOLOGNA' WITH DARK MAUVE 'CARDINAL DE
  RICHELIEU'

WHITE 'ALBÉRIC BARBIER' WITH CRIMSON
  'GÉANT DES BATAILLES'
WHITE 'MME PLANTIER' WITH MAUVE
  'ANAÏS SÉGALAS'
MAUVE 'VEILCHENBLAU' WITH LIGHT YELLOW
  'GOLDFINCH'

ROSES FOR THE WIDE BORDER

The taller species roses are most effective here, especially where very long borders are involved, for their luxuriant growth quickly fills up the space and they need very little maintenance once established:

THE HYBRID MUSKS
R. ALBA SEMIPLENA AND R. ALBA MAXIMA
R. CHINENSIS MUTABILIS
R. GLAUCA
R. HUGONIS
R. LAEVIGATA
R. MOYESII
R. PIMPINELLIFOLIA GRANDIFLORA
R. ROXBURGHII

These can be interplanted with the taller shrub roses to good effect:

'BARONNE PRÉVOST'
'CÉLINE FORESTIER'
'GÉANT DES BATAILLES'
'INDICA MAJOR'
'JAUNE DESPREZ'
'MME CAROLINE TESTOUT'
'SACHSEN GRUSS'

263

1 Remnants of an old *R. laevigata*
   hedge at Daljosafat.
2 An 'Old Monthly' hedge at Swellendam.
3 'Dorothy Perkins' and 'Excelsa' on
   the road banks at Knysna.
4 'Dorothy Perkins' on a road fence at
   Klein Drakenstein.
5 Old roses and herbs in a border at
   Boschendal.
6 The 'Kaapse Roos' on an old Muslim
   grave at Malmesbury.
7 'Celsiana' and foxgloves at Boschendal.
8 Pink 'Louise Odier' and mauve
   nicotiana look well together.
9 'The Bishop' is useful for lighting up
   a spring border.

Shrub roses look best when grown together with companion plants that offset and so enhance their colour and foliage. Shrubs effective in the wide border among the taller roses are:

ABELIA CHINENSIS
VARIEGATED ABUTILON
THE LARGER BERBERIS VARIETIES
CEANOTHUS
CISTUS (ROCK-ROSES)
FUCHSIAS (LARGER VARIETIES)
HIBISCUS (PALE PINK, WHITE AND
   PALE YELLOW)
HONEYSUCKLE
LEMON VERBENA
MOONFLOWERS (WHITE AND YELLOW)
OLEANDERS (PINK AND WHITE)
PETREA
PHILADELPHUS (MOCK-ORANGE)
VIBURNUM OPULUS (SNOWBALL TREE)

ROSES FOR THE HERBACEOUS BORDER

Because they produce flowers throughout the year, the Tea and China roses are particularly suitable here. They really are a constant source of pleasure. My favourite Chinas are:

'FABVIER'
'LOUIS PHILIPPE'
'OLD MONTHLY'
R. X ODORATA

As for the Tea roses, who can distinguish between so many beauties! I delight in all of them, not only for their lovely fragrance, but for their warm colours which fluctuate wonderfully throughout the seasons.

There are any number of plants which grow happily with these roses, but here are some of the best:

AQUILEGIAS
BORAGE
CAMPANULAS
CATMINT
DAY-LILIES
DIANTHUS
FLAG IRISES
FUCHSIAS (THE SMALLER KINDS)
FOXGLOVES
HELLEBORES
LAVENDERS
LARKSPUR
LILIES (ESPECIALLY THE WHITE ONES, LIKE
   ST. JOSEPH'S LILY)
LINARIAS
LOVE-IN-A-MIST
NICOTIANAS
ROSEMARY (DARK BLUE)
SALVIA (BLUE)
SANTOLINAS
THYMES (DIFFERENT VARIETIES)

CEMETERY ROSES

The many roses that have continued to grow and flower unattended in old cemeteries for so long prove that there are varieties that can withstand the long, dry Cape summers. Many cemeteries could be considerably improved by planting one of these hardy survivors. Those most commonly found on old graves are:

'BLUSH DAMASK'
'FÉLICITÉ ET PERPÉTUE'
'FELLEMBERG'
'FRAU KARL DRUSCHKI'
'GÉANT DES BATAILLES'
'GÉNÉRAL GALLIÉNI'
'MME HERBERT STEVENS'
R. LAEVIGATA
'ROSE EDWARD'

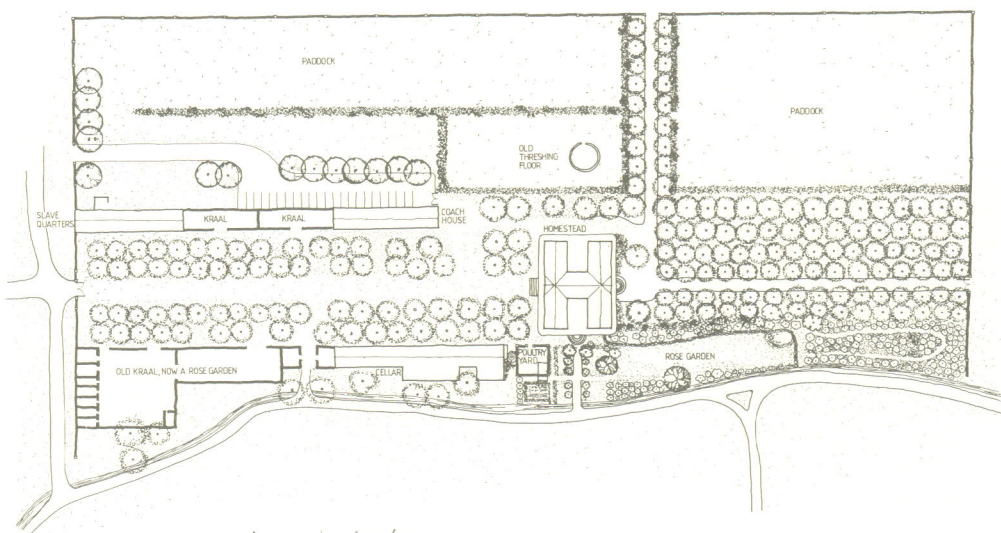

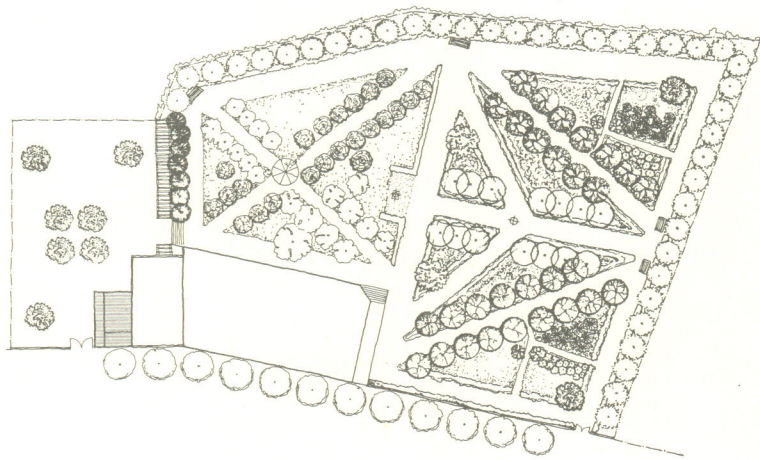

Top: The formal lay-out of the Boschendal werf with oak avenues and buildings arranged on either side of the main axis. The rose garden is below and to the side of the house.

Left: The Mayville memorial rose garden in Swellendam was designed to display the rose formally in chronological order.

Right: The Rust and Vreugd garden has been restored to the archival plan of about 1800. Hedges are of clipped rosemary, santolina and lavender; the beds are filled with old roses and other shrubs of the period.

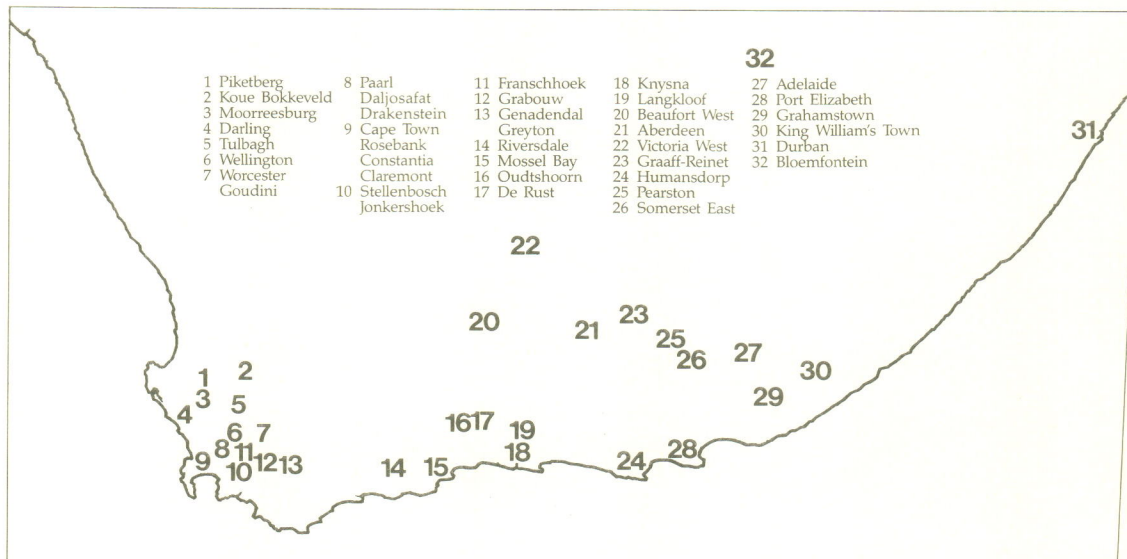

1 Piketberg
2 Koue Bokkeveld
3 Moorreesburg
4 Darling
5 Tulbagh
6 Wellington
7 Worcester
  Goudini
8 Paarl
  Daljosafat
  Drakenstein
9 Cape Town
  Rosebank
  Constantia
  Claremont
10 Stellenbosch
  Jonkershoek
11 Franschhoek
12 Grabouw
13 Genadendal
  Greyton
14 Riversdale
15 Mossel Bay
16 Oudtshoorn
17 De Rust
18 Knysna
19 Langkloof
20 Beaufort West
21 Aberdeen
22 Victoria West
23 Graaff-Reinet
24 Humansdorp
25 Pearston
26 Somerset East
27 Adelaide
28 Port Elizabeth
29 Grahamstown
30 King William's Town
31 Durban
32 Bloemfontein

INDEX

Numbers in bold type refer to illustrations

Aberdeen 160
Abu Man Sur 204
'Adam' 140, **140**, 177
Adelaide, Second International Heritage Rose Conference at 43, 98, 124, 150
'Adelaide d'Orléans' 252
African Court Calendar 226
'Aglaia' 234
'Aimée Vibert' 131, 164, 253, 263
Aiton, William 14, 15, 53, 80, 81
Alabandian roses 47
'Alba' 86
Albas (the White Roses) 47–55, 263
'Albéric Barbier' 194, 238, 240, **240**, 262, 263
'Albertine' 238
'Alister Stella Grey' 235
Aliwal North 215
Alphen 76, 156
Altyd Gedacht, Tygerberg 78
Amajuba, battlefield of 94
American Heritage Rose Society 93, 116, 256
'American Pillar' 234, 244, 248, **248**
Anacreon 47
'Anaïs Ségalas' 43, **43**, 263
'Anchen Müller' 86
Andrews, H. C. 88, 164
Andriessen, Jan 134
'Anemone' 208
Angela of Bengal 33
'Anna de Diesbach' 166–7, **166**, **167**, **262**, **263**
'Anna Olivier' 150, **150**, 156
'Annie Muller' 86
'Antoine Ducher' 202
Archbishop of Cape Town 93
'Archimedes' 137, 139, **139**
Arderne, Henry 126
Arderne homestead, Claremont 126
Attar of roses 9, 13, 26–7
Auld House, Swellendam 78, 86, 181
Australia 148, 229, 248
'Austrian Brier' *see R. foetida lutea*
'Austrian Copper Rose' *see R. foetida bicolor*
Autumn Damasks (Monthly roses) 57–60, **58**, **59**
Avontuur 188
Ayres, Charles (nurseryman), 142, 164

'Babiana' 258
Baccalhoa, Quinta da 229
Bainskloof 117
Balgowan district, Natal 126
Banhoek 215
Banks, Sir Joseph 81, 217
Banksia roses 54, 88, 156, 184, 216–19, **216**, **217**, **218**, **219**, 220, 234, 262, 263

Barbier, Rene 81, 238, 240, 246, 247
Barkley East 188
Barlow, Pam 64, 118
Barnard, Lady Anne 60, 93
Barnard, Prof. Chris 148
Barnes, Captain John 208
'Baronne Prévost' 160–1, **160**, **161**, **262**, 263
Barry, Joseph 78
Barry, Nina 111
Basson, Arnoldus Willem 33
Batavia 26, 48, 60
Batchen, Gillian 38, 201
Baumbach, Lydia 82
Beales, Peter 116, 134, 172, 173, 231
Bean, W. J. 238
'Beauty of Glazenwood' *(R. x odorata pseudindica)* 88, 251, 254–5, **254**, **255**, 263
Bedford 78
Beduduar 190
'Bela Portuguesa' **256**, 258
Belfast (Cape) 173
Bell, Leonie 232
'Belle de Crécy' 33, **33**
'Belle Portugaise' *see* 'Bela Portuguesa'
Béluze, J. 111
Belvidere church, Knysna **90**
'Bengale à bouquets' 94
'Bengale centfeuilles' 96
'Bengale Pompon' 86
Bennett, Henry 177
Bennetts, Basil 18, 120, 235
Bernadine de Saint Pierre, J. H. 80, 102
Bernaix, A. 134, 258
Bibliography 270–1
Biermann, Barrie 92
'Bishop, The' *see* 'The Bishop'
Bishopscourt 92, 120
Bizot, M. 118
'Black Prince' 88, 170–1, **171**
Blair, Mr 109
'Blairii No. 2' 101, 109, **109**
Blake, Mrs 98
'Blanc Double de Coubert' 207
'Blanche Moreau' 18
Blatt, R. J. 90
Blauwklippen 82
Bloemfontein 111, 134, 142
Bloemhof, Graaff-Reinet 98, 254
'Bloomfield Adundance' 98, **99**
'Blush Damask' 34, 57, 66–7, **66**, **67**, 184, **263**, 264
'Blush Hip' 66
'Blush Noisette' 232
'Blush Rambler' 232, **232**
Boerhaave 16, 34, 48, 62
Boland Farm Museum, Worcester **37**, 232
Bonfiglioli 119

Boschendal 4, **13**, 20, 32, 54, 62, 64, 76, 82, 97, 106, 109, 119, 120, 128, 137, 151, 168, 190, 194, 198, 214, 217, 222, 228, 232, 242, 261, **265**
Bosschaert, J. 11
Boston, Parks Dept. of 238
Botanical Magazine 14, 15, 16, 74, 86, **196**, **201**, **202**, 204, 210, **210**, **212**, 214, 217, 222, **222**, **238**, 254
Botha, Choppie 170
Botha, Elsie 124
Botha, Jacobus 124
Bottelary 117
Botticelli, Sandro 58
'Boule de Neige' 101, 112–13, **112**, **113**, 262, 263
'Bourbon Queen' 107, **107**
Bourbons 72, 81, 101–21, 263
'Bourgogne pompon' 15
Boursault, M. 229
Bouvet, Lozier 80
Bovlei 102, 198, 248
Bowditch, T. E. 59
Bowler, Thomas **70**
Bowles, E. A. 198
Bowles, Mrs 166
Boyeau, M. 126
Breiter 82
Bréon, M. 80, 102
Brickell, Chris 88
Brougham, Lord 256
Brown, John C. 22
Buist, R. 36, 71
Bulawayo 134, 142
Bunyard, E. A. 58, 66
Busby (gardener to Lord Brougham) 256
'Buttonhole Rose' *see* 'Homère'

'Cabbage Roses' 13, 166, 202
Cadet, M. T. 82
Cairns, Margaret 156
Calcutta Botanic Garden 11, 59, 76, 208, 210, 229
Camdeboo 131, 178, 254
Camps Bay House 78
Candolle, A. P. de 86
Canton 80, 88
Cape Almanac 13, 78, 204, 208, 212
Cape Amateur Gardener 16, 112, 118, 152, 181
Cape Garden 94, 131
Cape Peninsula *(see also under names of suburbs)* 210, 240, 258
'Cape Rose' *see* 'Kaapse Roos'
Cape sea route 79–80
Cape Town, roses in 117
Cape Town Botanic Gardens 20, 22, 23, 42, 54, 57, 70, 71, 86, 90, 92, 102, 104, 108, 111, 137, 138, 139, 160, 168, 190, 217

Cape Town Castle **12**
'Captain Christy' 177
'Cardinal de Richelieu' 43, 44, **44**, **45**, 263
'Cardinal Fisch' 101
Carter, George 234
Carthage, roses of 58
Cartier, Dr 229
'Catherine Mermet' 137, 144–5, **144**, **145**, 166
Catullus 58
Cayeux, Henri 258
'Cécile Brunner' 98–9, **98**, **99**, **180**
'Cécile Brunner' (white) 98, **99**
'Céleste' **50**
'Celestial' 88
'Céline Forestier' 88, 123, 124–5, **125**, 263
Cels, Jacques Martin 64
'Celsiana' 57, 64–5, **64**, **65**, **265**
Centifolias 9–23
Ceres 218
Ceylon (Sri Lanka) 26, 57, 234
Champney, John 123
'Champney's Pink Cluster' 123, 232
'Chapeau de Napoléon' 18, **19**
'Chapman's Crimson Rambler' 244
'Charles de Mills' 41, **41**, 263
Charleston 232
Chateau de Hex 96
Chateau de Neuilly 102, 252
Chelsea Physic Garden 66, 80, 256
'Chénédole' 42, **42**, 263, **263**
'Cherokee Rose' *see R. laevigata*
'Chestnut Rose' *see R. roxburghii*
Child, Daphne 92
China Roses 73–99, 226
Choisy, F. T. 48
'Chromatella' ('Cloth of Gold') 123, **126**, 164
Clare Valley (Australia) 188
Claremont 111, 126
Clarensville, Sea Point 22
'Clementine' 188
Cloete, Jacob 84
'Cloth of Gold' *see* 'Chromatella'
Clusius (Charles de l'Ecluse) 202
Cochet, M. 152
Cochrane, Colin 253
Colley, Gen. G. P. 94
Colombo 26
Colvill's Nursery 86, 210, 228, 229
Commelin Jan 48
'Common Pink Moss' 16, 17, **17**, 18
Companion plants for roses 43, 264
'Comte de Paris' 137
'Comtesse Bardi' 146
'Comtesse de Frigneuse' 126
'Comtesse du Cayla' 97, **97**
Conrad, Petrus 57
Conserve of roses 26, 27, 36, 190
Constantia 23

Coquereau, M. 92
'Coronation' **237**
Correvon, M. 86
'Coupe d'Hébé' 108, **108**
Cowan, Dr J. M. 204
'Cramoisi Supérieur' 92, **92**, 93, 262
Cranemere, Camdeboo 178, 254
Creole gardens 74, 86, 146
Crépin 238
'Crépuscule' 123, 130, **130**, 131, 137, 246, 263
'Crested Moss' 18
'Crimson Glory' 168, **168**, 244
'Crimson Moss' 18, **18**
'Crimson Rambler' 234, 236
'Cuisse de Nymphe' *see* 'Maiden's Blush'
Culpeper, Nicholas 190
'Cupidon' 22
Curtis, Samuel 254
Curtis, Wilbour 74, 212
Curtis, William 14, 15, 204, 210, 217
Cyrene, roses of 58

'Dainty Bess' 180, **180**
Dale, Mr 226
Dale, Mrs 217, 226
Daljosafat 208, 241, 264
Damascus, roses of 58
Damask hedges 58
Damask roses 12, 30, 57–71
Darling 58, 148
Darlington, Dr C. 204
Darlington, H. R. 180
Dauphine 192
Day, Mrs 16
De La Roche, Baroness 88
'De Meaux' *see* 'Rose de Meaux'
De Pronville 94
De Rust 170, 202, 204
De Villiers, Dr Con 13
De Villiers, 'La Mode' 178
De Villiers, Molly 253
De Waal, Manie 162
Deas, Stewart 142
Delavay, M. 214
Delhi 80
Department of Forestry 134
Desprez, M. 123
'Devoniensis' 88, 120, 124, 137, 138, **138**
Devonshire, Mr 20
Deze Hoek, Piketberg 208
Dickson, A. 180
Dodoneus, Rembertus (Dodoens) 12, 30, 47, 50, 188, 190, 194, 196
'Dog Berry' 190
'Dog Rose' *see R. canina; R. laevigata*
'Dog Rose' (of the Cape) 208
Dom Manuel Fort, Cochin 229
'Dorothy Page-Roberts' 98
'Dorothy Perkins' 234, 236, 238, **242**, 243–5, **243**, 262, **264**
'Double Delight' 69, **69**
'Double White Noisette' 253
'Double Yellow Rose' **204**
D'Oyly, Charles 93
'Dr Grill' **139**, 177
'Dr Huey' 248, **249**
Drakenstein, 57, 58, 84, 241
Drakenstein Mountains 90
Druid Lodge, Robertson 152
Du Cane, Ella & Florence 212
Du Monceau, Henri Louis 58
Du Plessis, I. D. 117
Du Pont, M. 34
'Duc de Chartres' 101
Ducher, M. 131, 146
'Duchesse d'Angoulême' 40, **40**
'Duchesse d'Auerstädt' 134–5, **134**, **135**
'Duchesse de Brabant' **142**
Duckitt family grave 58, **61**
Duckitt, Frederick (present owner of Waylands) 60, 128
Duckitt, Hildagonda (cookery writer) 60, 88, 117, 128
Duckitt, John 148
Duhamel, H. L. du Monceau 30, 58
'Duke of Angoulême' 40

Duminee, J. P. 183
Duminy, Johanna Margaretha **27**
Duncan, Walter 126, 248
Durban 92
Durban Botanic Garden 92, 22, 110
Durban Botanical Society 22, 164
Dutch East India Company 11, 22, 25, 26, 57, 96
Dutch East India Company Garden (*see also* Cape Town Botanic Gardens) 11, 13, 16, 25, 48, 160
Dutch flower painting 11
'Dutch rose' 12
Dwarsrivier, Banhoek 215

Eagle's Nest 22
Eastern Cape 138, 228
Eastern Province Herald 258
'Eclair de Jupiter' (*see also* 'Gloire des Rosomanes') 90, 101
Edwards, Walter 217
Eglantine *see R. eglanteria*
Ehret, G. D. 36, **36**
Elgin 20, 34, 41, 110, 119, 222
'Elinthii' 138
Elling, Gertrude 66
Ellis, Revd W. 78, 102, 138, 253
'Elvira' 188
'Emily Dupuy' **141**
'Empereur du Maroc' 170
Endt, Anne 96
'Engineer' 180
English, Mrs 152
English settlers at the Cape 13, 78, 138, 187, 188, 204
'Erinnerung an Brod' 236
Erskine, Philip 78, 104
Erskine, Rupert 78
Erythrina caffra 156
Estment family 38
'Ethel' 248
'Etoile de Hollande' 88, 115, 168, 244
'Etoile de Lyon' 151, **151**
'Euphrosyne' 123, 234
'Everflowering Multiflora' 232–3, **232**, **233**
'Excelsa' 234, 236, 238, 243–5, **244**, **245**, 262, **264**
Ezelfontein, Ceres 218

Faber, Mr 214
'Fabvier' 90, **90**, 264
Fagan, Jessie (Queenie) 16, 78, 236
'Fair Sultana' *see* 'Violacea'
Fairbridge, Dorothea 59, 76, 78, 84, 90, 93, 111, 152, 156, 212, 218, 238, 258
'Fairy Rose' 86
'Fantin-Latour' 23
Fa-Tee nurseries, Canton 82, 88
Faubourl, Madeleine 86
'Félicie' *see* 'Petite Renoncule Violette'
'Félicité et Perpétue' 120, 251, 252–3, **252**, **253**, 262, 263, 264
'Fellemberg' 94–5, **94**, **95**, 131, 181, 262, 264
Fernwood, **123**
Ferreira, Antonie Michael 166
'First Love' **242**, 244
Flemish flower painting 9, 11, 48
Flora rosarum 26, 27, 36
Fontaine, Governor Jan de la 124
Forenaughts, Wynberg 234
Fortune, Robert 88, 220, 254
'Fortune's Double Yellow' *see R. x odorata pseudindica*
Foster, Mr 138
'Francis Dubreuil' 170, **170**
'Francois Juranville' 130, 238, 246, **246**, 263
Franschhoek 43, 142, 151
French Hoek *see* Franschhoek
French Riviera 256
'Frau Karl Druschki' 88, 115, 120, 182, **182**, 183, **183**, 184, 264
French Hoek *see* Franschhoek
French Riviera 256
'Fun Jwan Lo' *see* 'Indica Major'

Gallicas (The Red Roses) 25–45
Galliéni, General 154, **154**

Garcon, M. 114
'Géant des Batailles' 164–5, **164**, **165**, 166, 168, 240, 262, 263, 264
Geissorhiza mathewsii (kelkiewyn) 148
Genadendal 20, 36, 54, 64
'Général Galliéni' 137, **137**, 146, 154–5, **154**, **155**, 166, 264
'Général Jaqueminot' 168–9, **168**, **169**
'Général Schablikine' 144
'Geneva' 242
Gerard, John 12, 25, 30, 32, 47, 58, 60, 188, 190, 197, 202
'Giant of Battles' *see* 'Géant des Batailles'
Gillespie, U. and S. 92
Glattwyn 228
'Globe Hip' 71
'Gloire de Dijon' 101, 104–5, **104**, **105**, 164
'Gloire des Lawranceanas' 86
'Gloire des Rosomanes' ('Jupiter's Lightning') 88, 90–1, **90**, **91**, 101, 164, 166, 168, 202, 262
'Glory of Paris' *see* 'Anna de Diesbach'
'Goldfinch' 235, **235**, 263
Gore, Catherine F. 38
Government House, Cape Town (*see also* Tuynhuys) 7, 13, 32, 60, 194
Gowie's Nurseries 18, 62, 97, 134, 142, 144, 152, 258
Graaff-Reinet 90, 98, 140, 160, 188, 198, 215, 217, 228, 254
Grahamstown 97, 112, 142, 148
Grahamstown Botanic Gardens 112
Grahamstown cemetery 38, 92, 112
'Grand Indienne' *see* 'Indica Major'
Grant, Baron 80
Grasse 146
'Great Holland Rose' **12**
'Great Maiden's Blush' 53
'Greater Rose de Meaux' 15
'Green Rose' (*R. chinensis viridiflora*) 54, 82–3, **82**, **83**
Greville, Sir Charles 36
Greyton 190
Grobbelaar, Mrs P. 124
Groot Constantia **84**
Groot Drakenstein 118, 220, 228, 241
Groot Paardevlei **258**
Groote Post, Darling 60, 117, 128
Groote Schuur 208
Groote Schuur Hospital 182
'Grootendorst', pink 207
'Gruss an Teplitz' 181, **181**, 187, 248
Guillot (father and son) 86, 97, 137, 144, 151, 164, 177, 178, 234, 226
Gulangabin 204

Hahn, Revd John 133, 210
Hakluyt 198
Handelwang, 'Tante Agnes' 82
'Happiness' 170
Hardy, J. A. 71
Harkness, J. 178
Harmansz, G. 47
Harrison, H. P. 92
Hartman, Jan Adam 7
Hartogh, Jan 26
Harvard Arboretum 238
Hazendal, Bottelary 117
Heany, Sheila 118
Hebe speciosa multiflora 137
Heckroodt, Mrs A. E. 107
'Hedge-hog Rose' *see Rosa roxburghii*
Helderfontein, Elgin 34, 54
'Hélène' 235
Hemsley, W. Botting 215
Henderson, P. 226, 241
Hermann, Professor 48
Herre, H. 200
Herschel, Sir John 48, 114
'Hessoise' 188
Hexriver Mountains 188
Heyns, Dr 178
'Hiawatha' 234, **234**
'Himalayan Musk Rose' *see R. brunonii*
Hoffman, J. B. 10
Hoffman, Klaas and Rachel 43

Hofmeyr, Isobel 156, 170, 254
Hofmeyr, Jan Hendrik 82, 254
Hofmeyr, John Murray 254
Hofmeyr, Leonie 156, 170, 254
Hogg, Thomas 207
Hohenort 156
Hole, Dean 104, 174
'Holland Rose' 12
'Homère' ('Buttonhole Rose') 120, 142–3, **142**, **143**
'Honorine de Brabant' 101, 106, **106**, 263
Hooker 238
Hooper, David 202
Hortus Cliffortianus 16, 188
Horvath, Michael 238
Hottentots 11, 57
Hugo, Jan Gysbert 170
'Huguenot Rose' (*see also R. damascena semperflorens*) 57, 58
Huguenots 30, 57, 58
Huijs te Marquette 124
Humansdorp 144
Hume, Sir Abraham 88
'Hume's Blush' (*R. x odorata*) 73, **73**, 88–90, **88**, **89**, 137
Hurst, Dr 86
Hybrid Musks 262, 263
Hybrid Perpetuals 73, 81, 159–75, 177
Hybrid Teas 177–85
'Hyménée' 137

Ida's Valley 4, 36, 64, 78, 118, 238
Ile de Bourbon (*see also* Réunion) 58, 80, 101
Immelman, R. F. M. 117
'Indica Major' ('Odorata') 84–5, **84**, **85**, 137, 224, 228, 262, 263
'Indica pumila' 86
'Irish Beauty' 180
'Irish Elegance' 180, **180**
'Irish Fireflame' 180
'Irish Glory' 180
'Isabella Sprunt' 140, **140**

'Jacob Cloete Rose' *see* 'Indica Major'
Jacotot, M. 164
Jacquin, M. 74, **76**, **77**, **80**, 192, **192**, 198, **199**, 203, 212
'Janet's Pride' 188
Jansen, Lysbeth 134
Jaques, M. 102, 252
'Jaune Desprez' 123, 124, **124**, 137, 263
'Jean Ducher' **142**
Jekyll, Gertrude 66, 144
Johnman, Mrs Dorothy 90, 116, 133, 139, 140, 141, 210, 220, 258
'Johnman's Cottage Rose' 116, **116**
Jonkershoek 134
Jooste, Dougie 200, 232
Josephine, Empress 88, 164
Josephine's Mill, Mowbray 156
Joubert, Revd W. A. 82
Joubertina 188
Jugreet, Nassar 74
'Jupiter's Lightning' *see* 'Gloire des Rosomanes'

'Kaapse Roos' ('Muslim Rose') 101, 117, **117**, **265**
Kabeljouwsrivier, Humansdorp 166
Karoo 166, 178, 202
Kashmir 196
Katberg 188
'Kathleen Harrop' 118, **118**
Keats, John 197
Keays, Ethelyn 162, 166
Kennedy, Mr 88
Kerr, William 210, 217
Kew, Royal Botanic Garden at 7, 53, 215, 232, 238, 248
Keynes, Williams & Co. of Salisbury 188
Killie-Campbell Museum 22, 92, 164
King, Mrs 173
King William's Town 104, 146, 234
Kingsley, Rose G. 137
Kirstenbosch Botanic Gardens 120, 256

Kirstenbosch cemetery 120, 156, 215, 256
Klapmuts farm 48
Klein Constantia 178, 200, 232, 241
Klein Drakenstein 128, 131, 244
Klipfontein, Graaff-Reinet 90, 140, 215, 217, 228
'Klipfontein Musk Rose' 198, **199**
Knorhoek, Sir Lowry's Pass 20
Knox-Shaw, Maisie 15, 20, 34, 41, 110
Knox-Shaw, Peter 20, 22, 234
Knox-Shaw garden 15, 34, 41, 119, 188, 212, 246
Knysna 90, 104, 210, 242, 244
Kolbe, Peter 13, 25, 47, 48
'Köningin von Dänemark' ('Queen of Denmark') 52, **52**
Koue Bokkeveld 188, 252
Krause, W. 241
Kromrivier, Koue Bokkeveld 188
Kromvlei, Elgin 20
Krussman, Gerd 238
Kuruman 252
Kuttel, M. 60, 88

'La Belle Distinguée' 188
'La Belle Marseillaise' see 'Fellemberg'
'La Boule d'Or' 128
'La Follette' 251, 256–7, **257**, 263
'La France' 124, 164, 177, 178–9, **179**, 202
'La Motte Sanguine' 128
'La Reine' 88, 162–3, **163**, 164, 166
'La Reine Victoria' 120, 121, **121**, 128, 164, 263
'La Rosiere' 128
'La Villes de Bruxelles' 57, 70, **70**
'La Virginale' **50**
Lacharme, M. 148, 166, 177
'Lady Godiva' 236
'Lady Hillingdon' 120, 137, 155–6, **156**, **157**, 166
'Lady Montagu' 101
'Lady Penzance' 188
'Lady Roberts' **156**
Laffay, G. 18, 44, 108, 162, 164
'Lamarque' 123, 126, **126**
Lambert, P. 181, 183
'Lane' 22
Langfontein, Koue Bokkeveld 252
Langkloof 53, 82, 88, 97, 140, 156, 168, 188, 254
Large climbers 251–9
Lategan, Felix 94
Lategan, 'Tant Mieta' 94
'Laurette Messimy' **156**
Lawder, Margaret 36, 128, 150
Lawrance, Mary 14, **14**, 15, 16, 49, 52, 86, 188, **196**, **202**, **204**, **207**, **252**
Le Blond, A. 58
Le Dru, M. 38
'Le Rosier de Philip Noisette' 123
Le Roux, Anne 202
Le Roux, Hanna 170
Le Roux, Marius 162
'Le Soleil' 128
'Leda' 69, **69**
Lee and Kennedy of Hammersmith 207
Leeuwenhof 246
Leibrandt, H. V. C. 11, 47, 271
Leiden Botanic Gardens see Leyden
Leighton's Nurseries 104, 146, 234
Lekkerwyn, Groot Drakenstein 241
Leliefontein, Klein Drakenstein 128
Lemery, Nicholas 30, 58, 196, 197
'Leon XIII' 128
'Leopold de Bauffrémont' 116
'Lésser Rose de Meaux' 13, 14, **14**, 15
Leyden (Leiden) Botanic Gardens 16, 34, 48, 54, 62, 81, 188
Libertas, Stellenbosch 10, 36, 42, 98
'Libertas Rose' 42, **42**
'L'Idéal' 128, 247
Liesching, Dr 20
Life at the Cape 100 Years Ago 208
Lindley, John 13, 16, 32, 81, 86, 196, 200

Lindley Library 2, 75, 188, 204
Linnaeus 16, 28, 188
'L'Innocence' 128
Lisbon 258
'Little White Pet' ('Little Pet') 128, 226, **226**
Liversedge, Dr 252
Lobel, Mathias de 188
Lockyer, Charles 57
Logan, Charles 218
'Lord Raglan' 128
Loudon 13, 192, 228
'Louis Leveque' 128
'Louis Philippe' 92, **92**, 93, **93**, 262, 264
'Louis van Houtte' 128, 146
'Louise Odier' 110, **110**, **265**
Lowe, R. T. 80, 229
Lowe, William & Son 156
Lowell, James 215
Ludwig, Baron Von see Von Ludwig, Baron
Ludwig's Nurseries 18, 28, 119, 178, 200, 207, 210, 226, 247
Ludwig'sburg Garden 20, 32
'Lusitania' 258
Lyons, rose conference at 177

'Mabel Morrison' 128
Macao 88
Macartney, Lord George 81, 212
'Macartney Rose' 48, 208, 212–13, **212**, **213**, 262
MacClaren, Mr 104
McFarland, H. 180
McFarland, J. H. 40, 64, 84, 98, 112, 115, 138, 150, 234, 248
McGredy, Sam 180, 184
'Ma Tulipe' 97, **97**
Madagascar 154
Madeira 58, 59, 80, 212, 229
'Mademoiselle Germaine Rand' 128
'Mademoiselle Helena Cambier' 128
'Magna Charter' 128, 148
Magon, Rene 80
'Maheka' see 'Violacea'
'Maiden's Blush' 47, 53, **53**, 128
'Mal Fleuri' 128
Malabar 57
Malan, Magdalena Johanna 117
Malan, Mildy 131
Malay Quarter, Cape Town 117, 164
'Malay Rose' see 'Kaapse Roos'
Malaysian slaves 117
'Maldensis' (R. centifolia parvifolia) 13, 86, 87
Malherbe, Maria Johanna 218
Malmaison 81, 88, 164
'Malton' 137
'Maman Cochet' 88, 137, 152–3, **152**, **153**, 166, 234
Manetti, Dr 132
Manget, M. 107
Manson, Hugh 148, 183
'Maréchal Niel' 123, 128–9, **128**, **129**, 131, 164, 263
Margottin, M. 110
'Marie van Houtte' 137, 146–7, **146**, **147**, 152, 166
Marquard, Susan see Van Zyl, Susan
Marquise Bocella 23
Mauborget 86
Mauritius 22, 26, 74, 76, 80, 81, 86, 102, 138, 146, 148, 253
Mayville, Swellendam 111, 265
Median Fire Worshippers 30
Meeding, Albertinia Sophia 53
Meeding, Capt. 53
Meeding, Maria Johanna Albertina 166
'Meg Merrilies' 188, **188**
'Memorial Rose' see R. luciae
Mercantile Advertiser 13
'Mermaid' 208, **213**, 262
'Merveille de Lyon' 183
Michaud, Serge 102
Middelpos, De Rust 170
'Mignonette' 86
Milesian roses 30
Mill River farm, Langkloof 53, 88, 90, 97, 114, 170, 254

Miller, Philip 9, 11, 13, 16, 26, 53, 80, 81, 190
Milton, John 197
Miniature roses 13, 86
'Mme Alfred Carrière' 123, 128, 131, 133, **133**
'Mme Berard' 128
'Mme Boll' 128
'Mme Bravy' 128, 177, 178
'Mme Bruel' 128
'Mme C. Joigneaux' 128
'Mme C. Kuster' 148
'Mme Camille' 128, 148
'Mme Caroline Testout' 183, 263
'Mme Charles Crapelet' 128
'Mme Cusin' 148
'Mme de Tartas' 98, 146
'Mme de Watteville' 128
'Mme E. Helfenbein' 128
'Mme E. Michel' 128
'Mme Eugene Verdier' 128, 148
'Mme F. de la Forrest' 128
'Mme Falcot' 98, 128, 146, 148, 150, 156
'Mme Gabriel Luizet' 128, 148
'Mme Georges Bruant' 207, **207**
'Mme Hardy' 57, 71, **71**
'Mme H. de Potworowski' 128
'Mme Hippolyte Jamain' 128
'Mme Honore Defresne' 148
'Mme Hosta ('Mme Hoste') 128, 148, 156
'Mme Isaac Pereire' 88, 101, 114, **114**, 131, 148, 263
'Mme Jacques Charreton' 128
'Mme Joseph Combet' 128
'Mme Jules Gravereaux' 182
'Mme Lambard' ('Mme Lombard') 128, 137, 148–9, **148**, **149**, 152
'Mme Laurette Messimy' 148
'Mme Legras de Saint Germain' **52**
'Mme Lombard' see 'Mme Lambard'
'Mme M. Lavalley' 128
'Mme Margottin' 128, 148
'Mme Marie Cirodde' 128
'Mme Moreau' 128
'Mme Norma' 128, 148
'Mme Pierre Oger' 120, **120**
'Mme Plantier' 43, 47, 54–5, **54**, **55**, 263
'Mme Rivers' 128
'Mme Schultz' 131
'Mme Verrier Cachet' 128
'Mme Victor Verdier' 128, 148
'Mme Zoetmans' 71
Mock-orange 43
Moffat, Robert 252
Molteno, Sir James Tennant 34
Mont Rose 156
Montague House, Woodstock 217, 226
'Monthly Rose' see 'Parsons' Pink China'
Moon (painter) **141**
Moorreesburg 115, 173
Moreau, M. 18
Morgan, G. 254
Morley, Dr 42
Moskonfyt 173
'Moss Adelaide' 16
'Moss Angelique' 16
'Moss Lanei' 16
'Moss Luxemburg' 16
Moss roses 9, 16–19, **16**, **17**, **18**, **19**
Mossel Bay 166
Mosselbank, Tygerberg **124**
Mottisfont garden 22, 146, 170, 252
Moutonsvlei 128
Mowbray 107, 156, 248
Mowbray cemetery **66**, 94, 140, 148
'Mrs Bousanquet' 142
'Mrs F. W. Flight' **236**
'Mrs Herbert Stevens' 166, 184–5, **184**, **185**, 264
'Mrs John Laing' 174–5, **175**
Multifloras 224–37
Muratie, Stellenbosch 134
Murray, Walter 228, 254
Murray, Anne 228, 254
Murray, Emma 111
Murray, Joyce 13, 111

Murray, Revd Andrew 111
Musk Roses 196–201, **196**, **197**, **198**, **199**
Muslim ceremonies 117
'Muslim Rose' see 'Kaapse Roos'

Nabonnand, H. 146, 154, 256
'Nagmaal huisie' 139
Nancy Steen Memorial Garden 74, **95**, 142, 184
National Rose Society 133, 177
Neethling, Helen 76
'Nemesis' 86
Nerard, M. 164
'New Dawn' 236
Newlands 115, 156
Newstead, Balgowan 126
New Zealand 43, 96, 142, 148, 152, 229
Niel, Adolphe 128
'Niphetos' 184
'Noémi' 57
Noisette, Louis 86, 123
Noisette, Philip 123
Noisettes 73, 81, 123–35
Non Pareille **170**
Nottle, Trevor 140, 141
'Nuits de Young' **16**, 18
Nur Jahan 196
Nylandt, Petrus 25, 30, 188, 194, 196

Oberkirch, Baroness d' 81
'Odorata' see 'Indica major'
Oil of roses 26
'Old Cape Rose' 16
'Old Double Yellow Scots Rose' see 'Williams' Double Yellow'
Old Garden Roses in Bermuda 146, 150
'Old Monthly' see 'Parsons' Pink China'
Old roses for historic and modern gardens 260–5
Oldenland, H. B. 13, 16, 25, 26, 34, 47, 48
Olivier, Emily 178
'Ophelia' 88, 178
Oranjezicht, Cape Town 154
Ordman, Gertrude 218
Orieux, Mary 76, 86
Orléans, Duke of 102
'Orphiline de Juillet' 38
Osbeck, Pehr 74, 80
Otto, Miss Maggie 202, 204
Oude Libertas 13, 98
Oudtshoorn 88, 90, 160, 166, 194
Oudtshoorn Courant 166
'Ouma Mietjie's Cabbage' 166

Paarl 84, 120, 178, 207, 208, 212
'Pacquerette' see 'Paquerette'
Paestum, roses of 58
'Painted Damask' see 'Leda'
Pal, B. P. 102
Palaka, Aroe 57
Palhinha, Dr Ruy 258
Palmer, Eve (Mrs Jenkins) 173, 178, 254
'Palmira Feifas' 258
Pampelmousse Gardens, Mauritius 22
'Papa Gontier' 156
'Paquerette' 86, 164, 226, 230
Parish, John 102
Park, Bertram 142
Parker, John 78
Parkes, Douglas 217
Parkes, G. D. 217
Parkes, J. D. 88
Parkes, Mrs 215
Parkes, Thomas 188
Parkinson, John 11, 12, 30, 36, 58, 47, 62, 190, **190**, **194**, 196, 197, 202
'Parks' Yellow Tea-scented China' (R. x odorata ochroleuca) 73, **73**, 89, 138
Parsons, Mr 81
Parsons, Samuel B. 92, 144, 162
'Parsons' Pink China' ('Old Monthly') 58, 73, **73**, 74, 78–81, **79**, **80**, **81**, 86, 101, 102, 109, 124, 166, 226, 254, 262, 264, **264**

Patraia garden, Florence **102**
Paul, William 13, 40, 42, 57, 64, 71, 86, 88, 116, 123, 137, 162, 164, 170, 188
'Paul Neyron' 172–3, **173**
'Paul Noël' 236
'Paul Ricault' 22–3, **23**
'Paul Transon' 247, **247**
'Paul's Carmine Pillar' 234
'Paul's Scarlet Climber' 244
'Peace' 152
Pears, Revd 254
Pearson, Dr 256
Pemberton, J. 88, 104
Penzance, Lord 188
Perichon, M. 102
'Perle de Lyon' 126
'Perle des Jardins' 150, **150**
'Perle d'Or' 98, **98**, **99**
Pernet-Ducher, M. 98, 137, 164, 202
'Perpetual White Moss' ('Quatre Saisons Blanc Mousseux') 18, **61**
Persian roses 13, 30, 202–5
'Persian roses' at the Cape 25
'Persian Yellow Rose' see R. foetida persiana
Petersen's nursery, Copenhagen 66, 138, 140, 164
'Petite Renoncule Violette' 38–9, **38**, **39**
Petrusfontein 104
'Phaloé' 123
'Philadelpha' 234, **234**
Pickstone, H. E. 241
Pickstone, Wendy 241
Piketberg 128, 173, 208
'Pink China' see 'Parsons' Pink China'
'Pink Dog Rose' see 'Anemone'
'Pink Monthly' see 'Parsons' Pink China'
Piquetberg, see Piketberg
Plain de Palmiste, Réunion 74, 82
Plantskole, Copenhagen 71
Pliny 11, 25, 28, 30, 47, 58, 190, 196
Pniel 33, 54, 97, 174, 231, 234, 235
Polyanthas 226
Pompadour, Mme de 33
Pompeian frescoes 58
'Pompon de Bourgogne' 15, **15**
'Pompon de Paris' 15, 86
'Pompone Rose' 14
'Pomponia' 13, 14
Port Elizabeth 107, 134, 258
Portemer 22
Portland roses 81
Poseidonia 58
Powis Castle 104
Pradel 128
Pratt, A. E. 222
'President Hoover' 244
Pride of India 107
Prince, William 123
Prince Albert 102
'Prince Charlie's Rose' see 'Williams' Double Yellow'
'Princesse Marie' **252**
Prodal, M. 164
Provence Rose 11–13
Provincial Roads Nursery, Paarl 207
Provins 30
'Psyche' 234
Pyrenees 192

'Quatre Saisons Blanc Mousseux' see 'Perpetual White Moss'
'Queen of Denmark' see 'Köningin von Dänemark'
'Queen of France' see 'La Reine'

Rabinowitz, Hymie 22
'Radio' 202
'Ragged Robin' see 'Gloire des Rosomanes'
'Ramanas Rose' see R. rugosa
'Rambling Rector' **232**
'Raubritter' 263
'Red Dorothy' see 'Excelsa'

Reddick, Terry 115
Redouté, P. J. 13, **14**, 15, 20, 34, 38, 53, 64, 81, 84, 86, 88, 102, 196, **198**, 202, 228, 232
Reeves, J. 75, 204, **205**, **210**, **232**
'Reine Emma des Pays-Bas' 154
'Reines des Vierges' 101
Rennie, Prof. John 112, 148
Retief, Dan 248
Retief graves 102
Réunion (see also Isle de Bourbon) 74, 76, 80, 81, 82, 86, 101, 102, 146
'Rêve d'Or' 123, 131, **131**, 137, 263
Rhodes, C. J. 118
Richelieu, Duc de 44, **44**
'Rival de Paestum' 156
Rivers, Thomas 20, 102, 132
Riversdale 116, 146, 258
Robert and Moreau 18, 137
Robertson 152
Rochon, Abbé Alexis 196–7
Romain mosaic depicting roses 11, **12**
Rondebosch 88, 131, 218, 258
Rookwood cemetery, Sydney 66, 164
Rosa alba maxima 47, 48, 51, **51**, 263
R. alba regalis 53
R. alba semi-plena 47, 48, 49, **49**, 54, 263
R. altaica 194
R. arvensis 47, 48, **196**,197
R. banksiae banksiae 54, 216–18, **216**, **217**
R. banksiae lutea 54, 88, 217, 218, **219**
R. bracteata ('Macartney Rose') 208, 212–13, **212**, **213**, 218, 262
R. brunonii 198, 200–1, **200**, **201**, 263
R. canina 48, 190–1, **190**, **191**, 207
R. canina borboniana see 'Rose Edward'
R. centifolia 11–13, **12**, **13**, 14, 16, 40, 53, 57
R. centifolia 'Muscosa' ('Common Pink Moss') 16, 17, **17**, 18
R. centifolia parvifolia 86
R. centifolia pomponia 14, **14**
R. chinensis minima 78, 86–7, **86**, **87**, 262
R. chinensis mutabilis **154**, 263
R. chinensis semperflorens ('Slater's Crimson China') 73, **73**, 74–6, **74**, **75**, **76**, **77**, 80
R. chinensis var. 'Grandiflora Hort' 254
R. chinensis viridiflora ('Green Rose') 54, 82–3, **82**, **83**
R. damascena semperflorens 18, 57, 58–9, **58**, **59**, 60, 61, 73, 80, 81, 101, 102
R. damascena versicolor ('York and Lancaster') 62–3, **62**, **63**
R. eglanteria ('Eglantine', 'Sweet Brier') 187, 188–9, **188**, **189**, 190, 202
R. ferox see R. rugosa
R. foetida bicolor 202–4, **203**
R. foetida lutea 202, **202**, 204
R. foetida persiana 204, **204**, **205**
R. fortuniana 54, 184, **220**, **221**, 228
R. gallica 28, **28**, 34, 40, 48, 81
R. gallica var. officinalis 26, 29, **29**, 30
R. gigantea 256, 258
R. glauca 192–3, **192**, **193**, 263
R. helenae **236**
R. holosericea multiplex 36, **36**
R. hugonis 215, **215**, 263
R. indica 75, 76, **78**, **80**
R. indica sulphurea 88
'Rosa Inglesa' 80
R. laevigata ('Cherokee Rose') 48, 54, 184, 187, 208–9, **208**, 212, 215, 220, 228, 241, 262, 263, 264, **264**
R. lawranceana see R. chinensis minima
R. luciae 238–9, **238**, **239**, 246, 262, 263
R. microphylla see R. roxburghii
R. moschata 54, 73, 81, **196**, 200
R. moschata flore semi-plena **198**
R. moschata multiplex 196

R. moyesii 222-3, **222**, **223**, 263
R. multiflora **164**, 224–5, **225**, 226, 230, 236, 262, 263
R. multiflora carnea **21**, **36**, 43, 228–9, **228**, **229**, 253, **263**
R. multiflora nana **73**, 226–7, **226**, **227**, 262, **262**
R. multiflora platyphylla 36
R. multiflora (unidentified forms) 231–3
'Rosa Mundi' 30, **30**, **31**
R. noisettiana 232
R. noisettiana manettii 132, **132**
R. x odorata ('Hume's Blush China') 73, **73**, 74, 84, 88–90, **88**, **89**, 137, 208, 264
R. x odorata ochroleuca ('Parks' Yellow Tea-scented China') 73, **73**, 88, **89**, 138
R. x odorata pseudindica ('Beauty of Glazenwood', 'Fortune's Double Yellow') 88, 251, 254–5, **254**, **255**, 263
R. omeiensis pteracantha see R. sericea pteracantha
'Rosa Portugueza' 58
R. pimpinellifolia 194
R. pimpinellifolia 'Grandiflora' 194–5, **195**, 263
R. provincialis sive Damascena **60**
R. roxburghii 88, 210–11, **210**, **211**, 262, 263
R. roxburghii hirtula 210
R. rubiginosa see R. eglanteria
R. rubiginosa zabeth 188
R. rubrifolia see R. glauca
R. rugosa 206–7, **206**
'Rosa Schoenbrunnensis' 20
R. semperflorens minima 86, **87**
R. sempervirens 164, 252, **252**
R. sempervirens major 253
R. sericea 187
R. sericea pteracantha 214, **214**
R. setigera 248
R. sinica anemone see 'Anemone'
R. spinosissima see R. pimpinellifolia
R. sulphurea **204**
R. triphylla (R. laevigata) 208
R. wichuraiana 238, **239**, 240, 241, 248
R. willmottiae 187
Rose Annual 84, 142, 200
'Rose Bradwardine' 188
'Rose de l'Isle de Bourbon' 102
'Rose de Meaux' ('Lesser') 13, 14, **14**, 15; ('Greater') **14**, 15, **15**
'Rose de Pompon' **14**
'Rose Edward' 101, 102–3, **102**, **103**, 264
'Rose of York' 47
Rosebank 156
Rosehill farm, Natal 92
Roseraie de l'Hay-les-Roses 90, 236
Roseraie du Parc de la Grange **242**, 244
'Rosette Delizy' 146
Rose-water 26, 30, 47, 57, 58, 60, 62
'Rosier de Cels' see 'Celsiana'
'Rosier du Bengale' 86
'Rosier Évêque' ('The Bishop') 20
Ross, Dean 140, 146
Ross, Helen 90
Rothman, Anna 220
Rothman, M. E. 16, 78, 117, 218, 220
'Rothman Rose' 68, **68**
Roulet, Dr 86
'Rouletii' 86, **87**
Rourke, Dr John 256
Roussel, M. 168
Roxburgh, W. 11, 76, 208, 210, 229
Rubidge, Capt. Robert Henry 228
Rugosas 206–7, 262
'Russeliana' 26, 34, 36–7, **36**, **37**, 54, 88, 228, 262
Rust en Vreugd **265**
Rustan, David 119, 124, 170, 248
Rustenberg, Ida's Valley 64, 118
Rutherford, H.E. 111
Ruysch, Rachel 64
Rycroft, Prof. B. 215

'Sachsen Gruss' 178, 182, **182**, 263

'Safrano' 140, **140**
Salomonsvlei 130, 131, 232
Salted roses 26, 36
Sampson, Mrs Victor 112
Savatier, Lucy 238
Savoy 192
Scallan, Father Hugo 215
'Scarlet Grevillea' see 'Russeliana'
Schmidt, George 36
Schmidt, J. C. 208, 230
'Schoenbrunnensis' 20
Schreyer, Johan 13, 25
Schroeder, Anna 133
Schroeder, Dr George 133
Schwartz, J. 120
Scott, Sir Walter 188
Sea Point 23, 110
Sea View, Tygerberg 183
Seal-hunters 47
'Sempervirens Major' 253, **253**
Sempervirens roses 252–3
'Seven Sisters' ('Cape Seven Sisters') 218, 231, **231**, 252
Seychelles 80, 102
'Shafter' see 'Dr Huey'
Shakespeare, William 197, 198
Shepherd, Roy 36, 38, 82, 86, 88, 123, 132, 138, 140, 168, 177, 207, 224, 253
'Shirley Hibberd' 240
Shohan, Lily 93
Shore, Mrs 139
Short, Hazel 188
Siggs, Miss O. 180
'Silver Moon' 241, **241**, 262
Simon's Bay (Simonstown) 96
'Simonstown Rose' 96, **96**
Sims (flower painter) 8, 86
Sintra, Portugal 229
Sir Lowry's Pass 20
'Slamse Roos' see 'Kaapse Roos'
Slater, Gilbert 74
'Slater's Crimson China' (R. chinensis semperflorens) 73, **73**, 74–6, **74**, **75**, **76**, **77**, 80
Smee, Alfred 120
Smith, Pauline 88
Smith Bros Nursery of Uitenhage 18, 53, 54, 82, 128, 148, 151, 152, 183, 188, 204, 207
'Smith's Yellow' 137, 138
'Snow Queen' see 'Frau Karl Druschki'
Society of Horticulture of Lyon 178
'Soleil d'Or' 164, 202, **204**
'Solfaterre' 126–7, **127**
Solomon, Saul 22, 92, 105, 110, 164
Somerset, Lord Charles 188
Somerset East 254
Somerset West 20, 226, 252
South African Quarterly Journal 32
'Souvenir d'Alphonse Lavallée' 115, **115**
'Souvenir de la Bataille de Marengo' see 'Russeliana'
'Souvenir de la Malmaison' 101, 111, **111**, 202
'Souvenir de la Princesse de Lamballe' ('Bourbon Queen') 107, **107**
'Souvenir de Madame Léonie Viennot' 137, 241, 251, 258–9, **258**, **259**, 262, 263
'Souvenir de Thérèse Levet' 154
'Souvenir du Dr Jamain' **170**
'Souvenir d'un Ami' **142**
Spath, Louis 238
Species roses 187–249
Speelman, Cornelis 57
Spitskop 94
Sri Lanka 80
St. Denis 74, 146
St. Helena 59, 76, 80, 208, 229
St. Mark at Staplefield 142
Stamford Hill 109
'Stanwell Perpetual' **195**
Staunton, Sir George 81, 212
Stavorinus, Johan Splinter 48
Steen, Nancy 33, 43, 66, 152
Stegman, G. W. 90
Stellenbosch 48, 57, 58, 64, 82, 84,

116, 117, 126, 128, 133, 134, 139, 140, 142, 162, 180, 184, 200, 208, 210, 212, 220, 226, 258
Stellenbosch Botanic Garden 200
Stellenbosch Drostdy 48
Stellenbosch Dutch Reformed Church 48
Stephen Brett's Nurseries 18, 78, 82, 107, 111, 127, 134, 146, 150, 151
Stevens, G. A. 208, 248
Steyn, Nita 111
Stone, A. 126
Stormberg 188
'Stud roses' 73, **73**
'Sultane Favorite' see 'Petite Renoncule Violette'
'Super Star' 202
'Sutter's Gold' 202
Sutton's Nursery 60
Sweet, Mr 86
Sweet Brier see R. eglanteria
'Sweetheart Rose' see 'Cécile Brunner'
Swellendam 16, 78, 86, 90, 111, 124, 181, 218, 220
Swellendam Drostdy Museum 84, 124, 188, 208, 238
Sydney, Australia 66, 164
'Sylvia' 98
Synstylae group 238

Tabernaemonteus 12
Table Mountain 47
Taillefert, Isaac 30
Tamboerskloof. Cape Town 154, 218
Tas, Adam 36, 42
Taschner, Ludwig 247
'Tausendschön' 230, **230**, 258
Taute, Babette 53, 88, 90, 97, 170
Taute, Clive 168
Taute, Grace 168
Tea roses 16, 73, 137–57, 177, 258
'Temple rose' ('Rose Edward') 102
Tennyson, Alfred Lord 197
'Thalia' 224, **224**
The Beadle 88
'The Bishop' 20, **20**, **21**, 54, **160**, **263**, **265**

The Oaks, Greyton 190
'The Vicar' (rose author) 192, 194, 214
'The Warrior' 96, **96**
Theophrastus 11, 28, 58, 196
Thibault IV, King of Navarre 30
Thim, Mr 66, 138
Thomas, A.S. 102, 146
Thomas, Capt. G. 248
Thomas, Graham 34, 36, 40, 47, 48, 86, 88, 115, 162, 197, 198, 200
Thompson, Richard 76
Thory, C. A. 15, 20, 34, 38, 53, 64, 81, 88, 102, 196, 229
Thunberg, Carl Peter 207, 224, 228
Tijmens, Wim 200
Tokai 218
Topp's Tea Gardens 13
'Triomphe du Luxembourg' 140, **140**
Trotter, A. F. 111
Tulbagh 16, 58, 78, 84, 218
Tulbagh Drostdy 7
'Tulip rose' **96**, 97
'Turner's Crimson Climber' 234
'Tuscany' 32, **32**
Tuynhuys (see also Government House) 12

Uitenhage 54, 107, 134, 166, 204
Uitvlucht, Tulbagh 84
'Ulrich Brunner Fils' 146
Unknown Tea Roses 140–1, **140**, **141**, **154**, **156**
Unknown Wichuraiana hybrid 248, **248**
Ursel, Count d' 96

Valentyn, Francois 48
Van der Byl, Mrs 156
Van der Groen, J. 25, 30
Van der Merwe, Capt. 258
Van der Stel, Simon 48, 57, 96, 134
Van der Stel, Willem Adriaan 36, 42, 48
Van Eerden, Corrie 82
Van Fleet 234, 241, 248
Van Goens, Ryklof 25, 57
Van Heerden, Helie 115

Van Huysum, Jan 64
Van Riebeeck (Riebeek), Jan 7, 11, 13, 25, 47, 93, 118
Van Swellengrebel, Governor 57
Van Zyl, Jacobus 124
Van Zyl, Susan 124
'Variegata di Bologna' 101, 106, 119, **119**, 263
Vatican Museum 12
'Veilchenblau' 235, 236–7, **236**, **237**, 263
Veitch & Sons 222
'Velvet Rose' see 'Tuscany'
Versfeld, Frank 128
Versfeld, Hildagonda 58
Versfeld, John 128
Versfeld, Walter 128
Verster, Izaak Charl 123, 124
'Vicar, The' (rose author) 192, 194, 214
Vibert, M. 18, 70, 90, 38, 164
Viburnum opulus 43, 90
'Victor Emanuel' 119
'Victor Hugo' 234
'Victor Verdier' 178
Victoria West 16
Victorian cottages 208
Villars 192
Villiersdorp 16
Vilmorin, Maurice de 214
'Violacea' 34–5, **34**, **35**
Virgil 58
Visser, Dirk 156
Von Ludwig, Baron 13, 14, 16, 20, 32, 53, 64, 76, 86, 204
Vondeling, Bainskloof 117
Vos, Andreas 86
Vredenburg, Mowbray 156

Wagenaer, Zacharias 57
Wait, Mrs C. 166
Wallich, D. 200
Walsh, Mrs 115
Walton, Erika 86, 244
Walton, Ian 244
Walton, Jessie 244
Walton, Kate 244
War of the Roses 30, 62

Watermeyer, F. G. 134
Waveren 57
'Wax Rose' see 'Duchesse d'Angoulême'
Waylands, Darling 60, 128, 148
Weber, Revd 82
'Weisser Herumstreicher' 230
Wellington 84, 102, 111, 226, 248
Wellwood 228
Welvanpas 36, 198, 248
'Welvanpas Musk Rose' 197, **197**, 198
Wheatlands, Graaff-Reinet 188
Whileman, Leslie 104, 139, 146
'White American Beauty' ('Frau Karl Druschki') 183
'White Bath' 16
'White Dorothy' 236, 243, 244
'White Moss' 164
White Roses (the Albas) 47–55
Wichura, Max Ernst 238
Wichuraiana roses 234–49
Wilbur, Donald 30
'William Lobb' 18
Williams, John 194
'Williams' Double Yellow' 194, **194**, 262
Willmott, Ellen 94, 188, **198**, 202, 220, 238, **239**, 254
Wisley 88
Witblits 173
Woodstock 217
Wolfe, Miss 234
Worcester 47, 102, 139
Wupperthal 76
Wynberg 156, 234

'Yellow Dog Rose' see 'Mermaid'
'Yellow Tea-scented China' see 'Parks' Yellow Tea-scented China'
'York and Lancaster' 62–3, **62**, **63**
Yorkists 30

Zanddrift 124
'Zéphirine Drouhin' 101, 114, 118, **118**, 131, 263
Zuurbraak 90, 253

BIBLIOGRAPHY

African Court Calendar & Directory, 1818–
AITON, W. T. Hortus Kewensis, London 1810–13 (2nd ed.)
American Rose Society Annual, 1916–
ARDERNE, H. 'A Cape Garden' (unpublished paper read before the Horticultural Club of Cape Town in 1896)
Australian and New Zealand Rose Annual, 1954–62
BAILEY, L. H. Manual of Cultivated Plants, Macmillan, New York 1924
— Standard Cyclopedia of Horticulture, Macmillan, New York 1914–17
BARNES, JOHN. A Tour through the Island of St. Helena, London 1817 (observations made during 12 years' stay in St. Helena)
BEALES, PETER. Classic Roses, Collins Harvill, London 1985
BEALES, PETER and MONEY, KEITH. Georgian and Regency Roses, Jarrold, Norwich 1978
— Early Victorian Roses, Jarrold, Norwich 1978
— Late Victorian Roses, Jarrold, Norwich 1980
— Edwardian Roses, Jarrold, Norwich 1980
BEAN, W. J. Trees and Shrubs Hardy in the British Isles, John Murray, London 1980 (8th rev. ed.)
BECKET, K. A. Roses, Dorling Kindersley, London 1984
BENTHAM, GEORGE. Flora Hongkongensis, London 1861
Bermuda Rose Society. Old Garden Roses in Bermuda, 1984
BLATT, REDVERS J. 'In a Californian rose garden' in Garden and Country Life, XXIII, Nov. 1933

BLUNT, W. and RUSSELL, J. Old Garden Roses, Part Two, Rainbird, London 1957
BOERHAAVE, H. Index Alter Plantarum quae in Horto Academico Lugduno-Batavo aluntur, Leiden, 1720
BOWDICH, T. E. Excursions in Madeira and Porto Santo, London 1825
BOWIE, J. & S. and PRITCHARD F. 'An Alphabetical List of Indigenous and Exotic Plants Growing on the Island of St. Helena, 1836' (unpublished)
BRADLOW, FRANK R. Baron von Ludwig and the Ludwig's-burg Garden, Balkema, Cape Town 1965
BUIST, R. The Rose Manual, 1844 (fac. ed. Heyden, London 1978)
BUNYARD, E. A. Old Garden Roses, Country Life, London 1936
BURCHELL, W. J. Travels in the Interior of Southern Africa, 1822 (fac. ed. Batchworth, London 1953)
Canadian Rose Annual, The, 1961–72
CANDOLLE, A. P. DE. Prodromus systematis naturalis . . ., Paris 1824–73
Cape Amateur Gardener, published by the Royal Horticultural & National Sweet Pea Society of Great' Britain, 1906, 1907, 1913
Cape Garden, The, 1909–10
CARTER, GEORGE. The South African Home Garden, Maritzburg 1914
CECIL, A. M., Baroness Rockley. Wild Flowers of the Great Dominions of the British Empire, Macmillan, London 1935
CONRADI, PETRUS. Batavia, Harlingen 1782
CULPEPER, NICHOLAS. Complete Herbal and English

Physician, 1653 (fac. repr. of the 1826 ed., Harvey Sales, Bath 1981)
Curtis's Botanical Magazine, 1789–
DARLINGTON, H. R. Roses, London 1911
DILLENIUS, J. J. Hortus Elthamensis, London 1732
DODONEUS, R. Cruydtboeck, Antwerp 1554
— A New Herbal of Plants, London 1619 (translated into English by H. Lyte)
DU CANE, FLORENCE. The Flowers and Gardens of Madeira, painted by Ella Du Cane, London 1909
DUHAMEL DU MONCEAU, H. L. Traité des arbres et arbustes, Paris 1755
DUMINEE, J. P. Twilight over Tygerberg, Kommetjie 1979
EAGLE, DAWN AND BARRY. Miniature Roses, Collins, London 1985
EDWARDS, G. Roses for Enjoyment, Collingridge, London 1962
— Wild and Old Garden Roses, David & Charles, Newton Abbot 1975
ELLIS, W. Three Visits to Madagascar . . . 1853, 1854, 1856, London 1858
ELLWANGER, H. B. The Rose, New York 1882
ENGLISH, D. A. South African Gardening Manual, Maritzburg Nurseries, 1916
FAIRBRIDGE, DOROTHEA. Gardens of South Africa, Maskew Miller, Cape Town 1924
FISHER, JOHN. The Companion to Roses, Viking, New York 1986
FORTUNE, ROBERT. A Narrative of a Journey to the Capitals of Japan & China, London 1863
— A Residence Among the Chinese (an account of his

third visit to China 1853–7)
— *Three Years' Wanderings in the Northern Provinces of China*, London 1847
FOSTER-MELLIAR, REVD A. *The Book of the Rose*, Macmillan, London 1910 (4th ed.)
Garden, The, Royal Horticultural Society, 1975–
GAULT, S. M. and SYNGE, P. M. *The Dictionary of Roses in Colour*, Ebury Press & Michael Joseph, London 1971
GERARD, JOHN. *Of the History of Plants*, London, 1633 ed.
GIBSON, MICHAEL. *Growing Roses*, Croom Helm, Breckenham, Kent, 1984
— *Shrub Roses for Every Garden*, Collins, London 1973
— *The Book of the Rose*, Macdonald General Books, London 1980
GORE, C. F. *The Book of Roses or The Rose Fancier's Manual*, 1838 (fac. ed. Heyden, London 1978)
GOWIE, W. *Gardening in South Africa*, Grahamstown 1912
Gowie, W. & C., Seed and Plant Merchants, Grahamstown. *Catalogues* (late 19th century)
GRANT, CHARLES, Viscount de Vaux. *History of Mauritius*, London 1801
GRANT, M. H. *Flower Paintings through the Centuries*, Lewis, Leigh-on-sea 1952 (an illustrated record of the Broughton Collection)
GRIFFITHS, TREVOR. *The Book of Old Roses*, Michael Joseph, London 1984 (English ed.)
— *My World of Old Roses, Volume 2*, Whitcoulls, Christchurch 1986
GÜNTHART, L. *The Glory of the Rose*, Harrap, London 1962
HARKNESS, JACK. *Roses*, Dent, London 1978
— *The Makers of Heavenly Roses*, Souvenir Press, London 1985
— *The Rose*, Macmillan, London 1979 (originally published by McGraw-Hill under the title *The World's Favourite Roses and How to Grow Them*)
HART, J. N. *The Culture of Roses*, Ward, Locke, London & Melbourne 1947
HARVEY, N. P. *The Rose in Britain*, Souvenir Press, London 1951
HENNESSEY, ROY. *On Roses*, West Coast Printing, Portland, Oregon 1943 (2nd ed.)
Heritage Roses, Heritage Rose Group U.S.A.
Heritage Roses in Australia, 1979–
Heritage Roses in New Zealand, Heritage Rose Society of New Zealand, 1986–
HIBBERD, SHIRLEY. *The Rose Book*, London 1864 (retitled *The Amateur's Rose Book* in later editions)
HILL, JOHN. *British Herbal*, London 1756
HOLE, DEAN S. R. *A Book About Roses*, Edinburgh 1869
HOLLIS, L. *Roses*, Collingridge, London 1974 (2nd ed.)
HOOKER, W. J. *British Flora*, London 1842 (5th ed.)
HUTCHINS, D. E. *Tree Planting*, London 1899
Index Kewensis, compiled under the direction of Joseph Hooker, Oxford 1893–5
Index Londinensis, compiled under the auspices of the Royal Horticultural Society of London at Kew. Oxford 1929–31
JACQUIN, N. J. VON. *Fragmenta Botanica*, Vienna 1809
— *Hortus Botanicus Vindobonensis*, Vindobonae 1770–6
JEKYLL, G. and MAWLEY, E. *Roses for English Gardens*, London 1902
KEAYS, F. L. *Old Roses*, Macmillan, 1935 (fac. ed. Heyden, London 1978)
KIAER, E. and HANKE, V. *Methuen Handbook of Roses*, Methuen, London 1966 (translated from the Danish)
KINGSLEY, ROSE. *Roses and Rose Growing*, Whittaker, London 1908
KOLBE, P. *Caput Bonae Spei Hodiernum*, Nürnberg 1719
KORDES, W. *Roses*, Studio Vista, London 1964 (translated by N. P. Hardy)
KRÜSSMAN, G. *Roses*, Batsford, London 1982 (translated from the German)
LAWRANCE, MARY. *A Collection of Roses from Nature*, London 1799
LE BLOND, A. *The Practice of Gardening*, London 1728 (2nd ed.; the English translation is by John James)
Leighton Nurseries of King William's Town. *List of Roses 1940*
LEMERY, NICOLAS. *Woordenboek of Algemeene Verhandeling der enkele Droogeryen*, 1743
LICHTENSTEIN, HENRY. *Travels in Southern Africa (1803–6)*, Van Riebeeck Society, Cape Town 1930 (reprint of Anne Plumptre's 1815 translation from the German)
LINDLEY, JOHN. *An Introduction to the Natural System of Botany*, London 1830

— *Rosarium Monographia*, 1820 (fac. repr., Coleman, New York 1979)
LINNAEUS, C. *Hortus Cliffortianus*, Amsterdam 1737
LOBEL, MATTHIAS DE. *Rariorum aliquot stirpium appendix . . .*, London 1605
LOCKYER, CHARLES. *An Account of the Trade in India*, London 1711
LOUDON, J. C. *An Encyclopedia of Plants*, London 1836
— *Arboretum et Fruticetum Britannicum*, Vol. II, London 1844
LOWE, R. T. *Manual of the Flora of Madeira*, London 1857
MCFARLAND, J. H. *How to Grow Roses*, J. H. McFarland Co., New York 1948
— *Modern Roses 8*, J. H. McFarland Co., Harrisburg, Pa. 1980
MCGIBBON, JAMES. *Catalogue of Plants in the Botanic Garden, Cape Town*, Saul Solomon, Cape Town 1858
MANSON, HUGH. *Rose Culture adapted to South African conditions*, Pietermaritzburg 1910
MAYHEW, A. and POLLARD, M. *The Rose: Myth, Folklore and Legend*, New English Library, London 1979
MECHLIN, STUART and BROWNE, JANET. *The Rose*, Mayflower Books, New York 1979
MILLER, PHILIP. *The Gardener's Dictionary*, London 1768 (8th rev. ed.) and 9th rev. ed. by T. Martyn, 1807
MITCHEL, P. *Flower Painters*, London 1973
MONEY, KEITH. *The Bedside Book of Old-fashioned Roses*, Degamo Productions, Carbrooke 1985
MURRAY, JOYCE. *In Mid-Victorian Cape Town*, Balkema, Cape Town 1968
— *Mrs Dale's Diary*, Balkema, Cape Town 1966
— *Young Mrs Murray Goes to Bloemfontein, 1856–60*, Balkema, Cape Town 1968
Natal Botanic Society. *Minutes 1867–71* (unpublished; Killie-Campbell Collection, University of Natal)
NOTTLE, TREVOR. *Growing Old-Fashioned Roses in Australia and New Zealand*, Kangaroo Press, Kenthurst N.S.W. 1983
NYLANDT, PETRUS. *De Nederlandtsche Herbarium of Kruydtboeck*, Amsterdam 1680
OBERKIRCH, HENRIETTE LOUISE D'. *Memoirs of the Baroness d'Oberkirch*, ed. Count de Montbrison, London 1852
PARK, BERTRAM. *Collins Guide to Roses*, Collins, London, 1956
— *The World of Roses*, Harrap, London 1962
PARKINSON, JOHN. *Paradisi in Sole Paradisus Terrestris*, London 1629
— *Theatrum Botanicum*, London 1640
PARSONS, SAMUEL. *Parsons on the Rose*, Orange-Judd, New York 1869 (1979 reprint)
PATERSON, ALLEN. *The History of the Rose*, Collins, Glascow 1983
PAUL, WILLIAM. *The Rose Garden*, 1848 (fac. ed., Heyden, London 1978)
PEMBERTON, REVD J. H. *Roses, Their History, Development and Cultivation*, London 1908
PERSOON, C. H. *Synopsis plantarum*, Paris 1805–7
PLINY. *Natural History* (Book XXI: viii.11–12; ix.12–15; x.16–20)
PRINCE, W. *Manual of Roses*, 1846 (fac. repr. Coleman, New York 1979)
RAVEN-HART, R. *Cape of Good Hope*, Balkema, Cape Town 1970
REDOUTÉ, P. J. and THORY, C. A. *Les Roses*, Paris 1817–24 (fac. ed. in 4 vols, De Schutter, Antwerp 1974–7)
RIVERS, T. *The Rose Amateur's Guide*, 1837 (fac. ed. Coleman, New York 1979)
ROBINSON, WILLIAM. *The English Flower Garden*, London 1883
ROCHON, ALEXIS. *A Voyage to Madagascar & the East Indies*, Paris 1793
RHODE, ELEANOUR SINCLAIR. *The Old English Herbals*, Longman Green, London 1922 (repr. Minerva, London 1974)
Rose Annual, The, Royal National Rose Society, 1907–
ROSS, DEANE. *Rose Growing for Pleasure*, Lothian Publishing Co., Melbourne 1985
ROTHMANN, M. E. *Uit en Tuis*, Cape Town 1946
ROXBURGH, W. *Hortus Bengalensis*, Serampore 1814
Royal Horticultural Society Journal (renamed *The Garden* after 1975)
SAINT-PIERRE, J. H. B. DE. *Voyage to the Island of Mauritius, the Isle of Bourbon & the Cape Of Good Hope*, trans. John Parish, London 1775
Sam Sly's African Journal, 5 June, 1848
SANDERS, T. W. *Roses and their Cultivation*, London 1904

SHEPHERD, ROY E. *History of the Rose*, Macmillan, New York 1954 (fac. repr. Heyden, London 1978)
SITWELL, SACHEVERELL, and RUSSELL, JAMES. *Old Garden Roses, Part 1*, Rainbird, London 1955
SMEE, A. *My Garden*, London 1872 (2nd ed.)
Smith Bros of Uitenhage. *Plant Catalogue 1904-5*
SMITH, C. W. *Rose Growing in South Africa*, C.N.A., 1953
South African Quarterly Journal, 1829–57
STAVORINUS, J. S. *Voyages to the East Indies*, London 1798 (translated by S. H. Wilcocke)
STEEN, NANCY. *The Charm of Old Roses*, A. H. & A. W. Reed, Wellington 1966
Stephen Brett Nurseries of Port Elizabeth and Uitenhage. *Plant Catalogue, 1905–6*
STEVENS, G. A. *Climbing Roses*, Macmillan, New York 1933
SVOBODA, P. *Beautiful Roses*, Spring Books, London 1965
SWENSON, A. A. *100 Oldtime Roses for Gardens of Today*, David McKay, New York 1979
TAYLOR, GEORGE M. *The Book of the Rose*, Winchester Publications, London 1949
Templeman's Nurseries of Cape Town. *Rose List 1940*
THEOPHRASTUS. *De Historia Plantarum*, Amsterdam 1644
THOMAS, A. S. *Better Roses*, Angus & Robertson, 1950
— *Knowing, Growing and Showing Roses in Australia*, Macmillan 1983
THOMAS, G. S. *Climbing Roses Old and New*, Phoenix House, London 1965 (and later eds)
— *The Old Shrub Roses*, Phoenix House, London 1955 (and later eds)
— *Shrub Roses of Today*, Phoenix House, London 1962 (and later eds)
THUNBERG, C. P. *Flora Capensis*, Stuttgart 1818–20
— *Flora Japonica*, Leipzig 1784
TOURNEFORT, JOSEPH PITTON DE. *Institutiones rei herbariae*, Paris 1700
VALENTYN, FRANCOIS. *Beschrijvinge van Oud en Nieuw Oost-Indien*, 1724
VAN DER GROEN, I. *Den Nederlandtsen Hovenier*, Amsterdam 1696
VAN PELT WILSON, HELEN. *Climbing Roses*, Barrows, New York 1955
VAN RIEBEECK, JAN. *Daghregister Gehouden by den Oppercoopman Jan Anthonisz Van Riebeeck [Diary]*, Van Riebeeck Society, Cape Town 1952
VAN ZYL, G. B. *Amateur Gardening*, Cape Town 1908
'VICAR, THE'. *South African Rose Book*, Speciality Press, 1940
Yellow Rose, The, 1986– (quarterly journal of the Dallas Area Historical Rose Group)
WALKER, ERIC. 'Catalogue of plants in the public gardens of Cape Town, 1938–9' (unpublished)
WARNER, CHRISTOPHER. *Climbing Roses*, Century, London 1987
WEATHERS, JOHN. *Beautiful Roses for Garden and Greenhouse*, London 1903
WHEATCROFT, HARRY. *My Life With Roses*, Odhams, London 1959
WILBUR, DONALD N. *Persian Gardens and Garden Pavilions*, C. E. Tuttle, Tokyo 1962
WILLMOTT, ELLEN. *The Genus Rosa*, Murray, London 1910–14
YOUNG, NORMAN. *The Complete Rosarian*, St. Martin's Press, New York 1971

PUBLISHED ARCHIVAL DOCUMENTS

Kaapse Archiefstukke lopende over het Jaar 1778–83, 7 vols, Archives Commission, Cape Town 1926–38
Kaapse Plakkaatboek, Deel 1–6, 1652–1806, 6 vols, Archives Commission, Cape Town 1944–51 (ed. Jeffreys et al)
LEIBBRANDT, H. C. V. ed. *Précis of the Archives of the Cape of Good Hope*, 17 vols, Cape Town 1896–1906
— *Letters Despatched from the Cape, 1652–1662; 1696–1708* (2 vols)
— *Letters Received, 1649–1662; 1695–1708* (2 vols)
— *Requesten (Memorials), 1705–1806* (Vols 1 and 2)
Suid-Afrikaanse Argiefstukke, Kaap 1–4, Resolusies van die Politieke Raad, 1651–1734, 8 vols, Archives Commission, Cape Town 1957–75 (ed. Jeffreys)

UNPUBLISHED ARCHIVAL DOCUMENTS

LEIBBRANDT, H. C. V. Manuscripts
— Letters Despatched 1707–1795
— Letters Received 1709–1794